Leo Tolstoy
and the
Alibi of Narrative

Russian Literature and Thought
GARY SAUL MORSON, SERIES EDITOR

CONTENTS

Acknowledgments

Research for this book was completed with assistance and funding from a Mellon Postdoctoral Fellowship at Northwestern University, the Senior Faculty Research Fund of the Davis Center for Russian and Eurasian Studies at Harvard University, the Davis Center's John F. Cogan Fund for Faculty Research in Russian Studies, and the Dean's Fund for Faculty Research at Harvard University.

Portions of chapter 8 first appeared as "Anna Incommunicada: Language and Consciousness in *Anna Karenina*" (*Tolstoy Studies Journal* 8 [1997]): 99–111. An earlier version of part of chapter 10 appeared in Russian as "Tema liubvi v pozdnoj proze Tolstogo" (The Theme of Love in the Late Prose of Tolstoy), in *Lev Tolstoy i mirovaia literatura: Materialy mezhdunarodnoi nauchnoi konferentsii*, ed. Galina Alekseeva and Nikolai Sviridov (Tula: Izdatel'skii Dom "Yasnaya Polyana," 2007), 63–70. Passages in chapters 2 and 8 were published as "Tolstoy Sees the Truth but Waits: The Consequences of Aesthetic Vision in *Anna Karenina*," in *Approaches to Teaching Tolstoy's "Anna Karenina*," ed. Liza Knapp and Amy Mandelker (New York: Modern Language Association, 2003), 173–79. And chapter 11 contains work published as "Tolstoy's *The Realm of Darkness* and Violence," in *Anniversary Essays on Tolstoy*, ed. Donna Tussing Orwin (Cambridge: Cambridge University Press, 2010).

I want to thank first and foremost Gary Jahn, who introduced me to Tolstoy over twenty years ago and advised my senior thesis on Tolstoy's "Death of Ivan Ilyich" and his essay *On Life*. Few intellectual experiences have had such a profound and lasting effect on me. Gary Saul Morson and Andrew Wachtel have been influential teachers, advisers, and sources of inspiration. Saul Morson's unique and sometimes provocative work has definitively shaped my view of Tolstoy, and he has helped me at every stage of this book.

I am very grateful to Harvard colleagues Jonathan Bolton, Svetlana Boym, Patricia Chaput, Michael Flier, George Grabowicz, John Malmstad, Joanna Nizynska, and especially Julie Buckler, Stephanie Sandler, and William Mills Todd, III, who offered help in ways big and small, from reading and commenting on my manuscript to providing teaching and leave opportunities that helped me to complete my work.

Tim Langen has been one of my most important interlocutors and collaborators. I would have never finished the book without his help. I am also in debt to Caryl Emerson, who has generously read my work on Tolstoy for many years. And many thanks to Galina Alekseeva, Vladimir Alexandrov, Michael Denner, Nina Gourianova, Peter Thomas, Liza Knapp, Ronald LeBlanc, Amy Mandelker, Robin Feuer Miller, Donna Orwin, David Sloane, and Paul J. Weir for reading and commenting on parts of my manuscript, answering questions, or providing help with different aspects of the book as it has taken shape. I appreciate, too, Andrew Frisardi's wonderful copyediting, the excellent advice from my anonymous readers for Yale University Press, and the assistance of my editor, Alison MacKeen. Alexander Gontchar, Ian Chesley, and Richard Freeman contributed crucial assistance in gathering and organizing materials for me.

In spite of the time I spent studying Tolstoy's increasingly dismal views on romance, my own happy family grew significantly while I wrote this book. I dedicate it to my wife, Joy, and our children, Fiona, David, and Daniel.

INTRODUCTION

When Tolstoy states dramatically in his aesthetic treatise *What Is Art?* that "the interpretation of works of art by words only indicates that the interpreter is himself incapable of feeling the infection of art,"[1] one forgets, for just a moment, that Tolstoy himself is using words to tell us how to understand art. For me, the exploration of this kind of mild contradiction is part of what makes reading Tolstoy enjoyable. Sometimes the contradiction is really nothing more than the thematic chiaroscuro of a story, as when Tolstoy celebrates fidelity in vivid stories of adultery, or cherishes the innocence of childhood by repeatedly dwelling on its loss. At other times, the contradiction may be more fundamental to Tolstoy's aesthetics, as when he seems to suggest that language both is and is not adequate for conveying an author's meaning. I use the term *narrative alibi* in this study to describe how Tolstoy creates a model of authorship out of these more fundamental contradictions.

A narrative alibi works in two ways. In the simplest sense, it can be a story that exculpates, removes blame or transfers responsibility. Many of Tolstoy's late stories rely on this kind of narrative, as they explain away the author's immoral youth and minimize his early literary career by telescoping the author's progress toward eventual religious conversion. Tolstoy's *Confession* (1879–82) describes the author's earlier dissolute life, crisis, and ultimate religious conversion, and it exemplifies this first sense of narrative alibi. Works such as "Father Sergius" and *Resurrection* also conform to this sense of narrative alibi, because their plots describe lives wasted early in the pursuit of pleasure and fame but later recuperated by moral reflection and action. These stories are redemptive, and we are meant to see that Tolstoy's very authorship of them is redemptive as well. In *What Is Art?* he claims his own aesthetic taste was "perverted" by his aristocratic upbringing, relegates his past work to the category of "bad art," and commits

1

himself to the notion that the only good art is that which communicates Christian ideals effectively.[2] Tolstoy's narrative alibis do not necessarily meet this narrow definition of art, but they share in its project of purifying and redeeming literature.

A narrative alibi can also be a story that uses the logic of the word *alibi*, which literally means to be "elsewhere." An alibi here is a meaningful absence, a place in the text where one is supposed to notice that the author has purposely bypassed or concealed an important aspect of the plot. He does this by diverting the flow of the plot around what is unsaid or concealed—in Tolstoy's case most dramatically, for example, in the early story "Sevastopol in December," where the second-person narration helps the reader see one thing but prevents him from seeing another. Such narrative maneuvering is usually more subtle, however, as when early in *Anna Karenina* Levin avoids situations that would remind him of Kitty's rejection of his marriage proposal, and we readers therefore experience the same lack of reminders. Although the novel is narrated by what we suppose is an omniscient narrator, the disclosure of the plot is shaped by Levin's willingness to be honest with himself. What goes unsaid is often a means of exposing the alibis and absences of language itself, especially in the great novels of Tolstoy's middle career, *War and Peace* and *Anna Karenina*, where we see the consequences of the failure to communicate as characters fall in and out of love. In more sinister fashion, a narrative alibi may be found in acts of purposeful concealment, as, for example, in the deceptive storytelling of Pozdnyshev, the murderous protagonist of "The Kreutzer Sonata." In order to understand the story, one has to listen to what Pozdnyshev is *not* saying.

I consider narrative alibi in this second sense as an instance of how Tolstoy inscribes significant absences into his narratives in order to retain authorial control over the interpretation of his texts. Tolstoy was never one to let readers simply make what they would of the meaning of a story. Early in his career, diversionary narrative tactics were part of Tolstoy's strategy of drawing his readers into his works of fiction, works he viewed as having a radical form. "Sevastopol in December" pushes and pulls the reader in order to impose an "experience" of the violence of war. Later in his career, Tolstoy found that by returning to the alibis of the early work, he could similarly assert control, not by directing the reader's perspective, as in "Sevastopol in December," but by re-appropriating his own authorial identity.

The older Tolstoy easily reinterpreted his early works, because, when he first became an author, not yet fully committed to the profession, he sketched an incomplete image of himself as author. Themes from early autobiographical works, such as *Childhood*, could be taken up anew, this time with Tolstoy subtly reminding readers that he was the most authoritative interpreter of his original authorial intention. Critics today rarely claim to have uncovered the author's intended meaning. Still, one is uncomfortable considering an interpretation that seems opposed to the author's stated understanding of his or her text. In the case of Tolstoy, this clash between interpreter and author is inevitable—if not actually designed by the author, then at least implicitly acknowledged by him and used for creative purposes. In order to dramatize his authorial evolution, the later, more didactic Tolstoy repeatedly returned to his early fiction, recasting in a moral light not only its themes but also its aesthetic assumptions—in such matters, for example, as the transparency and communicability of consciousness. Depending on the time, Tolstoy himself understood his work in substantially different ways, though he often composed an authorial history and identity encompassing many years of literary work that smoothed over those differences.

Over time, authors typically return to themes and methods, rethink them, and write new works. One could say that it is their job to do so. Yet Tolstoy is especially reflexive in his literary interests. He has always struck his critics as introspective, not just in the psychological sense but also in terms of his restrained references to literary history and his own authorial development. Of the early Tolstoy, Eric de Haard has written, "Tolstoi seems to be the most independent and 'rootless' writer of his generation, ignoring as it were the recent tradition of Russian prose, and at the first stage of his career also keeping aloof from literary life."[3] Authors, moreover, do not return to every work, theme, or practice, only to particular ones. What is it about a flirtatious conversation between a man and a woman in high society, to give a single example, that causes Tolstoy to return to the same literary situation even in patently antiromantic, religious works of fiction such as *Resurrection?* The answer is to be found not in *Resurrection*, nor in the religious philosophy that novel espouses, but in the earlier, more romantic works themselves. Tolstoy found the romantic conversation of true love to be so communicatively effective that it came to serve as shorthand for his changing aesthetic theories. He returns to this and other aspects of his early aesthetics again and again.

Reflexivity in an author's history poses questions that are not unique to Tolstoy. Early and late works in an author's oeuvre often enter into a complex hermeneutic relationship to one another. Hans Georg Gadamer uses the term *historically effected consciousness* to describe how a historical event shapes our later view of it.[4] How would such a process work for the career of a single author? The literary example may in fact be a more convincing case of historically effected consciousness than any other, because authors are real people with constitutive biographical pasts. There can be no question that the past affects how they subsequently think about the past, just as, for example, Tolstoy's various literary works on childhood continued to influence his later conceptualizations of childhood. By contrast, how the event of Napoleon's victory at Austerlitz affects my understanding of history is far less apparent.

With Tolstoy, I look to the early works as though future, possibly contradictory, reinterpretations were immanent in them. Especially the metaliterary and autoreferential passages in the early works appear as though they suggested to Tolstoy that he could and should return to them as touchstones of his mature aesthetics. I argue that we should interpret Tolstoy's fiction with the implicit clash between early and late interpretations fully in mind. He makes authorial intention unavoidable, yet not simple, and requires we (re)consider it in our interpretations.

Rearticulation, reevaluation—these are the words that come to mind for Tolstoy, but not necessarily *interpretation*. Tolstoy did not believe in interpretation, as is evident in the passage I quoted at the outset of this introduction. The pinnacle moments for him and for his characters are when characters grasp the truth without having to reflect, without having to interpret anything, as when Levin loses his self-consciousness while cutting hay in *Anna Karenina*. Tolstoy nevertheless enthralls readers who enjoy interpretation—Vladimir Alexandrov's recent book revels in the many points of interpretation available to readers of *Anna Karenina*.⁵ Yet there is also an undeniable resistance to ultimate interpretation in Tolstoy's novels, as Alexandrov also makes clear. Tolstoy's resistance to interpretation generates practices and themes he returns to often as he reconceives his literary aesthetics.

We can ask whether Tolstoy believed in genuine aesthetic pleasure, for example. Do people enjoy, should they enjoy, art in Tolstoy's fictional world? Or is it just a distraction from life's moral dilemmas? If we replace the word *art* with *sex*, we can ask the same questions. But we readers enjoy Tolstoy's art, and infidelity, sexual temptation, and romance in general are important aspects of his art. Tolstoy tells us in his art to avoid art. These minor readerly quandaries and a host of other points of resistance are not uninterpretable, but they are deceptively multivalent, representing opportunities for Tolstoy to reserve final judgment for himself, so that he can conjure an authorial identity that is similarly versatile. By actually emplotting significant lacunae in his fiction, as in the plotlessness of his early fiction, for example, Tolstoy leaves open the possibility to tell the story differently, should he so choose, and to tell the story of his own authorship differently. He sees the literary present as a future authorial past to be reenacted and re-accentuated. This process of sometimes obfuscatory authorial intervention realizes our metaphor of the alibi in Tolstoy's literature. The meaning of a text, and thus the author's intending self, may be "elsewhere," waiting for Tolstoy to return and uncover it.

I readily admit that Tolstoy generally gives the opposite impression. He disdained literary critics interpreting his works and emphasized the importance of communicating directly and clearly to readers. Although Tolstoy's aesthetics changed significantly over the many years he was an author, he discussed literature both early and late in his career primarily in terms of communication. He repeatedly wondered whether readers would understand the story or novel in the way he intended it to be understood. The comprehensibility of the author's intention was for Tolstoy an important measure of a work's success. Crucially however, comprehensibility does not imply simplicity in fiction or a lack of contradiction. Tolstoy would welcome Fitzgerald's notion that "the test of a first-rate intelligence is the ability to hold two opposed ideas in the mind at the same time, and still retain the ability to function." Even if Tolstoy wants us to understand his authorial intent, and repeatedly returns to emphasize it, that does not mean we will or could. Readers still cannot decide, for example, whether Tolstoy means us to condemn or sympathize with Anna Karenina, a feature that should be easy to discern given the novel's deceptively clear biblical epigraph: "Vengeance is mine, I will repay." If the author's intent is so important to *Anna Karenina*, we wonder, why does Tolstoy make it difficult to uncover? Why does he elide, hide, and otherwise disguise the very stuff that will create that meaning, not just in *Anna Karenina* but in much of his work?

There is good reason for this strategy, as I will argue repeatedly in the coming pages. Works of fiction are protean in meaning, and authors use this malleability as a way to craft a unique kind of identity. In this study I plan to discuss at length the significance of the narrative rationale for those absences, the narrative alibi. The development of Tolstoy's narrative techniques did not proceed in a straight line. It was a product of his continuous self-reflection. Therefore, although this book follows a generally chronological format, certain important themes will force us to leap back or forward in time, as Tolstoy revisits old concerns or plants the seeds for new ones. In part I—"Tolstoy's Narrative Alibi"—I consider the texts "A History of Yesterday," *Childhood,* and the late novel *Resurrection* in terms of how Tolstoy's outsider status in the literary establishment and repeated withdrawals from city life both legitimized his authorial aims and involved him, so he thought, in a cycle of guilt, by which he considered his authorship to be escapist and without social value. And yet, by virtue of Tolstoy's intense self-reflection, he came to use that perceived absence from society as the foundation of a more thorough aesthetics of absence, a subset of a larger philosophical tradition of negativity. What we see in part I is both an

institutional pose—Tolstoy as outsider, as nontraditional author—and a negative aesthetics that capitalizes on the identity suggested by that very pose. Part I
introduces the concept of narrative alibi more fully, and makes reference to the
broad course of Tolstoy's life and career. Extended interpretations of Tolstoy's
fiction do not begin until midway through part II.

Tolstoy's alternating devotion to and derision of literary authorship did not
help him to be understood the way he wanted to be understood. Farming and
teaching did little to make Tolstoy's literary aims more transparent to readers.
He needed to draw readers in and teach them how to understand in a new way
what he considered radically new literature. In part II—Legitimate Lives"—
examples from Childhood, Boyhood, "Sevastopol in December," "Sevastopol in
May," "Two Hussars," The Cossacks, and War and Peace illuminate how Tolstoy
developed a formal means of inviting readers to recognize his authorial posture
both inside and outside the literary establishment as both legitimate and meaningful. He did this by creating open-framed and broken-framed narratives, and
with other authorial gestures that invite readerly participation in the creation of
meaning. As in part I, we examine here an approach to the author's image and
to his intention. What is the nature of the truth that literature can convey? Is it
in the world or in the text? If readers are called upon to participate in the construction of literary meaning, does that make truth something that is temporarily, even contingently, constructed in the literary text? Tolstoy attempted to
answer these questions in his fiction. By repeatedly emphasizing and transcending the boundaries between the text and reality, Tolstoy forced readers to contemplate how art is diverting—something that entertains but that also distracts
one from the truth of the world.

Having made truth his "hero," as Tolstoy says in "Sevastopol in May," and
having asked readers to validate that truth and his role as truth teller, Tolstoy
was perhaps inevitably drawn to consider how author, character, or reader actually comprehends the truth. Is the truth something one figures out or decodes—
an interpretation—or is it something one simply recognizes when one sees it?
The early Tolstoy, who was more concerned with legitimation, wanted others to
join in his interpretation of the world, in the way he got at the truth. If others
understood him the right way, his own authorial identity would be legitimate.
From about Anna Karenina on, Tolstoy by contrast refocused on modes of
authenticity and on ways of remaining true to the source of honest being that
existed in childhood and that is subsequently spoiled, as he came to believe, by
sex and society. This is a truth that one recognizes rather than interprets.
Echoing a point he had made about Vronsky's view of Mikhailov's painting of
Anna Karenina, Tolstoy wrote in What Is Art? that "the receiver of a true artistic

impression is so united to the artist that he feels as if the work were his own and not someone else's—as if what it expresses were just what he had long been wishing to express." Part III—"Authentic Lives"—views that turn away from literary structures that force the reader's active interpretation in light of Tolstoy's dedication to authenticity and especially to the innocence of childhood as sources of genuine meaning in life and in literature. In that context, I interpret *War and Peace, Anna Karenina,* "The Death of Ivan Ilyich," and *Hadji Murad.*

Tolstoy's narrative alibi, the story he told about being a part of and absent from the literary institutions of his day, created an aesthetics that, by turns, reaches out to others for legitimation and recoils inward for self-authentication. The language of Tolstoy's fiction, especially in narratives of love and romantic betrayal, breaks down along similar lines. Part IV—"The Language of Love"— describes love as it is represented in "A History of Yesterday," "Lucerne," and *Anna Karenina* as a language in which no interpretation is necessary and comprehension is total. Love stories were an ideal form of fiction for Tolstoy precisely because they narrate perfect comprehension between the self and another (and by implication between the author and his reader). The betrayal of love, which is the subject of part V—"Suspicious Stories"—engenders fiction in which language becomes a kind of impenetrable cipher. In this context I interpret "Family Happiness," *Resurrection,* "The Devil," "The Kreutzer Sonata," and "After the Ball." Love stories were an ideal narrative form especially in the early half of Tolstoy's literary career. The late Tolstoy turned not just to the betrayal of romantic love but to its impossibility. Sexual desire, equated early and late by Tolstoy with the desire for stories, propels one further and further from a moral life. In Tolstoy's late fiction, romance was always romantic betrayal. The authentic life recollects the innocence of childhood and examines the utopian prospect of a Christian brotherhood of men. These stories repeatedly modeled a destruction of meaning in fiction, typically by citing Tolstoy's earlier stories and rephrasing their romantic dreams in an ominous key.

It is as though Tolstoy as a moral philosopher simply no longer pondered whether he needed literary institutions or the outside world at all. He accepted, as he says in *What Is Art?* "the indubitable truth that all compromise with institutions of which your conscience disapproves—compromises which are usually made for the sake of the general good—instead of producing the good you expected, inevitably lead you, not only to acknowledge the institution you disapprove of but also to participate in the evil that institution produces."[6] The purifying aesthetics of the late Tolstoy was predicated on reconsidering and destabilizing the aesthetics of the early Tolstoy. Part VI—"The Death of an Author"—examines Tolstoy's *The Kingdom of God Is Within You, Boyhood,*

"Why Do Men Stupefy Themselves?" *What Is Art?* and "Father Sergius" with the aim of making this implicit violence explicit by examining the role of violence in Tolstoy's fiction and in his development of a philosophy of nonviolence. The paradox here is that Tolstoy wanted his readers to understand perfectly his dismantling of traditional literary understanding. That seems not just paradoxical but untenable, and I interpret Tolstoy's most developed theory, *What Is Art?* as just such an untenable aesthetics. I call this a "death" of Tolstoy's fiction both because of his disavowal of almost all of his past work and because the literary guidelines he embraced prohibited him from writing in any way that paralleled his previous work. There is a death of the author in Tolstoy's work, but he is both culprit and victim.

Part I

---•◆•---

TOLSTOY'S NARRATIVE ALIBI

For many readers, Tolstoy is altogether too present in his fiction. He keeps telling us everything, rather than showing us. His narrators, when omniscient, are somehow too omniscient, and we are always being reminded that it is an all-knowing Tolstoy who authors the work we are reading. Yet this version of the oppressive authorial Tolstoy, while undoubtedly true, is only half the story, and not the more important half. Tolstoy also figures the author as a kind of absence—missing from the text in significant ways. Exactly how Tolstoy shapes and defines this absence is crucial for understanding his creative appropriation of his own authorial image throughout his career. The process of inscribing absence into authorship is what I call Tolstoy's narrative alibi.

GUILTY STORIES

He was not a libertine but neither, as he himself said, was he a monk.

— *"The Devil"*

Evgeny Irtenev, the recognizably autobiographical hero of Tolstoy's late unpublished story "The Devil" (1889), is destined for happiness: he has saved his family estate from financial ruin, he has married a woman who loves him, and he even has a lovely new baby girl.[1] One thing alone prevents him from achieving complete happiness: his dire need to continue an affair with a local peasant woman, Stepanida, the "devil" of the story's title. Ravaged by desire, he ultimately goes insane, vowing in the closing pages of the story either to kill Stepanida or to kill himself in order to end the agony.

Faced with the choice of authoring one concluding crime or another . . . Tolstoy chooses both. "The Devil" has in fact two endings, one in which Evgeny turns the gun on Stepanida, and another in which he kills himself. Who is to blame, the story asks, the society that tempts the man, or the man who succumbs to temptation? Is guilt to be attributed to an extrinsic cause or to an intrinsic cause?

Tolstoy's literary world seems to spin best on the axis of such oppositions and double encodings. *War and Peace*, "Master and Man," "Who Should Teach Whom to Write, We the Peasant Children or the Peasant Children Us?" are titles that underscore more substantial tensions in Tolstoy. Two influential monographs, *Hidden in Plain View* and *Leo Tolstoy: Resident and Stranger*, embrace Tolstoy's duality.[2] But for Tolstoy's Evgeny Irtenev, the contradictions are unbearable. Someone must account for them; someone must be held accountable.

Tolstoy was not Dostoevsky. His works are not filled with unthinkable murders and usually no one is on trial. Yet his stories and novels almost always call on characters (and sometimes readers) to answer for themselves. Tolstoy repeatedly asks himself the same questions. Has he lived a good life, a just life, a moral life? Can he do better? Can he help others be better people? Tolstoy memorably begins his 1884 profession of faith, *What I Believe*: "I have lived on this earth for fifty-five years and, with the exception of fourteen or fifteen years of childhood, for thirty-five years I lived as a nihilist in the true sense of the word, that is, not as a socialist or a revolutionary, as that word is usually understood, but as a nihilist in the sense of the absence of any belief. Five years ago I began to believe in the teaching of Christ—and my life suddenly changed: I stopped desiring that which I previously desired, and began to desire that which I previously did not desire. That which previously seemed good, now seemed bad, and that which previously seemed bad, now seemed good" (23: 304). Tolstoy's insistence on a dramatic division in his life prompts us to ask: what was the nature of his religious and spiritual beliefs before his conversion?[3] Did he really live in "the absence of any belief"? Five years previously, he had written in *A Confession* that he used to "conceal" his desire for good (23: 5). The author's nihilism notwithstanding, are we not obliged to ask whether we can in turn reveal and articulate the essence of the upright and moral life as it is presented in *Anna Karenina*, for example. Does this help one to understand the novel as fully as possible?[4] Tolstoy feels the need to characterize what his faith was at the time, but to what extent do we? What is more, the contradictions in the author and his works seem to go together. As one critic writes: "In the process of work, Tolstoy himself changed to such an extent that there was an enormous difference between his original plan and the final version. Thus, all his works, after careful analysis, seem incomplete or contradictory—moving within themselves."[5]

For this study the contradictions of literature, language, and belief that have plagued Tolstoy and his critics will be considered as problems of writing and authorship. In describing an alibi of narrative I intend to show how Tolstoy developed a mode of authorship that embraces those contradictions and uses them as a source of evasion, accountability, and, most important, creative inspiration.[6] By revising and revitalizing the concept of authorship itself, seeing it as a public and discursive practice that thrives on internal divisions throughout the course of a literary career, we may come to view such dilemmas as that between Evgeny Irtenev's guilty world and his guilty self as engines of Tolstoy's literary production.

A NARRATIVE ALIBI

Nobody is to blame, and yet the men are dead—murdered by these very men who are not to blame for their deaths. (*PSS*, 32: 349)[7]

—*Resurrection*

Consider Tolstoy's late novel *Resurrection*. The plot of this novel is a simple one (Tolstoy's earlier big novels do not so easily succumb to the schematic decoding I am about to give). The aristocratic hero of *Resurrection*, Nekhlyudov, repents of his past misdeeds toward a peasant woman, Maslova, after learning how her life subsequently became depraved. After having served as juror on a trial that convicts her of murder, he takes steps both to make amends to her and to live in a morally just way. His thoughts, as he becomes cognizant of the true path, closely resemble Tolstoy's own late philosophy, with its distinctions between man's animal and spiritual being, between belief in God and belief in religion, and so forth.[8] But the salient feature of *Resurrection*, the dilemma that propels the plot forward, turns on neither repentance nor reconciliation. What has happened in the novel is not nearly as important as what has not happened. To put it briefly, Maslova's sentence would have been a light one, if it were not for the fact that a single, crucial phrase was omitted from the verdict: "They were all so worn out and so muddled with arguing that nobody thought of adding the clause, '*but without intent to take life*'. Nekhlyudov was in such a state of agitation that he did not notice the omission. And so the answers were written down in the form agreed upon, and taken back to the courtroom. . . . This, instead of another verdict, was returned, not because all were agreed but because, first, the presiding judge, who had summed up at such length, this time omitted to say what he always said, namely, that they could find a verdict of 'Guilty—*but without intent to take life*' "[9] As a consequence Maslova is severely punished (her sentence is fifteen years penal servitude in Siberia) and Nekhlyudov resolves to accompany her into exile—that is the main plot. In *Resurrection*, Tolstoy engenders the plot by doubling an absence: what is missing in the verdict is the phrase that says the intention to take life is missing. The novel unfolds two explanatory narratives deriving from that plot kernel. The first explains the absence in the verdict politically, by repeatedly indicting the tsarist judicial system. Here, as Tolstoy demonstrates, the fault belongs to a corrupt and incompetent government, as well as to the society which tolerates it. Maslova is the victim of a corrupt government and society. The second explanatory narrative details the absence of intention psychologically, by narrating Maslova's spiritual rebirth as the revelation of her true self, buried by sin and the harsh realities of her life. What is missing is her spiritual self, which she must retrieve over the course of the novel. In order to explain Maslova's missing intention to take a life, the extrinsic and intrinsic bases for interpretation—the guilty world and the guilty self—are thus both invoked by Tolstoy's narration of exclusion.

I treat these kinds of explanatory narrations in Tolstoy's oeuvre as narrative alibis. Tolstoy's narrative alibis are often literary explanations for why the author in the past failed to behave in a morally defensible manner, even if we doubt the veracity of those biographical or autobiographical accounts. Tolstoy writes in A *Confession*:

> I cannot recall those years without horror, loathing, and heartache. I killed people in war, challenged them to duels in order to kill them, lost at cards, ate up the labor of the peasants, punished them, fornicated, deceived. Lying, theft, deeds of all sorts, drunkenness, violence, murder. . . . There wasn't a crime I didn't commit, and for everything I was celebrated; my coevals considered and still consider me a relatively moral man.
>
> And so I lived for ten years.
>
> In that time I began to write from vanity, self-interest and pride. In my writing I did just the same as in my life. In order to obtain glory and money, for which I wrote, I needed to conceal what was good and reveal the bad. And so I did. How many times I contrived to conceal in my writing, under the guise of indifference and even gentle mockery, those strivings of mine for good, which made up the sense of my life. And I achieved my goal: I was praised.[10]

Tolstoy puts his sinful life and his written work directly together: "In my writing I did just the same as in my life." Narrative alibis purposely conflate and confuse the author's biography and his literary psychological analyses or self-analyses.[11] In A *Confession*, Tolstoy recasts his life as criminal and his art as an act of concealing what was most important to him. And there is nothing wrong with that strategy. We cannot know more than the author, it goes without saying, when he chooses to reveal or rewrite his past authorial intentions—what others understandably view as "relatively moral," the author may retrospectively deem immoral. But we can examine the form and uses of that authorial past as it is creatively refigured and thus understand Tolstoy's authorship all the better.

We are all familiar with the contemporary use of the word *alibi*, usually in the context of a crime, whereby a suspect can remove suspicion by providing proof that he or she could not have committed the crime. The word *alibi* is, literally, an adverb for "elsewhere," deriving from the Latin old locative case of *alius*, "another." That is why to be "in another place" is essential for many of the best-known alibis. In a legal context to be elsewhere necessitates the supporting details and corroboration provided by a narrative account of being elsewhere. Here—reversing the cliché—it is deeds without words that are empty. Alibi is thus especially well suited for narrative, for there is always a story or relevant sequence of events that depicts being elsewhere. As in the case of Nekhlyudov and *Resurrection*, narrative alibis draw on the special significance of an absence.

Beyond the legal context, an alibi is thus something we can give whenever we are called to account for ourselves. When we speak of whether someone "has" an alibi or not, we implicitly allude to the importance that *having* a story, being able to tell the story of oneself, holds for modern identity (even if it is the possession of a kind of absence). Nekhlyudov has forgotten about Maslova—put her out of his mind. But Tolstoy, stretching realistic plausibility, seats him on the jury whereby she can not be excluded from his biography. The narrative calls on him to account for this attempted exclusion in how he describes himself and his life.

An alibi is an unusual form of narrative precisely because it is generated by absence, and thus alibi is a small, well-defined instance of the philosophical concept of negativity. Though a negative concept, an alibi does real work; it functions in a system of legally binding processes and confers a status upon those who employ it rhetorically. An alibi is a speech act rendering the real act, the crime, impossible, at least for the accused. The narrative opposite of a confession, it exculpates rather than implicates. An alibi is an account of not being there. So, an alibi is a kind of anticonfessional narrative.

In the case of literary authorship, however, alibi may be viewed from another angle. The very occupation of writing narrative itself may also create an alibi, providing an author with an excuse for being elsewhere, engaged in the creation of fiction rather than actively engaged in the world. Some authors, like Tolstoy, are inclined more than others to invoke this alibi, especially if they think a typical or normal life in society perpetuates injustice. Remember Tolstoy's dual ending for "The Devil": being in the world and not being in the world are both suspect. Tolstoy is famous for his tortured oscillations between "author" and "simple _____ (fill in blank with one of the following: landowner, teacher, husband, father, religious thinker, anarchist)," and thus one sees intuitively the advantage this duality in narrative alibi might hold for him.[12] The more he wrote, however, the more Tolstoy felt that his absence from the social world, however riddled that world was with sloth, immorality, and temptation, was a guilty absence, a significant absence. He consciously or subconsciously began to use accounts of such absences as a fundamental component of his fictional narratives. He used absences that tell stories and stories that explain absences in nearly all of his major fiction. And he repeatedly quit being a writer, though he had just become one.

THE BIRTH OF THE AUTHOR

I believe, my dear Alexander Vasilyevich, that you love me as a man, and not as an editor loves a hack writer who might be some good to him. As a writer I'm no longer good for anything. I'm not writing, and I haven't written since *Family*

Happiness, and I don't think I shall write in the future—at least I flatter myself
with this hope. Why is this? It's a long and difficult story. The main reason is that
life is short, and to waste it in my adult years writing the sort of stories I used to
write makes me feel ashamed. I can and must and want to get down to business.
It would be good if it could be the sort of thing which would tire me out, which
urgently needed doing and would give me courage, pride and strength—that
would be all right. But I really can't lift a finger to write stories which are nice and
pleasant to read, now that I'm 31. It's funny I should even think about writing a
story at all.

—*Letter to A. V. Druzhinin, October 9, 1859*[13]

Tolstoy began splitting his career into early and late phases from the very
start, and he gave up being an author, as we see in this letter to Druzhinin, not
long after he became one. By this time he was well known in literary circles.
Sending his first novel, *Childhood* (1852), off to be published, he sought to validate an authorial identity in a world of literary conventions and institutions. At
first he was mostly concerned to establish his uniqueness as an author and have
that uniqueness recognized by others. One imagines that his purposely infuriat-
ing Turgenev and others by denigrating the literary merits of Shakespeare or
George Sand has something to do with this.[14] Later in his career, however, he
chastised himself, as Andrei Bolkonsky does in *War and Peace*, for his desire to
be legitimated by any external authority, excepting his obligation before a
Christian brotherhood of man. As Jeff Love says aptly of Tolstoy: "Few could be
said to have sought authority more passionately, more violently, and more
immoderately."[15] In his later literary works, Tolstoy devised what he felt were
more authentic authorial postures that needed no outside recognition.[16]
Tolstoy's definition of artistic "sincerity"—the keystone of his late work on aesthetics *What Is Art?*—demands that the artist pay no regard to what others may
think, as Michael Denner has argued.[17] Both early and late, Tolstoy used many
of the same creative narrative strategies to achieve these goals, and even to overcome his own past, which he increasingly interpreted as misguided, as mere
preparatory work for his true self. Tolstoy's use of narrative alibi has its source in
his dissatisfaction with the norms of an authorial career, though later it serves
his desire to redeem an immoral youth.

Becoming an author offered Tolstoy, he soon realized, a fundamental advantage over all other careers he might have chosen: as an author he was given the
opportunity to participate in the social and political life of his country without
actually having to be present in the capital cities. Of course, Tolstoy spent plenty
of time in St. Petersburg and even more time in Moscow, which, in contrast to

the purely urban Petersburg, seemed a combination of city and country.[18] As a young author, he even embraced the Petersburg scene and his new fame. Yet first in his fiction, then in his own life, he turned away from the pressing immediacy of the city's cultural debates, and sought an alibi, a reason for being elsewhere. He cultivated myths of childhood and home life, and insisted late in his career on their absolute authentic reality. As a much older man, and in response to prompting by his biographer Pavel Biriukov, Tolstoy wrote that his return to Yasnaya Polyana was a way of resisting outside influence: "I always resisted involuntarily the epidemic influence from outside, and if at the time I was excited or happy, then it was for my own personal, inner reasons, those that I found in school and in contact with common people [общению с народом]."[19] Tolstoy was still interested in the city, in the center of cultural and political life, in the balls and dramas of society life—these were crucial for his novels, and he had a wife and children who did not want to be buried in the countryside their whole lives. But for Tolstoy to live that city life was fundamentally to misunderstand it: he celebrated distance and even absence, rather than presence, as the necessary condition for seeing the truth. Outsiders, not insiders, are the more compelling arbiters of meaning in Tolstoy's fictional worlds. *Anna Karenina*'s Levin, awkward outcast of both politics and the beau monde, points to several generations of noble forebears and declares he is the true aristocrat, not the more dashing Vronsky with his money and Petersburg connections. Right or wrong, Levin is empowered in the novel because Tolstoy gives him, not Vronsky, the distance to ponder the true meaning of life for all of us.

But there is no need to immediately question the meaning of life, when sometimes more simple questions go unanswered. For example, why did Tolstoy become an author rather than a military man, a lawyer, or a bureaucrat? Writing is not the same thing as publishing one's written work and thereby assuming the public identity of an author. Tolstoy could still have kept voluminous diaries and never become an author. We may know less than we think we know about this question, and yet a plausible answer could reveal crucial information about Tolstoy's methods and goals in authorship. N. I. Burnasheva characterizes the state of scholarship: "Literary scholars' current notions about Tolstoy's very first steps in his writer's career are chronologically very uncertain, vague and contradictory, frequently subjective and based on incidental notes taken randomly from the diary and unconvincing arguments; they do not provide an orderly and clear picture of the early stage in the creative development of the writer."[20] Part of the problem, Burnasheva notes, is that researchers who find Tolstoy remarking in his diary that, for example, he "wrote until twelve [o'clock]" assume that the "writing" refers to literary works, such as his planned childhood trilogy.[21]

The relationship between just plain writing and writing a work of literature, however, is not a simple one.

In general, the distinction between authorship and writing is important, but especially in the case of Tolstoy. Tolstoy was an indefatigable writer throughout his life. His diaries and letters make up many volumes of his collected works. But when he published *Childhood* he became an author in the widely understood sense of someone who has published his or her writing. For the purposes of this study, authorship, not writing, will be the main focus, because the former generates a version of the self that is shared publicly with readers and is constituted in part by their reception.[22] An author uses his or her biographical image as a device to help readers understand a single work of literature as well as the unity of an entire corpus of literary work. Boris Tomashevsky refers to this as the biographical "legend," the information about an author that is necessary in order to understand the text.[23] Moreover, the image of the author can evolve, and perhaps should evolve, over time. Although linked to the philosophical concept of personal identity, which is itself a model for authorial identity, authorial identity is not the same as personal identity.[24] Authorial identity is more protean; and it can be radically discontinuous without threatening personal identity. A novelist who after many years becomes a poet, for example, may be unusual but is not schizophrenic. The opposite trajectory is common: in the Russian tradition, Turgenev and Nabokov, for example, wrote poetry before becoming novelists.

There are several theories of authorship that consider writing, publishing, and the uses of authorial identity. How Tolstoy's example fits with those theories, and challenges them, is the explicit subject of the last chapter of this book, though it is worth previewing here. I argue that in contrast to recent influential theories of authorship, such as Barthes' "death of the author," Tolstoy views authorial intention as dynamic. Barthes dismisses the author's role in the creation of a text's meaning: the author, for Barthes, is merely the literal antecedent of the text as physical object. But this is a narrow vision of authorial intention. For Tolstoy, intention is not relegated to the past, like some ancient piece of glass that one unearths and uses to decipher a defunct civilization's practices. This is the premise that the Russian Formalists and American New Critics attacked, and which Barthes himself takes up in his celebration of the reader versus the author.[25] Tynianov, one of the most canny scholars of literary tradition, carefully separates the biographical genesis of a work of art from its derivation in literary and cultural history.[26] Tolstoy purposely mixes the two, as we have seen in the lengthy passage I quoted from *A Confession*. Tolstoy may or may not have immorally concealed the good in his literary work, but, regardless, others found him a relatively moral man. In other words, both the author and his milieu share some of the blame. Nor does Tolstoy consider the literary text a timeless servant to canon, as T. S. Eliot might have us believe in his famous essay "Tradition and the Individual Talent." Literary intention remains present and changeable for Tolstoy, and in time, because it was never finalized in the first place. That is why the absences and alibis of Tolstoy's early fiction are so important to his overall conception of authorship. They represent a future past, whereby he may return to an earlier text and reinterpret its meaning as his original authorial intention.

Tolstoy's decision to publish *Childhood* changed his view of literature markedly. He conceived a public authorial persona, joined social and political debates, and, within a few years, acted to change the literary environment itself by attempting to start his own military journal, *Voennyi listok* (Military Bulletin), in 1855 (the government denied him permission).[27] His war stories brought him prominence. Alexander II ordered that "Sevastopol in December" be translated into French.[28] In 1861, Tolstoy would start a pedagogical journal, *Yasnaya polyana*, drawing on his experience teaching peasants in the school he set up on his estate. Tolstoy wrote pedagogical articles and the journal put out twelve issues.[29]

As a young man, Tolstoy kept diaries and a Franklin journal, in which he tracked his moral weaknesses and goals for self-improvement. He crafted ambitious courses of self-study. Although his diary keeping was not continuous throughout his life, he returned again and again to the form until his very last days. He wrote thousands of letters, often filled with advice and instruction, especially in his later years. Beyond diaries and letters, yet still excluding Tolstoy's published fiction, are many reams of essays and other publicistic works that contain his pedagogy, philosophy, and moral instruction. "Even if one does not take into account all these drafts, corrections and copies, but just the overall quantity of printer's sheets and divides them by years (Tolstoy wrote for sixty years) it turns out that he wrote not less than fifty printer's sheets a year, which is more than four printer's sheets a month."[30] A printer's sheet was sixteen pages or so, which means Tolstoy averaged about two and a half pages per day. The sheer immensity of the ninety-volume Soviet Jubilee edition of Tolstoy's works is impressive.

Yet how Tolstoy became an author is more important than the fact that he wrote so much. It was not at all clear that he would become an author in the first place: "Do you remember, dear Aunt, a piece of advice you once gave me—to write novels? Well, I'm following your advice and the occupations I speak of consist of composing literature. I do not know if what I am writing [*Childhood*] will ever be published, but it is a work which amuses me, and at which I have persevered too long to abandon."[31] What makes this passage from an 1851 letter about Tolstoy's initial thoughts on *Childhood* attractive to biographers and others is that it seems to confirm an innate talent in the young Tolstoy. His dear Aunt Tatyana, who knew him better than anyone, must certainly have recognized something in the young man that made her think he could become a famous author. What was it, we wonder? His active imagination? His extreme sensitivity? His descriptive skill? His diaries?

We run into problems even as we ask those questions. Tolstoy was an avid writer before he became a published author. The contemporary reading public knew him, however, only as an author, and had little or no access to his diaries or letters, his literary fragments, and other miscellanea. Although such writings as Tolstoy's early diaries are both prior (they preceded the published work) and, in some general sense, causal (they were precursors to the published work), scholars and readers of today also generally know the author in published works first, then learn more about him through his written and unpublished work. Lydia Ginzburg illustrates how one may unify writer and author through an "autobiographic principle": "Tolstoi wrote neither autobiographies nor memoirs (except for the unfinished *Recollections of Childhood* begun in 1903), and the reason may well be that the autobiographical principle was already a pervasive part of his writing. His diaries served as the raw material for his moral maturation. The novels absorbed the detailed self-analysis, the introspection of the diaries, although that self-analysis was always summary in nature—a starting point for the work of self-improvement. That is why the diaries contain not investigations of Tolstoi's whole personality or character, but rather separate features, passions, and events as tests of that personality."[32] The novels and stories nevertheless create a problematic causal link for our reading of the unpublished material. We read backward to the unpublished material but assume its effect was carried forward.

Hans-Georg Gadamer described the awareness of such an approach to history as historically effected consciousness, and he argues that we must recognize that the past we study has itself shaped the way we look at it.[33] Tolstoy's diaries have affected how we look at them through the lens of the novels. The effect of the past, I would argue, has caused us to elide the important differences, in Tolstoy's case, between writing itself and writing for publication, between being a writer and being an author.

The past of a story or novel, its source, and its cause are all different things. Roland Barthes wrote that "the Author, when believed in, is always conceived of as the past of his own book."[34] We may equate Tolstoy historically with his writerly past, the early diaries, but we risk leaving out the most important variable of the equation: the man himself. He may not be the "past" of the text, but he is definitely the source. Tolstoy's relationship to his own authorial image was complex and sometimes paradoxical. He purposely uses the psychological forms he takes from early diaries and literary experiments to shape the image of the author that emerges in the later fiction.[35] Yet this mirror can be used as much to distort as to reveal. As an older man Tolstoy reinterpreted his early work and the authorial image that attended it. The later stories that deal with infidelity, such as "The Kreutzer Sonata," "The Devil," and *Resurrection*, reference the reader's knowledge of *Anna Karenina*, for example. Tolstoy also uses facts of his life to help shape a not entirely accurate authorial biography, for example, in the "Reminiscences" provided to his biographer Pavel Biriukov.[36]

The discursive connections that Tolstoy creates between his earlier and later works complicate how we view his authorship. The author here is not just the source of the text, nor simply something that accompanies the text like its shadow or reflection; in addition and more essentially, the Tolstoyan version of the author sustains a conversation about the text. This kind of authorship "establishes different forms of relationships among texts," as Michel Foucault says of the author's name.[37] Each time Tolstoy rearticulated an authorial identity, he reshuffled the relations among his various texts, elevating some while dismissing others. The easiest example of this sort of maneuver can be found in Tolstoy's repeated self-identifications with his fictional characters. Characters' names sounded very familiar to contemporaries who knew Tolstoy: Bolkonsky and Drubetskoi from *War and Peace* derive from Volkonsky and Trubetskoi (from Tolstoy's mother's and grandmother's names), and most notably Levin in *Anna Karenina* is unmistakably drawn from Tolstoy's first name, Lev (and the character Levin shares several of the author's interests and ideas). Another autobiographical character, Nekhlyudov, from *Resurrection*, stands out in particular, since Tolstoy repeats this name from several early works, thereby prompting the reader to posit connections between among this character and earlier ones.

A. N. Wilson makes the necessary, and perhaps too simple, point: "Tolstoy was profoundly self-obsessed, and it is this self-obsession which made him a writer. But the truth could be told the other way around. It could be said that it was only through the artifice of literature that he was able to comprehend or impose a shape on the inchoate business of existence."[38] That is a good explanation, as far as it goes; but Tolstoy himself was not unaware that man makes books and those books in turn help to make the man. One of the reasons soldiers explain their battle experiences in cliché, false ways in *War and Peace*, for example, is that they already know how war stories are supposed to sound. How the author influences the reader's understanding of a work of literature, and how the image of the author is formed in that reading, were always important to Tolstoy. He writes in 1853: "When one reads a work, especially a purely literary one, the chief interest lies in the character of the author as it expresses itself in the work. But there are some works in which the author pretends to a view, or changes his view several times. Most pleasing are those in which the author somehow tries to hide his personal view and at the same time remains constantly faithful to it wherever it is revealed. The most insipid works are those in which the view changes so frequently it is totally lost."[39] Tolstoy's suggestion that authors hide their personal views becomes a self-indictment of concealment twenty-five years later, in *A Confession*. As a newly published author himself, Tolstoy could, in the passage I just quoted, scarcely say such things without reflecting on his own authorial image. One must add, then, to Wilson's artifice of literature Tolstoy's own manipulative self-awareness—artifice squared, as it were.[40]

His notebooks testify to his transformation from a diary keeper to an aspiring author; in them, he pondered what this change meant. Tolstoy did not like the idea of becoming an author, for example, if it meant becoming a journalist. All of his relationships with journals were temporary and some were conflicted. In an 1871 letter he wrote: "To tell you the truth, I hate papers and journals—I haven't read them for a long time and consider them a harmful institution."[41] But a relationship with a journal was exactly what becoming an author tradi- tionally meant in Tolstoy's time. Only the most successful authors could pub- lish separate books. Any account of these early years must emphasize the institutional struggle Tolstoy built into his professional identity. His reluctance about an authorial career especially irked Turgenev, who was one of his early champions.

The humorous side of the sometimes affectionate, more often acrimonious, personal relationship between Turgenev and Tolstoy is well cataloged in the lore of Russian literature (how Tolstoy would refuse to get off Turgenev's couch, how Turgenev lent Tolstoy money to cover gambling debts, and how they quar- reled over George Sand—Tolstoy saying "that if her heroines actually existed, they should be tied to the hangman's cart and dragged through the streets of St Petersburg").[42] Turgenev was at one point romantically interested in Tolstoy's sister Maria, who was separated but not yet divorced from her husband. Yet any genuine friendship between Turgenev and Tolstoy ended in 1861, when Tolstoy criticized how Turgenev was raising his illegitimate daughter. (Turgenev had sent the girl to France, where Pauline Viardot looked after her education.) Several years later, in 1878, after Tolstoy's apparent conversion, they were reconciled—Turgenev again visited the Tolstoy estate at Yasnaya Polyana—but the two authors were never close.

Direct examples of Turgenev's literary influence on Tolstoy are rare.[43] In a late, retrospective statement, Tolstoy called *Notes of a Hunter* Turgenev's best work and linked it, obliquely, with his own *Childhood*. He says in 1902:

> I think that each great artist should also create his own forms. If the content of artistic works may be endlessly varied, so too may their form. Once in Paris, Turgenev and I returned home from the theater and spoke about it, and he agreed with me completely. We recalled all the best of Russian litera- ture, and it turned out that in these works the form was completely original. To say nothing of Pushkin, take *Dead Souls* by Gogol. What is it? Not a novel, not a novella. Something completely original. Then *Notes of a Hunter* by Turgenev—the best that Turgenev wrote. Dostoevsky's *House of the Dead*, then, sinner that I am, *Childhood*, Herzen's *My Past and Thoughts*, *A Hero of Our Time* and so forth.[44]

Tolstoy was fascinated with form and asserted the formal novelty of his major works. The structure, and especially the narrator, of Turgenev's cycle of stories no doubt caught his attention from the start. When asked in later years to list which authors and works had influenced him and how much, Tolstoy acknowledged *Notes of a Hunter* as very influential, one of just a handful of works that he said had an effect on him as a young man.[45] It is hard to know from such retrospective evaluations how deeply Turgenev's work actually shaped his own.

Nevertheless, the effect of Turgenev was, at first blush, stifling. In 1853 Tolstoy wrote in his diary: "Read *Notes of a Hunter* by Turgenev and somehow it's difficult to write after it [him]" (June 27, 1853).[46] Turgenev and just a few others were likely on his mind when he wrote the previous year in his diary: "Do I have talent compared to the new Russian men of letters? Definitely not."[47] A few months later (October 1852), Tolstoy began work on something entitled "Notes about the Caucasus. A Trip to Mamakai-Iurt," possibly under the influ- ence of Turgenev. (Nearly word-for-word excerpts from these notes eventually turn up in "The Woodfelling," which was dedicated to Turgenev, and in "The Raid," two early stories).[48] Nekrasov wrote to Turgenev of similarities between "The Woodfelling" and *Notes of a Hunter*.[49] As various critics have suggested, Tolstoy's novella *The Cossacks* was influenced by Turgenev's *Notes of a Hunter*.[50] Much later in his career, after listening to a reading of Turgenev's "First Love," the author of "The Kreutzer Sonata" remarked that "[Turgenev's] ending was a classic."[51] That ending includes, of course, a deathbed letter to the narrator from his father about the "poison" of women's love.[52] Such direct lines of contact between the two authors do little justice to how Turgenev affected Tolstoy's career. Turgenev was an early champion of Tolstoy, took him under his wing professionally, and later introduced him to a European audience.

More important, as pertains to our discussion of authorial identity, Turgenev also helped to establish the lasting image of Tolstoy as an unmanageable talent—brilliant, to be sure, but wild, unharnessed, uncultured, and uninterested in the typical responsibilities of authorship. He may have been one of the first to note what has since become a truism about Tolstoy: that he often performed his authorial identity, posing by turns as prophet or savage.[53] As he writes: "I have nicknamed him the 'troglodyte,' because of his savage ardor and buffalo-like obstinacy."[54] Turgenev's praise of Tolstoy is often couched in the conditional mood and future tense. He first wrote Nekrasov of the author of *Childhood*: "You're right—here's a promising talent. . . . Tell him, if he is interested, that I pay him greetings, bow, and applaud him."[55] And to Annenkov he writes: "If this young man continues as he began, he will go far,"[56] and, "I'll soon meet the sister of Tolstoy (the author of *Boyhood*—soon one won't have to add that epithet—only one Tolstoy will be known in Russia)."[57] Or, as he writes to Botkin: "He is, to be honest, the sole hope of our literature."[58] To others, he speaks of Tolstoy as the true successor of Gogol: "Read *Boyhood*. . . . There is the successor to Gogol at last!"[59] For Turgenev personally, Tolstoy represented an opportunity to mold an unformed and undeniable talent.

In advising Tolstoy, Turgenev reveals what he values in a contemporary author. His advice for Tolstoy falls into two categories. In the first, he urges Tolstoy to dedicate himself more thoroughly to the profession: "I simply love Russian literature too much not to want you to be outside the range of all kinds of stupid and undiscriminating bullets. . . . I repeat once again—your weapon is the pen, not the sword, and the Muses not only do not tolerate vanity but they are jealous mistresses."[60] He maintains this singularity of authorial identity when he writes again a few years later (1857): "You write that you are very glad not to have followed my advice and become only a writer of fiction. I do not want to argue the point—perhaps you are right. Only I, sinful man that I am and prone to error, no matter how hard I wrack my brains over it, for the life of me I cannot imagine what else you might be if not a fiction writer: an army officer perhaps? a landed gentleman? a philosopher? the founder of a new religion? a government official? a businessman?—be so good as to help me out of my difficulty. . . . I am joking, of course, but seriously—I really would so much like to see you go ahead full speed at last, with all sails set."[61] The second category of advice was more directly critical. "Turgenev," as Sorokin writes, "who thought of Tolstoy as a relatively pure product of savage ignorance and Muscovite bigotry, tried to prevent Tolstoy from injecting any messages of homespun philosophy in his work (he called it *mudrit'* —playing the wise man), in other words, from behaving like a prophet, until Tolstoy had improved his education and become civilized."[62] The question Sorokin leaves open is whether Tolstoy wanted to become civilized, especially in Turgenev's sense. For Tolstoy, Turgenev was a leading representative of the literary establishment that needed change.

Ernest Simmons notes, moreover, Tolstoy's early disapproval of the lack of morality in contemporary literature, and describes his resistance to becoming an author: "[While in the Caucasus] Tolstoy read with pen in hand, jotting down his reactions in the diary. His thoughts at the time about literature, and his own relation to it in the light of his dawning career, seemed to fluctuate with the uncertain state of his health. 'Literature is rubbish,' he wrote, 'and I should like to set down here rules and a plan of estate management.' . . . Contemporary literature was declining, he decided, because authors were producing too many light books for the sake of commercial gain."[63]

In short, Tolstoy had second thoughts about authorship as a career. He made plans in 1855 for reforming the army, for example.[64] Victor Shklovsky overstates the matter, however, when he writes of Tolstoy's authorial motivations simply that "he wanted to be like everyone else: if a man went to the Caucasus he had to come back covered, if only modestly, with military glory, or at least with some actions to his credit. Tolstoy did not realize yet that he was not like anyone else. He did not attribute much importance to his writing [in this case a second version of *Childhood*]."[65] On the contrary, Tolstoy was conscious of the steps he was taking toward becoming an author, and it shaped how he wrote his earliest works. His drafts to *Childhood* and his letters suggest he intended to control the process as much as possible.[66] He was unsure he wanted to be an author, perhaps, but when he did focus on becoming an author, he managed the process carefully.

I find it tempting to consider Tolstoy's becoming an author through the psychological lens of his diaries, Franklin journals, and efforts at self-improvement. As Ginzburg says, his analysis of a character's thoughts resembles the analysis of himself taken from his diary.[67] The problem with the interpretation is that, while it deepens our understanding of the development of Tolstoy's style of writing and the genius of his psychological insight, it provides a marginal explanation of why he actually became an author. At least since the time of Chernyshevsky, praise for the early Tolstoy nevertheless usually underscores his talent for psychological description.[68] Yet writing diaries, and writing as a means of self-improvement, are neither necessary nor sufficient to explain why Tolstoy decided to write the novel *Childhood*, to make it fictional, to imagine it as part of a longer work (*Four Epochs*), to send it to the most important publisher of the day, or to embark on the literary *career* itself.

OVERCOMING THE PSYCHOLOGICAL TOLSTOY

The past, no matter how it is revived, is already dead, killed by time itself.[69]

— *Boris Eikhenbaum*

Our interpretive approach to Tolstoy should avoid conflating two pertinent meanings of psychology: the author's personal psychology, as we know it through his biography, and the author's method of psychological characterization in his fiction. As a mature author of fiction, Tolstoy was unrivaled in his psychological descriptions, but to enthrone mimesis as the ruling mode of Tolstoy's fiction would be to elevate psychology above other explanatory systems. It is be better to question whether we get Tolstoy right, I will argue, than to wonder whether Tolstoy got the world right. Tolstoy's art transcends his realistic psychological descriptions. The implications of the traditional psychological approach to Tolstoy, especially in his early career, are far reaching. Tolstoy's entry into the world of authorship is influenced by his diary writing and by his nearly obsessive moral self-examination. But authorship, as I have argued, is also a public, rhetorical, and institutional process of positioning oneself in relation to other voices. Writing is not the same as authorship. So we must consider the psychological tradition in Tolstoy scholarship in order to distinguish more precisely writing from authorship. Tolstoy's narrative alibi begins when he connects the absences in his fiction with the ability to manipulate authorial identity.

The personal psychology of the author is closely related to authorship but is not a window into it. The fact that psychology can screen our view of Tolstoy and misrepresent his fiction and his authorial biography has certainly not been lost on critics. "Inasmuch as Tolstoy's personal reasons for writing fiction were partly confessional," Donna Orwin writes, "he resisted such writing (often unsuccessfully) as undignified. . . . My own opinion is that Tolstoy did not intend to make sense of his old age, and therefore cannot be reconstituted according to rules of psychological reason."[70] By refocusing on Tolstoy's aesthetics or his religious philosophy, for example, scholars have thematized the anti-psychological aspects of Tolstoy's prose. Thus, Amy Mandelker describes how literary framing techniques mediate the way we view Tolstoy's most famous heroine, Anna Karenina. Because Tolstoy views her as an embodiment of art and artifice, these framing techniques reveal Tolstoy's attitudes toward forms of literary art itself, and the Victorian novel in particular.[71] It is not a question of whether psychology pertains to the discussion of Anna Karenina's character; Tolstoy's portrayal of Anna has devastatingly accurate, realistic psychological detail. With Mandelker, we ask, rather, how Tolstoy's views on art (not his views on reality) shape that psychological portraiture. Anna's lack of a personal history strips her of a biography that would otherwise root her psychology, for example, thereby focusing us all the more on the aesthetics she represents. Form and psychology are not easily separated.

In his prefatory remarks to *The Young Tolstoi*, Boris Eikhenbaum defends his formal approach to literature by declaring the past already dead. And if the past is already dead, then formalist analysis, which concentrates on meanings immanent in the text, is not guilty of killing it. This interpretation of the young Tolstoy is Eikhenbaum's most methodologically formalistic; Eikhenbaum even uses the term *morphological* to describe his analysis. "The basic theme of this first part, as well as of the following parts will be Tolstoi's poetics. The central questions will concern his artistic traditions and his system of stylistic and compositional devices."[72] Eikhenbaum regrets that studies of Tolstoy are stuck on what he calls an "iconographic approach," which venerates the man and his ideas over his literary works. "At the same time," he argues, "many sense the necessity of 'overcoming' Tolstoi. Apparently we are entering a new region of Russian prose, one seeking new paths away from the psychological novel of Tolstoi or Dostoevsky. . . . Against this background, the study of Tolstoi strikes me as an immediate task. To 'overcome' an artistic style means to understand it."[73] An important reason for understanding Tolstoy, according to Eikhenbaum, is to overcome the psychological novel he represents—just as Tolstoy himself overcame the romanticism of Lermontov and others.

Overcoming Tolstoy can also be understood as overcoming both the imposing biography of the man and his psychological literary analysis. Thus there are two kinds of psychology to the iconographic Tolstoy: biographical and literary. Not just any Tolstoy scholar, Eikhenbaum was also an elegant summarizer and defender of formalism, as in his essay "Theory of the 'Formal Method,' " published in 1927. Yet there is something different in this preface to *The Young Tolstoi*. Eikhenbaum likely knew, even as early as 1921, that the formal approach was only a provisional means of overturning the iconographic Tolstoy. He complains in the first paragraph of his study of his inability to make use of manuscripts in the Tolstoy archive, "which continue to be inaccessible to 'outsiders,' even those interested not in the domestic but in purely literary materials."[74] (The domestic aspect of Tolstoy's biography has a way of insinuating itself into everything.) There is a missing connection between Tolstoy's biography and his decision to become an author: a link, unexplored by Eikhenbaum, between the psychology of the man and the psychological style deployed by the author. In fact, we do not know exactly how or when Tolstoy's psychological analysis of himself in his diaries was transformed into the means and desire to write fiction. We should indeed overcome psychology (of the man) in our study of Tolstoy, but not by imprisoning psychology in brackets, as it were, by intimating that it is a set of inconsequential facts about an iconographic figure.

In the transition from *The Young Tolstoi* to his later volumes on Tolstoy, Eikhenbaum was caught between immanent and contingent approaches to Tolstoy, between considering only the literary text and considering that same literary text through the prism of "a socially engaged Tolstoy who cannot abide the thought that any decision affecting Russia might be made without his participation."[75] Because the two methods seemed unbridgeable, the later approach was perceived, as Carol Any writes, "by both his Marxist opponents and his formalist friends, as a major concession, if not an utter capitulation, to official [Soviet] policy."[76] Even as early as in his first published novel, *Childhood*, Tolstoy plays these approaches off one another and seems to insist that we see his mind and autobiography behind the very works he most uses to hide himself. *Childhood* initiates a key theme in the interpretation of Tolstoy's works: to what extent is his fiction autobiographical? And how important is autobiography to understanding Tolstoy's fiction? Tolstoy's contradictions, long recognized as an essential part of his biography, were productive, not pernicious for his fiction.[77]

Examples of the remarkable psychological perspicacity that characterizes Tolstoy's fiction are everywhere in his unpublished writing. Ginzburg sees that connection as key to Tolstoy's art. She writes: "The documentary character of Tolstoy's writing consists of the fact that his heroes not only address the same problems of existence that he addressed, but that they address them in the same psychological form and in relation to virtually the same everyday circumstances that he himself was faced with."[78] That parallel, so influential in our appreciation of Tolstoy, creates problems when we turn our attention more exclusively to questions of authorship. Authorship is not just the production of a literary text, after all; it is the manipulation and management of a public persona.

Just as frequently noted is the relationship between Tolstoy's yearning for moral improvement and his literary activities. Here, the connection with psychology and, more exactly, with his motivation to become an author is in view. Tolstoy's self-analysis is not for psychological but for moral reasons, and the two are clearly connected. Henry Gifford writes: "He was genuinely concerned with his moral condition; he wanted badly to find something durable he could believe in. At the same time the act of recording his observations delighted him for its own sake. The diaries are also a writer's workshop, littered with sketches, notes, and projects. . . . The anxiety for betterment was real, but the keenest satisfaction came from his newly found art. It would remain always a problem to reconcile the demands of art with those of living."[79] Gifford infers this satisfaction on the basis of too little, I think, when we recall the lack of a record of Tolstoy's earliest thoughts about his own authorship. Was he self-satisfied? Can one write a diary without implicitly or explicitly recognizing the self as worthy of description? Orwin pairs Tolstoy's desire to improve morally with the birth of his fiction: "The failure of his early attempts to control and shape his own life (and the consequences of his own Rousseauist philosophical orientation) taught him that education had to take place not through reason and philosophy, but through the sentiments and, therefore, art. In the art that grew from his twin fascinations with details and philosophical generalization, the young Tolstoy may be said to have had two goals: to re-create reality and to order it according to higher moral truth."[80] Tolstoy learns from the philosopher Rousseau not to learn from philosophy. One can frequently see Tolstoy's attempts in the early fiction to combine art and morality, triangulating psychology, morality, and art.

Eikhenbaum worked with the assumption that the diaries have psychological form but no psychological explanation. In the preface to *The Young Tolstoi* we see that Eikhenbaum meant to overcome a psychological approach to Tolstoy, not to substantiate it further. Yet several years later, he wrote in a passage influential enough to be quoted at length:

> Evaluating his behavior with the help of a "Franklin" table of weaknesses, Tolstoy as a result sharpened his methods of self-observation and became interested in the paradoxical quality of mental life, the disjunction of it with the "rules." . . . Even if one does not know the early literary experiments of Tolstoy, it is possible to establish that they had to be closely connected to his diaries—as their design or summary. The fundamental elements of the diary, detailed and compared in the form of consecutive description, interrupted by general arguments, definitions and aphorisms—such was the construction of that "history of today," which Tolstoy undertook for several days before leaving Moscow for Yasnaya Polyana. He had no other material, but his "favorite" writer Sterne ("A Sentimental Journey") served as a suitable literary model for the reworking of this material.[81]

Here, though one senses a continued struggle between intrinsic and extrinsic explanations, Eikhenbaum leans more heavily on the psychological explanation, on the smooth transition from diary to fiction.

For Ginzburg, who was directly influenced by Eikhenbaum and the other formalists, there is little that separates the documentary from the novelistic.[82] She cites a proportional relationship between Tolstoy's writing (unpublished) and authorship (published) that turns on aesthetic structure. "Aesthetic structuring increases," she argues, "as one moves from letters and diaries to biographies and memoirs, and thence to the novel and the tale. . . . But there is a unifying principle. The letter and the novel, according to this view, represent different levels in the structuring of images of personality [*lichnost'*], and at any level in that structuring the aesthetic element is inevitably present."[83]

This interpretation of the difference between a diary and, say, a novel as one of degree of aesthetic structuring allows Ginzburg to treat all kinds of writing in a similar manner, and with similar sophistication and success. Yet Tolstoy himself did not think of the difference between a diary and a novel as a matter of aesthetic structure alone. Aesthetic structure fits within a larger set of Tolstoy's authorial concerns about the mediation of literary communication with readers.

THE MEDIATION IS THE MESSAGE

I have noticed that some people who are not only clever but capable of sparkling in society have lost out in the end because they lacked [a] sense of timing. If you speak heatedly and then become too bored and listless to reply, the last impression lingers and people say, "How dull he is . . ."

— "A History of Yesterday"

Tolstoy was often just as interested in the ways he could not access the inner workings of the mind as in the ways he could, and that boundary of accessibility to the mind remained at the center of his aesthetics. In his efforts to re-present, not reflect, reality in fiction, Tolstoy felt constrained by the barriers of language, genre, literary tradition, and social expectations of the author, and he seems to have become fascinated by the effect of mediation itself, as many scholars have noted.[84] The framing of a work of literature is one kind of mediation, but there are other kinds, too. Language itself emerges as one of the ultimate barriers to the expression of the contents of the mind, and Tolstoy used this sense of language as barrier, "contra semiosis," as one scholar puts it, in even his earliest works.[85] Liza Knapp writes, for example, that the inner monologue of Tolstoy's characters is not so much realistic psychology as "an attempt to formulate a mode of discourse that transcends 'external language' and evokes the abyss, the unknowable, what lies beyond death."[86] (In later years, Tolstoy would even describe how one's animal or material self conceals one's true spiritual self.)[87]

Tolstoy discovered, moreover, that he could use this unknowable abyss as a way to cloak and manipulate his own authorial identity, to become unknowable, or at least less accessible.[88] Once he evoked the darkness, so to speak, Tolstoy found it a convenient place to hide. Irina Paperno describes Tolstoy's encounter in his diaries with his "inaccessible self" as similar to an experience of death: "The search for the true self turned into an impossible mission of defining the non-self of the true being, which lay outside language. His last hope was death: it was in death that the author hoped to finally experience the truth of a selfless being. It would seem that, against reason, he hoped to leave a record of this experience."[89] The most essential aspect of being, death, is unknowable and unrepresentable. Yet Tolstoy endeavors to record his struggle to represent the unrepresentable. In his early diaries, Tolstoy attempted to improve himself morally by writing an account in the past tense of the current day (in large part what he did *not* do that day), followed by a schedule with infinitive verbs of tasks and goals listed under the next date. This clever analysis of life missed one thing only, as Paperno notes, the present: "not even one day was entirely present."

Tolstoy's encounter with the "non-self of the true being," as Paperno puts it, is an extreme case; authors respond in many ways to the alienation of the writing process, which relies on a language that always belongs at least in part to an other. Mikhail Bakhtin suggests that Tolstoy recognized the foreignness of language and tried to make it univocal, utterly his own. He entered into a kind of battle with the otherness of language, denying its alterity by bending meaning to his exclusive monologic will.[90] And it is true that Tolstoy's stories and novels sometimes leave readers with the impression that the implied author and omniscient narrator know and can put words to everything, from the meaning of Christianity to the tiniest thought that flashes through the mind of a single character. But for Tolstoy, language is neither an instrument to be wielded with absolute power nor a mirror of the self. He often idealizes it as a mode of being, a kind of practice. Consider, as a metaphor of language, the passage I just quoted as an epigraph: Tolstoy's description of how to play cards from his earliest extant story, "A History of Yesterday": "In the course of the game one may chat, gratify one's ego, and make witty remarks; furthermore, one is not obligated to keep to the same subject, as one is in that society where there is only conversation. . . . I have noticed that some people who are not only clever but capable of sparkling in society have lost out in the end because they lacked [a] sense of timing. If you speak heatedly and then become too bored and listless to reply, the last impression lingers and people say, 'How dull he is . . .' But when people play cards this does not happen. One may remain silent without incurring censure."[91] We are reminded here first, one should say, of Tolstoy's relative immaturity. An older Tolstoy would not find society life so profound. Nevertheless, children's games, such as the chalk-letter game Levin and Kitty play in *Anna Karenina*, are important to Tolstoy for similar, microcosmic reasons. Language in this ideal form of card playing in "A History of Yesterday," exists between talking (social action—the performance of words, the ability to "sparkle") and silence (isolated and mute ideation, the timing of a pause). For his entire authorial life, Tolstoy bears witness to the powerful boundary between silence and speaking, between nothingness and text; he struggles against it, and uses it in his experiments with narrative form. What Tolstoy discovers in his early autobiographical fiction is a narrative practice, how to be a writer between the said and the unsaid. The concluding paragraphs of "Sevastopol in May" (1855) literally asks: "perhaps I ought to have left it unsaid." And even a small text like the earlier "A History of Yesterday" (1850) is governed by the opposition between said and unsaid. The narrator wants to tell a history of yesterday, but so many impressions and thoughts occur in one day that he would never be able to. There would not be "ink enough in the world" to write such a history. And so the narrator tells us a history, but reminds us that the reality of that history, its entirety, is impossible to describe.[92]

Richard Gustafson's profound and influential work on Tolstoy's religious thought and its relation to his fiction focuses on another kind of mediation, both more and less elemental. If salvation is what one is seeking, then the stuff of real life itself intrudes, and is a kind of mediation between birth and the afterlife. For Gustafson, the Orthodox icon best symbolizes Tolstoy's art, precisely because of its mediated nature: "Tolstoy's emblematic imagination is iconic. . . . An icon of a saint, therefore, is an image of the Image of God. . . . In the Eastern Christian tradition art is thrice-removed from reality. An emblem is just such an image thrice removed."[93] Tolstoy was thus engaged in a project of continual enunciation, of clarification and reclarification of his most cherished ideas: "The pattern of this relationship is shaped by the process of articulation. The primary rule in reading Tolstoy, therefore, is that the later clarifies the earlier."[94] Gustafson rejects strictly biographical and psychological readings of Tolstoy's fiction (and especially notes Tolstoy's critique of the philosophy of empiricism), and relies on a structuralist analysis that derives key concepts from the whole system of Tolstoy's works.[95] This strategy tends to collapse our sense of Tolstoy's authorial development and, by valuing later statements over earlier ones, renders significant conflicts in Tolstoy's thought as detours on the road to further clarification.

Some contemporary Tolstoy critics, several of whom I have not yet mentioned here, consider directly Tolstoy's problem with the mediating relationship of art to reality. Gary Saul Morson argues that Tolstoy confronts an inconceivably complex real world and strives to replicate that complexity by means of his ingenious creative strategies: "Narrative necessarily falsifies, and yet, of course *War and Peace* is itself a narrative. . . . How does one write a narrative exemplifying the falsity of all narratives?"[96] Vladimir Alexandrov treats mediation as one of the fundamental aesthetic and critical problems of our day. While admitting that in interpretation some mediation is inevitable, he argues that "not all mediations are equal, and the criterion for choosing among them is ultimately ethical: *that mediation is best that mediates least.*"[97] Especially later in his career, Tolstoy disparages aesthetic ornamentation on ethical grounds. Sometimes, however, Tolstoy purposely uses more mediation rather than less—to comic (Pierre as a mason) or profound (the red square of "Diary of a Madman") effect.

The concept of mediation is best considered in such contexts when it directly pertains to Tolstoy's aesthetics. In its most important and basic sense, mediation created for Tolstoy an either-or dilemma: he could have either art or life. His solution was to reject the dilemma and to create narrative structures that embrace a rhetoric of both-and: *both* art and life. With the notion of narrative alibi, I hope to evoke both the crime that, as Tolstoy came to believe, belletristic literature perpetrates as well as the impossibility of his committing it. Tolstoy gets his art and rejects it at the same time.

AN AUTHOR OF ABSENCE

FORMS OF NEGATIVE CREATION

From youth I prematurely began to analyze everything and to destroy mercilessly.

— *Diary, November 6, 1873*

All authors confront an empty page that needs to be filled with words, just as all struggle from paragraph to paragraph in deciding how much information the reader requires to understand settings, plots, and characters. Tolstoy was different from most in his extensive use of that which cannot be said or written as the negative space against which his fiction takes shape. For example, in *War and Peace* he asserts so often and so fervently that one can neither plan a battle nor describe it accurately that one wonders how the story grew to the length of four or five novels. The play of absence and presence in Tolstoy's work — in this case what cannot be told and what can — reminds us of how frequently he puzzled over the ontological status of fiction. Early in his career, he would have been pleased if readers took his fiction as a piece of life simply to be experienced rather than interpreted according to one set of literary conventions or another. Later, though, Tolstoy almost completely abandoned traditional belletristic literature for moralistic tales and essays. Paradoxically, these tales always seem to require the kind of decoding, or elaboration of the moral, that the earlier author would have rejected as both cumbersome and reductionist.

Traditionally, the notion of negativity and negative space has been far more important for the plastic and visual arts than it has been for narrative fiction. The outline of a statue takes shape in relation to the empty space that the chisel leaves behind. A photograph places its subject in relation to foregrounded and backgrounded images, and the image itself becomes perceptible only to the degree that it is differentiated from the objects it is not. Artists have often taken advantage of this essential characteristic of the image by contrasting object and shadow. Both presence and absence are necessary for the image to be perceived.

In *Anna Karenina*, Mikhailov paints, for want of a better term, by negation or subtraction.[1] He tries to eliminate what prevents an image or idea from appearing fully to the viewer; he "removes the wrappings": "He knew that much attention and care were needed not to injure one's work when removing the wrappings that obscure the idea, and that all wrappings must be removed. . . . In all he painted and ever had painted he saw defects that were an eyesore to him, the results of carelessness in removing the shell of the idea, which he could not now remedy without spoiling the work as a whole. And in almost all the figures and faces he saw traces of wrappings that had not been entirely removed and that spoilt the picture."[2] This idea of removing the wrappings creates a visual metaphor not only for the artistic process but also for more substantial questions of existential truth. In the chapter devoted to the death of Levin's brother Nikolai, the last thing the dying man does is "clutch" at his clothing: "And Levin noticed that all day long the sick man really kept catching at himself as if wishing to pull something off."[3] This narrative sequence follows directly after the chapters devoted to Anna and Vronsky's visit to Italy and to Mikhailov's studio, thus allowing the original image of wrappings to broaden into a philosophically profound metaphor, an overarching metaphor in Tolstoy's fiction: clothing, furnishings, and material objects in general obstruct and obscure the truth. In later stories, such as "The Death of Ivan Ilyich" and "Master and Man," Tolstoy returns again to the idea that a main task of illness and death is to strip away the material and egoistic impediments to spiritual salvation.[4]

It is a remarkable characteristic of *Anna Karenina*, and of Tolstoy's novels in general, that seemingly peripheral subjects such as painting or aesthetic vision become, on closer inspection, crucial to Tolstoy's most cherished ideas. The notion of aesthetic vision emerges, at first, from Tolstoy's curiosity about the vagaries of visual perception—that vision can be deceptive—and subsequently matures into a key metaphor of salvation. This is a different sort of truth from that associated with Tolstoy's "absolute language," those generalizing, authoritative dicta that one comes across from time to time in the novels and stories.[5] Morson notes that Tolstoy's absolutes (e.g., "But pure and perfect sorrow is as impossible as pure and absolute joy") tend to be negative.[6]

The truths of Tolstoy's absolute statements often reside in the "negative space" that prepares the reader for an important image or visual composition. Rudolf Arnheim writes that negative spaces—the emptiness created by the chisel that gives shape to the stone—require "sufficient figure quality to be perceivable in their own right."[7] What one cannot visualize in the language of the novel prepares one for what can be visualized. Take the opening to *Anna Karenina*, in which the Oblonsky household, and ultimately Stiva on the leather sofa in his study, materialize out of the context of two of Tolstoy's most authoritative statements in the novel—the biblical epigraph, "Vengeance is mine, I will repay," and the famous opening lines, "All happy families resemble one another. Each unhappy family is unhappy in its own way." Pause for a moment and visualize just what those lines depict. "Everything was upset in the Oblonsky household" is somewhat better, but still too colloquial and vague to put before the mind's eye. In fact, the entire second paragraph of the novel, while effectively creating a general image of domestic chaos, contains little visual detail. It is not until Stiva, with his "plump, well-kept body," appears on the "morocco leather-covered" sofa with springs that readers have anything substantial to imagine.[8] As Stiva opens his eyes so do readers—but what a difference there is between what he sees and what we see (we see *him*)!

Tolstoy's language seems to support Stiva's plump body by placing his fleshy infidelity in the verbal context of the novel's broader ideas; but his indulgent physicality also tempers Tolstoy's language and the absolutism of the epigraph.[9] For there can be no question: this happy man will not really suffer vengeance for this or any other infidelity. The novel's epigraph thus creates an imageless discursive space that prepares for Stiva's bodily appearance. When he first opens his eyes that morning, Stiva is disappointed to find the real world in place of his dream, truth instead of fiction. We too are meant to see the truth instead of fiction in *Anna Karenina*, but not to share Stiva's disappointment.

The language and imagery of the novel play on the tension between presence and absence, even at moments that would seem to be psychologically particular and exact. In part IV, chapter 17, the narrator says of Vronsky: "And in fact in a moment his thoughts grew confused and [Vronsky] began to fall into the abyss of forgetfulness [пропасть забвения].[10] The waves of the sea of unconscious life were beginning to close over his head when all at once he felt as if he had received a violent electric shock." Tolstoy uses the word *пропасть* just six times in *Anna Karenina*, but does so in a particular way. The Russian пропасть has two divergent meanings: an abyss or precipice, and a mass or abundance; the verb проПАСТЬ, rather than ПРОпасть, means to disappear, vanish or, more idiomatically, to perish or die. Thus one does not stretch the meaning of the Russian noun пропасть too much by underscoring the contradictory significance here of absence versus presence, and scarcity versus plenitude. Tolstoy plainly drives a wedge between the two meanings: for Karenin (129; *PSS* 18: 151), Vronsky (379; *PSS* 18: 437), and Anna (389; *PSS* 18: 450) пропасть is an abyss or precipice; for scenes involving Levin, пропасть means a mass or an abundance. For Levin, пропасть means "a mass of thoughts and feelings" (146; "пропасть мыслей и чувств ," 18: 169), "lots of elk" (402–3; "лосей пропасть," *PSS* 19: 10) to be shot with his hunting companion, not to mention "quantities of snipe and double-snipe too" (536; "Бекасов пропасть. "И дупеля есть," *PSS* 19: 165). Notice how the translator changes the tone of the same word as it appears in different English equivalents alongside "thoughts and feelings" versus "elk" or "snipe." No matter how it is translated, however, the vacuum of meaning that threatens Karenin, Vronsky, and Anna has no analogue in the idiomatic use of the word by Levin.

Tolstoy appears to use these opposite meanings of пропасть in significant ways. In "Two Hussars," for example, there is an abundance (*пропасть хоро-шеньких*) of lovely girls. In "Family Happiness," a precursor to *Anna Karenina*, Masha approaches an abyss (*пропасть*) of destruction wrought by infidelity. In *The Cossacks* the bottomless abyss (*бездонная пропасть*) into which a young man is willing to throw himself is in fact considered by Olenin to be a source of vitality. Pierre, by contrast, is terrified of the inexorably approaching abyss (to wit, his marriage to Helene) in *War and Peace*. Tragedy is given to Pierre's comedy when Andrei describes to him the horror of facing his own wife's death as the "abyss"; but Andrei also soon thereafter—after meeting Natasha, to be more precise—realizes that his wealth of experiences would "be abundantly gratu-itous/in vain [проПАСТЬ даром]" if he were not to take an active role in life again. Not too surprisingly, Ivan Ilyich also approaches the abyss as he begins to guess at the conclusion of his illness. Pozdnyshev in "The Kreutzer Sonata" describes his arguments with his wife as revealing an abyss between them. In "The Devil" there is an "abundance" of reasons why Evgeny chooses Liza as his wife, and she has an "abundance" of taste and tact. Tolstoy often uses this word to describe the fear and faith one has in love's ability to transform us.

In *Resurrection*, пропасть is a marker of Nekhlyudov's moral transformation, and Tolstoy emphasizes its role in Nekhlyudov's personal identity (note that he repeats Nekhlyudov's name three times in two sentences): "Then he used to have to devise things to do, and the interest of his work was always one and the same—Dmitri Ivanovich Nekhludov; and yet, notwithstanding the fact that the entire interest of life had Dmitri Ivanovich as its pivot, all this work was boring. Now all his work concerned other people, and not Dmitri Ivanovich, and it was all interesting and absorbing, and there was an abundance [пропасть] of it."[11] These two meanings, an "abyss" and an "abundance," are not inherently opposed to one another—though clearly Tolstoy intends to contrast absence with presence, nothingness with near excess. Were the significance of absence not so obvious, one could consider both under the rubric of the "dangers of plenitude" (the Russian phrase *бездонная пропасть*, a bottomless or fathomless abyss, contains this sense of dangerous infinity). For example, Tolstoy not infrequently used the narrative trope of disaster striking the happy man, like Job. When a man (it is usually a man) has everything he could want and more (ПРОпасть), then he seems most at risk of losing it all (проПАСТЬ). Prince Andrei when he has Natasha's love, Karenin when he triumphs in politics, Levin when his son is born (and he feels newly vulnerable), and Ivan Ilyich with his promotion and new home are good examples.

It is also true, however, that facing the abyss can provide a moment of rejuvenation, an opportunity for self-creation that flickers briefly in the dark and disappears. Woe to the man, Karenin, for example, who sees nothing in that moment of illumination. This creative possibility suggests the analogue to authorship. Tolstoy does seem to relish the creative opportunity of the experience of nothingness in life, and one wonders how much of this experience Tolstoy himself shared—not in a life-threatening situation but in an artistic one. Did he ever "remove the wrappings," as Mikhailov did, and discover nothing?

AN ALIBI FOR BEING

There is no alibi for being.

—Mikhail Bakhtin

The critic most responsible for drawing early attention to Tolstoy's thematization of negativity was Apollon Grigoriev. In a well-known review from 1862, he ascribes Tolstoy's remarkable uniqueness to his "analysis of spiritual movements which no one had analysed before."[12] Although this kind of psychological analysis was first noted by Chernyshevsky, Grigoriev sees in it "only one thing in common with the methods of our time—negation."[13] Grigoriev ties Tolstoy's psychological observations to a social problem of the day, and Tolstoy's psychology is authenticated and all the more significant for its social implications. The target Tolstoy chooses above all else, according to Grigoriev, is "elevated" or "extraordinary" human feelings. Tolstoy's analysis of these feelings goes too far, says Grigoriev, and Tolstoy slips into a kind of, as the critic phrases it, "pantheistic despair" in "Lucerne," "Albert," and "Notes of a Billiard Marker." Moreover, "this analysis turns into something with no content, into an analysis of analysis, which through its lack of content leads to skepticism and an undermining of any spiritual feelings. The key to the ultimate destination of this analysis is the death of the oak tree in 'Three Deaths' which is presented on a level of consciousness superior to that of the sophisticated landowner's wife and that of the simple peasant. From this there is surely but one step to Nihilism."[14] In our own day it is difficult to imagine the shudder that the word *nihilism* could send down the collective spine of nineteenth-century Russian conservatism.[15] But Grigoriev misses the fact that Tolstoy developed nihilism's psychological and aesthetic rather than philosophical and sociological implications, and thus misses the aesthetics Tolstoy defined by plumbing the depths of nihilism: Tolstoy's "contentless" analysis produces a veritable world in fiction while undermining and transforming traditional mimesis. Tolstoy was aware that his version of realism was no passive mirror to the world; he often chose to emphasize the real world's potential for meaning and transformation. Andrei in *War and Peace* contemplates the unfathomable sky, as Levin does in his own way (he makes metaphors of the clouds) while resting on the hay in *Anna Karenina*. They both remake themselves by contemplating that nothingness. Tolstoy's story "The Diary of a Madman" figures the negative space of unknowability as a red square. Unable to conceive of the meaning of life, and fearing the inevitability of death, the narrator of the "Diary" slips into a feverish delirium. "Life and death somehow merged into one another. Something was tearing my soul apart and could not complete the action. . . . Always the same horror: red, white, and square. Something tearing within that yet could not be torn apart."[16] Echoes of the apocalypse sound throughout the narrator's crisis, as opposites (life and death) merge and the indivisible (the soul) divides. What persists in this delirium is the image of the square, meaningless and foreboding.

Tolstoy often returned to the conception of death as an experience of nothingness.[17] Kathleen Parthe, who has devoted a number of articles to the theme of death in Tolstoy's oeuvre, compares the square of "Madman" to other equivocating grammatical devices Tolstoy used in his descriptions of death: "At first glance, the square seems to be a marked departure from Tolstoy's usual repertoire of devices for signifying death, which consist of personal pronouns (*ona* 'it [fem.],' *ono* 'it [neuter]'), indefinite pronouns (*chto-to* 'something'), demonstrative pronouns (*eto* 'this,' *to* 'that'), and certain third-person verb forms with 'something' or the neuter 'it' in subject position or with no subject at all. Tolstoy relied on various means of grammatical 'masking' available in Russian to achieve the desired effect of namelessness and the appearance of actions (as Shestov said) 'without a cause.' Indirect signification of death is appropriate and effective because death is difficult to understand, frightening, and taboo."[18] By "masking," Parthe is referring to Tolstoy's practice of obscuring the agent of an action in order to disorient the reader.

Tolstoy's symbols of death, and of the dying process, have frequently been noted for their inscrutability. In "The Death of Ivan Ilyich," which Tolstoy was working on while writing "Madman,"[19] Ivan is thrust into a "narrow, deep black sack" as he dies.[20] In *War and Peace*, Tolstoy describes Andrei dying and imagining something ("it") outside the door, trying to get in. As Nikolai Levin lies in bed dying, in *Anna Karenina*, he begins clutching at himself, as though trying to remove some kind of covering or wrapping. In "Master and Man," the snow-storm, elusive and unknowable, pushes and pulls Vasily Andreevich and Nikita until they finally have to stop.

. The image that captures Vasily Andreevich's last moments is both remarkable and characteristic of Tolstoy: "At first, impressions of the snow-storm, the sleigh-shafts, and the horse under the shaft-bow, . . . all presented themselves to [Vasily Andreevich's] imagination. Afterwards all these impressions blended into one nothingness [в одно ничто]. As the colors of the rainbow unite into one white light, so all these different impressions mingled into one, and he fell asleep."[21] Death itself takes no perceptible shape but blends into an illuminating "nothingness," like white light, showing Vasily Andreevich the way to self-sacrifice and salvation. Note how the "nothingness" here is not opposed to something; absence does not take meaning from its opposition to presence but is itself primary.[22] Like many of Tolstoy's later narratives shaped by alibi, the plot of "Master and Man" describes an arc whereby the main characters intend to travel "elsewhere" but in fact traverse a path from nonbeing (an inauthentic life) to being.

Being, in this instance, is not a form of social existence. Tolstoy's thinking about this runs directly counter to that of Mikhail Bakhtin. As David Sloane puts it: "If one's primary aim were to understand Tolstoy, one would say that the Bakhtinian model of discourse is simply incapable of describing the dynamics of non-verbal and preverbal thought so crucial to the experience of Tolstoy's characters."[23] Caryl Emerson considers Bakhtin's thoughts on Tolstoy before he turned to linguistic analysis (and to seemingly utter condemnation of Tolstoy). The notes of an early student of Bakhtin show that Bakhtin considered Tolstoy's failed attempts to balance two aspects of selfhood in his fiction, the I-for-myself and the I-for-the-other. Emerson explains: "But Bakhtin's point seems to be that Tolstoy's swollen 'I' refuses on principle to credit the self that *others* see, need, reach out for, attempt to implicate, with any legitimacy at all. What is more: Tolstoy sees the I-for-the-other as a fallen, depraved state precisely *because* it is sensitized to the needs and pressures from others. Ideally, one's 'I' should not respond to and incorporate these outside pressures, but strive to outgrow them. 'Throughout the rest of his creative work,' we read in Mirkina's notes, 'Tolstoy will distribute the world between these two categories; "I-for-others" will become all of society, while "I-for-myself" will be isolated and alone.'"[24] In

Resurrection Nekhlyudov's experience of the abyss is split in just this way; his conversion separates his selfishness from his selflessness.

"There is no alibi for being," as Bakhtin liked to say, emphasizing what he believed was a person's responsibility to participate fully in the individualizing processes of the social world of discourse. To be is, for Bakhtin, first and foremost to be an interlocutor; and to be an author of literature is to be a special kind of interlocutor, one who confronts the essence of authentic experience by aesthetically shaping the word. Some authors keep close to this truth-bearing path, Bakhtin went on to theorize, as they bravely maintain a "dialogic" openness toward the unknown world. Other authors shrink from the challenge of dialogue. Dostoevsky is a hero for Bakhtin, and Tolstoy by contrast almost a coward. Dostoevsky created a new novel that celebrates a dialogic multitude of voices, whereas Tolstoy drained the life from language in his novels, forcing it into monologic, univocal quiescence. Afraid of life itself, Tolstoy merely nudges the cold carcass of his prose into a vivacious simulacrum of life.

Though Bakhtin's disdainful interpretation of Tolstoy is unwarranted, it does provide an insight into the way that Tolstoy exerts authorial control over his fiction. Tolstoy uses narrative structure to exemplify a kind of authorial despair, his doubt in his own ability to overcome the mediation of literary language and convention, to reach others. By tearing down the structures of meaning he builds in his fiction, Tolstoy reveals the deception he himself has created in those seemingly realistic worlds. He refuses to let narrative verisimilitude convince and reassure his readers that their problems are but a few pages away from (generalized and fictionalized) solutions. That is why his fictional works are not simply imagined solutions for our problems.[25] It is also why *Anna Karenina* does not end with Anna's death, nor *War and Peace* with Pierre and Natasha's marriage.

Bakhtin notwithstanding, Tolstoy alternately embraced and rejected the belief that there was in fact an alibi for being—narrative fiction, in which the "I-for-myself" might find forms of self-legitimation. Tolstoy became fascinated with that narrative alibi, explored its potentials, and in his late essays and moralistic tales ultimately succumbed to its logic: real meaning can never be here, is always elsewhere. The narrative alibi, that "alibi for being" Tolstoy availed himself of, was his occasional excuse for not participating in the world of others, at least (but nevertheless essentially) inasmuch as it created an aspect of self he ultimately refused to admit was authentic. In his story "Gooseberries" Chekhov takes Tolstoy to task for his alibi: "To leave the city, the struggle, worldly noises, to leave and hide oneself on one's estate—this is not life, it is egotism, laziness; it is a sort of monasticism, but monasticism without good works. Man needs not six feet of earth [the answer in Tolstoy's story 'How Much Land Does a Man

Need?'], nor an estate, but the entire globe, all of nature where he can have scope to develop all the characteristics and features of his free spirit."[26] Chekhov is too strident, but not entirely unjust. In fact, he could have taken this critique from Tolstoy himself, who was well aware that he used his literary calling to escape the world, knew himself to be hypocritical, and yet was willing to make the compromise "to show how incompatible this life is with people's inherent possibilities."[27] To be and not be in the world, to be both a resident and a stranger, as Gustafson appropriately called him, Tolstoy authored works of literature with structures that acknowledged his absence.

THE ABSENT CRITIC

> To write or say such things about a person that you would not say to his face or write him means to say offensive things . . . means that you are writing libel.
>
> — *"To Those Gentlemen Critics Who Care to Consider It"*

In his earliest fiction Tolstoy had not yet thought about aesthetics in overtly theoretical terms, but he had pondered at great length the relationship of author to reader, partly because a more intimate, experiential form of fiction was what Tolstoy saw as realistic, and partly because Tolstoy was consumed by the idea of controlling his authorial image. As to the former, his first literary plan, entitled "From the Window," aims to describe the events the narrator actually sees from his window and uses the boundary between private and public spaces to motivate the near plotless accumulation of subjective (witnessed) and objective (street-level) detail.[28] We do not have an extant version of "From the Window," unfortunately, but we do have *Childhood*. The publication of *Childhood* (1852) provides an excellent example of how Tolstoy first managed his own reception. By examining this early authorial episode we can see how Tolstoy used the absence of a real interlocutor to create his vision of the anti-institutional author.

Opting to sign only the initials L.N. to the manuscript, Tolstoy sent it to Russia's leading journal, *The Contemporary*, asking only that if it were to be published the editor Nekrasov would change nothing. It was both published and changed, slightly. Tolstoy's touching, if mythologized, portrait of childhood was greeted with acclaim by the reading public. Nevertheless, while unsigned, or cryptically signed, publications were not all that rare at the time, in Tolstoy's case, a decision about signing, and thus taking responsibility for one's words, was part of a larger group of theoretical problems in the reader-writer relationship that interested him. I have in mind, in particular, Tolstoy's reservations about describing publicly his thoughts on the reigning literary institutions themselves. Even as Tolstoy sought his first publication, he questioned the entire mechanism that brought the author's work before the eyes of readers.

To sign a work is to vouch explicitly for the mode of communication the work itself implicitly advocates. Tolstoy was just an inexperienced author, but his drafts for *Childhood* demonstrate how little he wanted to legitimate the current literary institution.[29] He believed, for example, that the mode of publishing in 1850–52 created a kind of criticism that was paradoxically at once intensely personal and suprapersonal. Much later, as a religious philosopher, Tolstoy came to regret publishing, because it continued to support a system he considered unjust. In *What Is Art?* he writes: "I have narrated all this [history of the publication process for *What Is Art?*] in such detail because it strikingly illustrates the indubitable truth that all compromise with institutions of which your conscience disapproves—compromises which are made usually for the sake of the general good—instead of producing the good you expected, inevitably lead you, not only to acknowledge the institution you disapprove of, but also to participate in the evil that institution produces. I am glad to be able by this statement at least to do something to correct the error into which I was led by my compromise."[30] As with much of his later writing, Tolstoy "corrects" the earlier thought, here translating what once would have been simply irritating or offensive into something "evil." Resistance to institutions was a touchstone for his aesthetics both early and late.

The early, unpublished drafts of *Childhood* illuminate the broader institutional context that Tolstoy confronted. Especially significant is "To Those Gentlemen Critics Who Care to Consider It," the penultimate chapter in an early draft of *Childhood*. Along with the final chapter of that manuscript, "To Readers," "To Those Critics" provides crucial testament to Tolstoy's early ideas about the entire literary process and the author's reception by an audience. They are his final words, so to speak, on the to-be-published work that precedes them—that is, until he decides to conclude the work differently. This entire exercise is theoretical and hypothetical for Tolstoy—he has not yet been published. His defensive address to the "critics" is thus itself a kind of fiction, following in the tradition of Gogol and Lermontov's attacks on the critics. It is metafiction, which would literally be separated from its fiction, since Tolstoy eventually removed from his literary text the conventional address to critics that Gogol and Lermontov leave in *Dead Souls* and *A Hero of Our Time*.[31]

"To Those Critics" testifies to Tolstoy's early interest in literary politics and literary institutions, and it signals, moreover, his desire to join the exalted ranks of Gogol and Lermontov among a membership of authors. Its opening rhetorical gesture underlines Tolstoy's haughty and heightened self-consciousness even in this, his first literary "act": "I embark on a literary career with great reservation and distaste. . . . Why? Because you, Dear Gentlemen, are for me those from whom in my literary career I am afraid to receive offense. The word 'offense' I speak here not at all in a metaphoric sense, but in a direct one. . . . When you write criticism . . . of all readers you have most in mind the author, and sometimes him alone."[32] One immediately notes Tolstoy's rejection of the metaphoric. He takes offense directly and personally, like the district police captain in Gogol's "Overcoat." Yet what reason does Tolstoy have to be concerned so much with what the critics might say? He is still, we recall, a writer who has never published anything, let alone been on the receiving end of unfair criticism. Looking back at the pages of *The Contemporary* in 1852, one rarely finds any sort of harsh negative criticism, and certainly nothing of the sort that appeared in the following decade under the leadership of more radical critics.

Tolstoy would have been familiar with the renowned critical attacks on Russian authors in recent memory—the debates on language in Pushkin's time, Belinsky's letter to Gogol, the bad reviews of Lermontov, and Turgenev's political interests and involvements. Yet Eikhenbaum links Tolstoy's works of fiction closely with external events, and thus overstates his social engagement. Eikhenbaum writes: "During the Crimean war he went to Sevastopol and wrote stories about war. When the dispute about 'fathers and sons' began, he wrote the story *Two Hussars*. When a controversy arose over 'art for art's sake' he wrote *Albert*. When the question of the emancipation of women cropped up, he wrote the novel *Family Happiness*."[33] One gets the sense that Tolstoy's callow rejection of criticism arises, on the contrary, more directly from an engagement with imaginary enemies. He tilts at windmills. He strikes a pose in order to see how it will look on him. Tolstoy frequently lamented his vanity. Moreover, as Tolstoy interpreted the critical experience in more intimate terms than most, the metaphor of posturing is not so inappropriate. Tolstoy does not just imagine himself a particular way; he wants others to perceive him that way as well. Thus he insists upon the singular activity of the author and the critic and the personal nature of their relationship. The reason *personal* control over the text is so important is that Tolstoy equates authorial identity with the governing intellect of the text, thinking perhaps that if the text is understood correctly then the image of the author formed by the reader will also correspond with how the author wants to be seen.[34]

Tolstoy relates to authorial identity in divergent ways. If he is attacked by critics, he wants there to be no distance between himself—Count Tolstoy, a nobleman with rights and privileges—and his authorial identity.[35] Later in his

career he uses his own biography—recast as a fall from real not mythical innocence—as the basis of a notion of authorial *authenticity*. Yet he wants creative
control over his authorial identity, the ability to shape an identity for public
consumption that is separate from his own. This notion of authorship,
frequently requiring the participation of readers, suggests Tolstoy's interest in
authorial *legitimacy*. He modulates the distance between these identities,
thereby expanding and collapsing his authorial alibi as he deems necessary.

Tolstoy conceives of his own identity as multiple when he needs it to be, but
the identity of others must be singular. With his peculiar request in "To Those
Critics" that the editorial first-person plural "we" be eliminated from reviews,
Tolstoy hopes, however naively, to individualize the critics and to force them to
assume a single answerable identity. He uncovers their alibis. In "To Readers,"
he writes: "Any author—in the broadest sense of that word—when writing
whatever, invariably imagines what effect his writing will have. When the entire
work pleases one person, then that work, in my opinion, is perfect in some
sense."[36] The idea of writing for a single reader stuck with Tolstoy—one can
even imagine that the idea of aesthetic "infection"—from his late essay *What Is
Art?*—derives in part from his notions of the intimacy of aesthetic reception.[37]
Ishchuk remarks wryly on Tolstoy's early notion of the reader, "By the way, it is
not difficult to guess that [Tolstoy's] 'imaginary reader' looks very much like the
young Tolstoy himself."[38] In 1857, Tolstoy writes to Botkin: "You know my belief
in the need for an imaginary reader. You are my favourite imaginary reader.
Writing to you is as easy for me as thinking; I know that any thought of mine
and any impression of mine is grasped by you in a purer, clearer and higher
form than that in which I expressed it."[39] Tolstoy's story "Lucerne" (1857),
accordingly, originates as a letter to Botkin.

By interpreting negative criticism as offensive—not wrong, or ignorant, or
misguided—Tolstoy forces what was an institutional relationship into an inter-
personal one. He is obsessed with his image. He wants to retain the control of
guiding a single reader's experience, although, of course, he wants more than
one reader. Thus he chooses as an example "libel," alluding to a legal system
that, by definition, governs many people, to discuss his mano-a-mano theory of
author-reader-critic relations. He writes: "To write or say such things about a
person that you would not say to his face nor write to him means to say offensive
things . . . means that you are writing libel. . . . Although those beginning a literary career, as on the stage, are subject to the judgment of all, yet whistling is not
allowed, just as engaging in personalities and slandering should not be
allowed."[40] An accusation of libel is not necessarily an idle one in the 1850s.
Tolstoy himself nearly fought a duel in 1856, and the deaths of Pushkin and

Lermontov in duels—hardly for literary reasons—were still relatively recent.[41] Tolstoy means to collapse the space between reader (critic or public) and author. The idea of "speaking one's mind to another face to face" fits not just Tolstoy's ideas of unmediated, direct, and proximate address in literature but also his haughty beliefs about nobility and honor. Thus the autobiographical hero Irtenev's famous passage about comme il faut people that Tolstoy will write a few years later, in *Youth:* "At the time of which I am writing my own favorite and principal system of division was into people *comme il faut* and *comme il ne faut pas*. The latter I subdivided into those inherently not *comme il faut* and the lower orders. The *comme il faut* people I respected and looked upon as worthy to consort with me as my equals; the *comme il ne faut pas* I pretended to disdain but in reality I hated them, nourishing a sort of injured personal feeling where they were concerned; the lower classes did not exist for me—I despised them utterly."[42] Tolstoy's hostility toward the critics combines his views on literature and his barely concealed disdain that such people have the right to address him in any manner. Recall that he wants to be an author of belles lettres, not a journalist (or, to be sure, a literary critic).

Tolstoy's early ideas of literary reception are worth considering in a biographical context. He was, to some extent, personally marginalized, since he lived in the Caucasus (Tbilisi) and served in the army at the time (1851), rather than residing in the capital. Demoralized, without a military commission, without medals or other testaments to his bravery, without even the documents to get his commission, without money to go out in society, deeply in debt—these are the conditions under which Tolstoy worked on much of *Childhood*. No wonder he valorizes absence and distance: he is nowhere near the center of the Russian literary universe. He was a literary novice, and his letter to the publisher Nekrasov is meek enough; yet whether by sheer ego or by some innate sense of his own genius, Tolstoy already imagines himself a force, a presence, in contemporary literary politics. He sees himself as having every right to address the literary milieu.

The important lesson to draw from these tactics is that Tolstoy anticipated critical responses in ways that are often hidden in the final redaction. We could not possibly know from reading the published version of *Childhood*, for example, that Tolstoy was so intent on battling potential critics, as individuals, before he even put the manuscript in the mail. The complaint he ultimately keeps from the final manuscript is that of which he accuses critics: leaving the real meaning (libel) unsaid. This example of Tolstoy's early rejection of certain institutional norms sets an important precedent for all those occasions in the future when Tolstoy will behave not only unconventionally but also in radical contravention of literary institutions—such as when he relinquishes copyright to his work, or helps to establish the Intermediary publishing company, or redefines the genre of the novel completely. From the start Tolstoy believed he was at odds with the literary establishment; the anticipation of a hostile response is part of what defines his work.

Yet Tolstoy does more than posture in this regard. He shapes narrative form in relation to the goals he sets for authorial self-creation. In working to subvert literary institutions, Tolstoy simulates an immediacy, a presence, in his narrative voice that some readers eventually find suffocating. In general his omniscient narrators are rarely cold and distant in a Jamesian way; if they were, perhaps one could more easily ignore them. On the contrary, Tolstoy's omniscient narrators, even embedded first-person narrators such as Pozdnyshev of "The Kreutzer Sonata," can be insufferable know-it-alls. They make themselves unavoidable and unignorable. Collapsing that distance between "elsewhere" and "here" is part of Tolstoy's narrative alibi in these first narrative attempts. He constructs his presence both literally (as a voice from the Caucasus) and rhetorically (as a voice that speaks directly to readers). The author writes his way into contemporary political and cultural discourse. In terms of the literary mores of the day, Tolstoy considers this move toward presence to be a kind of realism. His unpublished essays "To Those Critics" and "To Readers" reveal the large stake that Tolstoy has in institutional disintermediation. What is more, pure presence in a work of literature (inasmuch as one can imagine it) and realism, ideally, have no set generic boundaries or, in theory, any conventional demarcations at all.[43] To that extent the "spoken voice" of Tolstoy's apostrophic address is both medium and message: it transcends convention and preaches its own transcendence. It is not at all surprising that Tolstoy goes on to use the highly rare second-person narrative voice in his early military story "Sevastopol in December" (1855).

"To Readers" and "To Those Critics" thus efface the typical boundaries between fiction and reality, since they force the impersonal conventional relationship between author and reader or critic into a real, acknowledged, and personal relationship. They also reinforce the boundaries between fiction and reality by rhetorically substantiating the institutions governing the relationship between author, text, and reader. Tolstoy is not the first, after all, to address critics and readers. What is more, Tolstoy frets so much about potential criticism, he may invite it; perhaps he himself ultimately recognizes as much, since he chooses, in the end, to remove these essays.[44] Tolstoy may have anticipated the negative effect his efforts would engender, or he may have seen that his rebellious gesture was, in the end, far too typical. But the crucial point is that in his subsequent literary attempts to define himself he would continue to use institutional resistance in creative appropriations of his authorial identity. *Childhood* appears without those essays that seem initially to be merely the author's vain posturing, but traces of the argument of the essays are still evident in the structure of the text itself, where they exert a detectable influence. Let us briefly examine a couple of examples, focusing on *Childhood* and "A History of Yesterday," in part because (at the risk of stating the obvious) autobiographical texts must balance the said and the unsaid, presence and absence.

One's whole life cannot be told. Tolstoy's "History of Yesterday" makes this point explicitly: "Only God knows how many diverse and diverting impressions, together with the thoughts awakened by them, occur in a single day. Obscure and confused they may be, but they are nevertheless comprehensible to our minds. If they could be told in such a way that I could easily read myself and others could read me, as I could, the result would be a most instructive and absorbing book; nor would there be ink enough in the world to write it, or typesetters to put it into print."[45] The author needs to choose which stories do and do not get told—thereby not only creating a coherent image of the author, or adhering to a particular narrative structure, but also modulating the reader's experience of the text. Yet it is not just selection, choosing one word, one sentence, one event, out of ten or twenty. Tolstoy makes selectivity itself a key component of his aesthetics.

A careful anticipation and manipulation of the reader's response form a key aesthetic moment in the final version of *Childhood*. In the opening paragraphs, Tolstoy attracts the reader's attention, which is aligned with the narrator's, yet he also performs a narrative sleight of hand: "On the 12th of August 18—, exactly three days after my birthday, when I turned ten, and for which I had received such wonderful presents, Karl Ivanych woke me at seven in the morning by hitting at a fly just over my head with a swatter made of sugar-bag paper fastened to a stick. His action was so clumsy that he caught the little image of my guardian angel, which hung on the headboard of my oak bedstead, and the dead fly fell right on my head. I put my nose out from under the bedclothes, steadied with my hand the ikon which was still wobbling, flicked the dead fly on to the floor, and looked at Karl Ivanych with wrathful if sleepy eyes."[46] Notice how conventionally Tolstoy's first published work begins: with a date, obscuring the exact year, the hero's age, the time of day. Yet Tolstoy does not even devote a complete sentence to this conventional specificity, as the opening lines hurry on to almost grotesque specificity in the image of the dead fly and the fly swatter that killed it. With this shift is an awakening not only of the hero but also of the reader, who is also roused to the sensory world of the wakeful child.

The space between the narrator and the reader's perception is collapsed into simultaneous experience—readers do not know any more than Nikolai—but the reader soon learns not to trust this gesture of simultaneity. There is in the novella, first, a narrative gesture of misdirection, contained in both the smack of the fly swatter that grabs the reader's attention—and wakens our hero—as well as in the false lead of Nikolai's subsequent accusing thoughts about Karl Ivanych, his German tutor. What we forget as we read the opening of *Childhood* is just what Tolstoy wants us to forget: that we are crossing a substantial boundary when we enter this fictional world. It is one example, in a series of examples, that minimizes the links between the text and the actual referential world that is supposed to be its source. All works of fiction require a willing suspension of disbelief, and *Childhood* is no different. What is different is that by removing his addresses to readers and critics from the final draft and by misdirecting the reader's attention at the beginning of *Childhood*, Tolstoy reduces as much as possible the framing gestures that call attention to that suspension of disbelief. Tolstoy is trying out authorial strategies here. His other early works of fiction do not all do this: the Sevastopol stories, for example, have strong framing gestures, though they break those frames in other ways.

In *Childhood* a crucial example of the ontology of Tolstoy's creative work is given just a few paragraphs later. Crying out of shame that he wrongfully accused his beloved tutor, if only in his mind, Nikolai explains his tears by saying he dreamed that his mother had died. But this story leads to new tears, "now for a different reason," he explains. His very real emotion has its basis in the recollection of something that never happened. Nevertheless, a cycle of events based on the nonexistent dream of his mother's death has been set in motion; these events acquire their own reality. Thus, one concludes, the fictional *Childhood* is composed of events which, though they may never have existed, are meant to evoke genuine emotion.

Tolstoy creates opening paragraphs that are purposely misleading and disjunctive. As far as he was concerned, one of the most irritating changes made by the censor in the first publication of *Childhood* was to replace in the opening paragraphs the words "image of my guardian angel" with "image of my mother." By pointing too soon to Nikolai's mother, the censor actually prepares the reader for Nikolai's fake dream of her death and thereby creates continuity where Tolstoy wanted discontinuity. It is a rare example of Tolstoy losing control over his text. He shapes the reader's experience so vigorously because he wants the reader to legitimate or validate the text and his identity. This concern for readerly legitimation does not extend through Tolstoy's career to the late stories, where he is more concerned that his characters live authentic lives true to their inner core of being. His early struggles with literary institutions and conventions are a struggle for legitimacy.

Part II

Legitimate Lives

From the very start of his career, Tolstoy demanded much from his readers, but his themes were traditional. The early fiction often described how characters come to terms with the world, how they mature from childhood to adulthood. Tolstoy drew deeply on his favorite authors, Sterne and Rousseau. The scope and philosophical profundity of his later, grander novels were either missing or less skillfully created in the early fiction. Turgenev in fact hoped that Tolstoy would drop his habit of psychologizing and philosophizing. For Tolstoy in these early works, becoming an author was like becoming a man through travel, battle, or by outliving myths of childhood. Tried and true paths to a legitimate role in society as a soldier, bureaucrat, or landowner existed, but such well-worn paths provided few opportunities for uniqueness, for separating oneself from the others. Tolstoy therefore devoted himself to formal innovation. These innovations aimed to create a new kind of literary realism that collapsed the boundaries between the text and the world and drew readers into an active role in the creation of the text's meaning. In theme, authorial rhetoric, and formal innovation, this early fiction invited readerly legitimation.

LEGITIMATE FICTIONS AND NARRATIVE DIVERSIONS

In my opinion, the personality of the author, the writer (composer) is an antipoetic personality.

— *"To Readers"*

LEGITIMATING FICTIONS

Tolstoy's authorial personality, even in the antipoetic guise quoted above, was the fruit of much thought and creative imagination. He considered how his fiction created a public perception of him, and realized that perception would affect how people read his fiction. A work of literature invariably presents some kind of image of the author to the reader, and publication is an opportunity for authors to shape and manage their presentation of a self. What kind of self does Tolstoy craft for his reader? Neither an entirely accessible, unmediated essence (an ideal of the diary), nor an opaque and impersonal source of text. Recall his signature for *Childhood*: L. N. To the people who knew Tolstoy had authored the work, these were the initials of his name and patronymic, but to the vast majority of readers the initials were little more than a cipher. I intend to argue that Tolstoy's authorial personality oscillates between those extremes of accessibility and opacity, and that each direction has its own specific narrative devices. Tolstoy mediates his authorial self via conventions of legitimacy (especially early in career) and authenticity (especially later in his career).

These conventions of legitimacy in principle garner more than public approval and critical praise. Texts with legitimation as part of the author's motive for self presentation rely upon narrative structures that appeal for special readerly participation and authorization; and they often require specific knowledge of the literary tradition in order to be fully understood. In his early attempts to describe the Caucasus, Tolstoy writes: "It may be that the imagination of the reader supplements the deficiency of the author's expression. Without that assistance how banal and colorless would all the descriptions be."[1] The reader could not be ignored, especially in tales of the Caucasus, since the literary precursors by Pushkin and Lermontov would immediately present themselves. The second-person narration of "Sevastopol in December" requires intensive readerly participation, for example, but so too does a work like *Childhood*, as we witnessed at the end of the previous chapter. Tolstoy at this stage is not yet the converted moralist he would become. For now, his maxims and truths about the world are contextualized by the events of his stories and novels. Even his youthful ideas of morality are subordinated to an overriding concern for literary novelty.

Legitimation turns our attention to the close relationship between author and reader. In literary theories of metafiction and reader response, one often encounters the notion that by shaping the reader's activity an author helps to create an ideal reader.[2] Iser quotes Booth: "Regardless of my real beliefs and practices, I must subordinate my mind and heart to the book if I am to enjoy it to the full. The author creates, in short, an image of himself and another image of his reader; he makes his reader, as he makes his second self, and the most successful reading is one in which the created selves, author and reader, can find complete agreement."[3] I mean to suggest in my interpretations of Tolstoy's narratives of legitimation that successful reading, "complete agreement" between and author and reader, creates and defines not just the identity of the ideal reader but also that of the author.

Later in his career, however, when he turns to authenticity as his primary mode of self presentation, Tolstoy valorizes authentic characters and relies more on narrative structures that are self-legitimating, seemingly requiring no readerly confirmation in order to be true or valid. That authentic life is a core moral self from childhood which degrades in adult social life, though one may recall or recognize traces of it. Consider "Master and Man" (1895), one of the best of Tolstoy's late stories, for example. In it Tolstoy substantially reworks his early story "The Snowstorm" (1856), notably removing those aspects of the text where the reader shares in the perceptual disorientation of the first-person narrator. "Master and Man" contains a Christian truth realized by its main protagonist. There is no open-endedness to the reader's experience of the text—except, perhaps, what Tolstoy hoped: that the reader would be moved by the example of the story and realize a similar truth in his or her own life. But this is different from a story that appeals to the reader's participation to become fully meaningful. *Childhood*, the Sevastopol stories, and other early works need the reader's response and participation to become meaningful. They rely much more upon the gaps in the narrative that Iser suggests elicit increased readerly activity and identification.[4] Having elaborated theories of nonviolence and Christian love, Tolstoy in his late fiction uses narrative forms that speak an absolute answer for those willing to hear it. But this hearing isn't necessary for the story's truth to be told.

At issue is how much control over the constitution of a self Tolstoy believes is or should be relegated to others and, more particularly, to readers. In his book *Hidden in Plain View*, Morson discusses the relationship of self and habit in Tolstoy, arguing, for example, that "the self . . . is a cluster of habits and memories," or that "for Tolstoy, selves are unrepeatable because the myriad accidents, habits, and memories that compose, shape, and alter them from moment to moment fit no pattern and can never be duplicated."[5] In contrast, I mean to emphasize not the unrepeatability of selfhood but its consistency—Tolstoyan characters, even Tolstoy himself, strive for an invariable core of selfhood, often inventing it in the process and telling or presenting it to themselves and to others. The question is whether these wavering, striving characters merely provide an index of error for Tolstoy. It is doubtful that they are merely the liars, poseurs, and killers of Tolstoy's fiction. We must go beyond considerations of Tolstoy's representation of the self in the real world to examine his struggle to tell the truth through fiction, or to represent honest or moral being. Between truth and fiction, habit and the missing core of being, are those processes of legitimation that point us toward the self as validated by social and cultural institutions. This is the self Tolstoy feared would have to pass through a gauntlet of libelous criticism, and that is why Tolstoy's struggle to articulate his position vis-à-vis his critics and readers predates even his first publication, as we saw in the previous chapters. In narratives of legitimation, the imagined core of being requires an other to validate it by sharing an emotional experience with the implied author or key character. In the narratives of authenticity, by contrast, that core of being is not imagined but recollected. It only has to be sought. The older Tolstoy, who so often shared his desire to merge with others in Christian brotherhood, ends his career by needing only the self.

Legitimacy itself, the legal imprimatur of belonging to a family, is a theme that resonates throughout Tolstoy's works.[6] He lost his own parents, of course, but Tolstoy also referred to his own mother and his beloved aunt as orphans.[7] More to the point, he purposely conflates legal legitimacy, being a lawful heir, for example, with telling a credible story. To tell the lives of orphans is also to rework a sentimentalist trope. Tolstoy thus blends the personal, thematic, and metaliterary in his reworking of orphanhood. "Four Epochs of Development," for example, which most scholars consider the first draft for *Childhood*, turns specifically on the notion of legitimacy, and describes the troubles of illegitimate children whose mother, of noble birth, has divorced her first husband and lives in an "unlawful" marriage with the hero's father. The children have neither title nor inheritance, and their father sends them to a commercial school.[8]

Only six pages are ultimately taken directly from "Four Epochs" into the manuscript of *Childhood*, significantly including those on the mother's death.[9] Among the new passages in the chapter on Nikolai's mother's death are the lines about Nikolai's indignation at being referred to as an "orphan"—thus the broken family theme supplants illegitimacy. Orphans, like Masha and her sister from "Family Happiness," or Nikolai himself in *Childhood*, are scattered throughout Tolstoy's works.

The great drama of the initial chapters of *War and Peace* is whether Pierre will be made the legitimate heir to a fortune. A single document, the old Count Bezukhov's petition to the tsar to make Pierre a legitimate heir, changes Pierre's life and the entire novel. Here we have not just a plot, but the very possibility for plot in the novel. What would become of *War and Peace* without Pierre's wealth? His money gets him married to Helene and, more important, gives him the ability to peek into those interesting corners of affluence and power in Russia that Tolstoy wants to illuminate. He has the time and the resources to do what he wants; his flexibility as a character is useful for an author who has previously never written a novel with such broad temporal and spatial scope. In *Anna Karenina*, Anna is not encumbered by a family history—and we have to wonder whether she would act so boldly were she presented in the context of a traditional family with her parents and other relatives fully engaged in her life and well-being. Her daughter Annie "realizes" Anna's experience of social ambiguity literally in her own illegitimacy. Later, in *Resurrection*, Nekhlyudov's dalliance with Maslova produces not only an illegitimate child (who dies) but also engenders her own illegitimate sinful life. She is exiled from society.

Legitimacy may involve validating or realizing metaphoric connections, based on similarity, rather than metonymic ones, based on contiguity. Gilbert and Gubar use metaphor to discuss the rhetoric of paternity in their theory of authorship in *The Madwoman in the Attic*.[10] This pattern can be extended to Tolstoy's treatment of aristocratic tradition. His aristocratic myth-making in *Childhood* would have little sense if readers were to refuse to accept these myths as legitimate versions of their lives.[11] Tolstoy's readers are encouraged to accept a similarity between fiction and reality. In "Sevastopol in December," we read: "The tales of the early days of the siege of Sevastopol are no longer beautiful historical legends . . ., but have become realities."[12] In *War and Peace*, Natasha is neither illegitimate nor does she have any false memories, but there is her celebrated peasant folk dance. Her spur-of-the-moment dance is an "emblem," a broadly resonant metaphor, according to historian Orlando Figes, who makes the evident point that "there is no *quintessential* national culture, only mythic images of it, like Natasha's version of the peasant dance."[13] Yet Natasha's dance is depicted as quintessentially Russian. Prince Andrei, who more than any other character in *War and Peace* mulls the meaning of his nobility, notices his father's framed genealogical chart demonstrating the family connection to Prince Rurik. Adjacent to the chart is a poorly done painting of a Bolkonsky family ancestor and descendant of Rurik.[14] Andrei laughs at how like his father the chart is.[15] The Old Prince so denigrates marriage that perhaps this visual clue of successive male generations symbolizes his desire to overcome the need for wives altogether. Marriage both enables and problematizes family traditions: witness the jam-making scene in *Anna Karenina*. There is no unbroken chain of family tradition for Levin, though his brothers, when feeling charitable, are sympathetic to his familial nostalgia. Levin is quick to point out what he believes is Vronsky's false aristocratic status—he cannot point back, like Levin, to "three or four honorable generations"—but Levin confuses his own honesty and decency (his willingness to provide for his children, for example) with nobility, which may very well be defined as service "to God and Country"—a definition in whose terms Levin is less noble than he believes.

Is the past a badge of authenticity one can display like a genealogical chart or a mark of illegitimacy to be hidden until overcome? What separates Levin from the Tolstoyan characters who follow him is that he realizes he has been living well but thinking wrongly. By contrast, most subsequent Tolstoyan heroes are forced to realize that their lives as well as their thoughts have been false. Usually, as in "The Death of Ivan Ilyich," "Master and Man," or "The Kreutzer Sonata," the hero recognizes that his childhood was good but was spoiled by the awakening of sexual desire, greed, and deception.[16] In this sense, Anna Karenina, with the momentary realization of childhood joy that accompanies her as she crosses herself, is a better precursor to the late Tolstoyan hero than Levin.[17] Ivan Ilyich, for example, unlike Levin, has *not* been living well. He must endure unthinkable pain until he disavows every last bit of life since puberty. But Ivan Ilyich does not need to imagine a past to sustain a moral core of his identity; he has an actual happy childhood to remember, even better than the one mythologized by Nikolai Irtenev. Recall that Ivan Ilyich rejects the abstract syllogism "Caius is a man, men are mortal, therefore Caius is mortal" because Ivan is a real man, not some abstraction: "He had been little Vanya, with a mamma and a pappa, with Mitya and Volodya, with toys, a coachman and a nanny, afterwards with Katenka and with all the joys, griefs, and delights of childhood, boyhood, and youth. What did Caius know of the smell of that striped leather ball Vanya had been so fond of? Had Caius kissed his mother's hand like that, and did the silk of her dress rustle for Caius? Had he rioted in school when the pastry was bad? Had Caius been in love like that? Could Caius preside at a session as he did?"[18] If, for Nikolai, Pierre, Levin, and others we had to speak of legitimacy, for later heroes we are more concerned with the category of authenticity. Tolstoy's notion of authenticity is understood here as being true to the core of honest self that really existed in childhood and was spoiled by sex and society.

NARRATIVE DIVERSIONS

Regardless of which convention Tolstoy uses, either legitimacy or authenticity, he connects literary structure and the presentation of self with something I will call narrative "diversion," using that word both in the sense of distraction and in the sense of entertainment or amusement. Diversion is a kind of narrative alibi that pushes or pulls the reader in a certain direction, creating an absence or interpretive gap by bypassing those aspects of a story the author wishes to keep unsaid. Tolstoy uses narrative diversions to distract readers, for example, from noticing the transition to a world of fiction, which forces them to ponder it retrospectively. This is one way in which he aims to create a kind of experiential realism. By isolating the moment of transition, he questions whether fiction, as entertainment, is an integral part of the (social, political, personal) fabric of life or separate from it. Can fiction be entertainment and political engagement at the same time, for example, or entertainment and inspired art? Is fiction something that distracts us from our authentic lives by making us forget the big questions or problems of our existence? Ivan Ilyich, for example, is angry that his family can discuss who is singing at a concert in the evening, while the question of death remains unsolved and unmentioned. Or is fiction a social convention that, among many other things, allows us to consider the role other people must play in legitimating our narratives of identity? These are not new questions for literature—Pushkin considered them in "Egyptian Nights": "'Here is a theme for you,' said Charsky, 'the poet himself chooses the subjects for his songs; the crowd does not have the right to direct his inspiration.'"[19] Still, it was important for Tolstoy personally, especially when he first decided to become an author. Diverting the reader, guiding the reader in general, is a kind of narrative skill Tolstoy honed in his early fiction. But divert how? With entertaining trifles? And will weighty philosophical digressions, by contrast, distract the reader so much from the fiction that there will be hardly any point in continuing to write it? Is Tolstoy giving his readers a break from life or forcing them to confront it more directly? Literary diversions cause us to focus on these central questions of legitimacy and authenticity.

The early stories frequently break narrative framing conventions, or contain asymmetrical frames, so as to disrupt the reader's suspension of disbelief. The second-person address of "Sevastopol in December" forces the reader to perceive directly what is often a less immediately relevant fiction. The closing paragraphs of "Sevastopol in May," which claim the story's hero is "truth," lead us to reconsider how we interpreted the preceding story. One is implicated in the fiction, forced to legitimate it and see it as connected to one's life. Tolstoy wants to deliver a didactic message, but he will not be able to if the reader is able to pretend that it has no relation to his or her life.[20] Broken conventions in Tolstoy's early works tend to take the form of confusing gaps in the plot, unmet generic expectations, and other narrative lacunae.[21] In "Two Hussars," for example, the reader is drawn into the expectation that the two parts of the story will align in some plot. What we are given instead is a kind of comparison of father and son: the protagonists are literally and metaphorically related, but they do not compose a traditional plot, as we expect. These broken conventions are a crucial aspect of how Tolstoy uses narrative absence to generate the readers' legitimating activity, and they are important to what I have called Tolstoy's narrative alibi because they force us to look at what the author is leaving out of his stories. Iser writes: "Blanks and negations increase the density of fictional texts, for the omissions and cancellations indicate that practically all the formulations of the text refer to an unformulated background, and so the formulated text has a kind of unformulated double. This 'double' we shall call negativity."[22] I associate the negativity of that unformulated background with a kind of hidden freedom in Tolstoy's relation to his own authorial identity. It is as though in his early works Tolstoy is laying the groundwork for his own subsequent revisions of his identity.

In the later works, by contrast, one encounters far more stories with complex—yet unbroken—framing techniques. This is because Tolstoy now worries less about authorial or characterological legitimacy and more about authenticity and depicting an authentic life. In *War and Peace, Anna Karenina*, and "The Death of Ivan Ilyich," for example, Tolstoy cultivates not myths of childhood, which would require societal legitimation, but narratives that ask us to recognize childhood as a source of innocence to be recollected and recovered. He therefore turns to those conventional metaliterary techniques that create self-legitimating texts. For example, the origin of a story, its telling, and its reception (thus the entire code of the literary process) is re-represented within the artwork.[23] Think of "The Kreutzer Sonata," for example, in which the narrator witnesses and describes both Pozdnyshev's telling of his murderous story and his own behavior while listening to it. Or consider the circular structure of "The Death of Ivan Ilyich," which begins with news of Ivan's death, circles back to review his entire life, and ends with his death, the reaction to which is found in the opening chapter. *Hadji*

Murad, which has a perfect opening and closing structure, as well as several involuting interpolated narratives that replicate that closed structure, is another example.

Tolstoy, turning to a realistic and objective accumulation of detail in his fiction, and generalizing from it, defines his work against both Romanticism and the burgeoning genre of journalistic prose, against both the sentiment of the poet's inner world and the utilitarian factuality of the journalist's outer world. Boris Eikhenbaum calls the time a "crisis," writing: "Tolstoi's work marks a crisis in artistic prose, and for a long time Russian literature lives under the yoke of the canonization of this crisis."[24] How did Tolstoy intend his new fiction with its plotless, unmotivated detail to supplant Romanticism? Because he was so uneasy about the relationship between text and world, Tolstoy frequently employed narrative misdirection—diversion, as I have been calling it—when encountering the boundaries of fiction—beginnings and endings, for example, but also other edges of his fictional worlds, such as those created by the interpolation of alternate art forms (e.g., painting, music).[25] This frequent misdirection not only manipulates and shifts the reader's attention but also suggests that there is an important ontological barrier between text and world. There are two ways in which he considers this problem. First, like many other authors, Tolstoy wondered whether language itself was capable of representing reality. Tolstoy generally tries to get his readers to forget there is language that mediates the world he is representing. Second, there is the confusing line between the unreal, fictional world that Tolstoy narrates, and the possibly real world referred to by memoir—in *Childhood* for example. Literary text and truth stand apart from one another, and Tolstoy often seems to suggest that the two may be entirely incommensurable. Although I take examples from many of Tolstoy's stories and novels, I want to focus here mostly on his historical and political fiction (the Sevastopol stories, *The Cossacks, War and Peace, Hadji Murad*). As Tolstoy ceased exploring whether fiction could or should entertain (be diversion in one sense), I believe he created more and more difficult obstacles (diversion in the other sense, i.e., distraction) to the easy consumption of his fiction. This conclusion contradicts, among other things, Tolstoy's notion that, because of its didactic and moral purpose his later fiction forges a more direct relationship between author, text, and reader. In *What Is Art?* accordingly he decides that only his "God Sees the Truth but Waits" and "A Prisoner of the Caucasus" are good works of art.[26]

Diversion and revelation form a literary practice that has its roots in Tolstoy's first publication, *Childhood*. Diverting or revealing the identity of the author is a constant theme in Tolstoy's autobiographical works. As the previous chapters have indicated, the present study examines what Tolstoy's entry into literary traditions and institutions and his ultimate exit from them tells us about his changing attitudes toward authorial self-presentation. How does a man envision himself who sees as potentially impossible his professional task of translating art and reality into one another? At one end of the half-century that separates *Childhood* and *Hadji Murad* we encounter an unknown Tolstoy working away in secret on his first publication, worrying all the time about how he will be perceived by the world of Russian high culture so far away to the north; at the other end of that half-century, we observe a very well-known Tolstoy—one of the most famous men in the world—*also* working away in secret. He is worrying about how he will be perceived both by his religious followers, who have his assurances that such childish things as belles lettres no longer occupy him, and also by the world of Russian high culture, which, despite everything, has kept its collective nose to the wind in case there should be a brief whiff from Yasnaya Polyana of the former literary genius.[27] The young man takes exceedingly great care as he begins to craft an authorial persona; the old man has, frankly, too much persona, and he is trying not to damage the image, that antipoetic personality, which he has honed to perfection for thirty years.

We do not want to mistake such similarity in authorial strategy and habit for unified theme and philosophy. I reject the view of Tolstoy, encouraged by Tolstoy himself, that reinterprets his earlier work according to the ideas of his later work. As Gustafson remarks, "The primary rule in reading Tolstoy, therefore, is that the later clarifies the earlier."[28] Tolstoy might have thought Gustafson right: as an older man Tolstoy ceaselessly reinterpreted his earlier work.[29] This approach by both author and critic shows us Tolstoy's ultimate religious philosophy, but effaces the art and philosophy that occupied him at the time of those original works. Tolstoy is such an authoritative critic of his own work, moreover, that his voice tends to drown out the responses of contemporary readers and critics. Witness his famous response to Strakhov, for example, that if he were to explain what *Anna Karenina* was about he would have to write the same novel all over again:

> If I wanted to say in words all that I had in mind to express by my novel, I should have to write the same novel which I wrote all over again. If near-sighted critics think that I wanted to describe only what I like, how Oblonsky dines and what shoulders Anna has, they are mistaken. In everything, in almost everything I have written, I was guided by the need to bring together ideas linked among themselves, in order to achieve self-expression. But every idea expressed by itself in words loses its meaning, becomes terribly debased when it is taken alone, out of the linking in which it is found. This linking is

based not on an idea, I think, but on something else, and to express the
essence of that linking in any way directly by words is impossible, but it is
possible indirectly, with words describing images, actions, situations.[30]

Tolstoy reduces to the absurd the very idea of reductionism, and he battles
against paraphrase from the earliest days of his career. Thus even though he
suggests that younger work be seen again in light of later work, Tolstoy also
insists, as in the statement above, on the singularity of the authorial word.
Misdirection and paraphrase: how Tolstoy can champion the one and abhor the
other is one of his primary authorial puzzles. Both tactics, I will argue, aim to
assuage Tolstoy's ceaseless doubt that art can say something meaningful about
the world.

As Tolstoy grows older, he continues to create difficult obstacles to the easy
consumption of his fiction. There is the "Afterword," for example, to his story of
1889 "The Kreutzer Sonata," in which he explains the radical ideas of the story
and how he feels about them personally. On the one hand, Tolstoy clarifies the
theories of sexuality and marriage in the story. His "Afterword" does not, on the
other hand, make the story any easier to read. Now the reader has to read story
and poststory and reconcile the two. Is this "Afterword" not a kind of paraphrase? What are we to make of this change of core aesthetic belief? We must
recognize, first, that Tolstoy purposefully destroys many of his old ideas in his
later writing. More than that, he destroys old forms of ideas and forms of writing. This destruction is paraphrase by other means. "A Few Words on *War and
Peace*," like the "Afterword," also comments on what the reader just finished
reading. Tolstoy makes no serious attempt at paraphrase, however. In fact, in an
oft-quoted passage, he asserts the irreducibility of *War and Peace*: "What is *War
and Peace*? It is not a novel, even less is it a poem, and still less an historical
chronicle. *War and Peace* is what the author wished and was able to express in
the form in which it is expressed."[31] As with his comments on *Anna Karenina*,
here Tolstoy insists on the inviolability of the artistic text. But, plainly, he was
not always consistent on this point.

Tolstoy cultivated his skill at destroying things and later admitted his penchant for destruction like this: "From youth I prematurely began to analyze
everything and to destroy mercilessly. I have often feared and thought that nothing would be left whole, but here I am getting old, and there is much more
whole and unharmed in me than in others."[32] In his *Confession* (1879–82), he
makes the implication more terrifying by widening the scope of the author's
destruction to include the author himself. He refuses to exclude himself from
the doom he sees in the world. He writes: "The third method of escape [from

the search for meaning in life] is through strength and energy. It consists of real-izing that life is evil and senseless, and of destroying it. This is what a few strong and consistent people do. Having understood the utter stupidity of the joke that is being played on them, and realizing that the blessings of the dead are far greater than the blessings of the living, and that the best thing of all is not to live, they act accordingly and instantly bring an end to this stupid joke, using any available means: a noose around the neck, water, a stab in the heart, a train on a railway line."[33] As Tolstoy describes an escape from life, we cannot help notic-ing how much stronger a suicidal Anna Karenina seems in this particular retro-spect. Traditional stories and traditional lives, or "ordinary" lives, such as Ivan Ilyich's, are chosen for destruction. A few paragraphs later in *Confession*, Tolstoy delivers the memorable line: "Can it be that only Schopenhauer and I have been intelligent enough to understand the senselessness and evil of life?"[34] Grigoriev had warned of Tolstoy's nihilism much earlier in a review of the short work "Three Deaths." By the time of Tolstoy's late aesthetic theory in *What Is Art?*—which describes communication between author and reader as infection and thus implicitly likens art to disease—it is quite clear that the life Matthew Arnold tells us Tolstoy was creating may have been a very unpleasant one. At least that is the way Tolstoy chooses to reinterpret it.

Tolstoy's lifetime fascination with the boundary between life and art, and with the possibility of passing from one to the other and back again, yields a series of oppositions, some of which Tolstoy openly addressed and some of which echo faintly beneath the noisy surface of his aesthetic ruminations. Orwin comments generally that "the early Tolstoy sought to occupy the middle ground between subjective and objective experience."[35] For example, within his writing itself he frequently opposes literary narrative to factual description, and within that division distinguishes between mediated and unmediated forms of communication.[36] The former diverts, the latter directs. As these kinds of dis-course take rhetorical shape, we find related tropes, notions of spatial distance versus proximity (e.g., "escape" versus the "instant end" of suicide), or, more abstractly, of metaphor and metonymy.[37] These images hang flesh on the bones of Tolstoy's language.

TOLSTOY'S FALSE MEMORIES OF CHILDHOOD

Childhood returns again and again as a touchstone for Tolstoy's evolving aesthetics. Andrew Wachtel has commented at length on Tolstoy's *Childhood*. He sees the truth-versus-fiction opposition of autobiography-versus-novel as presaging one of Tolstoy's main authorial dilemmas: how to generalize from

individual experience to universal truths.[38] This approach has the advantage of
explaining Tolstoy's dedication to truth in his fiction (for example, at the end of
"Sevastopol in May," the narrator states: "The hero of my story . . . is truth"), but
it gives too little attention to a second, increasingly important aspect of his work:
Tolstoy as truth teller. Tolstoy complains in an unsent letter to Nekrasov about
the latter's editorial change of the title from *Childhood* to *A History of My
Childhood*, "who is interested in a history of *my* childhood?" Wachtel takes this
complaint as a sign of "the extent to which fiction and autobiography were
intertwined for Tolstoy when he was writing *Childhood*."[39] I view this as Tolstoy's
preoccupation with the authorial image that his work produced and his fear of
losing control of it. Remember how concerned Tolstoy is with the status of the
author as one individual writing to another. The final lines of the same letter to
Nekrasov read: "I can only console myself with the fact that I have the opportunity to publish the whole novel separately under my own name, and to renounce
completely the story *A History of My Childhood*, which by rights belongs not to
me, but to an unknown employee of your editorial staff."[40] Wachtel elsewhere
sees Tolstoy's repetition in *A Confession* of the passage in *Anna Karenina* where
Levin describes hiding rope for fear of hanging himself and not going hunting
for fear of shooting himself as: "a radical trick to achieve the goals of realism."[41]
Tolstoy retroactively makes Levin more real; and thus perhaps his happy ending
could be read as "wish fulfillment," as Wachtel puts it, on Tolstoy's part.[42]

If we are going to psychologize Tolstoy, I would focus attention less on wish
fulfillment and more on false memories and their repetition. The genuine
emotion Nikolai derives from the false memory or reported dream of his
mother's death, as well as the false memories that music evokes, are part of a
much larger pattern in Tolstoy's work whereby characters, and sometimes
Tolstoy himself, compose new or ideal identities by repeating a false past. I do
not have in mind here the lies characters knowingly or unwittingly tell when
they report on what happened in battle.[43] Rather, I am interested in how falsehood is incorporated into being through a sort of false repetition—for example
a memory that recapitulates an event that never happened.[44]

Let us consider again Nikolai's recollection of the false dream of his mother's
death. He tells the story of a memory about something he did not really experience; yet he does experience real emotion. Later, as his mother plays the piano,
Nikolai remarks: "I well remember the feelings [those pieces] aroused in me.
They resembled memories—but memories of what? It almost seemed as if I
were remembering something that had never been."[45] Tolstoy was fascinated by
the causeless emotion of music. Music plays a large role in the early stories
"Lucerne" and "Albert," as in this description of those listening to Albert's

violin: "Now a calm contemplation of the past arose in their souls, now an impassioned memory of some past happiness. . . . It was as if each would have liked to express what all this meant, but was unable to do so."[46] Albert's supreme vision, while he is later near death, merges desire and memory: "It was more than reality: it was reality and recollection combined."[47] As Natasha Sankovitch, Patricia Carden, and others have noted, Tolstoy uses "imagination" for "memory."[48] In a late diary entry Tolstoy writes: "Music is the stenography of feelings. . . . Music without speech takes those expressions of feelings and their nuances and unites them, and we receive the play of feelings without that which called them forth."[49] And Pozdnyshev, the protagonist of Tolstoy's "Kreutzer Sonata," complains that "[music] merely irritates me. How can I put it? Music makes me forget myself, my true condition, it carries me off into another state of being, one that isn't my own: under the influence of music I have the illusion of feeling things I don't really feel, of understanding things I don't understand, being able to do things I'm not able to do."[50] Tolstoy, himself so keen on controlling his reader's experience, is disturbed by the uncontrollability of music, its unpredictable effect on the listener, its shaky ontology.

But the pattern extends well beyond music. In the early story "Two Hussars" (1856), Count Turbin speaks falsely of his service in the cavalry: "He transformed his desire first into a reality and then into a reminiscence and came to believe firmly in his past as a cavalry officer—all of which did not prevent his being, as to gentleness and honesty, a most worthy man."[51] The reminiscence twice removed from reality is all the more believable, especially when it is not simply told but retold. It makes one wonder about the link between *Confessions* and *Anna Karenina*. There is, so far as I know, no mention whatsoever in Tolstoy's diaries or letters of these suicidal temptations until *after* he has appropriated the story from Levin.[52] Tolstoy tells Gorky: "I know that people sometimes think up things unconsciously, completely unacceptable things, and then it seems they dreamed them and didn't make them up."[53] Tolstoy kept the narrative habits of self-creation throughout his career, even as he provided the possibility for changing an imagined core of his authorial identity from legitimacy to authenticity. He gave up on what Irina Paperno describes as his intention to accomplish "the complete textualization of self," but he kept the narrative strategies he developed in that quest.[54]

The source of a work of art, like the source of authorial identity, can be missing entirely, false, a kind of nonsequitur. As I mentioned earlier, Tolstoy sees the boundary between life and fiction as a barrier, and he is always drawing our attention away from how he crosses it and creates the artwork. The main protagonist of "After the Ball" begins the story: "So you are saying that by

oneself one is unable to understand what is good and what is bad, and that
it is all a matter of environment, that we are victims of environment. But I
think everything depends on chance. I can speak of my own experience."⁵⁵ Yet,
in fact, as the narrator of the story remarks, no one was saying anything of
the sort. The quoted speaking voice that begins the story is so instant, and nearly
apostrophic, that one hardly notices the beginning of the story—which, when
we read the title "After the Ball," begins only after it ends. The story begins not
in medias res, as in classical epic, nor in the middle of a conversation, as with
War and Peace, but literally as the answer to a question no one has asked. In
Truth and Method Gadamer says we must reconstruct the question to which the
text is an answer—things get complicated, though, when the text pretends it
answers no question.⁵⁶ This is not an isolated event for Tolstoy. "The Kreutzer
Sonata" really gets going as Pozdnyshev announces, "Aha, I see you've discovered who I am," but no one does know who he is. In "Two Hussars," "After the
Ball," and "The Kreutzer Sonata," these rhetorical gestures are directly associated with identity, and in each instance the protagonists repeat stories they
have invented about themselves and come to believe.⁵⁷ Tolstoy develops a pattern of how to articulate an identity that only seems grounded in memory, but
the content of that identity can vary as needed for self-creation. The repetition
of a false memory hollows out an absence, a space in which a narrative alibi can
be enunciated.

The ontological pattern was evident even in *Childhood*, and Tolstoy returns
to it again in *Boyhood*. In the chapter "Karl Ivanych's Life-Story," there is the
following explanation by Nikolai (it is worth paying attention to what stays the
same and what changes in this passage): "As Karl Ivanych was afterwards to tell
me his story more than once, using the *same* sequences and the *same* phrases
and never departing from the *same* unvarying intonations, *I think I can repro-
duce it almost word for word, except of course for mistakes in language*. . . .
Whether it really was the history of his life or whether it was the product of his
imagination evolved during the lonely time he spent in our house, and which
he had from endless repetition come to believe in himself, or whether he
merely embellished the actual events of his life with fantastic additions, I have
never been able to decide."⁵⁸ These reservations do not prevent Nikolai from
repeating the story. Whether it is history or imagination is not insignificant, but
it is less significant than one might think. As one repeats a repetition, whether
the first articulation is true seems to matter less and less.

Repetition, like reflection, need not be unreal. Nabokov, a great reader
of Tolstoy, provides a good example. Tolstoy influenced Nabokov in many ways,
and in his course lectures Nabokov championed Tolstoy's prose. Nabokov

perhaps also learned from Tolstoy that illusion and misdirection are not incompatible with the aura of realism. Thus, in *The Gift*, Fyodor's father sees mirages in which real mountains are reflected: the point is, the reader infers, that literary fiction may also reflect or convey real truths. Nabokov makes a similar point in *Invitation to a Beheading*, in which the hero is trapped in a world that is a poor reflection of reality (art in the hero's world offering, by contrast, much greater verisimilitude). What Nabokov realized is that literary devices that seem at first to distract or divert the reader's skeptical attention may lead to more substantial revelations of the relation between art and reality.[59]

Much of Tolstoy's early work ponders the role of diversion in realistic fiction, asking whether there is such a thing as genuine aesthetic pleasure. Although Tolstoy spent much of his life at his country estate, he believed strongly in art that engages society rather than looking upon it disinterestedly. Tolstoy rejects notions of aesthetic pleasure that demand the viewer's or the reader's detachment.[60] One frequently detects two movements in the early stories, the first toward entertainment, in the broad sense of rewarding the reader's expectations and providing literary escape, the second toward moral censure for that entertainment. Tolstoy was himself torn by impulses toward dissolution and subsequent repentance of it, though this oscillation hardly makes him unique among other young, socially conscious noblemen of his generation. He embeds that duality in his fiction, however, and he continues to do so for most of his career. Typical of Tolstoy are literary scenes that dwell at some length on the licentious details of a man's weaknesses, followed by attempts, unsuccessful as well as successful, to reform. To foster an alibi, in Tolstoy's world, is not to give in to moral escapism; it is to cultivate a ceaseless possibility for rebirth and, ideally, self-perfection.

SOLDIERS' STORIES

Gazing into Napoleon's eyes, Prince Andrei mused on the nothingness of greatness, on the nothingness of life, of which no one could comprehend the significance, and on the nothingness—still more—of death, the meaning of which
could be understood and explained by none of the living.

—War and Peace

EARLY WARS ON FICTION

As one reads this famous passage about how Prince Andrei finally meets
Napoleon, one may easily assume the narrator's, and Andrei's, point of view.
But I do not think it would be difficult for me to ignore my hero if I were slowly
bleeding to death on the battlefield. It is as though Tolstoy, whose thoughts of
death were sometimes all-consuming, purposely imagined an event in fiction
in which another would be struck by the enormity of death in a way he himself
was. Napoleon fails to interest a man who is dying—to which one wants to say,
of course. The more fascinating aspect of this passage is how certain Tolstoy is
of the incommunicability of the experience. Why bother trying to explain the
meaning of death if none of the living will understand?

The early stories, especially "Sevastopol in December," do try to explain it,
and they address the reader directly and forcefully. Tolstoy's attempt to imagine
a real reader, which he first mentions in "To Readers," continues to shape his
aesthetics throughout his early years as an author. "Sevastopol in December"
(1855), an early military story, is written in the second person with a style that
resembles that of a tour guide. The narrator takes the newcomer by the hand,
as it were, and introduces him to the sights, sounds, and smells of the battlefield. Although the story sounds outlandishly sensationalistic, and is sensationalistic in some respects, it aims mostly to spoil the reader-tourist's romantic
expectations. Like more personal narratives of dissolution and repentance,

"Sevastopol in December" gives readers the sordid detail before chastising them for it.

Morson interprets such voyeurism—the reader's struggle against it as well as submission to it—as central to Tolstoy's didactic fiction: "Tolstoi's violation of the principles of 'framing' and 'aesthetic distance' is strategic; he assumes that his readers expect to read fiction with a set of conventions that separate it from reality and therefore deliberately encourages those expectations so *that* he may violate them later. For it is precisely aesthetic detachment that these stories seek to challenge. Their recurrent theme is that the aesthetic experience is itself immoral, that to observe is to act—and act badly."[1] Observing may be acting badly, but participating in art is not, at this juncture, itself a bad thing for Tolstoy. We recall that the reader's participation is crucial to Tolstoy's notion of authorial legitimation. Besides, there are many kinds of aesthetic experience in Tolstoy's fiction in addition to watching (structured experiences of the beautiful are found in scenes of dancing, playing music, even hunting). Nevertheless this is an especially strong argument as it tracks Tolstoy's preoccupation with the boundary between reality and fiction. Morson sees, moreover, the unobtrusive narrative beginning by Tolstoy as part of conventional literary framing; when the narrator later becomes more active, and breaks the frame, the reader is reminded that the story is literature and thus feels "off the hook" morally. Tolstoy sets this trap to lull the reader back into a position of culpability for the misdeeds depicted by the story.

The problem is that much, if not most, "realistic" fiction of the time was not at all as conventional as Morson supposes. The prose fiction of Pushkin, Gogol, Lermontov, Dostoevsky, and even Turgenev (not to mention Tolstoy's favorite, Sterne) was frequently strongly marked at the beginning by epigraphs, framing narratives, outbursts by the narrator, and other metaliterary breaks. Very many of Turgenev's stories from *Notes of a Hunter* are framed. Tolstoy does not in fact, as Morson suggests, encourage the reader to separate fiction from reality.[2] The inevitability of convention is the approach to understanding litera-ture Tolstoy was dismantling, or trying to dismantle. This effort includes the disintermediation effects of *Childhood*. As in the opening scene of *Childhood*, in "Sevastopol in December" the narrator startles the reader, here with his second-person address, by which he draws our attention away from what is, frankly, a much more radical strategy in the context of this story: the use of the present tense in an attempt to create near cinematic simultaneity of text and experience as the reader is immersed in the realistic world of Sevastopol. (The analogy with cinema is anachronistic, but Tolstoy did embrace advancements in photographic technology. As an old man, he enjoyed being filmed.)

It is this vivid experience of Sevastopol that makes the story enjoyable for readers, who relish the realistic details of the battleground, and rewards their expectations, for their beliefs and first impressions are otherwise assaulted at almost every turn. Tolstoy's use of the second-person address is ultimately subjugated by realistic presentness. The main rhetorical feature of the story is: You may think x, but really it is y. Turn by brutal turn, Tolstoy narrates disenchantment, severing the relationship not between literature and truth but between inaccurate perception and truth. (You are thus encouraged to forget that you are reading literature.) This technique of correcting misguided impression is similar to the correction of Nikolai's mistaken perceptions of Karl Ivanych in the opening passage of *Childhood*. Both instances prefigure that key aspect of Tolstoy's narrative alibi: the need, possibly inevitability, of revisiting one's interpretation. Consider these exemplary passages from "Sevastopol in December":

- Your first impressions will certainly be most disagreeable. . . . But look more closely at the faces of these people moving and you will get a very different impression.
- Yes, disenchantment certainly awaits you on entering Sevastopol for the first time.
- Do not trust the feeling that checks you at the threshold; it is the wrong feeling.
- "So this is Fourth Bastion! This is that awful, truly dreadful spot!" So you think, experiencing a slight feeling of pride and a strong feeling of suppressed fear. But you are mistaken, this is not the Fourth Bastion yet. This is only Yazonovsky Redoubt—a comparatively safe and not at all dreadful place.[3]

One wonders whether the poor reader (object of the second-person narration) will ever get it right, but it does seem possible that the reader-tourist may learn something by the end of the story:

- Now you begin to understand the defenders of Sevastopol and for some reason begin to feel ashamed of yourself in the presence of this man.
- "That's the way it is with seven or eight men every day," the naval officer remarks to you, answering the look of horror on your face; then he yawns as he rolls another yellow cigarette.
- It is only now that the tales of the early days of the siege of Sevastopol are no longer beautiful historical legends for you, but have become realities.[4]

Yet this rhetorical process is not what ends the story, and the second-person address fades in the last paragraph, as the narrator paints a lovely sunset to the accompaniment of a military band playing an old favorite. The musical denoument provides a kind of cathartic realignment of the reader's senses with nature, closing the distance the story has created between society and nature. Readers familiar with Tolstoy's other works incorporating music may read this ending with some trepidation, and may doubt that Tolstoy has actually closed the gap here between an experience of presentness and detached observation.

Something happens in the Sevastopol stories, between "Sevastopol in December" and "Sevastopol in May" (both published in 1855), that reveals a particular pattern of narrative experimentation in Tolstoy.[5] Many people read "Sevastopol in December" as a narrative experiment first and a publicistic, military tale second—or perhaps vice versa. Yet Tolstoy is experimenting with how personal observation and moral growth can be integrated into a social (even natural) background. Here alienation from the horrible truth of which he was a part horrifies Tolstoy. Nevertheless, this alienated form could serve, if not for ultimate self-knowledge then for knowledge cast in the shape of a new realism. This is what happens in the Sevastopol stories. "Sevastopol in December" is an ordinary story of self-alienation and, perhaps, loathing, but the story and its techniques are rescued by the author's transformation of much material on his earlier life into the present experience of another person—making it no longer an alienating subjective experience. Tolstoy strives for a new form of realism.

Just as Tolstoy worked against the notion that all reading is already framed by literary conventions and expectations, his strategies to transform realism adopt a view of language that facilitates pure experience. Throughout his career, Tolstoy oscillated between divergent views of language as perfectly transparent and capable of conveying the author's intended impressions, or as a troublesome obstacle to be overcome by narrative invention. This dual view of language is revealed most dramatically by his romance narratives, but even in the Sevastopol stories one can see Tolstoy struggling with broader definitions of language in literature. The adoption of the second-person voice in "Sevastopol in December" is an attempt to see past the obstacle that language might raise between experience and its representation. "Sevastopol in May" goes much further than its precursor, by announcing—immodestly, even for Tolstoy—that the real hero of the story is "Truth." Yet, as opposed to "Sevastopol in December," the later story creates readerly obstacles rather than removing them.

There is an important difference between digression, which is a narrative aside, and diversion, which is, as I have been describing it, both a misdirection and a play on our expectations of enjoyment. Readers of Tolstoy know that he loved to include digressions in his stories and novels from the very beginning of his literary career. With such digressive talents as Laurence Sterne and the Pushkin of *Evgeny Onegin* as his models, Tolstoy frequently left the straight and narrow path of basic plot to wax philosophic or to describe characters and objects in abundant detail. In "Sevastopol in May," for example, as he is describing aristocratic characters, he interjects: "Vanity! vanity! vanity! everywhere, even on the brink of the grave and among men ready to die for a noble cause. Vanity! It seems to be the characteristic feature and special malady of our time. How is it that among our predecessors no mention was made of this passion, as of small-pox and cholera? . . . Why did the Homers and Shakespeares speak of love, glory, and suffering, while the literature of today is an endless story of snobbery and vanity?"[6] This passage clearly digresses from the plot, even diverting our attention from it. But the reader is not idly enjoying the distraction of this digression. Thus it diverts in only one sense of the word, presaging Tolstoy's late didactic essays.

Tolstoy no doubt understood that there was something a bit vain about his digression on vanity—the metanarrative aspect of the digression tells us something about vanity and about the author's relationship to vanity in "Sevastopol in May" (i.e., it may be indulged, so long as it is simultaneously denounced). Similarly, narrative diversions are frequently also metanarrative expressions. In other words, they break from the plot, gesture toward idle entertainment, and meditate on the relationship of the larger novel to plot and entertainment. Digressions that form a symbolic pattern of some sort are no longer really digressions. Some of Tolstoy's favorite literary devices, such as repetition, are transformed into networks of meaning in precisely that way. Marya's "heavy tread" in *War and Peace* is less descriptive each time that Tolstoy repeats the phrase, yet more indicative of how motifs and patterns are formed in the novel.

Compared to "Sevastopol in December," "Sevastopol in May" is a more complex narrative, and also a more sophisticated and mature story in how it deploys its sometimes tendentious themes. With its omniscient narrator, the story integrates several perspectives, implements new descriptive narrative techniques, and explores the limits of how the personal experience of violence and war may be conveyed. The narrator follows the experiences of several people that day, ranging from Mikhaylov's drunken servant to generals and princes. He juxtaposes the divergent perspectives of various characters. He tracks the last few instants of thought passing through Praskukhin's mind. He charts the disjunction between these men's intentions and their actions. He lays bare the petty motivations of so-called heroes. He unmasks his hypocritical heroes. He digresses on the nature of vanity, and he declares that "Truth" itself is the real hero of his tale. Such numerous authorial interventions suggest we view the story as a countermovement away from the presence championed in "Sevastopol in December."

These themes will become important to *War and Peace*, for which "Sevastopol in May" is an important precursor; thus the story is crucial in the development of Tolstoy's aesthetics. Any one or two of these themes or narrative techniques may be seen in earlier stories, but never before had they all existed in such close proximity and intertwined narrative purpose. More than any work up to this point, "Sevastopol in May" forces the reader to wonder why the author includes some events and excludes others, why he has put the story together the way that he has, and what he hopes to achieve by these narrative combinations.

The most significant passage of "Sevastopol in May" is located at the very end of the story. The narrator, having switched from the third-person back into the first-person voice, closes with the following paragraphs:

> There, I have said what I wished to say this time. But I am seized by an oppressive doubt. *Perhaps I ought to have left it unsaid.* What I have said perhaps belongs to that class of evil truths that lie unconsciously hidden in the soul of each man and should not be uttered lest they become harmful, as dregs in a bottle must not be disturbed for fear of spoiling the wine. . . .
>
> Where in this tale is the evil that should be avoided, and where the good that should be imitated? Who is the villain and who the hero of my story? All are good and all are bad. . . .
>
> The hero of my tale—whom I love with all the power of my soul, whom I have tried to portray in all its beauty, who has been, is, and always will be beautiful—is Truth.[7]

Others have seen in these words a kind of summing up of Tolstoy's early aesthetics. Kupreianova writes: "'Where in this tale is the evil that should be avoided, and where the good that should be imitated?'—by concluding with these words the story 'Sevastopol in May' (4, 59), Tolstoy staked the fundamental question of his life and activity and the compositional core of his 'new philosophy' and his early philosophical experiments."[8] But, of course, those are not really the final words, as we can see above. The story ends with the narrator's declaration of love for the Truth, his real hero.

Between the expression of good or evil and the Truth runs a second axis dividing the said from the unsaid. By declaring, at the end of his story, his fear that perhaps he should have left all unsaid, Tolstoy switches the logic of the story's enunciation around completely. By the time one reaches the end of the story, there can no longer be any question of the narrator's having remained silent. It is too late, and Tolstoy, typically, insists on having it both ways: the story spoken and unspoken. Although the story has been told, by declaring his fidelity to Truth at the conclusion, Tolstoy ultimately undermines the fiction that has preceded it. "Sevastopol in May" leads to a dead end, where fiction leaves off and truth begins. By forcing us to confront the removal of fiction, Tolstoy reveals a hidden or absent meaning in the text, an alibi in the story, of which the author was presumably always conscious.

"Sevastopol in May" has particular resonance for the topic of diversion, because misleading passages in the story function as metafiction and model how the entire story itself can mislead. In the third chapter, Mikhaylov, who has a presentiment that he will die that day at the bastion, approaches a group of noblemen, his superiors both militarily and socially (a prince is among them). Knowing that they often have inside information on military operations, Mikhaylov hopes to learn whether there will be action that day or not. He asks: "How about today? Will anything happen today?"[9] No one replies, perhaps because it is a secret but more probably because the question shows such bad form on Mikhaylov's part. The circulation or noncirculation of knowledge, like money, reinforces class distinctions. Rather than continue to talk about a question, remember, of life and death (as far as Mikhaylov is concerned), Galtsin directs everyone's attention to a young woman walking past. And Mikhaylov is diverted from his worries: "Lieutenant-Captain Mikhaylov found it so pleasant to walk in this company that he forgot the nice letter from T— — and his gloomy forebodings at the thought of having to go to the bastion."[10] He forgets, but we are reminded.

In this instance, and in others, a pleasant diversion offers escape from one's difficult, gloomy life, and plunges one into waking forgetfulness, though ultimately charting one's error or weakness. Numb disregard for how life passes by is an important theme in much of Tolstoy's fiction. In "The Death of Ivan Ilyich," Ivan hangs a medal from his watch chain that reads *respice finem*, "look to the end," recommending, in other words, exactly that which Ivan fails to do. By allowing himself to forget his own mortality in his pursuit of the conventional trappings of success, Ivan ultimately loses hold of the meaning of life itself. Mikhaylov makes a similar mistake, though it does not cost him his life, since another officer, Praskukhin, is the one who dies when the shell explodes. Nevertheless, Mikhaylov has a near-death experience on the psychological level—from which, one must suppose, he learns something, even as he continues to try to impress the group of noblemen who treat him shabbily.

In "Sevastopol in May," the narrative itself mirrors the idle diversions of Mikhaylov and other characters. The final meandering chapter, for example, mimics the conversations between French and Russian troops. Those conversations additionally serve as models of superficial narrative communication, driven as they are by which French words the Russian soldier knows rather than by an interior logic in the conversation itself. Why does Tolstoy include these passages in the story? Because here the narrator imitates the kind of idle observation that poses as realistic storytelling. These idle diversions are not "Truth," in Tolstoy's sense, because they contain no guiding logic of moral value. Mimesis by itself is insufficient for art. Although several of Tolstoy's early stories have the facade of realistic sketches, a kind of pure witnessing of people and events, he prefers to allow moral judgment to shape what makes it into the story and what is excluded from it. Simple, inadvertent selection does not say enough for Tolstoy. Even the most plotless of his stories limit the amount of physiological sketch that emerges in the final version.

Rules for inclusion in the narrative, as well as rules for exclusion, explain how these stories work as art, and compose an important dimension of their thematics. We do not find the present tense in "Sevastopol in May" as often as we did in "Sevastopol in December," but we do ponder presence itself. Narrative inclusion, simply making it into the story, is one way that Tolstoy develops the connection between realism and presentness. Some realistic parts of a story are there because of their temporal aspect (present tense); others because of spatial proximity (they are simply present); and still others for logical reasons. When confronting idle diversion, readers are invited to question, not just why characters are thoughtless in the story, but why readers themselves can be distracted or entertained by that diversion. In "Sevastopol in May," Tolstoy writes, "*Eh sussy oo ashtay?*"[11] quoting the soldiers as they try out their French and engage in other idle behavior against a background of scores of dead bodies being removed from the field of battle. Here the failure to look at death is blamed on the waking sleep of life, where one is engaged in diverting idle conversation instead of confronting one's mortality.

"Sevastopol in May" in this final chapter returns to the present tense, and death itself is likewise omnipresent. Yet as the story diverts to idle conversation, it follows the soldiers and retreats elsewhere, away from the corpses who tell the needed story of needless death. This final diversion is a crucial element of Tolstoy's more general use of a narrative alibi. Alibi—meaning literally "to be elsewhere"—provides the story its moral imperative. Although the focus of the narrative shifts to the chatting soldiers, the gravity of the story derives from the barely visible background of corpses scattered across the landscape. By announcing that his hero is Truth, Tolstoy attempts to reveal the heretofore hidden locus of real aesthetic value in the story. Speaking for the dead soldier, Tolstoy says the unsaid. It is a real story of fictional truth.

TWO HUSSARS, NO PLOT

Chiastic narrative forms (real or true fictions versus fictive or false realities) continued to interest Tolstoy to the very end of his career. His late moral parables depict the eternal truth of the world, but in fiction. Such experiments were more urgent early in his career, because his legitimacy as an author seemed to turn on the realism he was developing and on his psychological perspicacity. As in *Childhood*, in "Two Hussars" (1856) Tolstoy tests the formal ways an author may cross into the world of fiction. The introductory paragraphs are propelled forward by a negative description more far reaching than in any other of his works. "Two Hussars" is almost Gogolian in tone. As in *Dead Souls*, where Chichikov is introduced mainly by what he does not resemble, Tolstoy in this story describes not what is but what is not: "Early in the nineteenth century, when there were as yet no railways or macadamized roads, no gaslight, no stearine candles, no low couches with sprung cushions, no unvarnished furniture, no disillusioned youths with eye-glasses, no liberalizing women philosophers, nor any charming *dame aux camellias* of whom there are so many in our times, in those naïve days, when leaving Moscow for Petersburg in a coach or carriage."[12] And so he continues in a sentence stretching two or three times as long as this selection, spurred by clauses, such as: ". . . на балах в канделябры вставлялись восковые и спермацетовые свечи, когда мебель ставили симметрично, когда наши отцы были еще молоды . . . [3:145] [when ball-rooms were illuminated by candelabra . . . when furniture was arranged symmetrically, when our fathers were still young . . .]," and so on and so forth. The story uses negation to clear an imaginative space for the reader, and then fills it in with a series of *whens*. Tolstoy replaces the metonyms of contemporary life with reminiscences of a wholly different life. Thus one form of transition from reality to fiction may be found in the rhetorical transition from metonym to metaphor, from spatial proximity to temporal distance and comparable times.

In this diverting beginning, as one may call it, the narrator dances among descriptions and evocations of a previous era, coaxing the reader to visualize a time and place different from the contemporary world (especially the contemporary world of a particular milieu). These sentences divert the reader in the second sense of the word also, as the narrator calls to mind contemporary images of railways, roads, gaslight, candles, couches, and eyeglasses only in order that he may snatch them away by negation. This twisting line of images disappears as quickly as it appears. More important, especially when we consider that Tolstoy will begin writing *War and Peace* in just a few years, the introduction to "Two Hussars" is steeped in nostalgia, recollecting a time or place that never was.[13] The setting Tolstoy so vividly introduces is one that never really existed in such harmony but was created by the narrator in order to generate a mood of readerly expectations unshaped by conventional literary framing.

The plot of the story complements the diversions of the introductory paragraphs almost perfectly. The young uhlan Ilyin originally has no intention of staying in the town of K——. Yet the superintendent of the posthouse has an agreement with the hotel owner to waylay travelers for a day. Thus Ilyin is purposefully and deceitfully diverted from his original trip, and he ends up gambling for four days straight. He loses both his own money and the government money entrusted to him. When the main protagonist of the first half of the story, Count Turbin, arrives he cries out that Ilyin is being cheated. Any gambling story with such an announcement in the middle of a game should bring the plot to a crisis—a duel, or some other dramatic confrontation—but here nothing happens. Turbin leaves the recalcitrant Ilyin to lose the rest of his money. Again, at the ball, Turbin angers a young man so much (by flirting with the woman the young man is courting) that the latter makes public accusations. Naturally, Turbin declares he is willing to provide satisfaction . . . yet still no duel. Nor again, when Turbin takes advantage of Zavalshevsky's sister and then rudely abuses Zavalshevsky when the latter alludes to it. Nor later, when Turbin strikes Lukhnov, steals back all of Ilyin's money, and leaves the room announcing his availability should Lukhnov demand satisfaction. The plot of "Two Hussars" deceives readers much as the superintendent of the posthouse did Turbin. We are reading a story that, by every convention and indication of convention, should end in violence after only a handful of pages. Tolstoy taunts his readers, as though we, too, should call him out.

When Count Turbin finally does leave the stage, we realize that the narrator has severed the story into two distinct parts. The first ends with Turbin's departure; the second begins twenty years later, long after Turbin has finally been killed in a duel, though not one that is described. Our question, as we read, inevitably addresses the form of the story. Just what kind of story could this be? It does not fulfill generic expectations in the first half, and the second half begins without any special denouement to the first half. By subverting the plot expectations of the first half so thoroughly, Tolstoy heightens the reader's generic expectation for the second half of the story, as though it should compensate for the frustrated expectations of the first. But the second half of the story is itself a kind of diversion from the line of the plot: the officers are drawn from their intended quarters to Anna Fedorovna's, and, once there, the young Turbin circles round the house to the garden in his attempt to seduce her daughter.

The second half of the story cannot focus on the development of the protagonist, who has since died in a duel; but when his son appears, the plot asks us to look for aspects of similarity between father and son. In other words, the plot functions according to metaphoric relationships of similarity, rather than according to a metonymic relationship of contiguity. It thereby repeats the opening gesture of the story. There is nothing that connects father and son other than name and possible similarity of character. The beginning of the second part of the story presages change and difference, however, rather than similarity: "More than twenty years had gone by. Much water had flowed away, many people had died, many been born . . . much that was beautiful and new had grown up and still more that was immature, monstrous, and new, had come into God's world."[14] Nevertheless, Turbin's son was "as physically like him as one drop of water to another."[15] Balancing similarity and difference is the challenge before the reader. The similarity is this: just as the dashing Count Turbin once pursued Anna Fedorovna romantically, so too does his son cast his net for her daughter Lisa. Neither the daughter nor (despite his physical resemblance to his father) the son matches up well to their parents. In the place of his father, the irresistible Count Turbin, his son is tastelessly impolite, cheating the easily misled Anna Fedorovna in cards and taking her money. He misinterprets Lisa's naive musings as a sexual invitation, and when he touches her hand while she is sleeping, she responds to his touch as to an unexpected assault. As for Lisa, she herself seems aware of her limitations as a character. She wants to meet Turbin and wonders: "And if he goes away he'll never know that I was here and thought about him. And how many such have already passed me by? Who sees me here except uncle and Ustyushka?"[16]

Lise invokes a frequently encountered line of nineteenth-century literary philosophy that we might call "Romantic existentialism"—if she or he doesn't love me, do I exist? In *War and Peace*, Tolstoy describes Anatole Kuragin's visit to the Bolkonsky estate in similar terms: "As always happens when women lead lonely lives for any length of time without male society, on Anatole's appearance all the three women of Prince Bolkonski's household felt that their life had not been real until then. Their powers of reasoning, feeling, and observing immediately increased tenfold, and their life, which seemed to have been passed in darkness, was suddenly lit up by a new brightness, full of significance."[17] All of a sudden, it is as though they are in a novel. But that is just the point. The narrative that makes demands on us to respond, to fill a role, or resist one, is a form of legitimation. Characters rise, or fail to rise, to the occasion when the spotlight hits them.

In "Two Hussars," Lise in fact barely exists in the story, legitimately or otherwise; her character is basically cliché. (There are few full and realistic women characters in Tolstoy's fiction before *War and Peace*.) Though she is present during much of the second half of the story, she serves mainly to unmask young Turbin as a "scoundrel," which is what Polozov finally calls him at the end of the story. Instead of a plot, Tolstoy has offered terms of comparison between past and present in order to constitute a sort of transgenerational notion of identity.

It is a less noble version of Andrei's connection to Rurik. Such narrative lines of identity are examined still further in *The Cossacks*. Diversion from plot, as well as the diversion the story enacts for the reader, swirl and knot that narrative line. In "Two Hussars" diversion accounts for those twists of heritage, behavior, and fortune that tangle the rope of the past one pulls into the present in order to account for one's self, one's vocation, and one's identity. It is a narrative alibi, rather than just a narrative. To write about continuity and difference between father and son in "Two Hussars" is to establish a narrative line that supplants an absent plot. Much later, in "After the Ball" (1903), Tolstoy will return to this strategy of juxtaposing the past and present, of creating a metahistory of authorial identity in place of narrative plot.

CROSSROADS: THE ROLE OF CHIASMUS IN *THE COSSACKS*

On and off throughout the 1850s Tolstoy worked on his novella *The Cossacks*, which follows a young, dissolute nobleman who enrolls as a cadet in the Caucasus in order to remake his life. Olenin vows to have no more relationships with women whom he does not love; no more gambling debts; no more aimless living. The story is personal for the author—how many times had Tolstoy himself tried to begin anew, without gambling debts or fear of venereal disease? "Olenin was a youth who had never completed his university course (having only a nominal post in some government office or other), who had squandered half his fortune and had reached the age of twenty-four without having done anything or even chosen a career. He was what in Moscow society is termed a 'young man.'"[18] To resemble a young Tolstoy completely, one might add only that he was also comme il faut. Yet the novella is also metaliterary and deeply committed to reworking literary tradition. Pushkin, Lermontov, Marlinsky, and others had written of military life in the south, perhaps the most important of Russian Romantic topoi.[19] *The Cossacks* is a confrontation of self in relation to literary tradition. Envisioning himself as a unique author vis-à-vis the Romantic tradition, Tolstoy uses *The Cossacks* as a way of defining his membership among the literary elect. The Sevastopol stories, *The Cossacks*, *Hadji Murad*—all provide that southern canvas on which Tolstoy can depict himself anew. He is not like the others, he is an original.

Tolstoy similarly describes Olenin's freedom, his ability to remake himself, in negative terms, as though an alibi were available to him at his very literary conception: "At the age of eighteen he was free—as only rich young Russians in the forties who had lost their parents at an early age could be. Neither physical nor moral fetters of any kind existed for him; he could do as he liked, lacking nothing and bound by nothing. Neither relatives, nor fatherland, nor religion, nor wants, existed for him. He believed in nothing and admitted nothing."[20] Nothing binds the man liberated by these negative freedoms; he is alone. Tolstoy makes clear, however, that such liberation is also why Olenin's life is so morally vacuous. The moral life demands more from these negations, these absences: mainly, that Olenin recognize the importance of others. His epiphany occurs in the absent space of the stag's empty lair, but it is a significant absence. Here Olenin recognizes his own uniqueness, and his relative irrelevance in a world of other individuals, each with their own unique experiences, needs, and wills.

Like Tolstoy, Olenin in this scene seeks legitimation of his individuality and his desires. He reasons: "The desire for happiness is innate in every man; therefore it is legitimate [законна]."[21] Satisfying the desire for happiness, and desires per se, strike Olenin as "illegitimate [незаконны]," because they may be thwarted by external circumstances. Olenin then asks himself which desires can be satisfied despite external circumstances, and he answers that love and self-sacrifice fit these criteria. The language of legitimation, literally "lawfulness," which requires almost by definition the recognition of others and of their needs and desires, is satisfied by Olenin solipsistically. He seeks out a legitimating philosophy satisfied entirely by the self, incapable of being thwarted by external circumstances. He is like the young Tolstoy, who wants to be a legitimate author but wants the circumstances of his reception by critics entirely in his control. What has changed is that the implied author of the novella, Tolstoy, seems to recognize his own sophistry. Using such explicitly logical terms as "it follows [следовательно]," Olenin reasons himself away from his recognition of the legitimate sovereignty of other persons to a tyranny of selfish altruism. Tolstoy himself uses his reliance on the literary tradition, by contrast, in an increasingly sophisticated manner.

Given the already multivoiced generic register of literature of the south, *The Cossacks* complicates its literary rhetoric by using narrative diversion more substantially than any previous Tolstoyan text. Many of the best examples of this are to be found at the thematic level in this tale, rather than at a formal, narrative level. Yet several formal, narrative diversions are easily adduced: the tale is marked at first as a Moscow story, for example, rather than one of the Caucasus (the opening scene of the party celebrates an end, after all, not a beginning); crucially, the end of the novella abandons Olenin in the south, rather than allowing him to return home, to complete a narrative circle, as the reader certainly expects he will. Tolstoy in fact intended to write a trilogy about Olenin.[22] The story begins with a juxtaposition of silence and speech (replicating that initial moment of no story, then story) and silence is valorized throughout the story. The Cossacks do not let their weapons jingle, for example: "A Cossack always carries his weapons so that they neither jingle nor rattle. Jingling weapons are a terrible disgrace to a Cossack."[23] Olenin, by contrast, is noisy: he "rustled and clattered with his heavy boots and, carrying his gun carelessly, several times caught the twigs of trees that grew across the path."[24] It is no surprise that his epiphany in the stag's lair follows his stopping and sitting quietly. The noise in his mind continues, which is part of the problem. Noisy Olenin represents the story, but the story values silence and its representative heroes.

Just as important as the juxtaposition of silence and sound is the contrast of light and dark. At the novel's beginning the chiaroscuro of the well-lit tavern and the darkness outside is dramatized by the contrast between idle noblemen celebrating one of their own in the tavern and the commoners getting up in the dark and going to work. As the story moves to warmer climes, no chapter integrates Olenin's arrival in the Caucasus with his introduction into the Cossack village; the chapters introducing the Cossacks and then Lukashka directly, the first ones taking place in the south, simply overlap with his arrival. There is a kind of temporal slippage. Thus when the narrator describes Olenin's appearance in the village, three days have passed since Lukashka's shooting of the *abrek*, but a full three months have elapsed since Olenin's arrival in the Caucasus. The story purposely elides Olenin's crossing over into his new life. Life in the Caucasus does not fit Western and Russian plots for it, Tolstoy reminds us. Thus the Moscow part of the story can have a conventional beginning but the Caucasian part cannot. No need to try to make such disparate senses of time mesh together.

In contrast to the novella's understated formal, narrative transitions, actual boundaries and borders of all sorts are met so frequently in *The Cossacks* as to be unmistakably significant. Settlements were usually heavily guarded, with armed men at the gates and others conducting watches. Yet the many lines of demarcation in the novella have thematic significance well beyond what could be reasonably expected, even in a genre where geographic tropes are commonplace. The two sides of the Terek River, the mountains versus the steppe, the hedge surrounding the village itself, fences surrounding the village properties — all are forded, crossed, or traversed in meaningful ways. To be able to cross freely from one side of the boundary to the other is the mark of belonging. Chiasmus is the ruling trope for *The Cossacks*.

Yet this thematic grouping of borders and boundaries still says nothing of the primary "crossing" of the entire novella: from one culture to another. Consider the example of Lukashka, who first triumphs at the river, where he detects the enemy in the unnatural movement against the current of a piece of wood. The river must be crossed, however, by Lukashka himself for him to prove that he is a true Cossack and capable of stealing horses. Lukashka and other Cossack heroes, both real and imaginary, pride themselves on their adoption of the enemy's clothing, language, and other characteristics. "Everything on a real [Chechen] brave is ample, ragged, and neglected, only his weapons are costly. But these ragged clothes and these weapons are belted and worn with a certain air and matched in a certain manner, neither of which can be acquired by everybody and which at once strike the eye of a Cossack or hillsman. Lukashka had this resemblance to a brave."[25] His beautiful horse is both the symbol of transgression—horse thieving—and the vehicle of transgression. Lukashka's story, the challenge before him as the novella begins, is to obtain a horse in order to enter service fully, in order to marry Maryanka. Yet, as we discover in the story, Maryanka creates obstacles for Lukashka: he is kept outside her window, never to be admitted before their marriage.

Among the many examples of the traversal of boundaries in *The Cossacks* is Daddy Eroshka's story of how to obtain "stone-break" grass. He tells Lukashka how to trick a tortoise into getting the grass for him: "Find her nest and fence it round so that she can't get in. Well, she'll come, go round it, and then will go off to find the stone-break grass and will bring some along and destroy the fence. Anyhow next morning come in good time, and where the fence is broken there you'll find the stone-break grass lying. Take it wherever you like. No lock and no bar will be able to stop you."[26] How exactly should the reader interpret this instruction? Since Eroshka is the local font of wisdom, instructing not only Lukashka but Olenin (in his own way) on how to become a Cossack warrior, one feels obliged to take his instructions seriously. The myth is naturalized, in the sense that both Eroshka and Lukashka see the story of the tortoise as a true one. The two Cossack men are united culturally by how they value the ability to break through a fence or lock. Eroshka when he was young had also crossed the river at will and stolen horses.

Olenin is handicapped in two ways: he is unable to cross boundaries easily, as Lukashka can, and he is uninterested in cultural praxes of boundary crossing. True, at times he would like to become a Cossack, but he has no interest, for example, in moving freely between aristocratic Russian society and the Cossack villages of the Caucasus. There is a typical form to life for the officers, as Tolstoy writes: "The life of officers stationed in a Cossack village has long had its own definite form. Just as every cadet or officer when in a fort regularly drinks porter, plays cards, and discusses the rewards given for taking part in expeditions, so in the Cossack villages he regularly drinks *chikhir* with his hosts, treats the girls to sweetmeats and honey, dangles after Cossack women, and falls in love, and occasionally marries there. Olenin always took his own path and had an unconscious objection to the beaten tracks. And here, too, he did not follow the ruts of a Caucasian officer's life."[27] This is not to say that Olenin transformed himself into a Cossack: "He wore Circassian dress but did not wear it well, and anyone would have known him for a Russian and not a Tartar brave. It was the thing — but not the real thing."[28] The narrator always notes his difference: "He thought himself handsome, agile, and like a brave; but he was mistaken. To any experienced Caucasian he was still only a soldier."[29] This simultaneous lack of rootedness and changeability is what puts other people off. They cannot tell exactly who he is, or even who he wants to be; they wonder about his motives and subsequently cease trusting him. Beletski, a typical Russian aristocratic officer, by contrast, appeals to the locals: "The Cossacks, to whom a man who loved wine and women was clearly understandable, got used to him and even liked him better than they did Olenin, who was a puzzle to them."[30] Although Olenin provides Lukashka with a horse and thus the means to move freely across the river and back, he shows no interest in either the horse or the reason Lukashka needs the horse.

To cross, or to be prevented from crossing (diverted) — these are the narrative options thematized by *The Cossacks*. Olenin at first has moderate success on both counts. Having learned from Eroshka the ins and outs of moving through the village, Olenin climbs the hedge. "Instead of passing round through the gate he climbed over the prickly hedge, as everybody else did."[31] Thus begins one of Olenin's most successful days. He has great success hunting, and his subsequent experience in the lair of the deer that day is transformative. As though recognizing his newfound identity of communal belonging, Olenin examines the swarming mosquitoes and says:

> "Here am I, Dmitri Olenin, a being quite distinct from every other being, now lying all alone Heaven knows where . . . above me, flying in among the leaves which to them seem enormous islands, mosquitoes hang in the air and buzz: one, two, three, four, a hundred, a thousand, a million mosquitoes, and all of them buzz something or other and each one of them is separate from all else and is just such a separate Dmitri Olenin as I am myself." . . . And it was clear to him that he was not a Russian nobleman, a member of Moscow society, the friend and relation of so-and-so and so-and-so, but just such a mosquito, or pheasant, or deer, as those that were living all around him. "Just as they, just as Daddy Eroshka, I shall live awhile and die, and as he says truly: 'grass will grow and nothing more.'"[32]

Like other famous moments of self-transcendence in Tolstoy's fiction—Pierre while in French captivity in *War and Peace*, or Levin while speaking to a peasant late in *Anna Karenina*—here Olenin's ideas include much of what Tolstoy thought philosophically sound but lack practical insights that would help him live his life in a reasonable manner.

Ironically, right after his epiphany, he gets lost in the woods. When Olenin tries to cross the boundaries between cultures and marry Maryanka, his limitations are revealed. He does not understand why she turns away from him, but, when she cries out simply, "Cossacks have been killed,"[33] the gulf between them is evident.

Thus a network of imagery of roads, trails, rivers, fences, and hedges limits the narrative direction of *The Cossacks*. Diversion, whether from a path in the woods or from one's resolve to live a life devoted to the happiness of others, is what interests Tolstoy here: crossing boundaries and borders successfully is a metaphor of changing or reshaping one's identity, of having an alibi. Tolstoy agrees with Olenin's optimism early in the story, with his belief in reform and changeability: Olenin "meditated on the use to which he should devote that power of youth which is granted to man only once in a lifetime: that force which gives a man the power of making himself, or even—it seemed to him—of making the universe into anything he wishes."[34] Yet Olenin is unable to create a new identity, or to cross back and forth between identities. (Once Tolstoy grew older he would disagree that youth was the only time to change oneself completely.) The reason he need not return to Moscow at the end of the narrative is that, in terms of his core behavior and identity, Olenin never really left. His failure in the end represents the dramatization of a philosophical problem Tolstoy examined in a narrative form. That problem, which has affinity also with his spiritual queries, is whether identity is singular or plural. Is identity fixed, or can one change, substantively, who one really is? How much does identity depend on others' legitimating our view of ourselves? More to the point for our interest in alibi: which absences may be retained for the purpose of reinventing ourselves and which are mere moral escapism? At the end of *The Cossacks* Olenin is not the Russian nobleman who became a Cossack who became a Russian nobleman—no, he is merely revealed as the somewhat shallow moral drifter he has been all along.

Olenin fails, a philosophy of shifting identity is undermined, and Tolstoy shatters the Romantic ideal of the self-created soul. Yet perhaps this point is not so apparent or uncontestable. Gustafson, arriving at the opposite conclusion, sees a divine love in Olenin's ultimate submission to his feelings of love for Maryanka. He writes: "Olenin proceeds to characterize this seizure of joy in a passage that is one of Tolstoy's most significant fictional articulations of the experience of the Divine. . . . 'Perhaps in her I love nature, the personification of all the beauty of nature, but I am not in control of my will. Some elemental force (*stikhijnaja sila*) loves her through me (*chrez menja*). The whole of God's world (*ves' bozhij mir*), all of nature, presses that love into my soul and says: love. I love her not with my mind, not with my imagination, but with my whole being. Loving her, I sense myself an integral part of the whole of God's joyful world.'"[35] I cannot help viewing the conclusion of the novella, however, as a judgment completely contrary to that ecstatic moment, which in itself may be valid. True, Olenin's attempted personal transformation is enunciated in a religious idiom (or perhaps in the last gasps of Tolstoy's Rousseauism),[36] but that spiritual rebirth is indistinguishable from Olenin's self-deception. Olenin loves an unrealistic ideal in Maryanka, and perhaps that ideal resembles a divine vision of nature and the world; but mostly Olenin's declaration of love to Maryanka serves as an index of his selfishness and narcissism. He fantasizes about his new life *through* his love for her; consequently, she is merely the means to an end, or, rather, the negative space against which he conceives his new identity.

I believe that rather than imagining *The Cossacks* as a precursor to the fundamental spiritual transformation that would take over Tolstoy's life, we can more easily see the secular message of a man who is convinced that some sort of stable family life will provide him with the meaning and sense of personal fulfillment that has heretofore eluded him. This secular Tolstoy will dwell on the theme of family happiness throughout the extended narrative of *War and Peace* in the 1860s. Domestic bliss makes the problems that formerly seemed insurmountable melt away. Late in *War and Peace*, Pierre reflects: "What had worried [Pierre] in old days, what he had always been seeking to solve, the question of the object of life, did not exist for him now. That seeking for an object in life was over for him now; and it was not fortuitously or temporarily that it was over. He felt that there was no such object, and could not be. And it was just the absence of an object that gave him that complete and joyful sense of freedom that at this time made his happiness."[37] As readers we do not know in *The Cossacks* whether Olenin will return home to Moscow and, if he does, whether he can be happy there; in *War and Peace* characters similarly fail in their repeated attempts to search elsewhere for happiness, and they return home only to depart once again. They divert not just from their plans for fame, fortune, and happiness, but also from the diversions they take from their plans—these diversions of a second order form a complex swirling pattern in the already swirling flow of the novel's plot, which otherwise surges directly from 1805 to the end of the Napoleonic wars. This unpredictable movement within the predictable forward progression of history characterizes the plot of the novel, and is not the same thing as Tolstoy's philosophical digressions, which have drawn a great deal of scholarly attention.

WAR AND PEACE: WAR

The historical thesis of *War and Peace* relates not so much to diversion as to the problem of scale and perspective in the construction of historical narratives. The novel examines the philosophical consequences of individual behavior considered from the perspective of the infinitely large scale of historical determinism and the infinitely small scale of human freedom to act. Jeff Love has argued, and proven conclusively, as far as I am concerned, the significance of calculus for Tolstoy's epic novel. He writes: "Calculus acts as a compelling master figure for the basic structural patterns that define the narrative form of the novel, one that moves beyond the limitations of Aristotelian poetics toward defining a new kind of narrative that hovers uneasily between the closure of epic and the openness inherent in the novel."[38] That human freedom to act is often defined as an absence of sufficiently particular detail to ascertain which causes determine behavior. In the composition of history, the greater the detail the more deterministic the explanation inevitably becomes. Causeless events are a myth deriving from a lack of detailed information. From the perspective of the individual actor in history, however, behavior springs from free choice.

The novel mediates these two extremes, speaking by turns from the perspective of deterministic history ("But there are laws controlling these events; laws partly unknown, partly accessible to us") and from the perspective of the individual ("[Pierre realized he] must remain in Moscow, concealing his name, must meet Napoleon, and kill him, so as either to perish or to put an end to the misery of all Europe, which was in Pierre's opinion entirely due to Napoleon alone").[39] Movement toward one or another of these poles dictates much of the content of the novel, to be sure, but that content is not the same as the plot of the novel. Pierre believes himself free to kill Napoleon and alter the course of history, but could we consider him similarly free to marry, say, Sonya? And if not, why not? Readers know the outcome of the Napoleonic wars, so there is no surprise ending to be expected in that context; but in the more romantic "peace" side of the novel there are also the conventions of genre to be considered.

The historical thesis of the novel has little to do with narrative diversion in a strict sense, but the more general progress of the novel follows a familiar pattern. In the minds of many readers, *War and Peace* is war *versus* peace. Do the passages of war take our attention away from the romantic narratives of the Rostovs and Bolkonskys? Or do the diversions into romance merely keep the reader happily distracted while Tolstoy delivers more important pronouncements about history and philosophy than can be delivered in an ordinary novel? Both Tolstoy's contemporary readers and current readers often find the novel deeply split between entertainment and philosophical instruction. Those who love the entertaining fiction of the novel find its historical digressions out of place.

In cinema, the dramatic juxtaposition of simultaneous events is known as cross-cutting, and one finds similar techniques used in (especially modernist) literature. For Tolstoy, the technique allows one to create a kind of narrative simile. Perhaps the most dramatic instances of this narrative simile in *War and Peace* transpire early in the novel. The Rostovs are celebrating Natasha's name day with a party, but Tolstoy undermines the happy dancing by juxtaposing it with the final hours of the old Count Bezukhov. One can imagine the camera matching the action of the tired footmen and cooks with the weary movements of those attending the dying man: "While in the Rostovs' hall they were dancing the sixth anglaise, while the weary orchestra played the wrong notes, and the tired footmen and cooks were getting the supper, Count Bezukhov had just had his sixth stroke. The doctors declared that there was no hope for recovery; the sick man received absolution and the sacrament while unconscious."[40] Much of *War and Peace* is devoted to dancing and death, and this early metanarrative paragraph signals Tolstoy's intention of revealing throughout the novel how we divert our attention from the horror of war (and in the Rostovs' case, the horror of financial ruin) by engaging in pleasant social activities that numb the mind to mortal thoughts. This scene is not entirely ponderous, however, as the impoverished Prince Rostov dances an invigorating Daniel Cooper, while the immensely wealthy Count Bezukhov slips from consciousness. If one could only have enormous wealth, be vivacious and yet marked by a true experience of death, and be wiser for it—well, this is Natasha by the end of *War and Peace*. She marries the enormously wealthy Pierre, betrays faintest glimmers, yet only glimmers, of her former love of life, and yet she has witnessed the devastation of death (Andrei's, her father's, and Petya's).

That early passage juxtaposing the Rostovs' party to Bezukhov's death is, in the simplest sense, just a transition from one storyline to another. Yet in terms of its metanarrative significance, it compels readers to consider it in a much broader context. Does death intrude, get in the way, divert one from a celebration of life? Or do social conventions of consumption, talk, and dance distract one from the greater truth of life, that one's mortality is everything? I think most readers would agree that this passage is not so much a transition as a wedge driven into the novel itself. Do we have to choose between one path and the other? Does the novel itself make this choice? Natasha's name-day party, in other words, leads readers to ask how the novel balances themes of life and death. One answer is that life lived provides a narrative thread by which readers pass from one extreme to the other. Much of Petya Rostov's life, for example, is contained in *War and Peace*, including his death. He helps us traverse the two extremes.

The novel also provides another more obvious model of diverting metanarrative thematics: history. History is a presence in *War and Peace* that, like God and the author, is everywhere felt and nowhere seen, except from the most lofty narratorial heights. It is a continually transpiring event in which one cannot simply and directly participate, which is why Tolstoy frequently shows the attendant phenomena of history, rather than history itself. When one looks at history directly, one sees extraneous incidents, Tolstoy argues, even amid the dead and wounded on the battlefield:

> But quite extraneous incidents that had nothing to do with the battle were what deserved the most notice; as though the attention of these morally overstrained men found a rest in the commonplace incidents of everyday life. A battery of artillery passed in front of their line. In one of the ammunition carriages a horse had put its legs through the traces. . . . Another time the attention of all was attracted by a little brown dog, with its tail in the air, who had come no one knew from where, and was running about fussily in front of the ranks. . . . But distractions of this kind did not last more than a minute, and the men had been eight hours without food or occupation, with the terror of death never relaxing for an instant, and their pale and haggard faces grew paler and more haggard.[41]

People can grow accustomed to anything, even battle, and be bored by it. Tolstoy also exhorts the values of "the commonplace incidents of everyday life."[42] This passage in *War and Peace* does not argue for the inclusion of commonplace incidents because they make up history. They react to the forces of history, but Tolstoy does not believe that the dog that squeals at bombs or the horse that trips in the traces actually composes history. These are fleeting diversions, distractions. Yet such diversions may represent the whole of the text itself. War dehumanizes the soldiers, and a faint distraction saves them, if only for a moment, from the terror that places them among the beasts of the world. War kills them, slowly or quickly, and the squealing dog averts their attention from their own mortality. In remarkably different context, then, one finds much the same metanarrative dynamics that operated in the scene at the Rostovs' name-day party for Natasha.

By the end of the novel, Tolstoy expresses one of his main theories, the idea that history progresses at a line tangential to what is generally perceived. A soldier's attention is diverted by dogs and horses, but what can one say about an entire army? Armies shape history, as even Tolstoy would concede. As the narrative perspective shifts to this collective group of armed heroes, Tolstoy concentrates on the "oblique movement" of the retreating Russian army as a metaphor of historical movement. "The famous oblique movement consisted simply in this. The Russian troops, which had been retreating directly back from the French, as soon as the French attack ceased, turned off from that direction, and seeing they were not pursued, moved naturally in the direction where they were drawn by the abundance of supplies."[43] Tolstoy refuses to accord to the commanders any sort of individual agency or control in the movement of the army. One is suspicious of Tolstoy's use of *naturally* in this context. He is eager to contradict the theory that a commander directs the army, but he is less willing to describe explicitly how the army moves. Tolstoy believes historical events are more determined the greater one's distance is from them, and he best describes the actual intervention of random uncontrollability in history in a specific context. These specific contexts are where the most literary freedom is to be found. Soldiers laugh at foolish animals, for example, and get distracted.

Given the metanarrative aspect of Tolstoy's discussion of history in *War and Peace*, one should not be surprised to discover the same diverting or distracting, oblique gestures at each remove of the novel's generalizing consideration of narrative and history. Beyond individual soldiers, and the Russian army, there is human being as such. A field stretching from the axis of what one can really know of causality in human nature to the axis of the unknowable activity of human will—this, too, is history: "For history there exist lines of movement of human wills, one extremity of which vanishes in the unknowable, and at the other extremity of which in space, in time, and in dependence on cause, there moves men's consciousness of free will in the present. The more this field of movement is analysed before our eyes, the clearer are the laws of its movement. To discover and define those laws is the problem of history."[44] Tolstoy's narrative calculus attempts to discover the unknown space of human will through time.[45] What makes this different from some ordinary narration is that "field of movement," which I understand to be his narrative gesture toward the unknown.

Tolstoy contemplates, in this last instance, the boundary between what can be known and what remains unknown in history. These are metanarrative passages, alluding not just to history but also to *Tolstoy's* history, *War and Peace*. *War and Peace* itself contemplates the boundary between historical and fictional characters. Tolstoy's critics, then and now, have paid close attention to which persons, families, and events the author adapted versus those he invented. Tolstoy saw the historical novel as a means to pursue his examination of the uneasy relationship between fiction and reality, evident from the earliest days of his authorship. In *War and Peace*, Tolstoy sees history already at one remove from reality, and yet clearly not so far removed as fiction. Both are shaped narratives that nevertheless struggle against a deterministic unfolding of events. Fictional characters in *War and Peace* sometimes stumble when they meet historical figures, yet the rough narrative ground created by their dilemmas supports the way the larger story is told.

Take, for example, Nikolai Rostov's encounter with the tsar. Nikolai has been dreaming of the moment when he might meet his hero; and yet when he has the opportunity, the obligation even, to approach the tsar to obtain orders from him, Nikolai declines to do so. Instead, his wordless contemplation of the tsar composes a visual tableau of untouchable grief, as the tsar privately acknowledges the Russian troops are defeated on the battlefield. There is an easy explanation for this tactic, skeptics might say, since Tolstoy must have been tempted to put words in the mouth of an historical figure at such a decisive moment in the history of the war with the French. The historical record has, after all, substantial account of the tsar's words after Austerlitz; and, one notes, even though Tolstoy has only scorn for the power of "great men" to affect history, he would scarcely want to distort history substantially by inventing too much language for the tsar. (Tolstoy makes a point of emphasizing in "A Few Words about *War and Peace*" the constraints of using historical figures and his fidelity to the historical record.) Consequently, Nikolai cannot speak to the tsar for both personal and metafictional reasons. The boundary between fiction and reality is not easily crossed in this instance, not least because the censor would never have allowed Tolstoy to speak for the tsar.

Tolstoy is so historically iconoclastic in *War and Peace*, however, one would not want to make too much of his fear of putting words in the tsar's mouth. What is more, the paragraph that describes Nikolai's feelings at this moment points beyond whatever reticence Tolstoy might have had: "But, as a youth in love trembles and turns faint and dares not utter what he has spent nights in dreaming of, and looks about in terror, seeking aid or a chance of delay or flight, when the moment he has longed for comes and he stands alone at her side, so Rostov, now when he was attaining what he had longed for beyond everything in the world, did not know how to approach the Emperor, and thousands of reasons why it was unsuitable, unseemly, and impossible came into his mind."[46] Patriotic fervor, like religious fervor, can paralyze as well as provoke. Tolstoy points to the unbearable height of emotion Nikolai endures.

Nevertheless, this display of the Romantic idiom and Tolstoy's novelistic contemplation of the boundary between fiction and reality coincide in a significantly productive way. When the barriers that separate Nikolai and the tsar are no longer present, he jumps to create new, imaginary ones. In other words, finding himself in the presence of the sovereign, Nikolai narrates reasons to be elsewhere; he nervously creates a narrative alibi. This burst of creativity is uncharacteristic: Natasha and Petya have more innate artistic potential, as witnessed by Petya's unconscious creation of orchestrated harmony: "Petya was as musical by nature as Natasha, and far more so than Nikolay."[47] Note also how the tsar is depicted—dejected, emasculated, physically incapable of crossing a ditch on his own. Rostov creates new barriers, not only because the distance separating him from the tsar has collapsed, but also because the height separating him from the tsar has collapsed. The tsar is literally on his level.

Tolstoy frequently laments the disruptive ratiocination that intercedes between opportunity and action, and he champions unconscious, near vegetative, immersion in the moment, as in the famous hay-mowing scene from *Anna Karenina*. Yet Tolstoy is unfair to himself and his most creative characters, nearly all of whom make altogether too much "of the moment." They think too much, suspect too much, and plot too much—in other words, they create the kind of multiple layers of nuanced meanings that we associate with the finest art. Tolstoy's autobiographical heroes share a tendency to amplify the slightest quiver of doubt into a symphony of suspicions (even Levin becomes intolerably jealous when a visitor flirts harmlessly with Kitty). In this scene with the tsar, Nikolai fails to act immediately, and Captain Van Toll approaches the tsar directly and comforts him. There is no story in this encounter between Van Toll and the tsar, however, but there is one in Nikolai's failure.

Tolstoy's analogous failure to cross successfully the boundary between fiction and historical reality in this scene with Nikolai and the tsar also makes a good story. Tolstoy adapts the aesthetics of the romantic obstacle—frustrated desire leading to heightened desire—to the story of Nikolai's missed opportunity with the tsar. The tsar's apparent weeping, inferred but not witnessed, creates the image of a leader both untouchable and yet "one of the people." Rostov sees Van Toll attend to the tsar successfully, and thinks, "And it might have been I in his place?";[48] yet this phrase also describes the position of Tolstoy's contemporary reader, born a generation too late. We might have been in their place, Tolstoy's readers undoubtedly react, while reading through *War and Peace*.

Real, historical personages do not succumb as easily to such acts of readerly identification. The main point to remember is that just as obstacles heighten the intensity of desire in romance, so too do obstacles between fiction and reality reinforce our expectation that they could or should meet.

Nothing signals the importance of this sequence between Nikolai and Tsar Alexander so much as the repetition of the same theme no more than a half-dozen pages later, when Andrei finally meets his hero Napoleon. Many readers pay close attention to the moment when Andrei notices the lofty sky above Napoleon and compares it to his hero's relative diminution. But a few paragraphs later Andrei comes face to face with his hero—there can be no question of avoiding meeting, as was the case between Rostov and the tsar. Nevertheless, even in response to a direct question from Napoleon, Andrei maintains his proud silence. But this is probably merely a matter of Andrei's pride—his recognition of the insignificance of his previous hero worship.

Here, on the contrary, as in the scene between the tsar and Nikolai, matters of history and fiction clash. Napoleon asks after two historical figures, and they answer in such perfectly quotable form that, frankly, it is hard to imagine the dialogue does not come directly from one of the history books that Tolstoy both uses and endeavors to undermine. That is to say, their answers to Napoleon's question are determined, even overdetermined, by Tolstoy. Readers can hardly take them at the same face value attached to other dialogue and action in the novel. In response to Napoleon's compliment, for example, Prince Repnin, commander of a squadron in the tsar's horse guards, replies: "The praise of a great general is a soldier's best reward."[49] As Napoleon remarks upon Lieutenant Suhtelen's youth, the latter answers: "Youth is no hindrance to valour." Napoleon counters: "A fine answer."[50] It is a fine answer, but the fact that clever repartee is valued here above so much else points to how similar this scene is to a drawing-room conversation. The rhetoric of both is conventional, highly aestheticized.

Here with Napoleon, Repnin takes the place of Van Toll in Nikolai's encounter with Tsar Alexander. Before his encounter with death, Andrei would have given his life for praise from Napoleon such as Repnin receives. Now, Andrei sees Napoleon: "Gazing into Napoleon's eyes, Prince Andrei mused on the nothingness of greatness, on the nothingness of life, of which no one could comprehend the significance, and on the nothingness—still more—of death, the meaning of which could be understood and explained by none of the living."[51] Instead of trading his life for Napoleon's, Andrei sees Napoleon is insignificant when compared with death. Unfortunately, Andrei overapplies his profound lesson on the role of death as a negative space giving shape to what is truly important in life—until happiness itself is degraded into the mere avoidance of pain. That is how he explains his new beliefs to Pierre when they meet later at Andrei's estate. They pause to speak of their most cherished ideas about life and death while crossing the emblematic boundary of a local river. Rather than crossing the Styx in his death, however, Andrei has clearly awoken to a new life, "something that had long been slumbering, something better that had been in him, suddenly awoke with a joyful, youthful feeling in his soul. . . . Pierre's visit was for Prince Andrei an epoch, from which there began, though outwardly unchanged, a new life in his inner world."[52] We know, as readers, that Andrei's joyful, youthful feeling will take the shape, in a few short chapters, of a young woman, Natasha.

Natasha, like Levin, prefigures Tolstoy's use of narrative diversion in order to promulgate an alibi of authenticity. No longer does Tolstoy seek to legitimate myth so much as narrate a childhood, and a cultural history, that is already authentic. It need only be witnessed, as the family spectators witness Natasha's dance. She is a boundary figure, like Anna, because she has little respect for boundaries. Even though her transgressive nature is domesticated in the end of *War and Peace*, she is a transitional figure for Tolstoy.

Part III

———————◆·◆·◆———————

AUTHENTIC LIVES

The category of authenticity probably seems so familiar to readers of Tolstoy that they scarcely notice how important it is or how long Tolstoy labored as a writer before he was able to compose the authentic characters we now celebrate. As a younger author, Tolstoy was unable to describe anything equal to Natasha's natural vivacity, Levin's aristocratic honesty, or Hadji Murad's bravery. There were precursors, of course, and Tolstoy had flashes of authorial brilliance from his earliest literary experiments. But he lacked confidence in how right he was about the world and in his ability to describe it rightly in fiction. As a mature author, by contrast, Tolstoy stated such things as: "*War and Peace* is not a novel," and, "If I wanted to say in words all that I had in mind to express by my novel [*Anna Karenina*], I should have to write the same novel which I wrote all over again." There is bluster here, but there is also Tolstoy's belief in his own ultimate aristocratic rectitude and, later, his belief in the immutable moral truths of Christianity. Confidence never made anyone a literary genius, but it did help Tolstoy redefine his aesthetics. With the convention of authenticity, Tolstoy imagines himself as an author who is able to say with Levin that he need not "cringe before anyone."

5

FAMILY HISTORIES

"I have never really considered what I am. I am Constantine Levin, that's all."

—*Anna Karenina*

AUTHENTIC ALIBIS

Tolstoy intended Natasha Rostova to be an authentic character. She was unique for Tolstoy, and represents a turning point. "Natasha, in her freshness and vitality, is absolutely unprecedented in previous writings," as Kathryn Feuer puts it, "which makes it all the more astonishing that Tolstoy seems to have created her so effortlessly."[1] Whereas Nikolai and Andrei dramatize the metafictional debate about boundaries between fiction and reality, the novel and history, Natasha lives along the boundary of art and life. Readers might at first assume that no such boundary can be distinguished in Natasha's life, since she is, of all characters, without artifice and pretension. She is introduced liminally: Natasha "was just at that charming age when a girl is no longer a child, though the child is not yet a young woman."[2] With Nikolai and Andrei, fictional characters crossed paths with historical figures; the division between them was inherent in the narrative process. Natasha, by contrast, is immersed wholly in the fictional part of *War and Peace*.

For Natasha the real and artificial are one, which is partly why she takes her childhood games so seriously: "Natasha did not like the visitor's tone of condescension to childish things."[3] Her earnest nature makes her genuine, but it leaves her susceptible to the feigned genuineness of others (she cannot recognize the falsity of others because she is so true herself). Nikolai, by contrast, immediately recognizes the braggart in others, because he is so ashamed of that characteristic in himself. As so often in Tolstoy, the world is measured by the yardstick of oneself. In *War and Peace* Tolstoy ultimately abandons his efforts to valorize unmediated presence, which was a strategy of legitimating the narrative alibi, of collapsing the real and the artificial. Natasha is our guide to the failure of that past method. She must learn to recognize the difference between the authentic and inauthentic, just as we readers must do, as Tolstoy implies in scenes such as Natasha's visit to the opera.

What is more, like many of Tolstoy's favorite characters, Natasha is loved by almost every other character in the novel (except, at first, Marya), perhaps in part because she has no respect for the artificial boundaries that other people set. She first appears as a harmless and exuberant transgressor. She spills giggling into the room where Anna Mihailovna is visiting, as though against her will: "She had evidently bounded so far by mistake, unable to stop in her flight."[4] Scarcely concealing her complete lack of embarrassment, Natasha evokes a force of nature, equally at home almost everywhere (dancing the quadrille in the ballroom, for example, or dancing a traditional dance at "Uncle's"). She is thus frequently shown pushing against limits and thresholds of all sorts, as with her initial entry into the novel, or when Andrei overhears her at the window exclaiming that the night is so beautiful she wants to fly away. In her naive iconoclasm, Natasha illuminates the conventions of social forms.

When she attends the opera later in the novel, her perception of the performance onstage is presented as though in a raw form (it is a painstakingly constructed simplicity, however). Since the time of the Russian Formalists, this scene has been referred to as a defining example of Tolstoy's use of the literary device they termed "estrangement" (*ostranenie*).[5] That is to say, Natasha's inexperienced view of the opera (people hopping around inelegantly and screeching) suggests the analogy that art is estrangement, a presentation of common and recognizable experiences in an unfamiliar or strange way, so as to render them more perceptible. Natasha thereby distances herself from the strange, perhaps inauthentic, art taking place onstage, but she is drawn to a more seductive, seemingly natural performance taking place in the box next to her at the opera house. She recognizes the flawed art of the opera, but misses the successful art perpetrated by Prince Vassily's children. Helene Bezukhova and her brother Anatole take turns reversing the *ostranenie*, making their strange behavior and seductive appearances seem totally natural to Natasha, often by collapsing the space that separates the performance (by Helene and Anatole) from the viewer (Natasha). As they collapse the space between performance and reception, they resemble Tolstoy in his early fiction. One suspects, in fact, that Tolstoy is drawn to their sinister aesthetic efficiency. Crucially, both kinds of space—that which widens, as Natasha watches the opera, and that which collapses, as she is seduced by Helene and Anatole—reinforce the boundary between art and life that Natasha has heretofore traversed so effortlessly.

This sequence of experiences and conversations is of the utmost importance not just to the overall aesthetics of the novel but also to Natasha's development as a character. As she herself claims, her whole existence now—the visit to Moscow, the meeting with Marya and the Old Prince, and especially the opera—all of it is a diversion from her true life. She is merely biding her time; she is following a tangent. She should, by rights, already be married to Andrei. The old Prince Bolkonsky knows, of course, that Natasha is unlikely to stay true to Andrei, no matter how much she wants to, because of her immaturity and her abundance of unfocused energy. He has managed his life to such an extent that it is unlikely that anything will ever divert him from his schedule; but Natasha lives in a world where desire curves space and warps time, not in the Old Prince's rational and rectilinear Newtonian world. One can fall off the map of that world, as Andrei learns when his father says he would refuse to know him were Andrei to act dishonorably on the battlefield.

The modulation of space is essential to the scene at the opera house—especially since we are not dealing with Tolstoy's usual (for *War and Peace*) discourse on perspective and historical narrative. Here the modulation of space, collapsing and expanding, itself models an artistic process that both intrigues and repels its audience. Little seems to be separating Helene and Natasha, both physically and literally, for example, as Natasha joins Helene in her box. The narrator notes again and again Helene's "nakedness," as though her putting on more clothing might interfere with the "simplicity and naturalness" of her intimate disposition toward others.[6] Anatole, similarly, appears out of nowhere, transported from the floor of the opera house to his sister's box. With both brother and sister, the key is a kind of sensual disintermediation (which echoes Tolstoy's early aesthetics of realism and acts as a precursor to later theories of the aesthetics of "infection"). Recall how Pierre falls victim to Helene's charms: "She was terribly close to him. She already had power over him, and between them there was no longer any barrier except the barrier of his own will."[7] And we know Pierre's will won't save him.

Is Natasha seduced by Anatole, or is she infected by a kind of fever? From the very start, she repeatedly notes the disappearance of barriers between herself and Anatole, whose eyes are like hands: "When she was not looking at him she felt that he was looking at her shoulders, and she could not help trying to catch his eyes that he might rather look in her face. But as she looked into his eyes she felt with horror that, between him and her, there was not that barrier of modest reserve she had always been conscious of between herself and other men. In five minutes she felt—she did not know how—that she had become fearfully close to this man. When she turned away, she felt afraid he might take her from behind by her bare arm and kiss her on the neck. . . . She glanced straight into his eyes, and his nearness and confidence, and the simple-hearted warmth of his smile vanquished her. She smiled exactly as he did, looking straight into his eyes. And again, she felt with horror that no barrier lay between him and her."[8]

Whereas in cases of true love, Tolstoy typically demonstrates how a lack of barriers emulates near supernatural mutual verbal comprehension, here the narrator points out the contrary: "Natasha did not understand what he was saying, nor did he himself; but she felt that in his uncomprehended words there was some improper intention."[9] Though she understates the matter, Natasha is on the right track. Later she receives a love letter from Anatole and understands nothing while reading it, save that it is from Anatole. Unmediated illicit love apparently has no communicative advantage. Not that the reader needs more hints to understand that.

There is a reverse rationalization in this directness, which Natasha makes in her romance with Anatole and which Tolstoy equates with falsity in historical discourse. Natasha, for example, works backward, telling herself that if she feels so close to Anatole (without barriers), then certainly she is in love with him. (Having fallen in love with Andrei, she looks back and sees the hand of fate.) Pierre, to give another example, challenges Dolokhov, and this retrospectively affirms his wife's guilt: "At the very instant he did this and uttered those words, Pierre felt that the question of his wife's guilt which had been tormenting him the whole day was finally and indubitably answered in the affirmative. He hated her and was forever sundered from her."[10] Similarly, Tolstoy suggests elsewhere, the soldier reconstructs from his postbattle vitality that he must have been a brave warrior. Natasha reasons: "But she loved [not just Andrei but] Anatole too, of that there was no doubt. 'Else how could all that have happened?' she thought."[11] What Natasha never realizes, though all those around her do, is that her direct, unmediated, barrierless love for Anatole needs some analogue for validation—either in their communication, in his romantic behavior toward her (deceit, misdirection, lies), or even in his behavior toward others. Sonya thus tries to convince Natasha that if Anatole really loved her he would approach the matter directly. But that analogue is missing. We recall how the collapsed present-tense narration of Tolstoy's "Sevastopol in December" relied on the conventions of travel literature and thereby matched the illusion of direct address to a more recognizable form. On another level, as part of a seduction narrative, Anatole's behavior toward Natasha is as apparent to readers as it is to Sonya.

At the opera, an alienating art allows Natasha to identify, dangerously, with Helene and Anatole. Natasha lets her guard down, and the disappearance of

barriers between her and Helene and Anatole is a metaphor for her vulnerabil-
ity. It is striking how far Tolstoy has come from championing unmediated presence in his realism: the immediate impression of the opera suggests a deformed
art, and the immediate effect of the Kuragins is dangerous seduction. It is not
that Tolstoy no longer values unmediated experience. On the contrary, he continues to develop the notion that consciousness itself is a kind of poison. Andrei
says to Pierre of his plans for educating the peasantry: "You want to raise him . . .
from his animal condition and awaken in him spiritual needs, while it seems to
me that animal happiness is the only happiness possible, and that is just what
you want to deprive him of. I envy him, but you want to make him what I am,
without giving him the means. . . . You can't help thinking. I go to bed after two
in the morning, thoughts come and I can't sleep but toss about till dawn,
because I think and can't help thinking."[12] The scene of Levin losing all self-
consciousness while mowing grass with the peasants in *Anna Karenina* is an
even more famous example.

　　The crucial difference between these examples of Andrei and Levin, on the
one side, and Natasha at the opera, on the other, is that only the latter involves
an experience of art. Tolstoy continues this line of criticism of dangerous presentness in art in *Anna Karenina*, where the real-seeming presence of Anna in
her painting by Mikhaylov is a potentially dangerous seduction for Levin. In the
case of Mikhaylov's portrait, the art itself is blameless of any seduction, if nonetheless a powerful vehicle for it. Staging is all-important. By greeting visitors in
such a seemingly candid image, Anna's portrait creates a false intimacy, which
Anna takes advantage of when she herself arrives to greet her guests. The difference between beneficial and harmful kinds of identification with art interests
the older Tolstoy, especially in *What Is Art?* but elsewhere too. In *What Is Art?*
the difference will be the Christian versus non-Christian content of the
message; here the difference is still mostly revealed by different kinds of love.

　　Natasha mistakes an alienating experience for an experience of inclusion.
Attending the opera should serve as entry for her into the warm embrace of
society. True enough, she does feel all eyes upon her, as though she is being
seized by the larger group: "The sensation that she had not experienced in a
long while—that hundreds of eyes were looking at her bare arms and neck—
suddenly came upon her both pleasantly and unpleasantly, calling up a whole
swarm of memories, desires, and emotions connected with that sensation."[13]
She feels a part of something larger than herself, but when she seeks confirmation of her emotions in others, that key analogue, she is surprised and put off:
"She looked about her at the faces of the spectators, seeking in them signs of the
same irony and bewilderment that she was feeling herself. But all the faces were

watching what was passing on the stage, and expressed nothing but an affected —
so Natasha thought — rapture."[14] This feeling of alienation, that she does not in
fact belong among the others, consequently opens the way for Anatole's seduction of her. She can recognize the affectation of unadulterated pleasure in the
crowd, in other words, but she cannot recognize the affectation of no affect
whatsoever, the "simplicity and naturalness" that Helene and Anatole share.

Not every diverting experience or narrative diversion in *War and Peace* is so
damaging. Readers have long recognized that part 7, which takes place at the
Rostov estate, and includes the wolf hunt, dining, and dancing at Uncle's, and
the holiday celebrations, forms a moral and aesthetic gravitational pole in the
novel. Part 7 constructs nearly a counternarrative to the plot of the rest of the
novel, not just "elsewhere" but almost another story to go with it, literally a narrative alibi. We find here an idealized representation of hearth and home, to be
sure, Tolstoy's last dramatic effort to legitimate his most cherished notions of
family. Many of the later stories seem to demonstrate his inability to live those
myths, that false life, as he would call it. Much of Levin's story in *Anna Karenina*
depicts his failure to create an ideal family life, as well as his efforts to find
something in its place that will suffice.

LEVIN AND THE RECOVERY OF THE AUTHENTIC

Tolstoy was not the first to discover that narratives themselves can be used
as models to reveal a more authentic self, a self that does not need to be legitimated so much as recovered from the negative space of what is already said
and done, from the unrepeatable events of one's life. Tolstoy was often drawn
to kinds of negativity, as though, like Nikolai in *Boyhood*, he were always looking over his shoulder to see if the world was still there.[15] His exploration of how
narratives may discover the truth as well as divert us from it led him further into
the realm of apophatic thought, traditionally defined as obtaining knowledge
(of God) by negation. In *War and Peace*, Tolstoy's narrative diversions are like
flanking maneuvers of the partisans, and similar geographical metaphors are
written large across the novel. In *Anna Karenina*, various diversions and narrative quests for a true self treat not geography but surface and depth, as well
as positive and negative spaces, as the governing metaphors for a recovery of
authenticity.

Early in *Anna Karenina*, Levin and Stiva walk back to Levin's country home
after hunting snipe at dusk. Levin has just learned from Stiva that Kitty did not
marry Vronsky, after all, and that she subsequently fell seriously ill. Though
frightened by the news that Kitty is unwell, Levin is elated that she remains

unmarried. He asks what caused Kitty's illness, and hearing Stiva mention Vronsky's name, immediately interrupts him: "I have no right to know such family details, and frankly I am not interested in them either."[16] The conversation ends. Stiva notices that Levin's face has become as gloomy as it was previously bright, and the remainder of the chapter is devoted to the description of Stiva's sale of his wife's forest to a local dealer. The entire episode asks us to consider the "right to know" in the novel. It is a small instance of the larger problem of how to read Tolstoy's narrative alibis. To what extent are we expected to recover the missing or absent information that shapes the plot?

In spite of his protests, Levin is clearly interested in "such family details," so why does the plot diverge from the main storyline at precisely this moment? The details of Stiva's sale of the forest advance neither Levin's plot nor Anna's. Is it that the diversion serves to heighten the suspense of the reader who, like Levin, is eager to know what happened between Kitty and Vronsky? No, readers already know what happened; and, in fact, having eavesdropped on Kitty's thoughts, the reader knows more about what happened to her than does her family, who must guess at the real reason of her illness. By raising a barrier to what can be said, Levin forces the story into a detour, which the narrator and we follow. The fact that we already know what happens makes the episode that much more metafictional. The chapter about the sale of the forest becomes a kind of parable in which Levin cannot see the forest for the trees—in this case, Dolly's trees. Our readerly suspense derives not from whether we will learn what happened to Kitty but from whether Levin will. The plot actually moves according to his obfuscating psychology, splitting the novel into two. One part follows the sale of the forest; the other unsaid part of the novel follows the real drama of Levin's unrequited love and desire to learn more of Kitty's fate.

By dwelling on the unsaid, Tolstoy illuminates how certain kinds of absence may shape a narrative. As we have seen, Tolstoy often explored the ontological status of fiction. One method Tolstoy continued to use throughout his career in order to create the illusion of fiction writing itself was to turn the agency of the narrative, though not the narrative voice itself, over to one of the characters.[17] In this instance from *Anna Karenina*, Levin takes virtual control of the narrative. He has a gravitational pull on the direction of the story. The conversation surrounding the sale of the forest demonstrates how this happens. Levin thinks that Stiva's sale of Dolly's forest is theft, since the dealer Ryabinin will pay far too little for it. Tolstoy implies that the sale is theft for another reason: Stiva cares little for true value of the land and thus "steals" it from Dolly through his inattention and spendthrift ways. Levin asks him, "Have you counted the trees? [Счел ли ты деревья?]," and Stiva counters: "'How can one count the trees?'

said Oblonsky, still anxious to dispel his friend's ill-humour. "'Count grains of sand, and planets' rays, E'en though a lofty mind were able . . .'" [—Как счесть деревья? —смеясь сказал Степан Аркадьич, все желая вывести приятеля из его дурного расположения духа. —Сочесть пески, лучи планет хотя и мог бы ум высокий . . .]."[18] A bit of poetry comes to Stiva's defense. This important exchange between Levin and Stiva says much about the logic that guides them personally, and yet even more about the kind of narrative strategy Tolstoy deploys in important passages such as this one.

Stiva quotes here the well-known eighteenth-century poem "God," by Gavril Derzhavin, and specifically the lines that ponder human knowledge of God (quoted in Russian and in my literal translation):

> Измерить океан глубокий,
> Сочесть пески, лучи планет
> Хотя и мог бы ум высокий, —
> Тебе числа и меры нет!

> To measure the deep ocean,
> To count grains of sand, the rays of the planets
> Although a great mind might be able, —
> You have no number or measure!

One might think at first that this is a relatively meaningless quotation by Stiva—who frequently quotes poetry to communicate pithy sentiment. Yet to know God by negation, by what God is not, is to assume a well known, apophatic approach to knowledge, the *via negativa* of Dionysius the Areopagite. In effect, Levin and Stiva represent in this exchange two different ways of knowing through negation.[19] Levin wants to know what happened between Kitty and Vronsky, but his sense of propriety, deriving as much from fear as from anything, dictates that he may not ask about it. Stiva ignorantly prices the land, but it is also true that no one besides Ryabinin will deal with him. (All the dealers collude with one another.) As the conversation progresses, the two close friends proceed to expose mercilessly one another's faulty logic; which is to say, if one follows the spirit of their exchange, both reveal that the absence the other assumes exists is actually a kind of willfully ignored presence. Each realizes, as good friends often do, that the other knows something but refuses to acknowledge it.

Levin understands that Stiva does not want to do the work of finding out how much the forest is worth; he simply wants to make sufficient effort to justify the purchase. When Stiva asks, rhetorically, why then, if the forest is so valuable, would no one else deal with him? Levin points out his friend's naiveté: "Because he and the other dealers are in league, and he has bought them off."[20] What was once the absence of available dealers now becomes the presence of several. Conspiracy thinkers like Levin (and occasionally Tolstoy himself), return again and again to apophaticism, because what is not there simply serves as additional proof of what has been hidden or of what cannot be known directly. Amusingly enough, Stiva's response, an ad hominem attack, is effective in this instance. "Oh, come!" Stiva interjects. "You are down in the dumps today."[21] Stiva identifies correctly that Levin is irritated not just by the missing money (the money Ryabinin will swindle from Stiva) but also by his lack of knowledge of Kitty. Like Tolstoy's narrative in this passage, Levin is motivated by what cannot be said.

The narrative does not depict Levin's psychology so much as it is shaped by his psychology. As I described in part I, Tolstoy often uses psychology for its narrative resources, sometimes dispensing with the psychological value altogether, or posing those psychological revelations as masks of more substantive self-delusion. The play of absence and presence we witness in this scene is precipitated by Levin's sense of decorum and propelled by the narrative digression of the entire chapter; it is a philosophical accompaniment to Ryabinin's visit. In *War and Peace*, Natasha worried that her life had been led astray from its right path. Here Levin worries that his visible life is an illusion, that the invisible life is the truer one. The examples from both *War and Peace* and *Anna Karenina* are diversions, but they take different rhetorical shapes.

When Ryabinin enters Levin's study, for example, he "looked round by force of habit as though to find the icon, but after finding it he did not cross himself."[22] To cross himself would signify something Ryabinin prefers to conceal from the two aristocrats, whereas an absent icon would signify something to him about them. Or consider another, plainer example. While arguing with Ryabinin about the price of grain, Levin simply retorts: "Why should I give you something for nothing [literally, 'Why should I make a gift to you out of what is mine']?"[23] Ryabinin serves as a symbol of elision—whether of Stiva's due diligence on behalf of his wife and family, or, in effect, of the knowledge of Kitty that Levin desperately wants to hear.

The crescendo of the visit follows a final reversal—a final revelation of presence—when Levin himself offers to buy the forest for a reasonable price, rather than allow Ryabinin to pay too little. Just as Levin exposed Stiva's negligence (and Stiva exposed Levin's foul mood), so now does Levin expose Ryabinin's corruption. This revelation releases the narrative and personal tension that has been building. Stiva and Ryabinin conclude their deal. And by simultaneously bringing decorum's necessary digression to a close, Levin permits the narrative to return in the subsequent chapter (part II, chapter 17) to the most important questions that plague him.

Here there is a brief repetition of the main motif and, finally, resolution. When Stiva asks again in disbelief whether Levin's wants him to count every tree before he will be satisfied, Levin responds: "Certainly count them! You have not counted them but Ryabinin has! Ryabinin's children will have the means to live and get an education, while yours may not have!" Stiva simply replies that "there is something mean in all this counting" and changes the subject.[24] But the main task has already been accomplished. Levin associates Stiva's financial lapse with his failure as a father and, ultimately, in Levin's opinion, as an aristocrat. "Try as Levin would to control himself, he remained morose and silent. There was one question he wanted to put to Oblonsky, but could not bring himself to ask, nor could he find the form to put it in or the moment to ask it."[25] There is nothing in the immediate context or putative plot to motivate Levin's question—one must simply know that he has been dying to ask it all along. Finally, with no segue, Levin asks what has become of Vronsky. The narrative digression is concluded.

Why now, at this particular moment in the subplot of Stiva's visit to the country to sell Dolly's property, is it possible for Levin to ask the question he has been waiting to ask since Stiva's arrival (and since his own departure from Moscow)? From one perspective, Levin's entire life in the countryside since Kitty refused his proposal has been a diversion, like Natasha's waiting for Andrei, so this narrative passage with Stiva and Ryabinin repeats the larger shape of the plot: it is an eddy within an eddy of the flow of the novel. Levin seems to recognize in his gratuitous (though accurate) abuse of Stiva the swerve of neglect that his own life has taken since his rejection by Kitty in Moscow. He recognizes a telling pattern, which is also why this small segment of the novel contains some of Levin's most telling self-description.

One suspects that Tolstoy concurs with many of Levin's opinions here. Tolstoy's authorial quest for a legitimating narrative reminds us, among many other things, that Tolstoy was not entirely satisfied with his status as an aristocratic landowner. The three years he spent teaching the peasants on his estate just before beginning *War and Peace* did not bring him closer to them. Noting the "deep sense of *otherness*, their difference from himself," Feuer sees Tolstoy's new understanding of himself as an aristocrat as an important moment for him as an author. She writes: "With Tolstoy's acceptance of himself as a nobleman and as an artist, the origin of *War and Peace*—not conceptually, but in time and in fact—has been reached."[26] Levin's rediscovery of aristocracy, how important it is for him, prepares the way for Tolstoy's rediscovery of authenticity as the governing mode of the true self (as opposed to the self legitimated by society).

The idea that Vronsky is a true aristocrat, to give a crucial example from the same episode, touches Levin to the quick. He says that he does not even consider a man like Vronsky an aristocrat, a "man whose father crawled up from nothing by intrigues and whose mother has had relations with heaven knows whom."[27] Yet Levin's concealed digression about Vronsky ultimately leads to revelation and self-revelation. He continues:

> No, pardon me, I consider myself and people like me aristocrats: people who can point back to three or four honorable generations of their family, all with a high standard of education (talent and intelligence are a different matter), who have never cringed before anyone, never depended on anyone, but have lived as my father and my grandfather did. I know many such. You consider it mean for me to count the trees in my wood while you give Ryabinin thirty thousand rubles; but you will receive a Government grant and I don't know what other rewards, and I shan't, so I value what is mine by birth and labor. . . . We—and not those who only manage to exist by the bounty of the might of this world, and who can be bought for twenty copecks—are the aristocrats.[28]

Clearly when Levin says to Stiva earlier in the chapter, "I have never really considered what I am. I am Constantine Levin, that's all,"[29] he is not telling the whole truth. He may have meant to say, "I have never considered what meaningless label others may attach to me," and yet even that seems inaccurate, when one reads this impassioned defense of his aristocratic birthright. Stiva, Ryabinin, and Vronsky—government ward, thief, and interloper—are all modern-day Judases, one gathers from Levin's outburst. Nobility is a birthright, though one entailing certain demands. The key phrase is: "never cringed before anyone, never depended on anyone." What a model for the self-reliant man — or, better still, for an author.

The crucial point is that this narrative diversion, a way of getting around the question Levin really wants to ask, ultimately serves his self-revelation. Narrative diversions and elisions similarly reveal the personality of the narrator (or author). Ralph Matlaw opines: "Tolstoy was one of the most integrated of writers, expressing at every point his personality through his art, and vice-versa. . . . [His] characters, who, when they are not satirically portrayed, are [also] completely integrated even in their shortcomings."[30] Although I have been arguing that Tolstoy was not in fact as integrated a writer as many suggest, there can be no question of the close relationship between artistic form and identity in this narrative sequence with Levin. What prompts Levin's soliloquy on his aristocratic nature is his confrontation with the plot itself. He recognizes with damning accuracy the metaphor—the cliché—of his recent life. Levin's escape to the countryside is mirrored by his escape into the conversation about the sale of the woods. Reminding himself that he can be neither bought nor sold is Levin's way of counting trees. As he finds the courage to ask more about Kitty, he finds the courage to confront the ideals he feels constitute his true self.

6

THE RECOVERY OF CHILDHOOD

Had Caius kissed his mother's hand like that, and did the silk of her dress rustle
for Caius?

— *"The Death of Ivan Ilyich"*

HAPPY CHILDHOODS REVISITED: "THE DEATH OF IVAN ILYICH"

Tolstoy's early stories use misdirection, diversion, in order to create the experience of real presentness for the reader, who, happily distracted, passes into a world of fiction perhaps without realizing it. The late stories, on the contrary, often feign the simplicity of pure readerly experience, while alienating that experience through complex narrative structures. In the former, Tolstoy struggles against the alibi of narrative, continually collapsing the distance between "elsewhere" and the present "here." In the latter, however, Tolstoy raises a narrative barrier to purely present meaning; and though his stories often contain what should be a simple moral meaning, they just as frequently convey to readers that truth is essentially inaccessible. Characters tend not to discover new ways to live, though they may recall the authentic lives of their childhoods. To the extent that Tolstoy's narratives are modeled on biographical lives, these late stories ultimately self-destruct. The truth is prior to the life depicted by the narrative, and once recalled, no longer needs the narrative.

By examining this remarkably alienating gesture by Tolstoy, I address not so much Tolstoy's populist moral fiction, such as "The Three Hermits," though sometimes those stories also contain surprising narrative features. I have in mind, rather, the semibelletristic short fiction of the later part of Tolstoy's career, such as "Master and Man," "The Death of Ivan Ilyich," "The Kreutzer Sonata," "After the Ball," and *Hadji Murad*. I will discuss "The Death of Ivan Ilyich" and *Hadji Murad* in this chapter, and "The Kreutzer Sonata" and "After the Ball" in chapter 10. The complex narrative structures of these and other late stories

belie the simplicity of Tolstoy's moral message, and suggest not just a philosophy radically different from the earlier Tolstoy but also an aesthetics that has
fundamentally changed. Here Tolstoy seems not only to embrace the alienating
narrative structures that separate reader from a more pure experience of the
text, but also to welcome the deferral of meaning that previously would have
been unthinkable for him.

Although one could equate Tolstoy's later fiction with a lack of equivocation
in its moral message, these stories are by no means univocal in their meaning.
Tolstoy places readers in "The Death of Ivan Ilyich" in the position of Ivan's
doctors, who disagree on the diagnosis of his illness even though they each
easily come to their own conclusions about it. Similarly, we all seem to know
exactly what the story means, yet we differ in our interpretations. As Gary Jahn
writes, "There are few stories whose intended meaning is so abundantly clear."[1]
There is an unequivocal meaning (that is, we know what Tolstoy wanted to
convey in this story) yet differing accounts of its significance (E. D. Hirsch's
term for the multiplicity of interpretations a story may have).[2] This tack works
well with "The Death of Ivan Ilyich," which is seemingly so insistent on conveying a single moral message. Hirsch's division of kinds of interpretation into
meaning and significance operates universally, however, and if there is a more
substantial interpretive division particular to Tolstoy's story, we may overlook it.
In other words, there is meaning and significance for any text, but what if a text
purposely confuses those categories as part of its narrative purpose?

Different kinds of interpretation take place in the story. Ivan makes judg-
ments in court, for example, that depend on his ability to sever his personal life
and feeling from his actions at work (and vice versa). Or, in another instance,
Ivan's wife, daughter, and her fiancé discuss the merits of Sarah Bernhardt
according to the refinement and "reality" of her performance. Ivan's colleague
and protégé Petr Ivanovich spends most of the first chapter trying to figure out
what exactly is going on at the funeral and how he should behave. When he
abandons his role as "observer and judge," readers are implicitly invited to take
over his duty in discovering the significance of Ivan's death.[3] Learning how to
understand people, situations, and events competently is one of the story's
primary objectives. Ivan himself returns repeatedly to the conclusion that he
alone understands the gravity of his illness; at best, others only subconsciously
understand yet pretend not to understand. They are simply unwilling to face
the existential abyss staring at Ivan Ilyich in his solitude.

A different kind of division informs interpretation as diagnosis in "The Death
of Ivan Ilyich." Petr Ivanovich says of Ivan's illness in the first chapter, "The doctors couldn't determine [what was wrong]. That is, they made determinations,

but different ones."[4] The *that is* creates a relationship of equivalence between the inability to determine and the differences in how they determined (mutually exclusive, one surmises). This equivalence (no meaning versus multiple meanings) proves to be relevant in a variety of ways as a marker of interpretive failure throughout the story. One can fail to understand either by failing to adduce an interpretation (no diagnosis) or by succumbing to multiple, possibly mutually contradictory interpretations (diagnoses that cannot be reconciled with one another). Ivan himself solves this dilemma in one way, when he interprets the failure of others to understand his illness as deception pure and simple. Siding with Ivan Ilyich, readers may also think the dilemma is a false one—that we are, again, confusing meaning and significance, in Hirsch's sense of the terms, when we really know what Tolstoy meant. The desire to know a single answer, as well as its invariable frustration, seems inscribed into the story itself. Why? Perhaps because the philosopher in Tolstoy was convinced the Christian teaching was a simple one, but each time he enunciated it the artist in him reconceptualized it. There is no reason, however, to oppose Tolstoy's art with his thought. In "The Death of Ivan Ilyich," each is impossible without the other, but perhaps we are also purposely diverted from one to the other.

"The Death of Ivan Ilyich" synthesizes and demonstrates Tolstoy's aesthetics of narrative diversion in its late-career iteration. One of the main questions of this aesthetics—is there such a thing as aesthetic pleasure, or does art merely distract us from the profound moral questions of life?—is what Ivan Ilyich, with Tolstoy's approval, asks as he faces his own mortality. "The Death of Ivan Ilyich" relentlessly demands that as readers we confront not just our own mortality but also the logical end of Tolstoy's early realism, with its tactics of disintermediation and goal of true presentness. Throughout this late story Tolstoy interrogates a principle of equivalence: that the world of the story *is* our world and is *inseparable* from our world. Remarkably, and paradoxically, at this thematic pinnacle, one also finds a dense network of aesthetic structuring in the story that is an unmistakable reminder of Tolstoy's craft. Here aesthetic mediation seems insurmountable.

This principle of equivalence may be found on all levels of the story. Tolstoy reveals it most dramatically, though, in the thematic parallel of the self and other, the individual and everyman. The narrator remarks: "The mere fact of the death of a near acquaintance aroused, as usual, in all who heard of it the complacent feeling that 'it's he who is dead and not I.' Each one thought or felt, 'Well, he's dead but I'm alive!'"[5] This refusal to equate another's mortality with one's own is generalized maximally in Ivan Ilyich's refusal to accept that the logic of the syllogism "Caius is a man, men are mortal, therefore Caius is mortal" applies to him: "He was not Caius, not an abstract man, but a creature quite separate from all others. . . . Had Caius kissed his mothers' hand like that, and did the silk of her dress rustle for Caius?"[6] Yet Ivan Ilyich is mistaken. He is both unlike *and* like other men, as his manservant Gerasim seems instinctively to know, saying of death simply: "We shall all come to it some day."[7] One person is like every other in death, and should be so in life, too, the story implies. But how alike?—the story seems to ask. The point, as Inessa Medzhibovskaya demonstrates, is that the syllogistic logic accounts poorly for the complexities of identity. "Ivan Il'ich unfolds a masterful case through direct demonstration of the flaw in Aristotle's syllogistic theory, primarily, its inability to discriminate between universal and individual statements."[8]

Not all similarities are good ones. Metaphoric equivalence was fine for Tolstoy's earlier stories, concerned as they were with legitimacy, with making the fiction an acceptable substitute for reality. Now, as Tolstoy devotes himself to representations of authenticity, he repeatedly destabilizes similarities and equivalences of all sorts. Whereas Ivan Ilyich believes himself to be unique in feeling, aspiration, and taste, the narrator makes clear that in his banality at least Ivan is indeed like everyone else. The narrator is deeply ironic in describing how Ivan falls and hurts his side while decorating. Ivan declares to his wife: "It's a good thing I'm a bit of an athlete. Another man might have been killed, but I merely knocked myself, just here; it hurts when it's touched, but it's passing already—it's only a bruise." In fact, Ivan will never recover. And the house that he has worked so hard to decorate is no more unique than Ivan himself: "In reality it was just what is usually seen in the houses of people of moderate means who want to appear rich, and therefore succeed only in resembling others like themselves: there were damasks, dark wood, plants, rugs, dull and polished bronzes—all the things people of a certain class have in order to resemble other people of that class. His house was so like others that it would never have been noticed, but to him it all seemed to be quite exceptional."[9] Similarity is a curse here, mainly because of Ivan's pretensions. Many aspects of Ivan Ilyich, including his name, suggest he is everyman, that he is the norm, the example for all of us. In other words, though he is not exceptional, he is exemplary.

The most intriguing, and in some ways the most important, use of equivalence in the story transpires at the level of syntax. Even simple sentences, on closer inspection, suggest that Tolstoy pays close attention to the role of equivalence as it shapes the narrative universe of his story. The best-known instance of this syntactical strategy is contained in the story's damning line: "Ivan Ilyich's life had been most simple and most ordinary and most terrible."[10] Tolstoy renders similar markedly dissimilar terms: simple, ordinary, and most terrible.

What has seemed at first to be a boon—the likeness of one man to another—is, as in the example of decorating, an index of moral devastation, or, more accurately, vacuity. Few readers miss the significance of the grammatical construction in this sentence. The sentence confirms its propositional logic irrefutably. Sameness in a morally vacuous world is not exculpatory. (Ivan Ilyich seems neither an iconic nor a symbolic sign, in Peirce's terms, but an indexical one. He neither resembles all people, nor substitutes conventionally for them—he relates to everyman through an unassailable logic that physically makes him one of many.)

Other examples of syntactical equivalence point toward the interpretive framework the story manifests—particularly, as I have mentioned, the narrator's judgment of the doctors' opinions, their diagnoses, of what in fact ails Ivan Ilyich. "The doctors couldn't determine [what was wrong]. That is, they made determinations, but different ones." We are confounded by the fact that the moral certainty in the text—Ivan's life was most simple and thus most terrible—is not matched by interpretive certainty. Tolstoy's language, likewise, is not simple and straightforward in the manner of a transparently realistic story, but rather is laden with multiple planes of imagery and symbolism. In a sense, the words то есть, "that is," are representative of Tolstoy's efforts. A common locution for him, то есть frequently precedes a moment of scathing irony. For example when Stiva loses himself in the cares of the day, Tolstoy adds, "то есть, забыться [that is, forgets himself]." For Tolstoy, the "that is" puts a spotlight on his unmasking the world, the way things really are. It is the lexical pause an audience makes before gasping at the revelation of the villain.

Tolstoy disliked doctors and rarely needed an excuse to level his most scathing criticism at them.[11] In his opinion, they use thinly veiled excuses to grope the naked bodies of young women. In the name of the general good, they commit particular evils. And, mainly, they offend, which is precisely the way that the younger Tolstoy described his, as yet nonexistent, relationship with the critics in "To Those Critics." Tolstoy sees in the differing diagnoses of the doctors the same relativism that threatened him as he contemplated embarking on his literary career. The only way for them to come up with such different opinions is for them to base their opinions not on science but on personal prejudice, or worse. Tolstoy's early response to the critics was to adopt a method of disintermediation, to try to circumvent the institutional barriers that he perceived as getting in the way. In "The Death of Ivan Ilyich," Tolstoy gestures toward circumventing typical literary interpretations.

Ivan learns to accept his mortality outside of rational processes and logic; though the syllogism of Caius is irrefutable, this alone cannot convince Ivan

Ilyich. Images of direct contact, the touch of Gerasim, for example, or Ivan's
own deathlike appearance, which tells his brother-in-law of his fate more com-
pellingly than any words: these suggest that truth is conveyed outside traditional
means of communication. And, in fact, even Ivan's last attempt to speak to
people is thwarted. He means to say, "Forgive me," *Прости*, but instead says,
"Let me pass," *Пропусти*. Not only is he thereby misunderstood, he also repeats
the more general syntactical rule of the story. The veneer of equivalence dis-
guises a profound difference. One can easily imagine, for example, a dying man
dropping a syllable, saying *прости* (forgive me) when he means *пропусти* (let
me pass). The other way around is counterintuitive. With his last ounce of
effort, Ivan Ilyich adds a syllable.

In this way direct address helps form the dense network of symbolic and
grammatical meanings in the story. Tolstoy intends that "forgive me" and "let
me pass" combine to indicate Ivan's acceptance of responsibility for his misled
life and his acceptance of his own death. But where we expect simplicity we
find an interpretive barrier, a wedge between the equivalent terms Tolstoy
invokes. Ivan does not mind this misunderstanding: "He waved his hand, knowing that He whose understanding mattered would understand."[12] Neither Ivan's
family nor Tolstoy's readers really do understand—but this is often forgotten. By
alluding to God's perfect understanding, Tolstoy would have us forget our own
difficulties and imperfect understanding.

As in many of Tolstoy's later stories, the focus is on his early aesthetics in
general and his past forms of narration in particular.[13] We must remember the
profound difference between "The Death of Ivan Ilyich" and something like
Childhood: Ivan Ilyich gets a *real*, happy childhood, not the mythologized one
of Nikolai Irtenev. "In returning to the past Ivan causes time to run backwards
and so cancels the direction in which he had been going. The luminescence of
his memory of childhood, which he is able to *recover* in imagination, anticipates
the dimensionless region of light, which is the figurative expression of his ultimate *recovery*."[14] In searching for the authentic meaning of his life, Ivan Ilyich
(like Anna Karenina in her last, fleeting thoughts) reaches back to childhood,
before he went astray. Nikolai Irtenev, by contrast, is an adult who understands
more and better than his child-self. He realizes that the unlikely dreams of his
childhood, explained and narrated as a generalizing example for others, must be
legitimated by an adult society of readers. In "The Death of Ivan Ilyich," the
narrator, and Ivan Ilyich, having revealed an authentic core of being, are not
worried who understands and who does not, so long as God understands.

In later works such as "The Death of Ivan Ilyich" Tolstoy's examination and
reworking of metonymic operations is key. Substitutability in "The Death of

Ivan Ilyich" is undermined throughout: as Ivan says, unfortunately, "another would have died." What, by contrast, is proximate, at hand in Ivan's life? What is exceptional, rather than exemplary? Peter Ivanovich is close to Ivan, and Medzhibovskaya shows how his "sense of debt is reinforced by the following categories of inclusion, massively repeated in the text. The irony of mutual belonging in the ontological community fraught with eventual dying is reinforced by the constant repetition of designators of membership (members [*chleny*], comrades, and co-workers [*so-tovarishchi*]) and by reflexive iterative verbs with a common destination (convened, got together [*soshlis'*, *s'ekhalis'*])."[15] There is also the family that loves him, his son in particular, and his servant Gerasim, whose touch and earthy wisdom bring so much relief to him. Proximity and constricting space are constructive principles in the narration of the story: Ivan moves from the provinces into the capital, for example. In fact, as Jahn notes, the entire structure of the story suggests a world closing in on Ivan . . . until he is actually trapped in a coffin, and even enclosed in the much smaller dark outlines of a newspaper obituary.[16] Such claustrophobic narrative movement is jarring and unpleasant, until one recalls that it is at the moment of maximal stricture within the dark sack that Ivan finally breaks through to genuine freedom and understanding. There is no knowledge Ivan gains that substitutes for his life; he merely traces his life backward and recalls what he has known all along. Levin's epiphany toward the end of *Anna Karenina* similarly points to a kind of inherent knowledge.

"The Death of Ivan Ilyich" works on Tolstoy's narrative alibi in two ways. First, Ivan's recovery of what is missing in his life points to Tolstoy's changing use of absence in the constitution of his characters' identities. Ivan cannot know fully how his death will define his life, but he can recover his childhood ideals. Second, Tolstoy uses the unexamined potentials latent in his earlier fiction to reconfigure his own aesthetics. In its reappraisal of Tolstoy's earlier fiction, "The Death of Ivan Ilyich" recalls Levin's epiphany and other scenes from *Anna Karenina*. Like Anna, Ivan has his moment of perceptual relativity: "What had happened to him was like the sensation one sometimes experiences in a railway carriage when one thinks one is going backwards while one is really going forwards and suddenly becomes aware of the real direction."[17] Gestures of crossing back and forth, instances of chiasmus, seemingly so important in the earlier fiction, such as *The Cossacks*, mark error in "The Death of Ivan Ilyich." As Ivan reflects on his life, "It is as if I had been going downhill while I imagined I was going up. And that's really what it was."[18] Where before there was possibility of life and art crossing, now there is impossibility. It was an error. Ivan asks rhetorically a few lines later: "'Then what do you want now? To live? Live how? Live as you lived in the law courts when the usher proclaimed, "The judge is coming!" The judge is coming, the judge!' he repeated to himself. 'Here he is, the judge. But I'm not guilty!' he exclaimed angrily. 'What is it for?'"[19] Unfortunately, the translation misses the inexorable logic of the chiasmus that leads Ivan to explode: "But I'm not guilty!" "Суд идет" (court is in session) is what is said when the judge enters. Ivan repeats to himself the untranslatable chiastic phrase "суд идет, идет суд," the second part of which can mean "court is in session," "the judge is coming," and "judgment is coming." The logic of the chiasmus tells Ivan he can no longer separate his work in the courts from his own judgment day before God.

"The Death of Ivan Ilyich" takes as a subject Tolstoy's own earlier principles of narrative. But Tolstoy is still saying something—we all agree on that—even if he undermines the way he says it. The symbols of the story do not cohere into an allegory, for example, but they are nevertheless telling. Ivan is the "phoenix" of the family, his medallion reads *respice finem*, and so forth. Similarly, looks and visual clues substitute for typical linguistic ones. Ivan's expression from the coffin said "that what was necessary had been accomplished, and accomplished rightly. Besides this there was in that expression a reproach and a warning to the living."[20] Forget what the necessary thing, the reproach, and the warning are; the expression communicates effectively, even if the message is lost (God understands, as in the story's conclusion). The story's expressive aesthetics is easier to identify than the meaning of the story itself. Peter Ivanovich responds to Ivan Ilyich's widow's tears, utterly conventionally, "Believe . . .," before she cuts him off. *Поверьте,* an imperative like those ending the story, *прости* and *пропусти* ("forgive me" and "let me pass"), at least grammatically urges us to believe, even if we're merely saying it. Tolstoy continues to write fiction even as he doubts its role in Christian art, as though the reader's suspension of disbelief were at least some step toward a personal conversion.

OVERCOMING FICTION: *HADJI MURAD*

Hadji Murad (1896–1904) is my final example of an important story of belief in fiction (in both senses). It was the final belletristic work of Tolstoy's career. He grants Hadji Murad such an unassailably authentic life that nearly all the Russians of the story seem totally weak and corrupt by comparison. Tolstoy's point is not Rousseau's notion that the native lives a natural life that we, who have been spoiled by society, should emulate. Tolstoy battled that Romantic idea for most of his career. But Hadji Murad nevertheless lives entirely in accord with the ideals of his faith and his being. Though he is self-absorbed and thus, in Tolstoy's moral universe, a severely limited model of instruction, he is undoubtedly a heroic figure in the novella.[21]

Tolstoy's first mention of Hadji Murad was to remark that he had "behaved basely" when he surrendered to the Russians.[22] (We won't mention that the far more honorable Tolstoy was at that time contracting venereal diseases and gambling away all his money.) They were both in Tbilisi in 1851, but they did not meet. Tolstoy was busy writing his first novel, *Childhood*. After fifty years of thinking about it, Tolstoy regards Hadji Murad more highly. Through *Hadji Murad*, Tolstoy revisits the earlier ideas of authorial self-presentation that first emerged in *Childhood*.

The plot of *Hadji Murad* is both simple and complicated, taking place in the context of mid-nineteenth-century Russian attempts to subdue Chechnya and the Caucasus. Hadji Murad betrays the imam Shamil, whom he suspects of wanting to kill him, and surrenders to the Russian forces. He hopes the Russians will help him free his family, which has been taken hostage by Shamil, and that they will also provide him with the military forces necessary to defeat Shamil, so that he may exact revenge. The Russians are unsure of Hadji Murad's intentions and delay helping him. They keep him prisoner, making an effort to treat him as their guest, until Hadji Murad fears he can wait no longer to attempt to save his family. He escapes from the Russians, but is quickly surrounded by a great number of troops and dies a brave and spectacularly violent death.

There are numerous important narrative branches in *Hadji Murad* that do not belong to the main story. Simplicity and naturalness, our ability to substitute the story for our world, are belied by the complex narrative structure:

1. The frame narrative is one of the most distinctive elements of the story. The narrator tells of how, while returning home through a field, he discovers examples of a remarkable thistle called a "tartar" that have been missed by the plow. The vitality of the flower reminds him of the story of Hadji Murad. What is unusual about this is that most of Tolstoy's late fiction frames are strictly invented. Here, by contrast, we have an entirely true framing episode, straight from the diary, so obvious in symbolic meaning in its new context that it seems totally artless, even overdetermined. This "true" episode rings more false than countless fictive passages that Tolstoy incorporated into his stories and novels.[23] If one wants to preserve the authority of the frame narrative and the moral and didactic aspect of the story, one highlights the unique and determinative role of the frame narrative.

2. We learn a great deal about Piotr Avdeev, a peasant who enlists in the army in place of his brother, who has children to support. Avdeev is killed

in a skirmish between the Russians and the Chechens, and an entire
chapter is devoted to his family and how they receive news of his death.

3. Hadji Murad's biography, as he tells it to one of the Russian officers,
occupies two chapters, separated by a single chapter. It is located in the
very center of the novella, and Tolstoy dedicated a great deal of time to
perfecting it.

4. The letter from General Vorontsov to Minister of War Chernyshov takes
a chapter.

5. Another entire chapter follows the movements of Tsar Nikolai throughout the course of a single day. Like Hadji Murad's biography, this section
occupied much of Tolstoy's effort, and was the special focus of his attention in his late revisions.

Tolstoy apparently envisioned individual and mutual goals for these separate
narrative strands. Autobiographical, publicistic, biographical, documentary,
and satirical fiction all have their place in this relatively short work, which
incorporates elements of Tolstoy's diary, historical facts and reminiscences, genuine historical documents, and court gossip. Critics sometimes make comparisons to *War and Peace*, but *Hadji Murad* is more collage-like in structure than
Tolstoy's great novel, and far more tightly structured.

The reason for this structure is revealed in Tolstoy's intended characterization of Hadji Murad. He writes in his diary: "There's this English toy, a peep-
show. . . . That's how one must show a person—Xadzhi-Murat: husband,
fanatic, and so forth."[24] Each narrative form reveals Hadji Murad in a new light.
What is more, while he was writing *Hadji Murad* and working on *Resurrection*,
Tolstoy had also become interested in the "fluidity [текучесть]" of personality:
"the fluidity of a person, that is, that he is one and the same: now a villain, now
an angel, now a wise man, now an idiot, now a strong man, now the weakest
being."[25] Obviously, Tolstoy intends to fracture our experience of Hadji Murad
in order that we form a composite view of him. This goal is not entirely new for
Tolstoy. He struggles in most of his major fiction not to let kinds of narrative
integrity imply a false wholeness of character.

But the imagined core of being that I have highlighted in novels and stories
is also here in *Hadji Murad*. Hadji Murad's autobiography occupies the center
of the novella (chapters 11 and 13 of 25). Although the autobiographical story he
tells is heavily mediated by the narrative structure of the entire novella, Tolstoy
took great care to craft Hadji Murad's language and the memories he would
retell. Autobiographical reminiscence has even greater resonance throughout
the novella, when one looks at the drafts. In the eighth redaction of the manuscript, Tolstoy rewrote the entire text in the first person; and he later mentioned

his dilemma in choosing between more subjective and more objective points of view for telling the story.[26] Ultimately, Hadji Murad's autobiography has a privileged position in the novella. It is the story within the story within the frame narrative—by enclosing it this way, Tolstoy keeps his modernistic "peep show" *and* his more traditional autobiographical inflected narrative.

A key detail reveals just how important Hadji Murad's autobiography was to Tolstoy. Though most of the biographical details about Hadji Murad's life are documentary, Tolstoy invents the story of Hadji Murad's mother nearly being killed by his father for refusing to be wet nurse to the Khansha's son so that she could nurse Hadji Murad.[27] Hadji Murad would later ask her repeatedly to show him the scar and sing the song about it for him. Here, as elsewhere in his fiction, Tolstoy seems to tempt us to make psychoanalytic interpretations of the relationship between a missing and mythologized mother and Tolstoy's authorial identity. Hadji Murad recalls, after recollecting the song, how his mother shaved his head for the first time and how he was astonished at his own reflection afterward.[28] In short, at the center of Hadji Murad's autobiography, which is the center of the novella *Hadji Murad*, Tolstoy creates a false memory for his true hero. We recall how central false memories were for the aesthetics of *Childhood*.

Yet Hadji Murad does not reveal the story of his mother or the song to anyone within the text.[29] This is in keeping with other interpolated stories in the novella, which are structured so that they do not require any legitimating process of a reader. As in "The Death of Ivan Ilyich," Tolstoy is mainly concerned with authenticity. He refuses to publish *Hadji Murad* altogether. The chapter (15) devoted to Tsar Nikolai's day is a good case of this structure whereby the story turns in upon itself. As the chapter opens, we learn immediately that the tsar will react differently toward the case of Hadji Murad than his minister of war would like. Then we get the tsar's "history of yesterday," the reason why he is in a foul mood (he was out late forcing sex on a twenty-year-old virgin), and finally the details of how what we already know happens happens. This is the repeated pattern of the novella. We already know that Avdeev is dead when we read the chapter that describes his parents learning the sad news. The past tense is given a past tense from which to view it as the ineluctable future. (Note that this is also the basic structure of "The Death of Ivan Ilyich": first we get his death, then we get the life that led to it.) We see Hadji Murad's severed head paraded around camp, and read the detailed description of it, before the final tale of his death is recounted by the officer Kamenev in a subsequent chapter. All of these self-sustaining, closed narratives within the self-sustaining, closed framing narrative remind us that Tolstoy no longer seeks narrative processes of legitimating an autobiographical past. The past is merely preserved—in the case of Hadji Murad, in an aspic of sensational bloodshed.

People knew that Tolstoy had written *Hadji Murad* and simply refused to publish it. Even Tolstoy's disciple Chertkov—was there anyone Tolstoy trusted more?—was only vouchsafed a copy of the manuscript as long as he promised not to let it out of his hands.[30] In 1909, a few years after the novella's completion, Sonya read Tolstoy a published interview with the writer Kuprin. Kuprin says in the interview: "Perhaps, by keeping in his desk such works of his as *Hadji Murad*, and not letting them see the light of day, [Tolstoy] harbors the notion of showing us when he has already died just what power he [still] had, and these most recent things of his—these sorts of 'Reading Cycles [Круг чтения],' these sorts of small wisdom for each day, will be shown to have been complete nonsense setting into relief his real greatness in artistic works."[31] Kuprin reads *Hadji Murad* a bit differently than I do. I see Tolstoy's sympathies lying with Hadji Murad. Yet Kuprin plainly sees Tolstoy in the tsar, who "dwelt on a thought that always calmed him—the thought of his own greatness."[32]

I think it is important to limit the extent to which we attribute a real psychological investigation of oneself or others in Tolstoy's authorial aesthetics. I have endeavored throughout this study to lay groundwork for that kind of reappraisal of psychology in Tolstoy. We discovered in Tolstoy's early fiction, for example, in his misdirection and destruction of boundaries between life and art, a hidden skeptical attitude toward reception and toward literary institutions per se. Tolstoy doubted that even his most sincere efforts would be properly understood. That hidden attitude was partly revealed in the use of false memories or sources with regard both to the constitution of a self for characters and to the ontology of the literary work. What seems at first to be psychological analysis in Tolstoy is more plainly an ontological investigation. And we can trace this ontological query thematically via the opposition of legitimacy to authenticity in Tolstoy's works. That opposition between legitimacy and authenticity is manifest in Tolstoy's complex use of literary structure, and especially evident in "The Death of Ivan Ilyich" and *Hadji Murad*. Ultimately, Tolstoy's attitude, even anxiety, about literary institutions accounts for much of the psychological analysis of his characters, and leads toward a philosophy of being that can dispense with the legitimating effect of the reader. Late works such as *Hadji Murad* demonstrate how Tolstoy resolves such matters in complex literary structures.

Part IV

A Language of Love

For many of us, reading Tolstoy means reading love stories, great love stories. We thrill at Tolstoy's descriptions of ballroom dances, the hopeful looks of potential lovers, cryptic conversations, marriage proposals, the smallest details about children and family life, as well as torrid affairs—though not necessarily in that order. In his love stories Tolstoy most successfully combined truly entertaining fiction, which he always viewed with suspicion, and philosophical reflection. Again and again, Tolstoy idealizes how lovers really understand one another. For them meaning is present and available, not hidden in a labyrinth of self-consciousness or trapped by elaborate convention. In love stories, Tolstoy discovers that elusive goal of his early realistic fiction: complete and total presentness. It is ideal, fleeting, maddening, but possible. Much of Tolstoy's mature aesthetics is built on that possibility of rendering utter presentness in romantic fiction; his most potent tragedies, such as *Anna Karenina*, erupt from its unsustainability and demise. The play of presence and absence in Tolstoy's early fiction, the alibi he cultivated in his narratives, is perfectly suited for the turn to romance in his mature fiction.

THE WORLD AS LOVE AND REPRESENTATION

Once, reading Schopenhauer, Levin put in place of his "will" the word "love," and for a couple of days . . . this new philosophy consoled him. But when he turned from life itself to glance at it again, it fell away, and proved to be a muslin garment with no warmth in it.

—*Anna Karenina*

TOLSTOJS WELT ALS LIEBEN UND VORSTELLUNG

Although it might at first seem a simplification, the passage about Levin in the epigraph says much about Tolstoyan aesthetics: love and language go together, and representing love is its own philosophical problem. "The world as *love* and representation" may compare poorly with life itself, but that keeps neither Levin nor Tolstoy from repeatedly trying similar philosophies. Tolstoy was never convinced of his power to communicate his ideas in and through language; he often doubted the ability of literature to break through barriers of social isolation; and he used motifs of romantic betrayal, infidelity, trust, and reconciliation to test the limits of communication and self-understanding. Love is the glimmer of hope Tolstoy has for language, suspicion its demise. True love facilitates nearly perfect communication, whereas the betrayal of love or illicit love can deprive one of even the simplest forms of communication.

Over the years, many critics have considered the relationship between Tolstoy's theories of art and language. On some level, all recognize the basic dilemma that for Tolstoy art is meant essentially to communicate ideas and emotions but that narrative (and perhaps language itself), literary tradition, and romantic love all work against successful communication.[1] In the previous chapters, I discussed how conventions of legitimacy and authenticity as well as an aesthetics of narrative diversion led Tolstoy to use absence creatively, to misdirect the reader at the boundaries separating life and art, and to create a series of false memories shaping his autobiographical fiction. Now I hope to demonstrate how Tolstoy's narrative alibi sinks to the level of language itself.

In his earlier stories and novels, Tolstoy associates with authentic love the kind of language that refers easily to ideas, emotions, and objects in the world; he associates the betrayal of love, however, with suspicion not just of another person but of the capacity of language to communicate important ideas and emotions. In the former case, language is perfectly transparent and comprehension immediate; in the latter, a "poetics of suspicion" emerges: language is a cipher that needs to be decoded, or a cruel deception that needs to be exposed.[2] By late in his career, this poetics of suspicion comes to dominate Tolstoy's aesthetics thoroughly, poisoning even the narrative itself, as in "The Kreutzer Sonata." Although in his late essay *What Is Art?* Tolstoy calls for an aesthetics of highly efficient narrative communication, his own repeated succumbing to the poetics of suspicion would seem to indicate its impossibility.

Even Tolstoy's first story, "A History of Yesterday" (1850), is devoted to testing many of the limits, however naively, of what can be conveyed in narrative. The narrator in that story decides to write a history of the previous day but fears it may be impossible. "Only God knows how many diverse and diverting impressions, together with the thoughts awakened by them, occur in a single day. Obscure and confused they may be, but they are nevertheless comprehensible to our minds. If they could be told in such a way that I could easily read myself and others could read me, as I could, the result would be a most instructive and absorbing book; nor would there be ink enough in the world to write it, or typesetters to put it into print."[3] Many students of Tolstoy are familiar with this passage — it reminds us of the infinite retreat of causality in *War and Peace* — but less frequently mentioned is that "A History of Yesterday" is also Tolstoy's first romantic narrative, though it contains much else as well. He does not in fact spend countless pages linking diverse and diverting impressions and thoughts to one another. Simple causality, in contrast to the complex models of historical causality he constructs in *War and Peace*, leads him to describe the day before yesterday. Yet even the day before yesterday is likely the object of his narrative only because of the woman who occupies his thoughts.

That woman, the wife of a friend, draws his unwavering attention, but she also eludes his narrative, even grammatical, grasp — the narrator's poor substitute for physical embrace. "Why does this woman love me (how I should like to put a period here!) to be confused by her?"[4] She affects, moreover, his very ability to communicate, not to mention his overall capacity for acting in a normal and polite manner. From the start, the narrator admits: "to show [convey; показать] what you want to is very difficult."[5] And he goes on to show both what he wishes and does not wish to convey. "She is a woman for me because she has all those endearing qualities which compel one to love them, or rather, to love her—because I do love her. *But not so that she could belong to a man. That does not enter my head.*"[6] Or again: "She is a coquette; no, not a coquette, but she loves to please, even to turn heads. *I won't say coquette*, because either the word or the idea associated with it is bad."[7] Tolstoy, like one of his favorite authors, Laurence Sterne, here creates a narrator who makes and unmakes his statements simultaneously. This narrative tactic approximates the uncertain, tentative behavior of an inexperienced young man (and author), and Tolstoy thereby fuses narrative and romantic gestures.

From the very start, Tolstoy associated romance with an investigation into the innate complexity of language, both verbal and nonverbal. Always implicit in this investigation is the almost magical ideal of total communication and mutual understanding. The narrator from "A History of Yesterday" continues: "Being embarrassed together and smiling together were very pleasant to me. A silly thing, to be sure, but together.—I love these secret relationships, expressed by an imperceptible smile or by the eyes, and which are impossible to explain. It is not just that one person understands the other, but that each understands that the other understands that he understands, etc."[8] Both statement and metastatement are crucial: love provides understanding but also an infinite spiral of understanding that one understands that the other understands, and so on. Love shades into epistemology and an endless self-other play of perspective. The autobiographical narrator of *Boyhood* (1854) highlights the epistemological aspect: "Asking myself: 'Of what am I thinking?' I would answer: 'I think of what I am thinking. And now what am I thinking of? I think that I am thinking of what I am thinking of.' And so on. To my wits' end."[9] So goes a boy's self-analysis. But do we really intend to be understood in love through a dizzying oscillation of perspective? The two passages are similar but they probably should not be. Real love, and genuine communication, require us to transcend that oscillation, if we are not to remain forever (and perhaps dangerously) isolated.

We may be tempted to think of Tolstoy's romance narratives in one of two ways. Perhaps we should concentrate on the highly dramatic, and violent, stories of romantic disaster in *Anna Karenina* and especially in "The Kreutzer Sonata," which follow characters who defy society in their notions of romance; or, by contrast, we could pick up the "family happiness" motif of the Rostovs and Scherbatskys, which yields more normative variations on Tolstoy's ideas of love. By a "poetics of suspicion" I mean to illustrate not only the transgressive— infection, adultery, blindness, trauma, murder, evasion—but also, with a corrective emphasis on *poetics*, the linguistic divide created by Tolstoy's romance narratives, which generate both a language of trust and a language of suspicion. I believe there is more at stake in Tolstoy's romances than happy and unhappy families.

THE MUSICAL PAST OF LANGUAGE

Music is the stenography of feelings. Here is what that means: a fast or slow succession of sounds, their pitch, their intensity, all of that in speech supplements words and their sense, indicating those nuances of feelings that are connected with parts of our speech. Music without speech takes those expressions of feelings and their nuances and unites them, and we receive the play of feelings without that which called them forth. Because of this, music acts especially strongly, and because of this the coupling of music with words is a weakening of music, it is a return backward, a copying out with letters of the stenographic marks.

—*Diary, January* 20, 1905

Tolstoy's notion of romantic language evolves out of a more primary conception of the direct relationship between speech and emotions, arising from his knowledge of music and the influence of Rousseau's belief that music conveys emotion.[10] I turn to the early story "Lucerne" to outline an early view into how music provides a prehistory to Tolstoy's linguistic themes. Paragraphs of facile nature philosophy mar this story; nevertheless, that philosophy serves as a substrate of the later, more sophisticated, romantic fiction.[11] We still see traces of it, for example, in *Anna Karenina*, where Levin's work in the fields represents his sexual vigor;[12] and, less overtly, in how his marriage to Kitty is compared to the surprisingly difficult activity of rowing a boat: "It only looked easy, but to do it, though very delightful, was very difficult."[13] Koznyshev and Varenka's failed proposal-engagement while mushroom picking in the woods is in fact a direct reference to ideas of nature, music, and romantic communication germinated early in Tolstoy's career.

"Lucerne" (1857; written first as letter from abroad to Botkin) demonstrates the often mentioned chasm between Tolstoy's art and his philosophy, and accordingly has been referred to as half treatise and half story.[14] Eric de Haard notes that the full title of the story, "From the Notes of Prince D. Nekhlyudov. Lucerne," "conveys the general 'carelessness' concerning genre, characteristic of the fifties, 'zapiski' ('notes') being the most unspecific, casual and less circumscribed type of written text, while 'iz zapisok' further stresses the fragmentariness."[15] Taking the consequences of this innate division of the text further,

Boris Eikhenbaum calls it Tolstoy's "first moral tract": "This is the first 'moralis-tic' treatise of Tolstoy, preparing for his break with journal literature, the attrac-tion of pedagogical work in the country, and the transition to new things."[16] For such an apparently important text, however, even its early reception by enthu-siastic readers of Tolstoy was mixed, leading Turgenev and others to fear for the development of Tolstoy's literary gift. Recent characterizations have been more forgiving: Olga Slivitskaia, pointing to how well it characterizes Tolstoy's art, calls "Lucerne" "a fractal of Tolstoy's entire integral aesthetic world."[17]

Part travelogue (Eikhenbaum mentions Radishchev's "Journey from Petersburg to Moscow" as a precursor), part short story, and part philosophical essay, "Lucerne" is most of all an early investigation by Tolstoy into the relation-ship between (subjective) space and (intersubjective) narrative discourse. In other words, the author considers how setting and point of view establish bases of narrative communication. Visiting Europe for the first time as a young man, Tolstoy was himself keenly aware of the influence the social and physical envi-ronment had on him. He was horrified by a public execution in Paris, but also shocked by the extent of his own horror. Though his reactions varied and he was by turns elated and repulsed, Tolstoy was often uncomfortable abroad. He writes in a letter to Botkin (April 5, 1857): "I am a complete ignoramus; nowhere have I felt it as strongly as here."[18] "Lucerne" derives from another of Tolstoy's personal experiences from this trip—when he witnessed an itinerant musician go cruelly unrewarded by the callous tourists who were his audience.

"Lucerne" is a first-person narrative in the form of a diary entry. It tells the story of Prince Nekhlyudov (frequently a stand-in for Tolstoy himself) as he visits Lucerne and attempts to befriend a musician who has been the object of ridicule by a crowd of tourists. In order to confront the prejudices of the tourists, Nekhlyudov invites the musician to join him for a drink in the hotel; but nei-ther Nekhlyudov nor the embarrassed musician are pleased by the unpleasant results. They are confronted by hostile waiters, barely understand one another, and seem to have in common only their mutual humiliation. The story closes as it began, with Nekhlyudov's musings on nature and art.

On the surface, "Lucerne" is symptomatic of Tolstoy's undigested reading of nature philosophy.[19] He immediately confronts the reader with his desire to create beauty similar to what he sees in God's creation: "When I went up to my room and opened the window facing the lake I was at first literally blinded and shaken by the beauty of that water, those mountains, and the sky. I felt an inward restlessness and a need to somehow express the surplus of something that suddenly filled my soul to overflowing."[20] Here is the Romantic task: how to make the externalized work of art replicate the affective contours of the interior world, inspired as it is by beauty in nature. Paraphrasing this "expressive" aesthetics, Patricia Carden writes, "It is the artist's mission to testify in his works to the truth of his own inner experience."[21] Emotional overflow more often than not makes a poor story, however, something even the young Tolstoy knew perfectly well. Throughout "Lucerne," natural landscape is juxtaposed again and again to the harshly imposed, rational, anglicized setting of the town and, moreover, to the rationality of the Swiss republic itself. Yet the story thereby takes on its own sort of contrary order; the hero is purposefully not English and the story is purposefully not rational, but emotional. One of the narrative challenges, then, is to overcome mere contrariness as a literary device.

The beauty of the landscape overwhelms Tolstoy's autobiographical narrator, Nekhlyudov, who tries subsequently to convey that overwhelming emotion in his story. In "Lucerne," there is an implicit economy of feeling (one may put a real value on the ephemeral singing of the musician) in a setting where the economy proper fails to reward its participants humanely and economic differentiation or class is to blame for social injustice. This aesthetics does not quite conform to the idea of "art for art's sake," popular at the time with Druzhinin and others, which opposed Chernyshevsky's radical aesthetics. The successful communicativeness of art serves here as proxy for failed commerce, and yet Tolstoy hopes to oppose Chernyshevsky more convincingly.

The story makes politics unavoidably, even embarrassingly, present, and aims to make up for the injustice of the tourists' behavior as can no bottle of champagne bought for the singer by the narrator in a fine restaurant.[22] Nekhlyudov (and presumably Tolstoy) shamefacedly recognize that Nekhlyudov's act of charity does little more than massage his own ego. The singer himself would have much preferred that Nekhlyudov buy him a drink in the modest bar on the street, rather than in the luxurious hotel. Yet Nekhlyudov does not want to be *in another place*, the literal meaning of alibi, with the singer, and thus somehow out of sight. He wants to be there, right in the face of the waiters and porter, in the midst of the society of tourists in the dining room, trampling on misguided English morals. And his story continues to do so, as though in Nekhlyudov's place. One hardly misses that Tolstoy intends to trample on our uncertain behavior as readers, too, for we are placed in the same position as the people who listen to the song. Thus Tolstoy's communicative aesthetics are at cross purposes in this story—the narrative creates a community among readers, but destroys it, as we are transformed from jurors into the accused.

Tolstoy is concerned here with how to chart a path, via narrative, that moves the reader's experience from elsewhere, safely removed from involvement in the story, to right here in the midst of the action. But he finds the traditional communicative conventions of the short story to be limiting. The exchange economy that should reward the singer for his work does not square with Tolstoy's notions of art, which are in no way egalitarian. Tolstoy expects his audience to know Rousseau, be familiar with European culture, and so forth. The contemporary reader may have fared little better than Nekhlyudov in making conversation with a common street singer. In other words, there is a limit to the comparisons we can make between the art in the story (the singer's song) and the art of the story. Nevertheless, "Lucerne" is strangely prophetic: just as the poor singer blames his own failings rather than his audience, so too would Tolstoy blame himself for the missteps of his literary career (among them, in his mind, "Lucerne," but also stories of about the same time and theme, such as "Albert" [1858] and "Family Happiness" [1859]). "Lucerne" is considered (by critics as well as by Tolstoy himself) to be one of his early failures, but that does not mean that the literary methods used in it were subsequently rejected. Tolstoy simply improved on them.

Recall that "Lucerne" begins in fact not with expansive nature descriptions, but with the private gesture of a diary: first the date, "8th July, 1857," then a first-person framing sentence: "Last night I arrived at Lucerne, and put up at the Schweizerhof, the best hotel."[23] The story ends, however, with a universalizing philosophical diatribe, tempered only by a slight first-person corrective gesture ("'No,' I said to myself involuntarily"),[24] weakened further still by the reflexive verb (*сказалось*), that harmonizes human and universal law. While ostensibly directed at the narrator himself, the addressee of the diatribe is clearly the reader, who has been following a story about how one person cannot make contact with others. At one point the porter mutters, "What is the use of talking? [Э! Что говорит!]."[25] This could be said of the whole story, which ponders how art forges (or does not forge) connections among people. As Galina Galagan says, it is the "*artificial* integrity of the world of people" the story subjects to the narrative process.[26]

Late in *Anna Karenina*, Anna exclaims to herself: "How is it possible to tell another what one feels?"[27] She loses her ability to communicate meaningfully with others: perhaps she is to blame, perhaps others are to blame. But it matters little, because Tolstoy apportions linguistic ability through romance in the novel. Authentic love facilitates near superhuman abilities to communicate; illicit love, by contrast, nearly always renders lovers painfully mute. Anna's case is not a general one, at least not in the way she thinks it is. She mistakes her particular situation for the human condition. Anna's isolation is self-imposed, in large part, and not a philosophical statement on the existential loneliness of human beings in the world. In fact, part of her problem toward the end of the novel is that she assumes everyone else feels the way she does; and because she fails to speak sincerely with anyone, she finds no counterargument to her generalizations.

Nekhlyudov's isolation in "Lucerne," however, undermines our preconceptions of how well or easily we can break through our isolation to reach other human beings in some meaningful way. This isolation is often a conventional barrier in travel narratives, which seek mutually comprehensible aspects of different cultures and places where mutual comprehension may occur. "Lucerne" adopts this convention. Although his isolation is also more or less self-imposed, Nekhlyudov intends his experiments in crossing social boundaries and eliminating differences to have a much more profound, even universal, effect. He notes early on how the other (mainly English) guests have "a reserve [literally, 'incommunicativeness'] not based on pride, but on the absence of any necessity for intimacy."[28] And yet, putting his Anglophobia aside, he is willing to acknowledge that "not all these frozen people are stupid and unfeeling, on the contrary many of them, no doubt, have an inner life just such as my own, and in many of them it may be much more complex and interesting."[29] All the more surprising, he reasons, that they seem to have no interest in sharing their inner worlds with other people. Tolstoy's formal treatment of the English and the Swiss differs little from how he will treat the more "exotic" cultures of the Caucasus. In each place, the hero remains alienated from the local population.

One can retell the basic plot of "Lucerne" in a very simple way: the narrator ponders a city he is newly arrived in; he tries and fails to connect with other people; he notices another person who also fails to connect (verbally, not musically) with others; he tries to befriend that person and yet fails to establish grounds for mutual understanding; the narrator thus subsequently addresses comments to himself as a generalized interlocutor.[30] Failure to understand is the theme that permeates the work. If the story itself is also a failure in some way, then we can say, with a modicum of seriousness, that it succeeds in its task. By breaking the conventions of fiction, moreover, Tolstoy forces readers to consider his art seriously as moral teaching. It is not a story, it is life.[31]

At first, however, nature seems to provide a model by which art will bring everything together: "All the confused and involuntary impressions of life suddenly received for me meaning and charm."[32] One may imagine that individuals each have their own separate inner worlds, which verbal language is often inadequate to render, but nothing of the sort could be true of music: "They all seemed to experience the same sensation I did, and they all silently stood around the singer, and listened attentively. All was quiet".[33] And, as long as the music lasts, one can easily imagine that no difference, let alone cultural difference, separates one person from another or from the world at large. The Russian captures this perfectly, as the repetition of "all or everyone [все]" becomes "all or everything [все]," typographically indistinguishable in modern orthography but distinct in Tolstoy's time.[34]

Once the music ends, however, misunderstanding returns and, worse, so too does the humiliation of one human being by another. The singer asks for money and is met by silence: "And again [he] said his incomprehensible phrase: '*Messieurs et Mesdames, si vous croyez que je gagne quelque chose—*' which he evidently considered very smart and witty, but in his voice and movements I now detected a certain hesitation and childlike timidity which were especially striking with his small stature."[35] Notice not only how the singer fails to find the correct phrase (the fact that Nekhlyudov analyzes him first in terms of his command of French signals Nekhlyudov's own class-based empathetic limitations), but also how his body and demeanor are affected by his linguistic competence.

Because the singer is misunderstood by the crowd, as Nekhlyudov is by the English, Nekhlyudov believes he shares a common experience with him: "I was totally confused. . . . I felt pained, grieved, and above all ashamed for the little man, for the crowd, and for myself, *as if it were I* who had been asking for money and had received nothing, and had been laughed at."[36] But empathy alone is not sturdy enough grounds for mutual comprehension in language. The misunderstanding is contagious, for after he befriends the singer, Nekhlyudov himself is scarcely understood for the rest of the story:

- "He [the singer] did not understand my remark."
- "The waiter did not understand me and my German speech was wasted on him. The rude porter tried to take the waiter's part, but I attacked him so vehemently that he pretended that he, too, did not understand me and waved his hand."
- "The singer presented a most piteous, frightened appearance and, evidently without understanding why I was excited or what I was aiming at, begged me to go away quickly."[37]

When all fail to understand him, or pretend they cannot understand him, Nekhlyudov begins to address himself as he walks: "'There it is, the strange fate of art [poetry]!' I reflected."[38] But one feels drawn to challenge Nekhlyudov's interpretation: is this really the strange fate of art or poetry?

Nekhlyudov's inner conversation uses the second-person form of address for much of the remainder of the story, and his soliloquy is meant primarily as an indictment of would-be friends of English tourists and other scoundrels. Perhaps music really is the only form of reliable communication, one assumes. The ending of the story seems to imply such a conclusion. "At that moment, in the dead stillness of the night, I heard somewhere in the far distance the little man's guitar and voice."[39] That is to say, art itself is the rejoinder to the narrator's tirade. The narrator adds, however: "And who knows the inner happiness that resides in the souls of each of these people?"[40] As it turns out, only God knows, Nekhlyudov reasons at the end, in an explicit deus ex machina. The story endeavors to find grounds for connectedness and fails. In future stories, love will replace music as the grounds not only for connectedness but also for communication.

True, God is one way to solve the dilemma of communication posed by "Lucerne." Descartes similarly turns to God in order to ground his first principles of epistemology in the *Meditations*. Another, more plain, allusion here is (as in *Anna Karenina*) to Derzhavin's poem "God" and its apophaticism. Nekhlyudov exclaims: "Only to you, insignificant worm, who rashly and wrongly try to penetrate His laws and His intentions—only to you do they seem contradictions [Только тебе, ничтожному червяку, дерзко, беззаконно пытающемуся проникнуть его законы, его намерения, только тебе кажутся противоречия]."[41] The key line from Derzhavin is: "I am a king—I am a slave— I am a worm—I am God! [Я царь—я раб—я червь—я бог!]," and the stanza containing that line begins "I am the connection to worlds existing everywhere [Я связь миров, повсюду сущих]." Unity of people in the story may fail to hold, but Tolstoy manages to convey a complex message about communication via his final volley of allusions.[42] Mutual understanding is possible, and that may be the most important point about the story. As I read it, "Lucerne" is about failure to communicate; as it fails, it also succeeds to some extent. Yet art, perhaps art alone, facilitates communication, whether it be listening to music or understanding a dense network of literary allusions and self-referentiality. Strangely, following this logic, we may conclude that Tolstoy trusts his reading audience in general more than his fellow man or woman in particular.

The younger Tolstoy likened authentic love to music, even though he recognized it was a cliché analogy; and this connection between love and music anticipates how he would go on to describe the communicative capacity of language in both licit and illicit love affairs. His affectionate letters from 1856 provide a telling example. Consider the following "love" letter to Valeriya Arsenyeva, written about three months before "Lucerne." In letters to Arsenyeva, whom he considered marrying, Tolstoy referred to the part of him that wanted to fall romantically in love as *"the foolish man* [глупый человек]," whom he opposed to the more reserved and practical Tolstoy himself.[43]

Forgive me this foolish comparison: to love as *the foolish man* does is to play a sonata without keeping time, without accents, with the pedal always down, but with *feeling*, giving no true pleasure thereby either to oneself or to others. But in order to allow oneself to give way to the feeling of the music, one must first hold oneself in check, work and work hard—and believe me there is no pleasure to be had in life without doing so. But the harder the work and the privation, the higher the reward. And the hard work ahead of us is enormous—to understand each other and to retain each other's love and respect. Do you really think that if we had given way to *the foolish man's* feelings we should have understood each other now? We might have thought so, but later we would have noticed a huge gulf, and having wasted our feelings on foolish endearments we should have nothing left to fill it up with. I guard my feelings like a treasure, because they alone are capable of uniting us firmly in all our views on life, and without this there is no love. In this respect I expect a great deal from our correspondence; we shall discuss things calmly; I shall try to fathom every word of yours and you will do the same, and I don't doubt that we shall understand each other.[44]

The same contradictions one finds in "Lucerne" are evident here. Tolstoy insists that Arsenyeva understand how difficult it will be for them to understand one another. Yet emotion itself is not enough—to play the sonata with feeling may still mean to play badly. One must have skill. To give in, one must hold back—a modulation of spatial metaphor we have encountered frequently while examining Tolstoy's narrative alibi. As in "Lucerne," Tolstoy deflates the Romantic expectation that emotion itself, or its unskillful expression, suffices to bring people together. There is no tragedy in the failure to communicate, only failure itself, an inability to perform well enough.

The passages of *Anna Karenina* dealing with Koznyshev and Varenka begin almost paradigmatically with the perfect verbal clarity achieved by a man in love. Koznyshev has only to mention that he would like to join everyone for mushroom picking for all to know that he intends to propose to Varenka: "The intellectual and learned Koznyshev's offer to go and gather mushrooms with Varenka confirmed several conjectures that had greatly occupied Kitty's mind of late."[45] The women, except for Varenka, begin to discuss different wedding proposals. Dolly sees the similarity among them, which is that when a man proposes, "there is a sort of barrier, and suddenly down it goes."[46] All is implicitly understood. As Kitty talks to Levin about the impending proposal, he does not even bother to phrase his thoughts carefully, because "he knew at such loving moments as the present his wife would understand what he meant from a mere hint, and she did understand him."[47] Does this sound like the hard work of communication with which Tolstoy threatened Arsenyeva?

When Koznyshev and Varenka enter the woods, crucially, each is represented as being at one with nature. Here is the Romantic ideal Nekhlyudov might have imagined. Koznyshev steps behind a bush and pauses, "knowing that he could no longer be seen";[48] he becomes part of the environment. He sees sunbeams playing through the branches, and "the graceful form of Varenka in her yellow dress . . . merged into one with the view that had so struck him with its beauty."[49] She, too, merges with the surrounding nature. What could go wrong? There is true love, as both admit, and even rationality cannot intrude, as Koznyshev reflects: "If I had chosen by reason alone, I could find nothing better."[50] Just as he is about to propose, however, she speaks of mushrooms; he follows her comment with a response suited to it; and thus they continue speaking of mushrooms, until the moment for proposals has passed for good.

Nevertheless—and here is the key point—Koznyshev and Varenka continue to understand one another as lovers do. The failure of the proposal is not a failure of communication but an instance of the misery of convention, which now has its way with the unlucky couple.[51] "Both he and she understood that all was over, and that what ought to have been said would not be said, and their excitement, having reached its climax, began to subside."[52] By rationalizing in their conversation not their emotions, necessarily, but nature (even the modest mushroom), Koznyshev and Varenka shatter the near-mystical unity of nature, self, and the transparent language that describes both. To be at one with nature, as both Koznyshev and Varenka are early in this scene, is to play the sonata with feeling alone, but without skill and work. They betray their love because they think it will develop on its own.

8

ANNA INCOMMUNICADA

"How they looked at me, as at something dreadful, incomprehensible, and strange! . . . What can he be telling that other man so warmly?" [Anna] thought, glancing at two pedestrians. "How is it possible to tell another what one feels?"

—Anna Karenina

Most readers of Tolstoy will recognize the tragic and angry meditation here as characteristic of Anna's final hours. Everything seems "dreadful" and "incomprehensible" to her as she loses herself in feelings of loneliness and estrangement. Anna's thoughts reveal her isolation from the rest of the world and lead her to believe that "to tell another what one feels," to foster genuine communication would be a sort of miracle.[1]

Chernyshevsky coined the term *inner monologue* for Tolstoy's technique of describing "the secret process through the mediation of which a thought or a feeling is worked out."[2] But Anna's final impressions go a step beyond the psychological perspicuity of the inner monologue, and the rendering of her thoughts in this scene is justly recognized as something approximating the "stream of consciousness" technique employed by later writers such as James Joyce and Virginia Woolf. Anna's stream of consciousness translates her outer silence—an inability to communicate—into the inner noise of her solipsistic detachment. This ambiguous relationship between consciousness and communication suggests that, as Anna loses control over the determination of meaning in external forms of discourse, she also becomes incapable of using language as an internal vehicle of rational thought and self-understanding. When we consider her death, then, we must recognize that *Anna Karenina* is not just Tolstoy's greatest love story; it is his greatest language story.

Tolstoy's novel seems a precursor to some twentieth-century thought and much modernist fiction in that he recognizes that consciousness is shot through with myriad linguistic forms. But Tolstoy is never willing to leave the integrity of personal identity to the unwieldy nature of ordinary, communicative language. Thought relies on no single language, Tolstoy seems to say, but on multiple languages, some of which are more trustworthy and more likely to lead to authentic ways of thinking than others.[3] The inherent variability in a language's capacity for authentic thought opens a door to relativism in Tolstoy's fictional world. Some kinds of language lend themselves more readily to the constitution of a moral self than do others, just as some kinds of love lead to happiness and others do not. Most important, though, is Tolstoy's notion that through love, language achieves its greatest transparency and availability of meaning.

The ethical implications of language in the constitution of self are visible throughout *Anna Karenina* but may be seen clearly in three examples: paradox, what I will call "translation," and prayer. Consider Stiva's paradox, "And worst of all is that it's all my own fault—my own fault and yet I'm not to blame."[4] As one element of paradox cancels out the other, so, too, does the proclamation of innocence undermine Stiva's claim of responsibility. Like paradox, Stiva's speech habits (and his thinking) sometimes carry little meaning beyond the event of their utterance. This is particularly true of Stiva at the beginning of the novel, where he "wakes" to a life of forgetfulness. Like other characters, however, Stiva assumes the admirable role later on in the novel of desymbolizing Anna's language; in effect, he begins to translate, or communicate, for her.

Stiva's reaction to one of Anna's suicide threats characterizes this flexible and ethically more positive relationship to language. On this occasion, Anna calls herself "an overstrained string that must snap," and warns that "it will end horribly."[5] Stiva's response to this threat is threefold. First, he answers her in her own language: "We must let the string be loosened, little by little."[6] Next, he translates her crisis into a socially acceptable idiom: "I'll begin from the beginning. You married a man twenty years older than yourself. You married him without love and not knowing what love was. It was a mistake, let's say."[7] Finally, by using the word *ошибка*, "mistake," Stiva bridges the communicative gap that is widening between Anna and others. The concept of error is acceptable to both sides; everybody makes mistakes. Anna need not take full responsibility for her actions, and society need not interpret her behavior as a total break with convention. Stiva confirms his new role as translator and intermediary by offering to procure for Anna a divorce from Karenin.

More than any other form of language in the novel, prayer is especially valuable in the constitution of an ethical self.[8] Prayer and self-assessment intersect frequently in Tolstoy's fiction. Two of the most famous examples may be found in *War and Peace*: when Princess Marya prays before the icon in her room and when Natasha begins to pray fervently in church. In *Anna Karenina*, prayer is most often associated with Levin, who, for example, breaks into prayer while Kitty is giving birth. Though he has often proclaimed himself an unbeliever, Levin is transported in this scene by his sudden devoutness, and only later does he realize that this relapse into prayer crystallized his understanding of his role and responsibilities. In less conventional ways, the language of prayer also touches Anna's life.

The story of Anna's loss of identity (initiated primarily by the consummation of her affair with Vronsky) and of her death is framed on both sides by prayer, which for Tolstoy often serves as an ideal form for other languages of self-understanding. In the postcoital scene we get a "false" prayer. Anna feels "so guilty, so much to blame, that it only remained for her to humble herself and ask to be forgiven; but she had no one in the world now except him, so that even her prayer of forgiveness was addressed to him."[9] Aside from the blasphemy implied here, Anna's identity, her determination of self, is formulated from this point forward in the novel within the relativistic world, in Tolstoy's view, of secular languages. Unlike prayer, these languages function primarily as a means of communication and thus make the constitution of a self within them dependent on social, and therefore potentially suspect, "forms of life."[10] Meaning for the self in such a world is temporary and mutable.

The second instance of prayer, and this time it is genuine prayer, occurs when Anna crosses herself out of habit and then jumps underneath the train. This prayer reverses the consequences of the first and restores to Anna her lost sense of self: "The familiar gesture of making the sign of the cross called up a whole series of girlish and childish memories, and suddenly the darkness, that obscured everything for her, broke, and life showed itself to her for an instant with all its bright past joys."[11] Prayer in this last instance—making the sign of the cross—evokes in Anna a series of memories that are clearly central to her momentary recovery of self; memory functions as one of the cornerstones of personal identity, uniting the often-interrupted flow of consciousness. For Tolstoy prayer assesses, glances backward and forward, and unites the self in a context of the divine.[12]

Thus prayer is connected with memory; memory provides the primary meeting ground for consciousness and truth in the novel, as, for example, when Levin cuts short his tirade against Stiva because he has remembered his own past transgressions (however minor they may have been).[13] Here Stiva accuses him of being "too much of a piece."[14] "Well, you see *you* are very consistent," said Oblonsky. "It is both a virtue and a fault in you. You have a consistent character yourself and you wish all the facts of life to be consistent, but they never are,"[15] which accusation goes to show that, for Levin, an authentic self is bound inextricably with honesty. This overanxious desire for consistency is one of Levin's "positive" faults.

Several languages in *Anna Karenina* seem to preclude the activity of memory; they take place within an impersonal time of abstract discourse. Consider again the language of paradox associated with Stiva early in the novel. Paradox frequently arrests the ability of language to transport the agent through time and to facilitate the kind of memory of self that is central to personal identity. The movement of paradox is circular; it continually cuts back on itself, as is evident in any of the versions of the liar's paradox: This statement is false. The paradox of Stiva's "honesty"—"he was an honest man with himself"[16]—thus both explains and condemns his forgetfulness, which makes it seem to him that he is honest and also makes genuine honesty on this occasion impossible.

A couple of famous instances of nonagency in the novel are connected with Stiva: his opinions "imperceptibly changed of themselves,"[17] and he is especially fond of his valet Matthew's phrase that "things will shape themselves [образуется]."[18] By contrast, when Stiva intercedes for Anna with Karenin—that is, when he becomes an "agent" in both the linguistic and ordinary senses of the word—he suddenly feels the weight of responsibility upon him: "The feeling [embarrassment] was so unexpected and so strange that he did not believe it was the voice of conscience telling him that what he was about to do was wrong."[19] The Russian word in this passage for "embarrassment" (*смущение*) is frequently used in the novel to describe Levin's awkwardness in society—excessive ease in society, though enviable, often suggests falsity in *Anna Karenina*, Stiva benefits from this descriptive association with Levin. It is an indication that he is remembering, rather than forgetting, himself, when he approaches Karenin about the divorce.

Anna differs from Stiva in that she consistently searches for a language of self that will, first, serve as a bulwark against society's attempts to define her and, second, provide her ever more vacuous life with some sort of meaning, however fleeting. Meaning is the important term here, because, having lost the absolute understanding of God as interlocutor in prayer, Anna ends up relying upon the other in the communicative act to help her determine her own identity. Jones writes: "However we conceive of the fundamental nature of Anna's tragedy, we shall miss a great deal if we do not also see it at least in part as a tragedy of communication."[20] When viewed from this perspective, Anna's progression toward insanity can be charted by her progressive loss of languages of communication: verbal, nonverbal, written, and symbolic.[21]

Several passages suggest that Anna gradually loses the ability to communicate verbally (especially to people other than Vronsky). This is clear in the scene which follows the physical consummation of her affair: "She felt that at that moment she could not express in words her feeling of shame, joy, and horror at this entrance on a new life, and she did not wish to vulgarize that feeling with inaccurate words. Later on, the next day and the next, she not only could not find words with which she would be able to express all the complexity of those feelings, but could not even find thoughts with which she would be able to reflect on all that was in her soul."[22] Of initial importance is the fact that these lines are immediately preceded by the "prayer of forgiveness" I cited earlier. The succession of the two passages confirms that Anna's loss of language begins here, as does the journey to outer silence and inner noise. It is also significant that these dramatic feelings of "shame, joy, and horror," which Anna cannot verbalize, should then come out in her dreams. Not only does she have no control over her feelings here, but they are trapped in the private forum of her mind: they never surface in communication and therefore have no context within which she might determine their meaning. Dreams become part of a symbolic language that Anna relies on heavily later in the novel.

When Anna does verbalize "all that is in her soul" to Karenin after the race in which Vronsky has fallen, she encounters something infinitely worse than her husband's obstinacy—her words, in effect, disappear, as Karenin's letter refuses to acknowledge them: "She had that morning repented of what she had said to her husband and wished only that those words could be unsaid. And now this letter acknowledged them unsaid and was giving her what she wished. But now the letter appeared more terrible than anything she could have imagined."[23] Why does the letter appear more terrible now? By refusing to acknowledge what Anna has told him, Karenin denies his role as interlocutor and therefore also the "definiteness [определенность]" which Anna almost achieved in this communicative act. The word *определенность*, which echoes throughout the novel in Anna's consciousness, has the connotation of "meaning" and derives from the word for "limit" or "boundary" (*предел*). Anna is quick to point out how much this "definiteness" (or "defined-ness") depends not only on herself but on others as well. She reacts by saying that it would have been better if Karenin had killed her, thereby unwittingly recalling the murder imagery of the postcoital scene with Vronsky. And by carefully dissecting her language in his letter, Karenin does manage to kill Anna, the old Anna.

Anna responds to her failure to communicate verbally by relying increasingly upon different forms of communication (written, nonverbal and symbolic): the fact that Karenin has, in a letter, easily disposed of her words is not lost on her. Within hours she successfully smuggles a note to Vronsky in Betsy's letter. Both Anna and Vronsky are more comfortable when they can transmit important messages indirectly, as when Stiva first asks Karenin to grant Anna the divorce and Vronsky implores Dolly to convince Anna to write to Karenin. The more Anna relies on others to communicate for her, however, the more she relinquishes control over the way in which various linguistic acts define her and her position. We think, for example, of the carelessness with which Stiva asks Karenin a second time, late in the novel, to grant her a divorce.

Anna's adventures with the written word are comic, tragic, and mostly unsuccessful. Anna writes many letters and notes that fail to achieve their desired results: her note to Vronsky telling him to visit her at home while Karenin is at Council leads to an unexpected meeting between the two Alexeis; her letter to Lydia Ivanovna requesting permission to see Serezha receives no answer at first and then receives an insulting refusal; her contradictory and misleading letter to Vronsky when he is attending the elections engenders his mistrust so that he grows cooler toward her; when she finally writes to Karenin about a divorce, she receives no answer; and her final note and telegram to Vronsky are tragically mistimed. Perhaps the only thing she writes successfully is her children's book, the most openly aesthetic form of written communication she attempts. Yet it remains unfinished.

The more aesthetic the form, the more expertly Anna uses it. That is why the method of nonverbal communication she cultivates in her new life with Vronsky is at first so effective, for the nonverbal unites the aesthetic perfection of Anna's beauty and social grace with the semantic capabilities of a language. She makes similar use of her portraits, as when she "bewitches" Levin, to use Kitty's word (*обворожила*), late in the novel.[24] Nonetheless, the language of looks and gestures has only a limited potential for the communication of important ideas, and still less is it able to express that crucial "complexity of feelings" in Anna's soul, which most requires language's power of clarity and definition.[25] The nature of this nonverbal communication and its relationship to an aesthetics of imitation shape the thematic content of the first chapters on Anna and Vronsky's life in Italy.

When Vronsky meets an old schoolmate, Golenischchev, and wants to introduce him to Anna, the significant looks the three of them exchange act as a means of identifying the way each understands Anna and Vronsky's position. The expression on Golenishchev's face tells Vronsky that the former has an "appropriate understanding" of Vronsky's relationship with Anna. The wording of this phrase in Russian, "какое должно понимание," blends together a sense of both decorum and responsibility. Tolstoy quickly gives the lie to this understanding:

"But if [Vronsky], and those who understood 'appropriately,' had been asked what this understanding amounted to, both he and they would have had great difficulty [responding]."[26] The question here, particularly as it relates to Anna, is whether gesture, manner, and look are capable of communicating, and therefore creating, genuine understanding, or whether these nonverbal means merely conceal a lack of understanding. More broadly, can they sustain the level of intimate communication necessary for her love affair with Vronsky?

Only the veil of genuine communication is evident when Golenishchev, responding to Anna's facial expression and manner, believes he "understands her completely." "It seemed to him that he understood that which she herself did not understand: namely how, having caused her husband's unhappiness, having abandoned him and her son and lost her good name, she was able to feel energetically cheerful and happy."[27] Inasmuch as Anna does not understand her new life and position, she is bound to rely more heavily on superficial modes of communication. She, Vronsky, and whoever happens to be with them, often appear to be playing roles.

This superficial understanding, which is based on nonverbal communication, reappears thematically in the next chapter, where we are told about Vronsky's "understanding" of painting—that is, his aesthetics of imitating art. Having grown bored with his new life, and unable to tell Anna this, Vronsky transfers his "desire for desires" onto painting. "He had a talent for understanding art and for imitating it with accuracy and good taste, and he imagined that he possessed that which is necessary for an artist."[28] When he paints Anna, we might say that here, too, Vronsky is imitating art; for in many respects Anna aestheticizes her life and becomes art in the novel.

Like Vronsky, Anna transposes emotions she does not understand and cannot communicate onto an aesthetic realm. After her pathetic visit to Serezha, Anna returns home, but "for a long time could not understand why she was there."[29] Unsatisfied with her feelings toward her daughter, she opens her locket with Serezha's portrait inside and pulls out of an album various pictures of him. When Vronsky walks in, first he turns to the pictures of Serezha and then he turns to Anna. Whereas Anna has previously used Stiva as a verbal intermediary, and Betsy's letter as a written one, now she uses pictures of Serezha as a means of communicating her unhappiness to Vronsky. Earlier in the novel when she contemplates taking Serezha and running away from Karenin, Anna enters the drawing room and sees the following: "Serezha, dressed all in white, was standing by a table under a looking-glass, and arranging some flowers he had brought."[30] All that would be necessary here is the image of "Anna as artist" in the mirror's reflection to perfect the implied self-referential composition (*Still*

Life with Child and Looking-Glass). Anna's gestures toward Serezha's pictures are similar in function to the way she uses her own portraits to communicate.

Later that day, when Anna attends the opera and the eyes of everyone are upon her as she stands at the front of her box, she herself resembles a picture in a frame (one of the reasons the title of Amy Mandelker's book, *Framing Anna Karenina*, is so apt). And although earlier in the day Vronsky did not understand the look on Anna's face, could not fathom why she wanted to go to the opera, now as he sees the utterly tranquil look on her face he perfectly understands, or believes he understands, the humiliation she is feeling. The system of nonverbal signs Anna relies upon imitates communication, just as Vronsky's painting imitates art. In genuine communication, as in the genuine art of Mikhailov's painting, a process of revelation is possible, "a removal of the coverings" from one's emotional self. The goal of communication in Tolstoy's romantic narratives is to let fewer obstacles get in the way of mutual comprehension.

Soon, Anna's inability to define those feelings of "shame, joy, and horror" becomes less a problem of communication than an emotional and psychological imperative. Failure to understand the other eventually harms one's ability to understand oneself. For Anna the act of articulating her emotions has been a necessity from the start, not in order that others understand her (others already believe that they do), but in order that she understand herself and her "new life." This is why Dolly's visit to Vozdvizhenskoe at first seems so important to Anna: Vronsky's estate represents yet another new start, after the debacle at the opera in St. Petersburg, and Dolly's visit gives Anna the opportunity to discuss her "position."

When Dolly tells her that she has no view on Anna's position and that one should love people as they are, not as they might be, "Anna, turning her eyes away from her friend and screwing them up (this was a new habit of hers and unfamiliar to Dolly), grew thoughtful, trying thoroughly to understand fully the meaning of these words. And evidently having understood them in the sense she wished, she glanced at Dolly."[31] This passage underscores an important development. Ever since the scene at the opera house, Anna has begun to divert her eyes in important conversations. This action, along with her new habit of screwing up her eyes, suggest a growing inability to comprehend the nonverbal communication that previously smoothed over the lack of definition in her life. Not only does she not hear Dolly correctly, she does not read her correctly, and she interprets the meaning of Dolly's words in her own private sense.

In fact, as if to make up for her growing inability to understand the language of gestures and looks, Anna has become a voracious reader of books. After she returns from her conversation with Dolly, one in which Vronsky has significantly asked Dolly to bring up the divorce, Anna misinterprets Vronsky's "questioning look" as a sign that he is feeling amorous. And though she may be losing her capability to interpret Vronsky's body language, Anna knows the right answers to his questions on agriculture and farming—she has been reading, "with the attention one gives only to what one reads in solitude,"[32] books and technical papers on subjects that interest him. What is important here is that Anna's successful participation in already crippled modes of communication has become occasional. Because understanding certain questions correctly means utter devastation, misinterpretation is not so much an option for Anna as it is a necessity.

It is striking how many times, in their last months together, Anna misinterprets Vronsky's looks and facial expressions. Consider, for example, the argument that erupts after Anna and Vronsky have received the telegram in which Stiva expresses his doubts about the possibility of divorce. Vronsky says he is interested in news of the divorce because he likes definiteness.

> "You want [the divorce] for the children, but you don't think of me," [Anna] pursued, quite forgetting or not hearing that he said: "for your own sake and for the children." . . .
>
> "Oh, I said for your sake! Most of all for your sake," he repeated, his face contorted as with pain, "because I am convinced that a great deal of your irritability is due to our indefinite position."
>
> "Yes, there it is! Now he has stopped pretending, and all his cold hatred for me is apparent," she thought, not listening to his words, but gazing with horror at the cold and cruel judge who looked out of his eyes provokingly.[33]

This passage highlights many of the themes addressed up to this point. To begin with, by sending the telegram, Stiva continues in his role as intermediary between Anna and Karenin. Anna is in another conversation about the "definition" of her situation. This time Anna, not Karenin, is the one who refuses to be the interlocutor, who refuses to acknowledge what the other is saying. Moreover, she mistakes the frustration in Vronsky's eyes for a sign that he hates her. Anna now lives wholly by a poetics of suspicion—believing that all action is pretense that needs exposure in order to be interpreted correctly. Here she believes that Vronsky has finally "stopped pretending." Most important, the outer forms of Anna's discourse—verbal, nonverbal, written—which I have been associating with her failed attempts to create a new identity, are now replaced by a depiction of her stream of thought, which characterizes both her emotional isolation and fractured sense of self.

Because the nonverbal language Anna and Vronsky have grown accustomed to using is highly aesthetic, even contorted into various codes, understanding is often described as the end result of multiple acts of "suspicious" decoding, rather than as the immediate comprehension of more transparent forms of communication that serve as an ideal in the novel. In other words, language becomes cipher, and an intervening poetics of suspicion operates both in self-understanding and in understanding the other. Anna could check with someone to see whether she is interpreting things correctly, had she anyone with whom to check. As it is, the only interpretive model she can consult, aside from the system of signs she has developed with Vronsky, which seems to mask genuine understanding, comes from Vronsky's gambler-friend Yashvin, who spouts a crude sort of social Darwinism: "He who sits down to play against me, wishes to leave me without a shirt, and I treat him the same! So we struggle, and therein lies the pleasure."[34] It is in terms of this "struggle" that Anna uses her "bright light" to analyze her relationships with Dolly, Kitty, and Vronsky. Anna's suspicions are a model of language for her.

The bitter irony of the final sequence of Anna's stream of consciousness is that, even as she is being driven to her death by the hateful discourse carried on in her mind, when we read and understand her most intimate thoughts, we engage in an implicit refutation of those very thoughts. We do understand her, and our understanding negates Anna's rhetorical question, "How is it possible to tell another what one feels?" and fosters a sense of tragedy: that her death was avoidable. Thus the novel communicates what Anna herself cannot.

Anna Karenina is an early example of the kind of modernist literature that purposely complicates supposedly transparent connections between language and consciousness. Mandelker also emphasizes this modern side of Tolstoy: "By creating a series of framed portraits of Anna—texts within text—[Tolstoy] repeatedly arrests his narrative flow in order to frame his heroine and alert the reader to the existence of the frame of beauty, corporeality, and the marketplace of both, that confines her. Tolstoy thus conflates the aesthetic question and the woman question in a manner that places him among the Symbolists rather than the realists."[35] Whether Tolstoy was a Symbolist or not, he criticized received realist paradigms in ways that we have come to associate with modernism.

The relation of modernism to the disjunction of language and consciousness is part of Anna's story, for it is she, rather than Levin, who experiences the full force of Tolstoy's criticism of realist aesthetics.[36] She is the embodiment of transgression against the conventional in the novel, a fact that by itself need not force us either to condemn or to celebrate her infidelity. Simply, when we speak of Tolstoy's modernism in *Anna Karenina*, we are speaking mostly, though not exclusively, about Anna. From my point of view, Anna's loss of language(s) reveals Tolstoy's growing fear that language is no longer capable of disclosing and conveying immutable truths about oneself and about the world. *Anna Karenina* is a turning point. Soon afterward, Tolstoy ceases to allow love to determine whether meaning is really present or deceptively present. All appearance is now treated as false; all conventions misleading. Anna's suspicious view of the world infects even her author.

As is well known, after his supposed conversion Tolstoy became enormously preoccupied with the Gospels, so much so that he undertook *A Translation and Harmonization of the Four Gospels*.[37] In the long career preceding this turn to the sacred language of the Gospels (and after it) Tolstoy was equally fascinated with charting the boundaries of non-"absolute," secular languages in his great works of fiction. He continually inquired into the capacity of these languages to constitute a self that still remains grounded in truth. Anna's romance is at the center of such an investigation into language; her tortuous passage through various communicative languages circumscribes the privileged forms of language in the novel that disclose the truth, facilitate a recollection of self, and yield complete understanding in communication.

The biblical epigraph, "Vengeance is mine; I will repay," the instances of prayer placed like bookends on either side of Anna's "fall," and the unthinkably perfect communication that brings Levin and Kitty together and that stands in stark contrast to Vronsky and Anna's oblique codes, all suggest that Anna's identity is compromised by the languages she is forced to use and which prevent such things as disclosure of truth, recollection of self, and complete understanding. On the one hand, the language of the "stream of consciousness" that best characterizes the content of her consciousness (for the reader) is highly subjective. On the other hand, language becomes alien and impersonal for Anna: she cannot adapt it to her own psychological needs. Both dramatize the difference between riddle and referent in Tolstoy's consideration of language for Anna.

Anna's identity is fractured by this paradox between highly subjective and highly impersonal forms of language, and she thus serves as a focal point for what is often considered a central modernist paradigm: that the traditional relation between the subject and the outside world, constituted by language's capacity to represent the world logically and transparently, is no longer tenable. In "Lucerne," this goal still seemed achievable in narrative art, and worth pursuing; by *Anna Karenina*, it is not. Levin, however, does not pay the same price as Anna for this modernist dilemma. Although he carries on what might be called Tolstoy's romance with authoritative languages, he does not find ultimate, immutable truths in these languages: he can sustain neither prayer nor perfect communication with Kitty, the wisdom of individual philosophies and religions escapes him, and his book on agriculture remains unfinished. Yet Levin, unlike Anna, does not commit suicide—he realizes that he has been "living rightly [жил хорошо]," and this saves him.[38]

"Living rightly," viewed within our linguistic context, seems like a completely unsatisfactory answer to the questions we have been posing with Anna. Are the problems of language and consciousness to be solved simply by silent, virtuous action? Not at all. Anna cannot repair her fragmented identity through language, because in Tolstoy's fictive universe, language, especially in instances of illicit romance, is itself often fragmented and untrustworthy. But personal identity need not rely exclusively on the unity of consciousness, whether this unity is conceived of linguistically or otherwise. That is why the modernist dilemma of the disjunction between language and consciousness is less important when we consider Levin. The self, in Levin's case, is treated differently, in a way that is in accord with realist rather than modernist paradigms.

Identity for Levin is found neither in the unity of subjective experience, consciousness, nor in the unity of the external facts of his existence. Here, the thread that binds Levin's life together into a meaningful whole derives from the consistency or honesty with which he lives his life; past ways of living are comparable, and require comparison, with the present way that life is lived. The unity of Levin's identity is not in him, or in his life, but in how he lives his life.[39] "Living rightly" thus only seems like an unsatisfactory answer to the questions we have been posing with Anna—rather, it is an answer, but to a different question. Whereas Anna has no past, or at least we find out little about her past in the novel, Levin's life on his estate is imbued with the past, with familial tradition. Naturally, this past makes demands on him—living rightly also means, for example, *loving* rightly—but in doing so it also provides his life with a meaning that does not have to be won from the chaos of language; it need only be preserved and nurtured. The danger of modernity in Levin's case is not linguistic but social. The encroachment of the culture of the city on the country, for example, is far more threatening. High society and politics in the capital celebrate the present and future in a way that causes Levin to worry that tradition will be effaced.

Because Anna is tested more rigorously than Levin is in the novel, one cannot help but conclude that in the end Tolstoy continues to privilege the novel's realist ideals. Sound relations between the subject and the outer world, even when they are established outside the rationality of language and thought, remain an estimable goal. Levin's epiphany that meaning is a product of living life and not of ratiocination leads him to accept, and (re)engage, reality. Later, in *A Confession*, Tolstoy will challenge the conciliatory, hopeful tone with which Levin ends the novel. Anna's anticommunicative aesthetics will go on to dominate much of Tolstoy's remaining belletristic literature; even if *What is Art?* condemns art that is unable to "infect," that adopts that anticommunicative aesthetics.

Part V

SUSPICIOUS STORIES

When romantic love goes bad for Tolstoy, language goes along with it. He decided that happiness could not be found in romantic love, and that therefore writing fiction that celebrated romantic love was immoral. I have argued throughout this study that Tolstoy's literary career is best separated into early and late periods, but that does not mean his aesthetic is forever sundered in two. In the romance narratives, early and late, the details of a love story in aristocratic society remain the same. But the late Tolstoy condemns what the early Tolstoy celebrated, and often repeats what he condemns, rather than passing over it in silence. The penultimate part of this study of Tolstoy is devoted to his destruction of the romantic narrative and its implicit aesthetics of communication. In these later stories Tolstoy uses his early oeuvre to contrast and redefine his later authorial identity entirely. We find many of the same devices as in the early work, but they have radically different meanings.

9

THE POETICS OF ROMANTIC BETRAYAL

"Now that is a thing I cannot understand," said the count.

"I know that you never understand what I say," began the countess, and went on, turning to Nekhlyudov, "Everybody understands me except my husband."

—Resurrection

THE BETRAYAL OF LANGUAGE: FROM "FAMILY HAPPINESS" TO *RESURRECTION*

For Tolstoy, love provides one with special abilities to speak and be understood, and in descriptions of love we find his most startling examples of communication. Contrariwise, the loss of love, the emergence of suspicion, infidelity, and betrayal, all take a terrible toll on communication. A jealous husband in Tolstoy's world has a difficult time communicating with his wife. Of course, that is nothing extraordinary to anyone who has ever been in love— groundless, or even well-grounded, suspicions somehow interfere with intimate conversations. Something more significant is at stake, however: the tenuous bond in Tolstoy's fiction between thought and language, and between intention and expression, is frequently seriously damaged as a consequence of doubt and jealousy.[1] Relationships between the unseen and the seen, the unspoken and spoken, the absent and the present are remarkably important for Tolstoy. They point to the very process of creativity, a process hobbled by the betrayal of love. The damage wrought by the betrayal of love—and Tolstoy's increasing pessimism that romantic love can sustain a person—signals a profound change in Tolstoy's aesthetics. The production of literary meaning itself is subject to doubt.

Pierre Brunel suggests that literary jealousy performs within the space of a hermeneutic hesitation: "Jealousy is neither healthy nor morbid in itself; it is not healthy in certain cases and morbid in others. But it exists as a constant hesitation between health and morbidity with which novelistic writing plays."[2] Real love does not hesitate. A moment's reflection will convince one that jealousy's hesitation is scarcely welcome in either literary or real-world romance. As Koznyshev and Varenka could attest, timing is everything. Jealousy shakes, for Tolstoy, that unsteady bridge between language and the world, intentionality in its broadest sense.[3] For Tolstoy, love and language both offer the possibility of transcending the self, which hesitation and suspicion render impossible.

This is not just a problem of romance for Tolstoy; it is also a fundamental problem of authorship and being. Suspicion eats away at the identifications a person forges between consciousness and expression: words no longer reveal the self but obscure it, and build, brick by verbal brick, a wall of interpretive confusion. For Tolstoy, the relationship between thought and language engenders mutually opposed theories of language as either revelation or cipher. Language transparently reveals the content of thought, like a glass onto the mind; or language encodes thought, making it a riddle that we must continually work to solve. The former vision of language serves the agenda of realism, which seeks to reveal the mechanisms of the mind and the world with the help of trustworthy language; the latter pays homage to Romantic conceptions of the self as tragically isolated, never rendered adequately accessible by imperfect words.

When suspicion intervenes, language as cipher operates both in self-understanding and in understanding the other. We begin to fear that consciousness itself conceals the truth. Paul Ricoeur writes of Nietzsche, Freud, and Marx: "What all three attempted, in different ways, was to make their 'conscious' methods of deciphering coincide with the 'unconscious' *work* of ciphering which they attributed to the will to power, to social being, to the unconscious psychism. *Guile will be met with double guile.*"[4] If the performance of language is itself deceptive, then perhaps treacherous diversion is necessary to understand it. No stranger to guile himself, Tolstoy generally considered such obfuscating consciousness the sign of a diseased rather than of a healthy mind, but he was willing to let his narratives be variously shaped by that disease. The romance narratives describe an etiology of expression.

This approach to language shares an attribute of the narrative alibi, as it accounts for absence in the productive process. Narrative marches on (in Tolstoy's case, sometimes for hundreds of pages) regardless of whether the language is inflected by deceptive riddles or not. The interpretive context of fiction offers Tolstoy an important venue for exploring the truth or authenticity values of opposing models of language; and romantic plotlines provide him with an opportunity to match his ideas of ethical behavior in love with an evolving philosophy of language. In the alibi of Tolstoy's romance narratives, the meaning of language is absent, deferred and encoded by illicit love.

Romance and its demise are at the center of the notions of self and society that Tolstoy valued most highly and continually tried to articulate. He tested not only his ideas of communication in the romance narratives but also his prized notions of community, and of how to form a community of love through love. "Lucerne" is an example of just such a failed community. More often we discuss nineteenth-century utopian ideas via Chernyshevsky and Dostoevsky. But Tolstoy also harbored visions of a perfect society, one governed neither by progress (the bête noir of *War and Peace* and *Notes from Underground*) nor politics, which lingers in the background of the major novels as an unrealistic escape for world-weary and otherwise misguided noblemen, such as Prince Andrei. Tolstoy sought utopia in love, and that is why his narratives of betrayal seem so cosmic.

These narratives of romantic betrayal chart a course through Tolstoy's fictional works along which a character may go from being merely delusional to being utterly mad. They reveal a hermeneutics of suspicion that at first asks one, in stories like "Family Happiness," simply to look past the obvious, but later demands that readers rewrite the story and, as in "The Kreutzer Sonata," match Pozdnyshev's proto-Freudianism with an interpretation that resists his initial act of encryption. From time to time, as readers, we need to be as suspicious as some of Tolstoy's characters. I believe that Pozdnyshev is, among other things, a deliberately deceptive storyteller, for example, and not the repentant wife killer he seems to be. Suspicion has deformed Tolstoy's very aesthetics.

To be in love is to live in a world where suspicion has no purpose. And yet the language of love at its most perfect is not therefore superfluous—rather it is unassailably transparent. In "Family Happiness" Masha remarks: "My love for my husband grew calmer, and I never wondered whether he loved me less. Indeed I could not doubt his love: every thought of mine was understood at once, every feeling shared, and every wish fulfilled by him."[5] This 1859 story narrates in the first person a young woman's growth into maturity—her romance with her husband, the temptations of infidelity, and her subsequent reconciliation not only with her husband but with the very idea of family life. The near perfection of understanding Masha experiences finds a match in the deservedly famous scene from *Anna Karenina* in which Levin and Kitty play their letter game; indeed they divine the thoughts of one another so well that it makes the reader somewhat incredulous. As Malcolm Jones puts it, "Some characters develop what seems to be almost a sixth sense about others with whom they have a particular relationship."[6] The letter game is worth considering, because it is often interpreted as a picture of love beyond language.

Conceived in such a way, language becomes literally an afterthought, possibly disruptive, so in concert are the movements of thought in the two lovers. As Tim Langen puts it, "The fantastically improbable proposal scene between Kitty and Levin is still a deeply satisfying emblem for the novel: they literally do *not* spell out their meanings, but instead trust one another to guess it. Spelling something out necessarily damages the contents, which is why Levin is so reluctant to discuss his feelings for Kitty."[7] Thus figured, language can become an obstacle to meaning, as Tyutchev would have it, "the spoken thought is a lie"; once approximated by language, the true thought is lost forever. But this reading of the letter game is not upheld by the rest of the novel. Levin eventually recognizes that love does not transcend language—after all, no matter how much he loves Kitty, he is never be able to divine her thoughts consistently— but that there is a workable, and work-intensive, relationship between the ideal and the quotidian. The sonata that Tolstoy described in his "love" letter to Arsenieva requires not just feeling but practice. In the end, he learns, love is a compromise between language and thought, just as marriage is a compromise between behavior and desire, reality and dreams for the future.

In Levin and Kitty's case, Tolstoy believes that language is infallibly capable of serving our communicative needs, but at other moments he seems to waver. As he grew older, Tolstoy trusted his ideal notions of language less and less, and gave into his suspicion that language was forever encoded. What was once an alibi became an algorithm of romantic misery. In *Resurrection*, for example, Nekhlyudov meets his sister after a long absence: "There passed between them that mysterious, indescribable, meaningful exchange of looks in which all was truth, and there began an exchange of words from which that truth was absent. They had not seen one another since their mother's death."[8] Even in this otherwise beautiful moment, a suspicious attitude toward language emerges, as though language and truth were utterly opposed to one another. This passage points not toward ideal communication, as one can read the language game between Kitty and Levin, but toward the total subsumption of language by falsifying convention, a nightmare of inexpressibility.

For most of his career, however, Tolstoy thought that language which emerged from strong and true love, a language of potential revelation rather than of riddles, could bring with it, ideally, clarity of self. This language fosters a kind of rebirth. Thought encounters thought in communication, perspectives shift and reform, and the world becomes a different place. In "Family Happiness" Masha remarks: "All my thoughts and feelings of that time were not really mine; they were his thoughts and feelings, which had suddenly become mine and passed into my life and lighted it up. Quite unconsciously I began to look at everything with different eyes."[9] Tolstoy here unmistakably recalls the language of religious conversion: reborn, one sees God's world and the self always in "a new light." Contrast that light with the "bright light" that Anna uses to see the world as inherently hateful; contrast that rebirth with the suspicious zealotry of Pozdnyshev's conversion in "The Kreutzer Sonata."

The betrayal and loss of love in Tolstoy's world invariably bring disaster; it is a death of language, rendering the subject incapable not only of eloquence but of understanding, and even, at the extreme, of ordinary communication. The most amusing example of this—it is really more of a parody of romance—is Pierre's proposal to Helene Kuragina in *War and Peace*, in which he allows himself to become engaged, though he knows he does not love her. Before they are married, Pierre can barely talk to Helene. He thinks that she is stupid and that she has had an affair with her brother; he wants to say something to her, but each time he can think only of her marble bust. Pierre's proposal is unique, because it is what he does not say—that is, that he does not want to marry Helene—that gets him married. To rephrase Austin and Searle, it is a "nonspeech" act.

In fact, throughout the novel, Pierre generally has too much to say, not too little, and so he is a good indicator of the linguistic dynamics I have in mind. Morson compares Pierre and Andrei: "Unlike Prince Andrei, Pierre has little mastery of language, but he has an inordinate respect for its power. For Andrei, one must escape [conventional] language to discover truth; for Pierre, one must embrace language, reach its essence, to discover truths hidden within its code. For one, language is a trap, for the other the profoundest mystery. If one only knew how to interpret the system, thinks Pierre, one could understand everything."[10] After his duel with Dolokhov, Pierre can "not conceive how he [is] going to speak to [Helene]," and when she confronts him, from anger he can do no more than make inarticulate noises, beg her not to speak to him, and finally shout: "I'm going to kill you!"[11] When we next meet Pierre, at the post station, he can neither hear, nor respond to questions, nor speak: "It was as though the mainscrew in his brain by which his whole life was fixed was loose. The screw moved no more forward, no more backward, but still it turned, catching on nothing, always in the same groove, and there was no making it cease turning."[12] Pierre's entire life, not just his language, has been thrown off by Helene's betrayal, and he hardly loved her in the first place. It is only in the aftermath of such a devastating reduction to silence that the formulas of the Masonic lexicon can come to occupy his speech and thought so thoroughly. Pierre's empty emotional world is filled by meaningless rhetoric, which Tolstoy satirizes.

By the time he writes *Resurrection*, Tolstoy has bypassed even Prince Andrei's mistrustful view of language. The narrative alibi has been completely normalized, in the sense that meaning is now not just possibly but always "elsewhere." Romantic love no longer offers any real distinction between truth and falsehood. All appearances are false; all romantic language perilous. The love of a society woman is equated to the drink an alcoholic takes. Both are relapses, an orientation toward delusions instead of reality. The society woman herself becomes an index of personal failure: Nekhlyudov "felt in this company that he was stepping back into the old ruts and, in spite of himself, yielding to the frivolous and immoral tone which held sway in that circle."[13] A childhood acquaintance, Mariette, serves in the role of temptress. A dramatic metaphor is meant to impugn the veracity of her comments, and Tolstoy is wickedly clever in his economical dismissal of her: "'Mind you come and see me, but *disinterestedly*, please,' she said, smiling a smile, the power of which she well knew; and then, the performance, so to speak, being over, she let down the curtain—she let down her veil."[14] Although she herself is anything but *disinterested*, Mariette decides to help her childhood friend. Their conversations are a record of the intimate transparency of two people in love; only now, Tolstoy no longer believes such things are possible. He brings both speakers to a dizzying peak of mutual comprehension, so that the fall may be more precipitous:

- "She was not pretending—she really had appropriated to herself that very same state of mind that Nekhlyudov was in, although she would not have been able to put into words what Nekhlyudov's state of mind actually was."
- "She said just what Nekhlyudov wanted to say."
- "[Mariette] gave Nekhlyudov a look that somehow established a full understanding between them of their attitude to the countess' words and to evangelism in general."[15]

In one passage, Mariette repeats the words "I understand [понимаю]" five times, as though insisting verbally on a state of being she would like to create emotionally.[16] Understanding between a man and woman, which once seemed like the pinnacle not just of emotional life but of its aesthetic depiction, has become its nadir, a sign of utter falsehood.

Ultimately, Tolstoy indicts not just her words but the whole communicative process taking place between Mariette and Nekhlyudov: "She seemed ready to cry as she said these last words. And though, if one were to analyse them, the words either had no meaning at all, or only a very vague meaning, they seemed to Nekhlyudov to be exceptionally profound, sincere and good, so attracted was he by the look in the shining eyes which accompanied the words of this young, beautiful and well-dressed woman."[17] Later on, Nekhlyudov recalls this conversation with shame, and Tolstoy agrees with his self-condemnation. By not battling falsehood (that is, by not assuming a thorough and unforgiving poetics of suspicion), Nekhlyudov is false to himself. "He would recall her words, which were not so much deliberate falsehoods as an unconscious echo of his own."[18] But the language used to describe these two is not really that different from Tolstoy's earlier descriptions of true love. In an earlier novel, Nekhlyudov and Mariette might have been happy together. They share the language of lovers, as in these summarizing paragraphs—which Tolstoy offers, taking on the perspective of a third party, as though to buttress the reliability of his account:[19] "When the countess returned, they were conversing not merely like old friends but like intimate friends, two people who alone understood each other among an uncomprehending crowd. They talked of the injustice of power, of the sufferings of the unfortunate, of the poverty of the people, but in reality their eyes, gazing at each other through the sounds of their conversation, kept asking: 'Can you love me?' and answering 'I can,' and physical desire, assuming the most unexpected and radiant forms, was drawing them together."[20] This "reality" is obviously no longer the reality of love that Tolstoy formerly offered his readers. Authentic communication and love are now impossible, though the passage above could once have described Levin and Kitty, right up to the clause "and physical desire . . . was drawing them together." Later in the novel, Tolstoy's demystification of Mariette takes a crude turn, as Nekhlyudov compares her to a prostitute on the street: "This street-walker is like filthy stinking water to be offered only to those whose thirst overcomes their aversion; but the woman in the theatre is like a venom imperceptibly poisoning everything it touches."[21] What more can one say?

As we saw in the previous chapter, in *Anna Karenina* Tolstoy makes a fundamental change in his poetics from possible trust to inevitable suspicion. If in "Family Happiness" suspicion is basically unfounded, in *Anna Karenina* its validity materializes like Vronsky out of the fog. Here language and plot are closely intertwined. Words ultimately turn against Anna and fail to serve her needs in her romance with Vronsky. Levin also struggles with language, but his romance with Kitty, free of the destructive suspicion that consumes Anna, at times suggests a near wordless (and sinless) way of life. So it is that talking and living diverge ever more radically in Tolstoy's evolving poetics. Between Anna's tragic heroine and Mariette's "streetwalker" come Tolstoy's most brutal attacks on love and language.

IN LOVE'S DETAILS: "THE DEVIL"

He felt that he was walking in the garden and saying to himself that he was thinking out something, but really he was not thinking out anything, but insanely and unreasonably expecting her; expecting that by some miracle she would

understand how he desired her, and would come here at once or go somewhere
where no one would see, or would come at night when there would be no moon,
and no one, not even she herself, would see—on such a night she would come
and he would touch her body.

— *"The Devil"*

Tolstoy's short story "The Devil" (1889) develops themes and attitudes
toward language that were left unresolved by Anna's story. Here the narrative
alibi devolves, literally, into criminality. The story begins: "A brilliant career
lay before Evgeny Irtenev."[22] Evgeny, however, decides to forgo this brilliant
career to save the family estate after the death of his father, who left it deeply
mortgaged. He works very hard and achieves modest, then total, success in
recovering the family wealth. Evgeny's one dilemma, the dilemma of a young
unmarried man, is how to fulfill his sexual urges. "He was not a libertine but
neither, as he himself said, was he a monk."[23] Sex is necessary, he believes, for
his physical health.

After much agonizing he turns to Daniel, the watchman, who procures a
peasant woman, Stepanida, for him; though she is married, her husband works
in Moscow and she and Evgeny are able to meet regularly. Evgeny promises
himself to break off his affair when he gets married, and indeed he does. His
new wife, Liza, adores him completely, though she is a madly jealous woman.
Within a couple of years, and after a tragic miscarriage, Liza is pregnant a
second time, when Evgeny sees Stepanida again and begins to burn with lust
for her. Thrice he attempts to avoid the inevitable: he begs the steward to
prevent Stepanida from working in the house, appeals to him again in vain
to have her family sent away, and finally he pleads with his libertine uncle to
save him. Disaster is averted: Evgeny, Liza, and the uncle go to the Crimea,
where Liza gives birth to a lovely baby girl.

But the Crimean cure does not take. On the third day of his arrival home, he
again experiences blood-boiling lust. He can no longer control himself and
lapses into mad raving, captured by an almost Anna-esque inner monologue:
"Really she is a devil. Simply a devil. She has possessed herself of me against my
own will. Kill? Yes. There are only two ways out: to kill my wife or her. For it is
impossible to live like this. It is impossible! . . . Yes, or else. . . . Ah, yes, there is
a third way: to kill myself."[24] At the last minute, Liza finds Evgeny in his study,
asks what is wrong, and leaves, having been given the promise that he will soon
explain all. . As soon as she walks out, however, there is a gunshot, and "no one
could understand or explain the suicide."[25] Afterward, the doctors say that
Evgeny was simply deranged, and the story concludes with a moral: "And

indeed if Evgeny Irtenev was mentally deranged everyone is in the same case; the most mentally deranged people are certainly those who see in others indications of insanity they do not notice in themselves."[26]

There are a few additional details one needs to know about the story. Although it was written in 1889, it was published only after Tolstoy's death. Its biblical epigraph, taken from Matthew, is the same as that in Tolstoy's play *The Realm of Darkness*, written three years earlier. As in *The Realm of Darkness*, there is a variant of the ending that was written a few months after the original; in it Evgeny tracks down a supernatural "laughing eyed [смеющийся взгляд]" devil (Stepanida), takes a revolver from his pocket, and shoots her "once, twice, thrice, in the back."[27] This version ends with the same moral as the other. But Tolstoy considered the story imperfect, and he hid it in his office so that his wife would not find it and recognize in it descriptions of Tolstoy's own lust for Aksinya Bazykina, a peasant woman from Yasnaya Polyana. In his diary, Tolstoy entitled the text "the story of Fredericks," referring to the well-known case of a court investigator who shot and killed a peasant woman with whom he had been having an affair. Fredericks was found two months later run over by a train (it was not clear whether it was a suicide). All of this sounds somewhat familiar.

But one does not need the train to connect Evgeny and Anna. He also ends his life after a deranged stream-of-consciousness monologue rationalizes his violence. Anna says: "We are all created to be miserable, and we all know it, and all invent means of deceiving one another. When one sees the truth, what is one to do?"[28] Evgeny: "Why, I thought I was free, but I was not free and was deceiving myself when I was married. . . . That [Liza] should know that I have exchanged her for a peasant woman, that I am a deceiver and a scoundrel! — No, that is too terrible! It is impossible."[29] The betrayal of love is enunciated in a harrowing language and logic, based on a suspicious mode of interpretation that sees inevitable fraud and deceit, and an ineluctable course of violent action. Evgeny's language has the guise of rationality, even its form (especially in the first example), but his conclusion that all is deceit twists logic completely. Debased language is thus the surface of a deformed and deforming mode of thought.

The demise of communicative language in "The Devil" is similar to that in *Anna Karenina*. First, true love creates all-but-perfect discourse: Liza "had the gift which furnishes the chief delight of interaction with a loving woman: thanks to her love of her husband she penetrated into his soul. . . . Things quite foreign to her . . . she immediately understood, and not only was she able to be an interlocutor for him, but often, as he himself said to her, a useful and irreplaceable counselor."[30] In fact, conversation in the story, not just between Evgeny and Liza, but also among the entire household, becomes a bellwether of psychological health.

Thus, as Evgeny's libido begins to overtake his mind and sense of marital duty, his control of language likewise suffers. He avoids conversations with his wife, the chatter between mothers-in-law unnerves him as never before ("it was as obvious to Liza that something was tormenting him as a fly in the milk"),[31] and three times he seeks to discuss his secret with select others, as though to find a communicative outlet besides his wife. Conversation is, in this manner, as much a psychological necessity for the lustful married man as sex is for the single man. It is Tolstoy's version of the "talking cure." "The moral effort he had made to overcome his shame and speak to [his steward] Vasili Nikolaich tranquilized Evgeny";[32] and a second time: "Though he knew that nothing would come of it, this [second] talk [with the steward] calmed Evgeny";[33] and a third: "The fact that Evgeny had confided his secret to his uncle, and still more the sufferings of his conscience and the feeling of shame he experienced after that rainy day, sobered him."[34] Like Anna Karenina, and like Pierre, he turns to reading: "He read a book and smoked, but understood nothing."[35] Like Anna Karenina, he proceeds from sex to reading and writing, and thence, somehow, to suicide and total silence.

Russian psychologist Lev Vygotsky described the child's transition from outer communicative speech to inner thought as a process in which language "goes underground."[36] For Evgeny, as for Anna, when failed communicative speech is forced into inner thought, language and logic go into a kind of Dostoevskyan underground. Here, to paraphrase Ricoeur, guile *should be* met with double guile.[37] In a world that one believes is constituted by veiled hostility, the real prophet is openly hostile; in the romance of hostility, the best way to punish a loved one is, obviously, to kill oneself. The shared dynamic of this extreme logic is: why tell the truth if language is invariably false?

Evgeny provides us with an aspect of the romantic betrayal narrative unavailable in *Anna Karenina*: namely, an alternate portrait of Levin in which the trials undergone bear consequences equal to those of Anna. Like Evgeny, Levin experiences love, nearly perfect communication, regret over the licentious behavior of his bachelorhood, a kind of destruction of language, and utter despair. Writing of Levin's crisis, Tolstoy underscores how terms that should yield greater meaning ultimately fail him: "The *organism*, its *decay*, the *indestructibility of matter*, the *law of the conservation of energy*, *evolution*, [these] were the words that usurped the place of his old belief. . . . But [these words and the ideas associated with them] yielded nothing, and Levin felt suddenly like a man who has changed his warm fur coat for [that] muslin garment, and, going for the first time into the frost, is immediately convinced, not by reason, but by his whole nature that *he is as good as naked, and that he must inevitably perish miserably.*"[38] And Levin is so tempted to kill himself that he hides the rope and ceases to go hunting. But Levin goes on living, and Evgeny and Anna do not. Why? Because Levin, who has passed through the gauntlet of temptation in meeting Anna, neither leaves his wife nor kills her, Anna, or himself. He persists by living for the demands of the moment, until the day a conversation with one of his peasants *reminds* him of what has known all along—that he must "live for his soul."

The key difference between Levin, on the one hand, and Anna and Evgeny (not to mention Pozdnyshev), on the other, is indicated by the inner mono-logues that describe their crises. The style Tolstoy uses, rather than the plot, suggests that Levin is never really knocked from the solid footing that the lan-guage of love affords him.[39] For Anna and Evgeny, elliptical, illogical, and vio-lent thoughts swarm in their inner monologues until the clear language of suspicion galvanizes them; for Levin, inner monologue is by and large a close representation of his everyday rational thought, even if that thought is often misguided. In fact, one would not compare Levin to Anna at all, if the narrator did not push the reader in that direction. Misguided thinking is not the same, after all, as totally irrational thinking. For Levin, "The words uttered by the peasant had acted on his soul like an electric spark, suddenly transforming and combining into a single whole the swarm of disjointed, impotent, separate thoughts that incessantly occupied his mind."[40] That "electric spark [искра]" will become in "The Kreutzer Sonata" an "electric shock [тольчок]" that wakes Pozdnyshev in the middle of the night with the homicidal assurance that his wife is in another man's arms.

What has changed in Tolstoy's poetics to lead us from the possibility of Levin's kind of salvation to the seeming inevitability of Evgeny's self-destruction? In *Anna Karenina*, one may recover from dangerously bad behav-ior, if it is sufficiently regretted and talked out (either openly or in a rational inner monologue). In "The Devil," however, real love and communication are apparently no longer sufficient—after all, Evgeny loves his wife and can com-municate with her. The price of saving oneself is now much higher. Must one give up the idea that language can yield truth, hitherto still a possibility in Tolstoy's romance narratives, in order to be saved from oneself or from others? Anna and Evgeny both kill themselves, but Pozdnyshev in "The Kreutzer Sonata" does not. What does he know about love—or, better, what does he *say* about love—that saves his life?

SUSPICIONS CONFIRMED: "THE KREUTZER SONATA"

"I see you've found out who I am!" said the gray-haired man softly, with apparent calm.

"No, I've not that pleasure."

— *"The Kreutzer Sonata"*

"The Kreutzer Sonata" provides Tolstoy with an apparent solution to the narrative dilemmas involved in writing about the triangle of language, love, and suspicion. For the first time, his narrative focus is primarily on the supposed "victim" of romantic betrayal, as one may temporarily call Pozdnyshev, the deceived (Pozdnyshev) rather than the deceiver (Masha, Anna, Evgeny), and he thereby draws his themes from a different perspective. "The Kreutzer Sonata" is thus truly in dialogue not just with one of the previous betrayal narratives but with all of them. Yet in this tale, more than in any other, an underground-like poetics of suspicion infects aesthetic structure, because Pozdnyshev is not only the deceived husband, and he is no traditional cuckold at all, having more or less pushed his wife into her lover's arms, but he is also the primary storyteller. Pozdnyshev nearly embodies suspicion, and thus for the first time Tolstoy's poetics of suspicion directly affect the narrative itself.[41] David Herman concludes, more dramatically, that "The Kreutzer Sonata" "as it was finally written is not a Christian work of art, not a work which strives to bring people together, but rather a work which intentionally strives to keep them apart."[42] Tolstoy purposely destroys the bond of love and language.

The plot begins as the previous stories have ended. For all his prolixity, Pozdnyshev is from the start communicatively crippled. His verbal signature, which the narrator repeatedly notes, is an incoherent sound that should carry semantic and emotive weight but that sinks below the threshold of comprehensibility. "A peculiarity of this man was a strange sound he emitted, something like a clearing of his throat, or a laugh begun and sharply broken off."[43] Moreover, although we are told how Pozdnyshev narrowly averts suicide, the fate of Anna and Evgeny, he is for all intents and purposes a *reborn* man who has passed through death and returned to life. He tells us that on the third day of his stay in prison he began to understand and a moral change took place.[44]

As in "The Devil," a rereading of "The Kreutzer Sonata" unmistakably reveals the underlying, presumably Christian, significance of the number three. Pozdnyshev can hardly speak without enumerating three qualities or objects, even in the most oblique fashion:

- "To be a libertine is a physical condition like that of an *addict*, a *drunkard*, or a *smoker*."
- Premarital sex is encouraged by the *state*, the *doctors*, and the *mothers* of young men doomed to libertinage.
- "Out of a thousand men who marry . . . there's hardly one who hasn't been married *ten*, a *hundred*, or even, like Don Juan, a *thousand* times, before his wedding."
- "Well, so these *jerseys, curls*, and *bustles* caught me!"
- "Everything was there on hand, *raptures, tenderness*, and *poetry*."
- "Of all the passions the *strongest, cruelest*, and most *stubborn* is the sex-urge."[45]

Such examples seem to pervade the story. The presence of the trio no doubt also derives from Pozdnyshev's obsession with the love triangle.

Tolstoy's noose around the neck of communicative language is tightened further. Whatever delusions of genuine love sustained the husband and wife are quickly and permanently dispatched by their growing hostility for one another, until a stage is reached where "it was not disagreement that caused hostility, but hostility that caused disagreement. Whatever she said I disagreed with beforehand, and it was just the same with her."[46] What could be a finer example of guile being met by double guile? *I disagree with you beforehand.*

A similar passage involving the disenchantment of love and enchantment of suspicious language may be found in "Family Happiness." At one point Masha says: "I was [so] convinced that I knew just what he would say and do, and how he would look: if anything did surprise me, I concluded that he had made a mistake."[47] Pozdnyshev and his wife are thus "doomed to silence."[48] But as opposed to Tolstoy's previous narratives of betrayal, in "The Kreutzer Sonata" we are led to believe that there never was real love, only sex, which Pozdnyshev equates with hostile silence: "The periods of anger corresponded quite regularly and exactly to the periods of what we called love," that is, sex.[49] Angry silence and sex are linked to one another for Pozdnyshev; thus his prolixity is, conversely, a kind of program for abstinence and salvation, another talking cure.

He rehearses and confesses his crime as he retells it, in order to assure his salvation. Yet as many readers have noticed, Pozdnyshev's imprint is left so strongly on his story that it certainly undermines the effect of his theory of salvation through celibacy. As Charles Isenberg puts it, "Pozdnyshev's language and manner reveal him as trapped by his obsession, unable to get the story to match his desire, to take on the satisfactory salvational meaning that could free him from his past."[50] In other words, his obsession with sexuality so inundates his story that Pozdnyshev re-creates the murder in his erotic telling of it. Moreover, his relationship to language is so debased, his story so overwhelmed by a poetics of suspicion, that Pozdnyshev cannot but narrate his life through the misprision created by his paranoia.[51] That paranoia is marked from the beginning by his revelation to the others in the train carriage that he is the man of whom they speak, the one who killed his wife, even though no mention of Pozdnyshev's case has been made.

The biggest problem in this story is how to account for Pozdnyshev's proto-Freudian narrative. Modern readers long familiar with the vagaries of desire exposed by psychoanalysis have no trouble recognizing Pozdnyshev's equation of sex with violence, of the phallus with a dagger; we are able to translate his discovery of his wife and Trukhachevsky together into the primal scene, his murderous hatred of his wife into a kind "countertransferred" homoerotic desire for her potential lover. The reader seems trapped in this reading: Pozdnyshev even travels by train to kill his wife, then travels by train again to tell the story. Is the Freudian picture of the psychic world simply a true one, or does Tolstoy anticipate Freud, or is it merely a happy coincidence?

At least initially, one need only accept that Pozdnyshev, betrayed by love, speaks and thinks as though all consciousness were false consciousness. That is, he interprets his own story within the "beguiling" language of suspicion, just as Anna and Evgeny interpreted their final hours. Pozdnyshev, the narrative artist of the story, is thus, to use Harold Bloom's term, a "strong poet": he misinterprets events according to the needs of his own assertion of identity.[52] He sees the world as determined by blind desire, and thus, to preserve the integrity of his own identity—assailed by falsehood, as it were—he meets guile with double guile. The only problem is that, rather than seeing Pozdnyshev as a victim of a debased form of language and consciousness, many readers assume that their own interpretive job is finished when they recognize how he perverts the objectivity of the narrative.[53] From there it is only a short step to characterizing Pozdnyshev's desire in the same terms with which he characterizes desire in the narrative. Both strategies see past the mere surface of objective truth, the objectness of the object.

Isenberg writes: "Pozdnyshev's state suggests just such a delusional remolding of reality, and Freud's descriptions of the jealous man's attitudes toward his wife and toward the social conventions governing behavior of married men and women fits him to a tee."[54] His repressed attraction for Trukhachevsky translates into raging jealousy: I don't love him, she does. And indeed, in support of this view, Pozdnyshev claims to read Trukhachevsky like a book, understanding him in ways that he might have understood his wife in other Tolstoyan narratives;

moreover, Trukhachevsky is scarcely threatened by the violence in the same way that Pozdnyshev's wife is. Along these lines, one might note also that Pozdnyshev is primarily concerned that men in general, and the narrator in particular, understand him and his story.[55]

But if we read through Pozdnyshev to the unconscious forces that determine how he views the world, and thus narrates it, are we not validating the poetics of suspicion he himself enacts? He is a delusional madman, but do we then become more rational by adopting his mode of suspicion? We recall Tolstoy's story "The Devil," written in the same year (1889) as "The Kreutzer Sonata." Its moral reads: "And indeed if Evgeny Irtenev was mentally deranged everyone is in the same case; the most mentally deranged people are certainly those who see in others indications of insanity they do not notice in themselves."[56] In other words, readers do not recognize that their demystification of Pozdnyshev is its own form of mystification: we use the same suspicious forms of interpretation that he does.

One must entertain seriously the notion that Pozdnyshev never committed any crime, never killed his wife, nor that he experienced any kind of conversion in prison.[57] His main transgression is to deceive the story's gullible narrator, intoxicated by Pozdnyshev's tea, and to implicate him, and by extension the reader, in a narrative that serves his own deranged creation of a salvational identity. In this way, he is not only like Dostoevsky's Raskolnikov (another murderer "saved" in prison), but most like the Underground Man, who, having convinced himself that modern existence is a kind of living death, continuously spins tales in order to live.[58] The primary reason for believing that Pozdnyshev's murder of his wife actually happened is predicated on his initial moment of self-revelation: *I am he!* But no one in the story knows who *he* is. The kernel of "The Kreutzer Sonata" comes from a story told by V. N. Andreev-Burlak,[59] and many people close to Tolstoy knew this; but it is clear that the characters in the story do not know what Pozdnyshev is talking about. Consider how the passage transpires. The lawyer suggests that "critical episodes" *in general* happen, but Pozdnyshev responds in the particular, as though they have mentioned some event *of his.* Pozdnyshev's overall fallacy is a confusion of the general and the particular: after all, he views his own hatred as a universal, though veiled, hatred of everyone for everyone: "'Yes, undoubtedly there are critical episodes in married life,' said the lawyer, wishing to end this disturbingly heated conversation. 'I see you've found out who I am!' said the grey-haired man softly, with apparent calm. 'No, I've not that pleasure.' 'It's no great pleasure. I'm that Pozdnyshev in whose life that critical episode occurred to which you alluded—the episode when he killed his wife,' he said, rapidly glancing at each of us."[60] Pozdnyshev's aesthetics is one in which prolixity leads to salvation. The moment of revelation is but an opportunity to start talking.

Pozdnyshev has passed through the suicide of Anna Karenina to the other side: he is Anna reborn. Thus the outer silence and inner noise that characterized her suicide are now reversed by Pozdnyshev's salvationism: he indulges in outer noise and conceals a morally vacuous and devastated inner world. The music that once seemed shorthand for perfect communication in "Lucerne" has become just another shared code of deception, mere foreplay in a false and illicit love. Now incapable of communicating, music stimulates to no good purpose or end. As Pozdnyshev puts it, music "irritates" ("она действует . . . раздражающим душу образом").[61]

Ruth Rischin generalizes from the musical metaphor that "The Kreutzer Sonata" is "a story of aggression against equivocation in language."[62] (Pozdnyshev tells the truth, for example, but conveniently ignores the truth he tells is that people always lie.) Herman similarly calls this linguistic ideal "semiotic purity."[63] Golstein further supports the argument: "At the time he was writing 'The Kreutzer Sonata' Tolstoj—striking a very modern note—was growing more impatient with the abuses of language than with the abuses of sex. He writes in his diary: 'Lately I am becoming terrified not by physical disfigurations, but rather by spiritual ones, the most obvious of which is the disfiguration of language that resorts to any means to hide the truth and replace it with lies.'"[64] But how do we henceforth tell truth from lie? Rather than interrogating Pozdnyshev's story for its veracity, we need to turn our critical attention more specifically to the language he uses.

The way that Pozdnyshev talks *seems* to prove how he has acted. Pozdnyshev eroticized his murder of his wife, and his retelling of the murder is similarly eroticized. As Isenberg puts it: "The repetitive jolting and banging of the onrushing train seem almost like a translation of the theme of sexual obsession into the speech of the machine."[65] But this kind of interpretation, noted by nearly every critic, assumes a distance between *fabula* and *siuzhet* that we have no reason to take for granted. That is, the reader assumes that there is a difference between the events as they supposedly happened and the events as they are narrated—that our task is to discover this difference and attribute it to Pozdnyshev's psychological peculiarities. But the best way to account for the difference between *fabula* and *siuzhet* is to stop assuming there is a difference. Pozdnyshev's story is the creation of his telling it; that is why the plot and narration accord so well with the violent staccato of the train, which is, of course, the perfect setting for a story of sex and murder if there ever was one.

An alternate version of the plot makes good sense: a strange man, Pozdnyshev, in the throes of a salvational theory of celibacy, which is equated on a more philosophical level with the need to reconstitute continually a narrative identity, turns his obsession from the woman on the train who refuses to countenance his oversexualized view of the world to a passive man willing to listen to a whole night's worth of talk. That man, the narrator, at first an active participant in the conversation, interrupting and asking questions, is seduced by Pozdnyshev's enthusiasm and strong tea and is soon quietly listening with understanding and sympathy: by becoming, moreover, the perfect sort of interlocutor usually confined to Tolstoy's narratives of idealized love, the narrator thus earns the words "forgive me [простите]" that Pozdnyshev initially reserved for the murdered wife of his story.[66] And these words conclude the narrative itself. A patina of love covers the poetics of suspicion, which are so strong here that the question "what *really* happened?" seems unanswerable and perhaps even naive.

Tolstoy could not leave his narratives of romantic betrayal entirely alone when they concluded by affirming a poetics of suspicion and the belief that what we take to be reality is merely deceptive appearance. Time and time again he establishes that conclusion, only subsequently to undermine it. *Anna Karenina* does not conclude with Anna's suicide, but goes on to tell of Levin's spiritual regeneration. *The Power of Darkness*, with its terrifying depiction of infanticide, is rewritten so that the murder remains unseen. "The Devil" is rewritten so that the hero does not kill himself but destroys a supernaturally described evil (he says she is a "devil" who has "possessed" him) woman. And "The Kreutzer Sonata," with its rejection of the future of humanity, is reinterpreted and recast by Tolstoy's afterword, appended to the original and softening its harsh demands.[67]

Nevertheless, of all of the works considered thus far, "The Kreutzer Sonata," with its deceptive narration, most thoroughly embraces a poetics of suspicion. "We are so accustomed to our own lies and the lies of others," Tolstoy writes in a contemporaneous essay, "it is convenient for us not to see through the lies of others that they may not see through ours."[68] But can one really tell a story so nihilistic that the very existence of the story itself is jeopardized? Perhaps the closest Tolstoy comes to outwitting this paradox is not even in "The Kreutzer Sonata" but in a story he conceived at the same time: it is "the story of a man who, having sought his whole life a good [just] life—in scholarship, in the family, in the monastery, in labor, and as a holy fool—is dying with the *consciousness of his ruined, empty, and failed* life. That man is a saint."[69] Perhaps, because that is one story Tolstoy never did write, it is the one that best represents his poetics of suspicion.

AFTER LOVE AND LANGUAGE

Beware the love of women: beware of that ecstasy—that slow poison.

—*Ivan Turgenev, "First Love"*

AFTER LOVE: TOLSTOY'S "AFTER THE BALL"

As I mentioned in Part I, after listening to a reading of Ivan Turgenev's short story "First Love" in 1896, Tolstoy remarked that "the ending was a classic."[1] That ending includes a deathbed letter to the narrator from his father about the "poison" of women's love.[2] Tolstoy no doubt appreciated how subtly Turgenev described the devastation wrought by illicit romance in "First Love." Yet Turgenev's art advanced and retreated several times, in Tolstoy's opinion. He later commented: "One page by Dostoevsky is worth a whole novella by Turgenev."[3] By the turn of the century, Tolstoy had taken full account of these two literary giants. In "After the Ball" he portrays the crippling impact of Turgenevian-tainted love as well as Dostoevskyan fascination with sadistic pleasure.[4]

In its political context, this 1903 story is an astonishingly blatant and effective critique of governmental cruelty and hypocrisy, based, to some extent, on a real event in Kazan that Tolstoy had mentioned as early as 1886. Tolstoy uses the provincial setting of the story to reconstitute and redefine his apolitical and more or less dissolute young adulthood. The story explains why the hero, Ivan Vasilyevich, is uninterested in politics, for those were the years of carefree youthful recreation: "I don't know whether it's good or bad, but in our university at that time there were no circles, no theories, and we were simply young and lived in accordance with youth: we studied and had fun."[5] Yet in spite of its hero, the story itself is politically active, thus acquitting the author of his earlier disengaged and feckless lifestyle. In essence, the narrative functions almost as an ordinary alibi, not just a metaphoric one; by explaining the actions of the young man, it acquits the old.

In "After the Ball," Tolstoy returns to fictions from his youth and about his youth. Alexander Zholkovsky has noted how he picks up on themes and motifs from *Childhood* (the gloves), *Youth* (boots and the notion of what is or is not comme il faut), as well as from an unfinished story of the same time, "A Christmas Eve" (1853), in which, after an evening at the ball, a young man visits a brothel for the first time. "A Christmas Eve" was also entitled, significantly, "How Love Perishes," and in manuscript, "The Ball and the Bordello."[6] At the end of "After the Ball," as an older man, Ivan reflects on the price he has paid for his worldly and political ignorance, for his "having fun," as he describes his university years: the loss of love, and a more exacting loss, one is led to believe, of his naiveté. What Tolstoy gains through Ivan's story, if we shift our attention to the autobiographical author behind the text, is a sophisticated relationship to narratives of love, loss, and betrayal.

The framing and genre markers of "After the Ball" focus it on the act of storytelling itself, on romance tales of youthful love, and on the genre of the society tale. The society tale provided inspiration for several of Tolstoy's romance narratives throughout his career, though one thinks especially of "Family Happiness" and the major novels.[7] Most of *War and Peace* and virtually all of *Anna Karenina* transpire "after the ball"—so the later story by that name is an epitome of one of his major themes. As in many of the late stories—after his "conversion," and after *What is Art?*—Tolstoy is characteristically and purposefully redefining here the aesthetics of his earlier work, just as he reworked a number of stories (such as "The Snowstorm" in "Master and Man"), and, more important, just as he reconfigured autobiographical moments of *Anna Karenina* in his *Confession*. Certain motifs associated with his work especially resonate.[8] The vicious colonel in "After the Ball" was actually based on Tolstoy's conception of what ultimately became of Nikolai Rostov from *War and Peace*.[9] What is more, the ball, that wonderful scene of socially prescribed behavior from *War and Peace* and other works, an analogue of life and love in the early fiction (for better or for worse), is transformed in "After the Ball" into a kind of *danse macabre*, a prelude to violence and death.

As in any good society tale, talking in "After the Ball" is at least as important as doing; in fact, the communicative dynamics of this short story are surprisingly complex. The story begins with the spoken line, "So you are saying," and ends with the words, " 'But you were saying,' he concluded."[10] Verbal discourse is meant to be foregrounded, and not just because the story is a framed first-person narrative. Multiple redactions of the manuscript point to Tolstoy's careful rewriting of the text until these mirroring lines of "talk" reflected one another at beginning and end.[11] The topic of the conversation that has ended just before

"After the Ball" begins is this: is there something in human nature that allows one to discriminate good from evil, or does it all depend on one's environment (*среда*)? Ivan Vasilyevich starts his story (and thus our story): "So you are saying that by oneself one is unable to understand what is good and what is bad, and that it is all a matter of environment, that we are victims of environment. But I think everything depends on chance. I can speak of my own experience."[12] The remainder of "After the Ball" recounts his tale of love for and disillusionment with a certain Varen'ka, as well as with her father. The society tale is thereby fused with philosophical and moral argument.[13]

This argument, though in many respects peripheral to the story that Ivan Vasilyevich tells, is nevertheless crucial to the interpretation of Tolstoy's narrative. In "The Kreutzer Sonata" and again here in "After the Ball," Tolstoy addresses one of Dostoevsky's favorite targets, particularly in *The Diary of a Writer*: that is, the supposed deterministic relationship of environment to crime or, more broadly, of context to culpability. Although his fictions construct crushing circumstances for his characters, Dostoevsky was a strident opponent of environmental determinism. Of jury trials he writes:

> Now is precisely the time we must tell the truth and call evil evil; in return, we must ourselves take on half the burden of the sentence. We will enter the courtroom with the thought that we, too, are guilty. . . . But to flee from our own pity and acquit everyone so as not to suffer ourselves—why, that's too easy. Doing that, we slowly and surely come to the conclusion that there are no crimes at all, and "the environment is to blame" for everything. We inevitably reach the point where we consider crime even a duty, a noble protest against environment. . . . So runs the doctrine of the environment, as opposed to Christianity which, fully recognizing the pressure of the environment and having proclaimed mercy for the sinner, still places a moral duty on the individual to struggle with the environment and marks the line where the environment ends and duty begins. In making the individual responsible, Christianity thereby acknowledges his freedom. In making the individual dependent on every flaw in the social structure, however, the doctrine of the environment reduces him to an absolute nonentity, exempts him totally from every personal moral duty and from all independence, reduces him to the lowest form of slavery imaginable.[14]

One is tempted to think that Tolstoy had this or similar passages by Dostoevsky specifically in mind as he formulated "After the Ball," which turns on the notion that Ivan, indeed all members of Russian polite society, are to blame for the crime Ivan witnesses against the Tatar. For Dostoevsky, and Tolstoy in "After the

Ball," both the individual and society bear responsibility. By allowing such a crime to be perpetrated, Tolstoy seems to suggest, society enslaves itself, thus metaphorically trading places with the Tatar who is beaten by the other soldiers.

Both the oral nature of "After the Ball" and the pairing of the social and martial settings allow Tolstoy to parcel out responsibility. As in "The Kreutzer Sonata," listeners to Ivan's story, and readers of Tolstoy's, witness the crime as it is re-created in narrative. In Dostoevsky's *Brothers Karamazov*, Fyodor Pavlovich is frequently offensive all over again as he reminisces about his past offenses. Yet a more penetrating discursive guilt also shapes the very structure of "After the Ball." In "The Kreutzer Sonata," even more than in "After the Ball," Tolstoy examines how environment (specifically society) provides for the criminal an alibi that he knows is available to him; similarly, Raskolnikov both battles and embraces the idea that his dire poverty and the environs of St. Petersburg have driven him to kill the old pawnbroker and her sister in *Crime and Punishment*. All these literary cases by Tolstoy and Dostoevsky test how one might translate physical environment into moral exculpation. In "The Kreutzer Sonata" and "After the Ball," the key violent moment is when the hero-narrator physically closes the distance between himself and the site of the crime, a collapsing of literal alibi, "elsewhere," into rhetorical alibi, a story that seems to eliminate responsibility for the crime itself. When both Ivan Vasilyevich and Pozdnyshev reject and thereby remove the environmental excuse, they point to an absent motive: if the environment is not to blame, then what is? Their narrative alibi is that absence in the form of a story, "After the Ball" and "The Kreutzer Sonata," which ultimately fails to acquit them.

One half of Ivan's story is devoted to describing dancing at the ball and his love for Varen'ka, and the other half of his story describes in horrifying detail how he sees her father, a colonel, direct the brutal punishment of a Tatar who has escaped from the army. The story itself brings those two spaces together, and its digressions are not unlike Ivan's perambulations through the town that night after the ball has ended. Characteristics that daughter and father share (the story was at one time entitled "Daughter and Father"), which had once endeared the father to Ivan, now prevent Ivan from continuing to love the daughter: every time he sees Varen'ka, he is reminded of her father's inhuman brutality. The colonel is there even when he is not. Such are the affairs that may direct a life, Ivan concludes—affairs of chance, he would have us believe. The Russian word for "chance" is *случай*, which means in most contexts an "event" or "incident."[15] Thus love has been derailed by chance, by the event Ivan witnesses.

Perhaps no reader misses the bald political point of the story: a "correct" reading equates high society at the ball with martial society at the parade

grounds. The "laws" or "rules" (*законы*) of dancing mentioned by both Ivan
and her father are thus implicitly connected to the "laws" (*законы*) of the state.[16]
Yet, and here is a crucial distinction, the ball does not *lead* to the scene of military justice in any way, and the plot seems purposely to avoid suggesting any
causal link: we recall that the story is told to demonstrate how Ivan Vasilyevich's
life has been determined by chance not circumstance. The causal link is
replaced by a poetic link. The nonplotted, nonplanned, possibly unforeseen
event is essential in *War and Peace*, but in other, later stories, such as "The
Death of Ivan Ilyich," for example, narrative structure and the life of the protagonist are more in lockstep with one another. In "After the Ball," Tolstoy
weighs his early and late aesthetics against one another. Ballrooms and chance
events—much of Tolstoy's fiction rests easily under this rubric.

In "After the Ball," our readerly interest in the events of the story proceeds in
the circular fashion of a hermeneutical argument: new information always
allows us to refine our previous understanding of the role of chance versus environment, until the very end, where it becomes clear that our plot line is really
a plot mirror, the end reflecting the beginning in a terrible glass. This mirroring
circularity seems, on the one hand, an inherent aspect of autobiographical
reminiscence, where the storyteller retreats into his past in order to return to the
present with a fresh understanding of himself. But the story is constructed so as
to prevent Ivan from causally connecting his past to his present. At a very basic
level, this obstacle is established by the framing narrator. As in "The Kreutzer
Sonata," there is a primary narrator in "After the Ball," though most of the time
Ivan is telling his story. But Ivan does not have complete control over the narrative, and his personal story is often, even abruptly, amplified by the primary
narrator's interjected descriptions.

Tolstoy provides a number of occasions where the listeners to Ivan's tale
actually object to his characterizations of his past. "'Well, there's nothing to be
modest about'—one of the women interrupted him. 'We know your daguerreo-
type portrait. Not only were you not ugly, but you were handsome.'"[17] Here, the
listener does not just interrupt and disagree with Ivan, she calls upon a specific
image to contradict him. Why, one wonders, do the women know his portrait so
well that they feel free to interrupt and challenge his assertion? Ivan's modesty
is probably a form of immodesty. One imagines that he is no better at concealing some handsome portrait of himself than he is at remaining silent, when, as
the narrator admits, "he told a story so sincerely and honestly."[18] Visual clues
frequently gainsay spoken ones in Tolstoy's work—we recall the smile of con-
tentment on Stiva's face that precludes his reconciliation with Dolly; his use of
ekphrasis to undermine Ivan's story therefore is not much of a surprise.[19]

As Ivan describes the numbing haze of dancing with Varen'ka, he is again interrupted: "Well, how is it that you didn't feel anything; I think you felt a lot when you clasped her by the waist, not only your body but hers too."[20] Here physical sensation, rather than visual sensation, contradicts Ivan. As in the previous example, the rhetorical contradiction (an appeal to a portrait and to a sensation) gestures toward what cannot be conveyed in fiction. That is to say, an author can neither show the portrait nor re-create the sensation in words. Thus, the rhetorical contradiction of Ivan functions also as a kind of narrative interdiction, alluding to what the narrative cannot accomplish. This too is an essential aspect of ekphrasis. For Ivan, the implied failure of narrative is one he goes on to correlate with his ability to serve or fit in with others. At the end of his story Ivan tries to conclude: "And not only did I not serve in the army [thereafter], but I didn't serve in any capacity at all, and as you see, did not fit in anywhere."[21] Here he is contradicted a final time by one of his listeners: " 'Well, we all know how it is you did not fit in anywhere,' one of us said. 'Better to say: how many people would not have fit in anywhere if it weren't for you.' "[22]

The listeners inside the text know as well as the readers outside it that linearity gives way in "After the Ball" to a mirroring between the two halves of Ivan's story. Rather than acceding to Ivan's re-creation of himself in the story, they actually demand to know what happened to love ("Ну,а любовь что?— спросили мы [Well, what of love?—we asked]"),[23] noting thereby the missing causal link between the story's beginning and its end. In other words, the narrative creates a desire for completion to the love story, unsatisfied by Ivan's conclusion and, one suspects, illicit from Tolstoy's perspective. The reader must recognize that violence in the story is done not only to the Tatar who runs the gauntlet but also to the narrative itself, and even to the communicative capacity of language. "After the Ball" may be a commentary in part on Tolstoy's earlier narratives of romantic betrayal, but it is also one of them and partakes of the metanarrative themes we have associated with them.

Most embedded first-person narratives, like "The Kreutzer Sonata" and "After the Ball," act to make an unknown person in the story known to the reader and better known to the other characters. But in "After the Ball" Ivan is trying to redefine himself entirely, and his interlocutors know him too well to let him get away with it. There is no uncomplicated line to be drawn from past to present, just as there is no easy causal line between the environment and the moral agent. Chance is the thing, as Ivan tells us.

But what exactly is chance in narrative? There is a slightly idiosyncratic understanding of it in "After the Ball." For chance is, at least in a basic sense, the way a single, perhaps seemingly unimportant, unexpected, or unintentional event (that other meaning of *случай*) comes to be invested with meaning out of all proportion to its apparent role in the causal chain of life. One could embark on the notion of chance in history, a topic occupying Tolstoy's thought throughout *War and Peace* and beyond. But I am more interested in the symbolic equivalent of the chance event in this story. What are the image or images, detail or details, that come to occupy too important a role in the construction of meaning in Ivan's story, out of all proportion to their "reason for being" there? How, to make the paradox explicit, is fortuity purposefully inscribed into the text itself? Fortuity is either a trace of aesthetic structuring in "After the Ball," a hint that Ivan is exaggerating the truth for effect, or else a sign that fate truly plays a role in Ivan's life.

Ivan is known for his attention to detail as a storyteller. At one point, a listener blurts out, "How Ivan Vasilyevich describes it."[24] The fact that this exclamation breaks the frame of Ivan's storytelling makes it that much more significant. Ivan is perhaps like a young Tolstoy, who, Eikhenbaum argued, was "especially interested in the problem of description, the technique of plot remaining peripheral."[25] This dialectic between description and narrative plot, where increasingly detailed description keeps the plot from moving forward, pertains mainly if one is thinking of plot primarily as a progressive, causal chain. But in this story the accretion of detail is meant to impart depth to the reflective surfaces of the two halves of Ivan's story. Perhaps an alternate interpretation will gain the reader more ground.

One must consider the motivation for such descriptive detail in the story. It characterizes Ivan, to be sure, but it also provides Tolstoy an occasion to redefine the role of detail in narrative. Detail describes two worlds: one is the world of Ivan's psyche—surely, there is something about *him* that drives him to spend so much time thinking about gloves, boots, and feathers, the metonymic details of his romantic evening at the dance. The second world is a metafictional one, though, where Tolstoy forces the reader to consider whether the story can sustain the burden of such symbolically meaningful detail.[26] That is to say, though Ivan invests great meaning, for example, in the colonel's boots, should we?

In "After the Ball," there is a significant example of how well Ivan can tell an entire story from the smallest detail: "The graceful figure of Varen'ka floated near him, imperceptibly lengthening or shortening the steps of her small white satin-shoed feet. The entire hall followed every move of the couple. I not only observed them, but watched them with ecstatic affection. I was particularly moved by the colonel's boots, which were fastened by foot-straps—they were good, calf-leather boots, though not of the pointed, fashionable kind, but with the old-style square toecaps and without heels. Obviously the boots were made by the battalion cobbler. 'In order to bring out and to dress his favorite daughter he doesn't buy fashionable boots but wears his home-made ones,' I thought, and those square toecaps continued to move me."[27] Reading this passage, one cannot help thinking of Gogol's "Diary of a Madman" and the dogs, whose letters begin simply enough, but then quickly devolve into talk about various kinds of food they have been eating. Ivan is drawn to the colonel's boots, then to the footstraps, the leather, the kind of toecap, the missing heels, and so forth. This is a very short story, maybe nine pages in all, and an entire paragraph is consumed by Ivan's description of boots (91 words of 3,178, to be exact, about 2.86% of the story, not including its other paeans to footwear).

Tolstoy uses Ivan's fetishistic attention to detail in the story in order to overburden the communicative capacity of language, in order to deny the productive junction between sexual desire and narrative. Wanting the woman and wanting the end of the story are both impeded. One thinks primarily of "The Kreutzer Sonata," but several other late texts could also be considered from this perspective, including *The Power of Darkness*, "The Devil," and "After the Ball." What these narratives share is a cascading breakdown of language both within the story (among characters) and in the narrative structures themselves.

Digression is, of course, a narrative technique Tolstoy loved and used with flair and wit from the days when he first read Sterne, and is just one strategy of several that undermine the story's linear plot. Another is the order of its narrative themes. Consider Zholkovsky's remarkable interpretation of the link between the first and second halves of the story: "It took a late Tolstoy to demythologize 'cultured love' by opposing it, in a stark reversal of the romantic *argumentum ad mortuum*, to 'death's body.' To subvert the myth of 'love as culture's way of overcoming death,' Tolstoy switched the order of episodes. . . . 'After the Ball' starts with love and ends with its refutation at the sight of a tortured body."[28] Morbid attention to detail prefigures the story's conclusion, in which death abides but love does not.

Ivan as storyteller is more interested in the metonymic details of his attraction for Varen'ka (and her father) than he is in Varen'ka herself, but this waylaid narrative attention seems at first to be in accord with realist aesthetics. Peter Brooks writes: "The aesthetics of realism does not bring the more graphic and detailed report of the naked body. . . . The object of attention and desire . . . is not detailed in its nakedness but rather approached by way of its phenomenal presence in the world, which means by way of clothing and accessories that adorn and mask the body. . . . An interest in the way, rather than simply in the endpoint, is indeed virtually a definition of narrative. . . . The body of the object of desire is the focal point of a fascinated attention. Yet this attention, the very gaze of literary representation, tends to become arrested and transfixed by articles of clothing, accessories, bodily details, almost in the matter of a fetish-ist."[29] Fixation on the metonymic details peripheral to the object of desire heightens narrative tension, creates suspense, and both "seeks and puts off the erotic dénouement," as Brooks puts it, that is the fulfillment of the narrative.[30]

The problem with this reading of the story is that Tolstoy seems to anticipate and reject it as part of that diseased coupling of illicit desire and narrative. Consider his reconceptualization of metonymy. "After the Ball" comes after the major realist fiction, a kind of metafictional commentary on its goals and meth-ods (including desire for the body displaced onto metonymical details—downy upper lips, heavy treads, porcelain busts, and locks of unruly hair). Ivan's listen-ers call him out on his attempts to avoid naming the body that is supposedly the object of his desire and his narrative. We recall that one of them exclaims: "Well, how is it that you didn't feel anything; I think you felt a lot when you clasped her by the waist, not only your body but hers too."[31] Ivan responds: "You see nothing except the body. In our day it wasn't like that. The more deeply I was in love, the more disembodied she became for me. Now you see legs, ankles and something besides; you undress the women you're in love with. But for me . . . over the object of my love there was clothing of bronze. [In our day] we didn't just not undress them, but tried to conceal their nakedness, like the good son of Noah. Well, but you won't understand."[32] Desire for Varen'ka does not have as its object the nakedness of her body, clad as it is in Ivan's psychic bronze armor, but rather is a desire for feeling itself—and its narrative counterpart, storytelling. At one point, Ivan even admits: "We never spoke of love. I neither asked her, nor myself even, whether she loved me. It was enough for me that I loved her. And I was afraid only of what could spoil my happiness."[33] He hardly cares, even as he retells the story many years later, what Varen'ka thinks, feels, or wants. She has virtually nothing to say in the story—Ivan's loquacity is at the expense of her silence.[34] In this economy of virtual love, their exchange of fan, feather, and glove replaces any genuine communicative exchange. Ivan's admis-sion of lack of interest in her is as close as he comes to even pondering the question. This indifference from a man who wants to answer the metaphysical dilemma of whether chance determines existence—one would think that the problem of "other minds" might be more compelling. But by this point in Tolstoy's career, the poetics of suspicion have so thoroughly vitiated the dream of connecting with the other that there is no longer even the pretense that one person could understand another. There are narrative rhythms and fragments, the sound of drums and boots, but nothing more.

What Ivan derives from his love for Varen'ka and its metonymic keepsakes is the ability to invest his life with special narrative meaning. There is something left to know, another chapter or adventure that impels him forward. After the ball, he returns home with the feather from the fan and one of her gloves, both of which receive nearly as much attention as the colonel's boots and gloves. Unable to sleep, he walks along the street, and everything he sees becomes charged with special meaning: the horses, the cab drivers, the cart shafts, the boots of the drivers, the houses along the street—"everything was especially dear and significant."[35] Yet his romantic storyteller's ability to see special meaning in everything is suddenly muted when he sees the colonel and his troops beating the Tatar. Now the droning music of the drummer and flutist, "that same unpleasant, shrill melody,"[36] is repeated over and over again until it becomes not only a death march but also the signature tune for a world divested of all special meaning or significance. The redundant melody is a retort to Ivan's creative vision.

The cruel idea of music as mere shorthand for a language devoid of meaning is surprising, when we recall how frequently music in fact moved Tolstoy to tears. In "The Kreutzer Sonata," his treatment of Beethoven, a great love of his youth, is tied explicitly to the notion of illicit romance.[37] Pozdnyshev remarks: "Under the influence of music it seems that I feel what I don't really feel, that I understand what I don't really understand, that I can do what I cannot really do."[38] For Pozdnyshev, to feel, understand, and do the impossible is exactly what creates a psychology through which moral transgression is permissible. Music is neither art nor prayer but incantation, facilitating not just sex, as in "The Kreutzer Sonata," but murder, as in "After the Ball." Whereas music was a symbol of an ideal community and of love in Tolstoy's early fiction, here it associated with death. One does not overstate the matter to suggest that now Tolstoy equates bad art, sex, and violence. The poisoned mind seems to permit their unification, rather than aesthetics proper. In reference to Tolstoy's treatise *What Is Art?* Caryl Emerson argues that "Tolstoy's aesthetics is closer to a psychology."[39] Perhaps his late literary works should be considered pathologically, a return to the psychology of his early fiction, only to discredit it completely.

Having seen the brutality of the colonel, having reassociated the details of his clothing and carriage not with Varen'ka, the object of his affection, but with a killer, Ivan repeats over and over to himself that the colonel must have known something he himself did not. "If I knew what he knows, I would understand what I saw and it would not torment me."[40] But try as he may, he is unable to convince himself of this truth; and consequently he can no longer join the army, or serve anywhere at all. What he can do is continue to derive temporary pleasure in the telling of the story, if not in the ultimate knowledge (that which the colonel knows) that is continually deferred by violence. Even many years later, Ivan does not simply conclude that the colonel is a blood-lusting villain; he returns to the same conclusion as before, where narrative leads into an epistemological as well as a moral dead end. This "if only I knew" attitude makes Ivan like one of Tolstoy's readers: he asks for the realist psychological analysis and explanation that a younger Tolstoy would no doubt have provided for his characters' behavior. That era has ended. "After the Ball" is post-Tolstoyan.

The final words of "After the Ball" seem to point to a new beginning, "but you were saying." Like Pozdnyshev of "The Kreutzer Sonata," and his Dostoevskyan cousin the underground man, telling stories is, for Ivan, a good substitute for life. The framing narrator explains at the beginning: "No one actually said that it was impossible on one's own to understand good from bad, but Ivan Vasilyevich had a manner of answering his own thoughts, which emerged as the result of a conversation, and from those thoughts he told [tales] from his life. Often he completely forgot the reason why he was telling them, distracted by the stories themselves, all the more so because he told a story so sincerely and honestly."[41] But, as readers know from the end of Ivan's tale, no matter how honest he is, he does not know the secret reason for the colonel's actions. Desire produces a narrative that leads not to knowledge, but turns violently back on itself.

There remains one final, crucial aspect of "After the Ball" to discuss fully. Perhaps Ivan's desire for Varen'ka, in spite of his protestations to the contrary, does lead him into metonymic digressions that dwell on fetishistic details in his story. Perhaps his desire for the body is revealed in those aspects of her phenomenal presence in the world, as Brooks would have it. Yet there is also in the story another body, revealed, described, and known with sympathetic and perfectly realistic thoroughness by Ivan—that is the flayed body of the Tatar who has deserted the army. Ivan's defamiliarized description renders the body newly perceived in all its horror: "I caught a glimpse," Ivan says, "through the rows of the back of the punished man. It was such a glistening, wet, red, and unnatural thing that I didn't believe that it was the body of a person."[42] Ivan contrasts this vision of dehumanization with the words the man cries out over and over: "Brothers, have mercy! Brothers, have mercy!"[43] repeated as if in time with the droning music. Ultimately, communication is what humanizes people in Tolstoy's world; the failure to communicate leads to a sub- (and very occasionally a super-) human existence.

Some literary theory would have one interpret this scene, psychoanalytically perhaps, as a narrative sleight of hand: Ivan sees and narrates the disrobed body of the Tatar soldier in place of Varen'ka, and what is truly the object of narrative desire thus remains concealed, covered, as the body of Noah is by his sons. One can also interpret this conclusion, however, as a sort of Tolstoyan punishment for Ivan's romantic narrative. An overburdened narrative of desire leads him into an epistemological dead end: he never learns what he needs to know for his story to make rational sense. Similarly, romantic desire leads to the destruction of one man by another; fetishized details of the colonel's wardrobe—his boots and gloves—are now incorporated into the scene of violence, as man destroys man. Varen'ka's wardrobe, and her need to be married off, moreover, explain her father's boots at the dance; and now those same boots have become the images of martial authority driving one man to raise his hand against another. It is difficult not to see the soldier, beaten over and over again with sticks, as a double for Varen'ka, since Tolstoy often equated, in later years, sexual desire for a woman with violence toward her. Moreover, as Stephanie Sandler remarks, "the homoerotic overtones are not subtle, but they are unspeakably taboo. Ultimately, 'After the Ball' is mostly about how men disable each other sexually and how they keep each other in line by inflicting violence on the body of another."[44] This emphasis on the "unspeakable" is entirely warranted, for, even as Ivan seems to speak endlessly, much in the story is elided, while much else is rendered narratively incommunicable.

There are two points still to make, both attempts to combine the retrospective glance that Tolstoy casts back at his earlier fiction in "After the Ball" with the narrative aesthetics he activates there. First, in "After the Ball" one witnesses a kind of "return of the repressed" metonym. All those characteristically Tolstoyan details from the major fiction no longer drive the narrative forward in a flurry of realistic description that integrates the environment metonymically. Rather, one gets detail as fetish, weighed down with unsustainable meaning, utterly unimportant to character development—an aesthetics, in sum, of antinarrative.[45] One sees Tolstoy trying to dismantle the aesthetics of his earlier novels, and the story itself thus becomes an object of violence. All those details from the early novels that did not serve a moral purpose, and which Tolstoy declined to use in many late tales, seem to return in "After the Ball" in a more gratuitous, even grotesque, form, as though exacting vengeance.

Second, I think it is illuminating to compare the loathing for traditional narrative that Tolstoy displays in "After the Ball" with the evident and utter joy he experienced writing *Hadji Murad* at virtually the same time (*Hadji Murad* from 1896 to 1904, "After the Ball" in 1903—neither was published until after Tolstoy's death). *Hadji Murad* was a guilty pleasure, Tolstoy recognized, in which he could not resist indulging. Similarities between both tales are easily adduced. Both stories contain well-marked narrative frames, and both cast a retrospective glance at Tolstoy's earlier work. Both stories rely heavily on similar parallelisms: ballroom and military field, for example, in "After the Ball"; Nicolas and Shamil, Russians and Chechens, and so forth, in *Hadji Murad*.[46] More important, while *Hadji Murad* is exquisitely crafted, the plot itself is less complex than one might imagine. As Donald Fanger writes, "Even allowing for possible amplifications, the conclusion seems inescapable that this is a *situation* more than a plot, and that the progress of the narrative amounts to a discovery of the context and ramifications of that situation."[47] That is a remarkable statement when one considers that *Hadji Murad* runs to nearly 120 pages in a popular translation.

The differences are more instructive. *Hadji Murad* is as aesthetically productive, even hopeful, as "After the Ball" is destructive and nihilistic. Compare the natural beauty of the thistle and the field that initiates *Hadji Murad* with the artificial conversation that frames "After the Ball," not to mention the horror of the military field. In *Hadji Murad*, Tolstoy renaturalizes violence, or at least puts it back into a setting he deemed more culturally acceptable. He also suggests a crucial difference between violence and authority that was missing in "After the Ball." There Varen'ka's father is violent by virtue of his actions, not just his authority (all are accountable, the story seems to say, regardless of rank). But authority is decisive in *Hadji Murad*, especially in the case of Nikolai. It thus seems fitting that Tolstoy should have come up with the idea for "After the Ball" while working on it.[48] Violence is not associated with one kind of story. It appears regularly in Tolstoy's fiction, forcing us to ask whether violence plays a defining role in Tolstoy's aesthetics.

Part VI

THE DEATH OF AN AUTHOR

Tolstoy depicted violence in his fiction throughout his career, and not just in his war stories. His late stories and the aesthetic theory of *What Is Art?* were violent in a related way, as they recalled his own earlier work and subjected it to brutal reconsideration. This late aesthetics derives not just from Tolstoy's evolving moral philosophy but also from an unusually creative approach to authorial intent, which Tolstoy viewed as open in subsequent years to authoritative revision. He thus provides a compelling rejoinder to twentieth-century criticism that banishes authorial intent from our literary interpretations. This study closes with a consideration of Tolstoy's position in the broader landscape of authorship theory.

THE ROLE OF VIOLENCE IN ART

A PRODUCTIVE HYPOCRISY

Although *Hadji Murad* (1896–1904) is, as we have seen, a story in which violence seems indivisible from fiction, Tolstoy spent most of the years of its authorship developing, publicizing, and trying to live by the precepts of his religious philosophy. His most important work espousing nonviolence in these years was *The Kingdom of God Is within You* (1893). Nonviolence united Tolstoy's dreams for a communal brotherhood of man with his increasingly strident opposition to the government and Russian Orthodox church. Was Tolstoy a hypocrite for preaching nonviolence while simultaneously writing sometimes lurid violent fiction? No, not in the ordinary sense of the word, though Tolstoy himself may have said he was a hypocrite—in later years he liked to point to his own aristocratic upbringing and profligate youth as proof of what was wrong with contemporary society. Like a preacher, Tolstoy often made his own hypocrisy into an opportunity for exemplary repentance.

A more productive way to look at Tolstoy's ideas about violence is to consider them in light of his bold revisions of his autobiography and his aesthetics. Violence plays an important role in Tolstoy's late purification of both.[1] There is no shortage of violence in Tolstoy's fiction, and I have had several occasions to discuss its role in specific texts. I ended the previous chapter by suggesting that, after the destructiveness of "After the Ball," *Hadji Murad* renaturalizes violence. There is horror in the violence of "After the Ball," but in Hadji Murad's horrific death there is something else: an undeniable dignity. His death is entirely fitting for his life. We readers may find Tolstoy's provocative imagery of Hadji Murad's severed head jarring. Because it inevitably fascinates us, it seems out of line with Tolstoy's rejection of violence, but Hadji Murad himself accepted this kind of death. For Tolstoy, the artistic value of the image outweighs any philosophical reservations he may have had. In this chapter, I consider the possibility that as Tolstoy turned to theories of nonviolence, he became more vehemently opposed, even violently opposed, to

his own aesthetic past. It may turn out that such distinctly different kinds of violence—real and metaphoric—are too incommensurate to be analyzed together.
The subject of violence is, regardless, an important one. Violence, like love, is a
touchstone in Tolstoy's aesthetics. Tolstoy returned to the problem of violence
repeatedly in autobiographical and nonautobiographical fiction, as well as in his
essays. Although Tolstoy's narratives of romantic betrayal evince a destruction of
meaning that one could link, metaphorically at least, with violence, a more fundamental link between violence and Tolstoy's narrative aesthetics may be possible. How, if at all, does Tolstoy's fiction presuppose or rely upon a kind of violence?
What kind of violence could that possibly be?

To ask such questions brings us close to a genre of criticism that thrives on
revealing discrepancies between the private words or life and the public statements of authors, politicians, philosophers, and others. Such discrepancies or
cases of hypocrisy may or may not be meaningful, but the fact of the matter is we
usually do consider the relationship between the speaker and the message.
Contradictions exposed on cross-examination in a trial are used to impeach a
witness, for example. And it is not unusual for us to take into account the stake
an individual has in saying one thing or another. Is the statement self-serving or
exculpatory in some way? Does the authority of the statement rely on a connection to the speaker's biography (e.g., the medical opinion of a doctor, the advice
of a well-seasoned traveler), which itself may come into doubt? Biography can
make something both more and less authoritative, both before and after the fact.
That connection is important for our discussion, because Tolstoy's biography
tends, at first glance, to make his ideas more authoritative: he seemed to live his
ideals, or at least tried to live his ideals, not merely to espouse them. We are
accustomed, as were Tolstoy's contemporaries, to the image of an iconic older
Tolstoy in peasant garb, for example. In the latter part of his career, he was known
at least as much for his moral and religious philosophy as for his literature, the
most famous of which had been published a generation previously. The force of
his belief was generated in large part from the conversion he described vividly
(and with threat of suicidal violence) in A *Confession*, and from his devotion no
longer to belletristic literature but to moral tales, philosophy, and practical aid
for victims of famine and government persecution. Tolstoy was known to have
spoken the truth to power—for example, in his 1881 letter to Tsar Alexander II,
asking him to spare the lives of assassins. His excommunication from the
Orthodox Church in 1901 only heightened that perception of him.

This perspective on Tolstoy emphasizes the coherency of his life and his writing, yet underestimates what has been my focus, the creative use that Tolstoy
made of his biography, even in the post–*Anna Karenina* era. Those same concepts

of identity and language that emerge early in Tolstoy's narrative alibi reappear and are reconfigured in relation to this later phase of Tolstoy's life. Again, Tolstoy was no hypocrite—not in the ordinary derogative sense of the term. He never promoted ideas or causes in which he did not believe. He did, nevertheless, make exceptionally productive use of the distance between his public image as a moral philosopher in his published writing and the self he seemed to acknowledge as more genuine. Again, in his narrative alibi Tolstoy modulates the distance between true, real, authentic presence and fictive, fictional, legitimating absence to structure the narrative use of violence in his fiction, and in his nonfictional essays.

In his late fiction in particular ("After the Ball," "The Devil," "Father Sergius," "The Kreutzer Sonata," *Hadji Murad*), Tolstoy reiterates a goal of ethical behavior but winds spectacular violence into the very fabric of his moral narratives. Today's reader might be surprised, especially in light of recent debates on the role of violence in the media, that Tolstoy does not worry whether scenes of violence or descriptions of violence, no matter how intensely they are described by him, will seduce his readers into becoming violent themselves. I do not mention this lightly. Tolstoy's concern for education reaches back to early in his career when he first opened peasant schools on his estate. Although *What Is Art?* addresses directly how literature may infect readers with non-Christian ideas, Tolstoy trusts that if the overall message is a Christian one, then a bit of dramatic violence will do no harm. The reader is not invited to emulate all of the Tolstoyan story but to learn from it. Like many religious writers, Tolstoy capitalizes on the dramatic potential of the narrative of sin and repentance. Many saints' lives make use of sex and violence.[2]

I have advanced two lines of argument thus far: first, that there is a relationship between Tolstoy's fiction and violence; second, that his ideas of nonviolence derive validity in part from his biographical image. I believe we may triangulate these two assertions and connect Tolstoy's use of narrative alibi in his authorial biography to his narrative violence. Tolstoy reinterprets elements of his autobiography, as well as his violent fiction, in this late hagiographic purifying style. The causes of violence, as well as Tolstoy's specific theories of nonviolence and aesthetics, form an interpretive background to Tolstoy's late fiction and non-fiction, where he dramatically reworks the motifs and themes of his early work.

BOYHOOD

Violence is an important subject for much of Tolstoy's fiction. The early military stories and *War and Peace* address the violence of war directly, and in *War and Peace*, Tolstoy demonstrates how unnatural, undignified, and disconcerting

it is for a person to act violently toward another human being. Yet the early connection between narrative and violence is made most strikingly in Tolstoy's
Boyhood (1854), where one can see connections to all the concepts of narrative
alibi we have been examining up to this point (narrative diversion, legitimacy,
authenticity, romance good and bad). At this early stage in his career, Tolstoy
views childhood as more myth than reality, not yet the past of the authentic life
his fiction aims to recover.

Tolstoy's narrator in *Boyhood*, Nikolai Irtenev, after seeing his brother kiss
Sonya, reflects on the predilection for violence of boys who are no longer children yet not adolescents. He suggests that violence is not a transitory but a
transitional, developmental stage in maturation. In other words, violence is a
component of becoming:

> I have read somewhere that children from twelve to fourteen years of age—
> that is, in the transition from childhood to adolescence—are singularly
> inclined to arson and even murder. As I look back upon my boyhood and
> especially when I recall the state of mind I was in on that (for me) unfortu-
> nate day [having seen the kiss], I can quite appreciate the possibility of the
> most frightful crime being committed without object or intent to injure but
> *just because* [так]—out of curiosity, or to satisfy an unconscious craving for
> action. There are moments when the future looks so black that one is afraid
> to let one's thoughts dwell on it, refuses to let one's mind function and tries
> to convince oneself that the future will not be, and the past has not been.[3] At
> such moments, when the will is not governed or modified by reflection and
> the only incentives that remain in life are our physical instincts, I can under-
> stand how a child, being particularly prone owing to lack of experience to
> fall into such a state, may without the least hesitation or fear, with a smile of
> curiosity deliberately set fire to his own house—and then fan the flames
> where his brothers, his father and his mother, all of whom he loves dearly,
> are sleeping. Under the influence of a similar absence of thought [мысль]—
> absentmindedness almost—a peasant lad of seventeen, examining the blade
> of a newly-sharpened axe lying near the bench on which his old father lies
> face downward asleep, suddenly swings the axe and with vacant curiosity
> watches the blood oozing under the bench from the severed neck. It is under
> the same influence—the same absence of thought, the same instinct of
> curiosity—that a man finds a certain pleasure in standing on the very brink
> of a precipice and thinking, "What if I throw myself down?" Or raising a
> loaded pistol to his forehead says to himself: "Suppose I pull the trigger?"[4]

I quote this passage at length in part to demonstrate how in such apparent
digressions miniature narratives are possible. The story stops, as though to point

out how stories begin. In the absence of reasoned plot, related to the boy's "black future," Tolstoy demonstrates a thoughtless origin of violence. The peasant lad examines the sharp ax—and don't we already know what will happen? Where is the aesthetic pleasure in this passage? Probably in the horrifying description of the peasant's vacant curiosity as he watches the blood flow, in our defeated expectations, and in our shock that this extermination of one's parent can take place entirely without affect. It is not violence toward others or violence toward the self, nor the theory or morality of violence, but violence per se that interests Tolstoy here. This fascination with violence persists throughout his career for both artistic and existential reasons. Here he explicitly correlates violence with one of his favorite existential topics: a curiosity about one's own death. One notices, also, how the lack of reflection, "absentmindedness almost," that yields violence is related to several of Tolstoy's most transcendent moments of pure consciousness without reflection (e.g., Levin mowing hay).

Although Tolstoy's interest in violence is an abiding one, its relation to his narratives changes. This passage from *Boyhood* suggests that the main difference in Tolstoy's treatment of violence early and late in his authorial career turns on how much Tolstoy allows that violence to penetrate or influence narrative itself. In *Boyhood*, violence does not seriously affect the story, how well we understand it, or narrative communication as such. This passage is a digression from the main narrative, but it is a harmless one; in fact, Nikolai's angry thoughts do little for the main narrative and do little damage to his ability to tell a story. Nikolai subsequently sticks his tongue out at his tutor St. Jerome and gets a few lashes with a birch switch for his efforts. Gorky later maximalizes the violent potential in his reworking of Tolstoy's *Childhood* myth. Gorky's protagonist, who suffers severe punishment from his violent grandfather, asks his grandmother: "Are small boys *always* beaten?" "Always," she answers.[5] One does not doubt the linguistic and narratival basis of *Boyhood* just because of the violence it depicts, as one does, I have argued, in "The Devil" and in "The Kreutzer Sonata." Nikolai says that violence emerges in boys of this transitional age because of an "absence of thought"—he implies that violence fills the negative space of poorly developed adolescent reason. Yet the violent rationale and rationalism of Tolstoy's late stories, especially "The Kreutzer Sonata," are precisely what is so terrifying.

In this single passage from *Boyhood* one sees aspects, which by now should be familiar, of Tolstoy's authorship of narrative alibi. Violence emerges here in a literary diversion. The passage is an aside, a digression from the plot, and poses questions of how violence becomes emplotted in the absence of narrative and how we should appreciate this kind of violent art. Idle curiosity, not thought or reason—these are the conditions of a violent distraction. Tolstoy characterizes violence as the potential outcome of this diversion. Nikolai's "portrait of the boy as murderer," however briefly, removes both legitimate and authentic versions of identity. Neither child nor adolescent, as Tolstoy writes, the violent boy has no interest in the opinions, and certainly not the approval, of outside authorities. His violent plots manifest no desire to engage the aesthetic reception by others. This is not a project of legitimation. It is imagined without a future. The violent boy also lacks, however, the experience of the world that would tell him which parts of his thinking and life are defensibly authentic. There is no salvation in "instinct" or innate goodness for Tolstoy, at least yet.

Tolstoy's digression on violence is a diverting and garish description—one wonders why this is so. There is really no need for the narrator to describe the details of a young peasant's ax-murdering impulses, the "blood oozing under the bench from the severed neck." Inside the philosophical digression on violence is a murder subplot that draws far more narrative interest than the narrative proper. Just as the larger digression (on violence) appears with little motivation—Nikolai is not really contemplating killing his brother over a kiss—so does the interpolated diverting description of a boy's murder of his father emerge from a lack of motivation. The murder is committed for no reason or "out of curiosity." In short, as Tolstoy suspends plot, he dispenses with motive.

Motive reveals being, as we see when we examine Tolstoy's later writings on violence. In *Boyhood*, looking inside the mind of the violent adolescent, we see nothing in particular. Tolstoy does not yet subscribe to an essential authenticity that corresponds with lost childhood. For the later Tolstoy, by contrast, one's internal moral compass must be disrupted in order for violence to occur. The voice of conscience must be quelled for one to become violent. And a main objective of the plot of the narrative is to recollect not the absentminded violence of adolescence but the core of goodness formed in an era of happy childhood. The plot of *Resurrection*, for example, leads to just such a recollection and its subsequent motivation of Nekhlyudov's life. "Father Sergius" also ends in the recollection of childhood ideals. What stops people from recalling these ideals?

THE REALM OF DARKNESS

Nikita, the main character of Tolstoy's late play *The Realm of Darkness* (1886), speaks of his loss of moral bearings and begins to provide us with an answer: "My dear Pa, you also forgive me, a sinner! Yuh told me at the beginnin' when I started this whorin' nasty life, yuh told me: 'If a claw gets stuck, the bird is lost.' I didn't listen t'yer words, no good dog that I am, an' it turned out like yuh said. Forgive me, for God's sake."[6] Unlike his fiction, Tolstoy's plays do not so thoroughly engage in psychological analysis and introspection and have gone relatively unstudied by scholars.[7] In cases of sinful, violent behavior, however, sometimes reason and rationalization cannot explain why a character acts the way he or she does, as we saw in *Boyhood*, and thus the stage is an ideal forum for conveying an aesthetic and moral idea. *The Realm of Darkness*, which has the subtitle *If a Claw Gets Stuck the Bird Is Lost*, is one of Tolstoy's most successful plays, and it exemplifies many of the artistic goals Tolstoy had for his fiction in the latter part of his career. The play sheds light on a key transitional phase in Tolstoy's thinking about violence, but it also allows him to bypass certain problems associated with his prose fiction, since it is a play, and with the social world of the aristocracy, since it focuses on the peasants.

Thematically the play treats sexual transgression, violence, and repentance — key motifs from Tolstoy's earliest works and crucial to his late fiction. Moreover, in its graphic treatment of infanticide, the play participates in Tolstoy's evolving philosophy of nonviolence and his ongoing investigation of the nature of sin. At every juncture the play also bespeaks not just the later Tolstoy's reexamination of Christianity but also his enduring interest in the peasants with whom he spent so much time. Their beliefs, ways of life, and especially their speech are brilliantly depicted in the play by Tolstoy.[8] Although individual idealized portraits of peasants may be found in Tolstoy's fiction, such as Platon Karataev in *War and Peace*, he strived to understand but not romanticize them. *The Realm of Darkness* starkly demonstrates that infidelity, violence, and moral despair are not restricted to the upper classes. It is a singular work with universal aims.[9]

The plot of *The Realm of Darkness* is as follows. Anisya, the young second wife of a rich old peasant, Pyotr, is having an affair with the hired hand, Nikita. (Nikita has previously had an affair with Marinka, an unmarried peasant girl, and abandoned her.) Anisya and Nikita, with the active encouragement of Nikita's mother, Matryona, conspire to kill Pyotr in order to obtain his money and to marry. Once Anisya has poisoned Pyotr, and Nikita has secured the old man's money, he marries Anisya but carries on an affair with Akulina, Pyotr's daughter from his first marriage. Anisya can say or do nothing to protest, since Akulina knows from Nikita that she, Anisya, killed Pyotr. The situation cannot continue indefinitely, and after several months Nikita agrees to marry off Akulina. But she is pregnant with Nikita's child. With encouragement from Anisya and again from his own mother (the play takes an especially harsh view of women), Nikita aims to conceal his sin. He crushes the newborn infant to death and buries it in the cellar. Now distraught, he nearly hangs himself from guilt but then reconsiders. As the play concludes, he appears before the people gathered for the wedding, confesses, and turns himself in, taking full blame upon himself and accepting his sins before God. The arc of the plot suggests that sin leads to violence and, fortunately in this instance, repentance—but it is the harrowing violence that sticks with many readers and viewers of the play.

The events of *The Realm of Darkness* were based on a real murder confession by Efrem Koloskov at his stepdaughter's wedding.[10] Tolstoy heard about the case from his friend, local prosecutor N. V. Davydov. Besides changing the names, Tolstoy made only a few significant alterations. He added the first murder, the poisoning of Pyotr, and chose not to depict an additional attempted murder by Koloskov of his sixteen-year-old daughter.[11] The addition of the poisoning of Pyotr is in accord with the sentiment underscored by the play's subtitle (and original working title) *If a Claw Gets Stuck the Bird Is Lost*; that is, even a single sin (illicit sex) can lead perilously to a life of sin (first one murder then another). Tolstoy designed the play to be realistic, but he worried about the reaction of the censor to the naturalistic violence of the fourth act, when the infant is crushed to death. He wrote a less explicit variant of the fourth act in an unsuccessful attempt to get the play staged in 1887.[12] Perhaps to highlight the play's realism further, Davydov subsequently wrote that Tolstoy had actually met twice with Koloskov; Tolstoy's scrupulous diary and other writings of that time record no such meetings, however.[13]

Tolstoy attempted to stage *The Realm of Darkness*. Tsar Alexander III liked the play when it was read to him, but he rescinded his approval at the request of Procurator of the Holy Synod Konstantin Pobedonostsev. The play was not performed in Russia until 1895, though it was staged to acclaim in Paris by the Théâtre-Libre in 1888 with the encouragement of Emile Zola.[14] In 1890 the play also opened successfully in Berlin; by the time the Maly Theater in Moscow staged *The Realm of Darkness* in 1895, therefore, it had already been influential in Europe.[15] Published in Russia in 1887 and widely read before it was realized onstage, it did, however, have an effect on the reading public in Russia well before the mid-1890s.[16]

Tolstoy took *The Realm of Darkness* seriously, though he remained ambivalent about whether plays in general could achieve the aesthetic goals he had for his other fiction. The relatively impoverished ability of drama (when compared to novels) to engage in psychological introspection was acknowledged by Tolstoy as a key limitation of the form: "Here [on the stage] it is impossible to prepare for the moments lived through by the hero, impossible to make him think and call up memories, or to throw light on the characters by referring back to the past. It all comes out dull, forced and unnatural. A ready-formed state of mind, ready-formed resolutions, must be presented to the public. But monologues and modulations of colours and scenes only disgust the spectator. It is true, I myself could not resist it and put a few monologues into *Vlast' t'my*, but while doing so I felt it was not the right thing."[17]

Tolstoy makes two points here on thought and memory that are worth emphasizing. First, showing how the character thinks is an aesthetic challenge for the dramatist.[18] In *The Realm of Darkness*, Tolstoy on the contrary accentuates how sin begets sin almost in spite of one's ability to reflect on one's behavior. Nikita's preliminary sins—having affairs with Marinka and Anisya—are within the scope of normally acceptable behavior. Nikita is just sowing wild oats, with his mother's approval. One cannot help recall how Tolstoy was told by his beloved Aunt Tatiana Ergol'skaia that nothing completes a young man like an affair with a married woman.[19]

The second point, on memory, is perhaps more important. For much of Tolstoy's career he would have considered not just thought but memory in particular as essential for the creation of art. Chapter 7 discussed the relation between memory and music. There is no overt music playing in *The Realm of Darkness*, though women singing in both the opening and closing scenes frame the play. But when Nikita repeatedly thinks he hears the murdered baby whimpering at the end of the fourth act, Tolstoy alludes to the unpredictable and multivalent nature of aural perception. The cries of the baby are imagined, not real, and thus characterize Nikita's despair and pain, which is real. The first thing said about Nikita in the play is in the opening scene when Pyotr calls out to him, asking if he's "gone deaf [Oglokh!]." Until his crisis, Nikita loses the ability to hear the voice of conscience. Like the cries of the dying baby in *The Realm of Darkness*, screams of pain merge with a droning inhuman music in the late story "After the Ball" (1903). The music in "After the Ball" and the whimpering cries heard by Nikita in *The Realm of Darkness* do not suggest meaning in memory, but rather a lack of meaning and a loss of memory, an existential crisis that has culminated in violence. As Pozdynshev says, the understanding in music is illusory not real. Since Tolstoy sees drama as somewhat limited in its ability to depict thought and memory, one is not surprised to find violence and sin represented in drama as counterrational: they are the result of a world rendered senseless by the loss of faith. If sin destroys thought and memory, two essential aspects of human being, then drama is an ideal medium to depict it. One wonders whether it was primarily the difficulty in getting *The Realm of Darkness* staged that dissuaded Tolstoy from authoring even more plays after it than he did.[20]

Whereas in early works Tolstoy's consideration of violence turns on psychological analysis and tests the rational or irrational basis for acting violently, his
later nonintrospective representations of violence are more often connected to
actual violent behavior. I purposely leave aside here dueling and the extensive
body of Tolstoy's war fiction, which have their own complex set of moral and
aesthetic issues, and which in some cases may contradict my general argument,
in order to focus on violence that is unsanctioned by political and social institutions, violence for which one can rarely share blame. Consider the violent
images from the postcoital scene between Vronsky and Anna Karenina: "He felt
what a murderer must feel when looking at the body he has deprived of life.
The body he had deprived of life was their love, the first period of their love. . . .
But in spite of the murderer's horror of the body of his victim, that body must be
cut in pieces and hidden away, and he must make use of what he has obtained
by the murder. Then, as the murderer desperately throws himself on the body,
as though with passion, and drags it and hacks it, so Vronsky covered her face
and shoulders with kisses."[21]

But Vronsky, unlike Nikita in *The Realm of Darkness* or Pozdnyshev in "The
Kreutzer Sonata," does not actually kill anyone. The violence is a metaphor
through which one glimpses Vronsky's moral horror, which he himself could
scarcely characterize in words. It is not just the dramatic form of the later plays
that causes Tolstoy to shift his analysis of violence, then, but also his shifting
ideas. In the later Tolstoy, sexual transgression does not lead to violent thought
but to violent action. In *Anna Karenina* the link between adultery and Anna's
suicide is not at all as direct and incontrovertible.

Especially in the latter half of his career, Tolstoy was of course an unparal-
leled advocate of nonviolence, and he wrote about it at length in his nonfictional work *The Kingdom of God Is within You*. But *The Realm of Darkness* is a
transitional point between early and late belletristic representations. There are
two murders that bookend the play: Anisya's poisoning of her husband, Pyotr, at
the beginning and Nikita's crushing of the baby at the end. In between, however, Tolstoy implies that through his sin Nikita has damaged himself: he has
perpetrated violence upon his soul that nearly erupts into the physical world as
he contemplates committing suicide at the end of the play. As Donskov writes,
"From the external events, so to say, the conflict becomes internal, as Nikita
utters 'I stopped bein' a man!' The fact that he recognizes this—and recognition, as the word itself indicates, is a change from ignorance to knowledge—
affects a change, a change toward his rebirth."[22] What is left unsaid and forms a
mystery throughout the play is the inner workings of the mind of Nikita, which,
as time goes by, is more and more dulled by drinking.

For the later Tolstoy one's internal moral compass is often profoundly disrupted as one passes out of childhood. In "The Death of Ivan Ilych" (1886), a work contemporaneous with *The Realm of Darkness*, puberty and social ambition push Ivan off course. He leads an immoral though not violent life. For violent behavior, in particular, the voice of conscience must usually be further quelled. The boundary between the innocence of childhood and the onset of sexual awareness, and with it, inauthenticity, is suggested in *The Death of Ivan Ilyich*, when Pyotr, a colleague of Ivan Ilych present at the funeral, recognizes in the tired eyes of the dead man's son an unspoken cause, his sexual maturation. In *The Realm of Darkness*, we are meant to blame Nikita's mother, Matryona, who early in the play encourages him not to marry but to enjoy his sexual freedom: "Why not have some fun? That's what young's for."[23] The use of stupefying substances—Nikita drinks heavily as the play goes on—gives conscience an alibi. Drowning out the voice of one's conscience, which Tolstoy discusses in "Why Do Men Stupefy Themselves?" substitutes for a missing motive. But it also makes a good, engaging, and exciting narrative.

Tolstoy is willing to give up his refined art of introspective psychological analysis, at least in *The Realm of Darkness*, if that is what a moral aesthetics requires. The first verse of the biblical epigraph of *The Realm of Darkness* (taken from Christ's Sermon on the Mount, Matthew 5: 28, 29) reminds us of the link between attentive consciousness and one's conscience: "But I say unto you, That whosoever looketh on a woman to lust after her hath committed adultery with her already in his heart."[24] The epigraph is unusual for the play. Not only is an epigraph unspoken in a work of drama, but the meaning of the verse, that lust means sinning in one's heart if not in one's deeds, is itself undramatic. The play actually contradicts the sense of the epigraph, since it opens with infidelity already ongoing and not just contemplated. Anisya and Nikita have long since moved from desire to deed.

The second verse of the epigraph speaks with violent and complicated imagery: "And if thy right eye offend thee, pluck it out, and cast it from thee: for it is profitable for thee that one of thy members should perish, and not that thy whole body should be cast into hell."[25] Like other late stories, such as "The Kreutzer Sonata," and "Father Sergius," *The Realm of Darkness* makes a clear and substantial link between sexual transgression and violence. The same epigraph here in *The Realm of Darkness* is used again by Tolstoy just a few years later in "The Devil" (1889). Along with the subtitle of the play, *If a Claw Gets Stuck, the Bird Is Lost*, the epigraph forces us (readers in the case of the subtitle and epigraph) to meditate on questions of mind-body connections as well as bodily integrity per se. Does an evil thought equal an evil deed? Can one really sever sexual desire from one's self as a whole? A younger Tolstoy would likely have equivocated: did Pierre's lust for Helene in *War and Peace* make him wholly bad? No. And Stiva's criticism of Levin in *Anna Karenina* that he is too much of a piece ("ты очень цельный человек") was a just one in the context of the novel.[26] In the later period we witness more frequent attempts by Tolstoy to integrate human being entirely through conscience; that is, to see contradictory and self-defeating behavior as an index of one's moral failing rather than as a sign of the breadth and fragility of human character.

Here the logic is all-consuming. To take one step down the road of sinfulness is to cross over into an irresistibly sinful life. His willingness to sin once makes Nikita much more likely to sin again. It is a slippery slope for Nikita, as one sin leads easily to another without an easily identifiable cause to blame. Of lying, he remarks: "What a break that somethin' told me t'swear before the icon. Right away I put an end t'the whole mess. They say it's scary t'swear t'a lie. That's all alotta bunk. Nothin' but talk. Plain an' simple."[27] The words "somethin' told me" (literally, "like someone nudged me [и как это меня как толконул кто]") are essential—an unnamed, unanalyzed, nonintrospective cause compelled him to act. Tolstoy transforms the inability to provide introspective analysis in a play into the dangerous infinite negativity of sinful life.

A cause is missing in Nikita's motivation to perpetrate ever greater crimes, because he has lost his memory in the deepest sense, the ability to recollect himself, his actions, and God.[28] The play asks viewers to make a dramatic jump from his dalliance with Marinka to his crushing an infant to death in order to hide his affair with his stepdaughter Akulina. Must sex lead ineluctably to murder? For Tolstoy the equation is never quite that simple, though it may seem so for characters like Pozdnyshev in "The Kreutzer Sonata." The crucial fact is that Nikita has forgotten his soul. Memory, that cornerstone of creativity in the fiction of the early Tolstoy, is now tied essentially to the maintenance of the spiritual self. In the important essay *On Life* (1887), which Tolstoy wrote along with *The Realm of Darkness* while convalescing from an injury to his leg, he distinguishes between the animal and spiritual sides of human being.[29] Through his sexual transgressions and other sins, Nikita extinguishes his spiritual side and gives in to the animal side of his being. He kills part of himself, Tolstoy would argue, before killing anyone else. Nikita's father, Akim, who approximates a *raissoneur* in the play, phrases it in terms of having "forgotten" God. He says: "It seems, d'ya, the end's at hand. . . . Oh, God's been forgotten. Forgotten, I mean. We've forgotten, forgotten God, God."[30] It is as though the action of the play realizes Nikolai's nightmarish thought from *Boyhood* that "the future will not be, and the past has not been."

Partly because it is in a different genre than his previous belletristic work, one that resists mnemonic narrative devices, *The Realm of Darkness* reflects Tolstoy's changing aesthetics, that memory is not just creative but essentially spiritual. Thus the following key exchange between Akim and Nikita portends the play's frightful climax:

> AKIM. I told yuh, d'ya, 'bout the orphan girl, that yuh wronged the orphan girl, Marina, I mean, wronged.
> NIKITA. Look what he remembered! Let sleepin' dogs lie. That's over'n done with.
> AKIM (*angrily*). Over? No, pal, 'tain't over. Sin, I mean, latches onto sin an' pulls yuh along, an' yuh're stuck in sin, Mikishka. Yuh're stuck in sin, I see. Yuh're stuck, yuh've sunk in it, I mean. . . .
> AKIM (*opens the door*). Come t'yer senses, Mikita. Yuh need a soul.[31]

Nikita does violence to himself by forgetting his soul. Half a man, he is destined to treat others inhumanly. Akim suggests he cannot live without a soul, and indeed Nikita is nearly driven to suicide before he ultimately confesses his crimes. Throughout the play, then, Nikita's lack of reflection bespeaks two authorial strategies. In terms of the play's broader themes, Nikita in his sinful behavior has forgotten God. In terms of the play's aesthetics, his lack of reflection, and thus introspection, accords with the demands of the dramatic genre.

"WHY DO MEN STUPEFY THEMSELVES?"

The relation between literary violence and missing motives, revealed first in the diverting digression of *Boyhood* and developed further in *The Realm of Darkness*, appears in unusual yet significant places in Tolstoy's oeuvre. "Why Do Men Stupefy Themselves," an essay written just after *Realm of Darkness*, in 1890, contains Tolstoy's argument against drinking alcohol, smoking tobacco and using drugs such as opium or hashish because of the muted haze of consciousness and conscience those substances create. He associates such lapses of conscience with all sorts of crime and degradation, from murder to prostitution to bad writing, during which tobacco silences the writer's internal editor. That authorship and murder exist on the same illicit continuum is both astonishing and telling. As in the case of violence in *Boyhood*, Tolstoy focuses on an act of violence without apparent motive. Why do people use stupefying substances and how is it connected to the perpetration of crime? He writes: "Ask a smoker why he began to use tobacco and why he now smokes, and he also will reply: 'To while away the time; everybody smokes.' Similar answers would probably be given by those who use opium, hashish, morphia, or fly-agaric. 'To while away time, to cheer oneself up; everybody does it.'"[32] What is the reason one begins smoking? No reason. Simply out of boredom, or for recreation. It's common. That is the story, a version of an alibi, the perpetrators tell when asked to report on their motives. But in an authorial strategy I have identified as Tolstoy's narrative alibi, he narrates both the surface and the true absent motive by retelling stories of violence in "Why Do Men Stupefy Themselves?"

There is a correlation in these violent retellings with Tolstoy's notion of the authentic life of childhood, ruined by sex and society. "When do boys begin to smoke? Usually when they lose their childish innocence."[33] In *Boyhood*, we recall, there was no cause for violence. Now Tolstoy suggests that the use of conscience-repressing substances has a purpose, in order to forget sexual transgression. This boundary between the innocence of childhood and the onset of sexual awareness, and with it, inauthenticity, appears similarly in "The Death of Ivan Ilyich," where Pyotr recognizes in Ivan Ilyich's son's tired eyes an unspoken cause, his sexual maturation. The missing motive for a variety of correlated acts that go against conscience is the reason for using stupefying substances: "The cause of the world-wide consumption of hashish, opium, wine and tobacco, lies not in the taste, nor in any pleasure, recreation, or mirth they afford, but simply in man's need to hide from himself the demands of conscience."[34] Hiding from one's conscience is not a motive for crime in the traditional sense. It is a behavior that accompanies illicit actions, and functions as narrative alibi both literally (I was not responsible for my actions because I was under the influence of x) and figuratively, as Tolstoy uses it to rework his older fictions. Violence, no matter how unthinkable and absentminded, was once just a stage of life (as in *Boyhood*) but is now a sign of absence, of missing authentic childhood and repressed conscience.

Drowning out the voice of one's conscience substitutes for the missing motive, but it also makes an engaging and exciting narrative, even better than the absentmindedness in *Boyhood*. Again, we cannot help but notice how Tolstoy is repeatedly drawn to sensational examples. In one memorable passage, he suggests how a cigarette provides a murderer with the strength to finish the job: "That cook who murdered his mistress said that when he entered the bedroom and had gashed her throat with his knife and she had fallen with a rattle in her throat and the blood had gushed out in a torrent—he lost his courage. 'I could not finish her off,' he said, 'but I went back from the bedroom to the sitting-room and sat down there and smoked a cigarette.' Only after stupefying himself with tobacco was he able to return to the bedroom, finish cutting the old lady's throat, and begin examining her things."[35]

Is it redundant to point out that Tolstoy did not need to describe how the murderer cut her, how she fell, her throat croaking, and the blood gushed out? The description has its own narrative features: introduction of character and plot, reversal, development of character, crisis, and denouement. In "The Kreutzer Sonata," written just a year earlier, Tolstoy frequently alludes to the presence of substances he deems intoxicating, such as tea and tobacco. Pozdnyshev's retelling of the story is similarly perverted by the strong tea he keeps drinking. "Why Do Men Stupefy Themselves?" thus revisits and revises "The Kreutzer Sonata," which itself revised earlier descriptions of violence, not to mention so much of Tolstoy's opinions on love and language. If this interpretation seems to attribute to Tolstoy too much authorial self-reflexivity in this essay, we can consider further that Tolstoy himself was an inveterate smoker who often struggled to quit.

Just as the work of stupefying substances blocks the enunciation of one's conscience, the revisionary meta-aesthetics that underlies Tolstoy's discourse on stupefaction untells his earlier fictional aesthetics by arresting the progression of metonymic narrative. That sort of realistic narrative ordinarily requires commensurability of cause and effect. It can be strained for dramatic purposes (e.g., a small mistake causes great calamity), but it cannot be annihilated without destroying narrative coherence. Tolstoy ultimately suggests that the reason the stupefaction of tobacco or alcohol is so dangerous is that the tiny (чуть-чуть) changes in consciousness they provoke have such great consequences. In the great chain of metonymic violence (related in its own way to the chain of being), the least of parts is potentially the most dangerous. What this means is that the idea of plot moving causally forward by the exposure of relevant details is undermined. *Any* of the details has the potential to serve as the causal lever of plot. The tiny bit is telling, but one never knows which tiny bit will tell. As mentioned earlier, in his late fiction Tolstoy begins to suspect the moral and aesthetic usefulness of metonymy, which, some would say, was the very literary substance of his great novels. In this essay on stupefaction, the metonym is the substance of great art but also of horrific crime.

Tolstoy cites the anecdote about the painter Bryullov, whose student, seeing Bryullov make a correction to his painting, remarks how much better it is, though Bryullov had touched the painting just a tiny bit. Bryullov responds by saying that art begins with the tiny bit (Tolstoy repeats the same illustration again in *What Is Art?*). He uses this anecdote to initiate his explanation of why Raskolnikov, from Dostoevsky's *Crime and Punishment*, decided to kill the old pawnbroker and her sister. What then follows is a striking counternarrative both to Dostoevsky's *Crime and Punishment* and to the works of the earlier Tolstoy himself. As Tolstoy writes, and I quote at length:

Raskolnikov's true life *was not being lived* when he murdered the old woman or her sister. . . . Raskolnikov's true life was not lived when he met the old woman's sister, but at the time when he had not yet killed any old woman, nor entered a stranger's lodging with intent to kill, nor held the axe in his hand, nor had the loop in his overcoat by which the axe hung. He lived his true life when lying on the sofa *he was not even thinking* about the old woman, nor even as to whether it is or is not permissible at the will of one man to wipe from the face of the earth another, unnecessary and harmful, man, but whether he ought to live in Petersburg or not, whether he ought to accept money from his mother or not, and on other questions not at all relating to the old woman.[36]

Tolstoy points to the ordinary moments of one's life, as Morson argues, as the potential source of the most extraordinary consequences.[37] More than that, however, with this stunning chain of negative actions Tolstoy wants us to believe that by not *actively* focusing his attention on the old woman, Raskolnikov allows himself to contemplate murdering her. Tolstoy continues:

And then—in that sphere quite independent of animal activities—the question whether he would or would not kill the old woman *was being decided*. That question *was being decided*—not when having killed one old woman, he stood before another, axe in hand—but *when he was doing nothing and was only thinking*, when only his consciousness was active: and in that consciousness tiny, tiny alterations were taking place. It is at such times that one needs greatest clearness to decide correctly the questions that have arisen, and it is just then that one glass of beer, or one smoked cigarette, may prevent the solution of the question, may postpone the decision, stifle the voice of conscience and prompt a decision of the question in favor of the lower, animal nature—as was the case with Raskolnikov. Tiny, tiny alterations—but on them depend the most immense and terrible consequences.[38]

Although I began my definition of narrative alibi in this book with an example of narrative from *Resurrection*—about the missing statement of the missing intention—I could just have easily begun with this description of Raskolnikov. Here Tolstoy tells an entire story first through negation, with a series of times when Raskolnikov was not doing something or not thinking of something. In place of the activity Raskolnikov is not doing, a process takes place, if not actually without him then at least grammatically without him ("his true life was being lived," "the question was being decided" using the reflexive verbs: "истинная жизнь . . . совершалась, решались вопросы"). Beyond his personal will, but still inside him, "tiny, tiny alterations were taking place [происходили чуть-чуточные изменения]" in his consciousness, while he is not doing anything, "only thinking [только мыслил]," though not thinking about murdering the pawnbroker. Tolstoy uses his narrative alibi here to reinterpret someone else's story, as demonstrated with *Crime and Punishment* and Raskolnikov. The fact that Raskolnikov decides to kill the woman for no particular reason opens the possibility for radical revisions of causality and motivation. Those tiny changes taking place in him are like dozens of little metonyms just waiting to assume metaphoric dictatorship over his conscious life, to thrust a crown upon his animal nature.

There is something not just revisionary but undeniably oppressive in wishing us to remain so attentive to consciousness that we will have perfect clarity if and when our big question arrives, which will presumably not be, whether it makes sense to remain in St. Petersburg? but rather: wouldn't it be better not to kill an old pawnbroker? Conscience must assume control over consciousness at just the right moment. Tolstoy writes unsympathetically: "People drink and smoke, not casually, not from boredom, not for merriment, not because it is pleasant, but in order to drown the voice of conscience in themselves. And if that is so, how terrible must be the consequences!"[39] What a pitiless condemnation from a man so moved by his own poorly controlled impulses—to gamble, smoke, womanize, and so forth. Knowing the reflexivity of Tolstoy's philosophy, however, and that he puts himself first among transgressors, we are forced to regard such statements not as the harsh condemnations they appear to be but as the radical self-censure we know them to be. Tolstoy makes knowledge of the decisive moments of one's life entirely retrospective. When *did* Raskolnikov decide to kill the old pawnbroker, not when *does* Raskolnikov decide to kill the old pawnbroker?

Assuming similar retrospection, one may proceed by analogy and ask which details in a novel are the most important ones? Tolstoy implores us not to allow anything to escape our attention, purged of all stupefaction. This turn in his philosophy suggests a distinct departure from both the aesthetics and the psychology of the mature novels, such as *War and Peace* and *Anna Karenina*, where a principle of selection trained by habit provided the crucial nexus between conscience and consciousness. Half-conscious habit, as opposed to the vigil of total consciousness, has now become a moral weakness. Imagine for a moment that early in *War and Peace* we are called upon to judge Pierre for his drinking or smoking, which dull his conscience, rather than for his habit of giving in to the will of others and his distaste for real work. No, in *War and Peace* it is clear that Pierre succumbs to temptation because he thinks in ways that habitually justify the wrong behavior. For the later Tolstoy, by contrast, all habits are bad habits.

In a well-known example from his essay "Art as Device," Victor Shklovsky examines a diary entry from 1897 in which Tolstoy ruminates about not recalling whether he had dusted his sofa. Shklovsky demonstrates how Tolstoy's unfortunate link between habit and literature contains a revisionary aesthetics. In the example Shklovsky quotes, Tolstoy writes that he cannot remember whether he has dusted the sofa or not, and he is horrified that habit has consumed so much of his conscious life: "If the whole complex lives of many people go on unconsciously, then such lives are as if they had never been." Shklovsky continues, memorably: "And so life disappears, reckoned as nothing. Habitualization devours works, clothes, furniture, one's wife, and the fear of war."[40] Tolstoy vows not to lose life to a habitualized loss of consciousness. Shklovsky in turn defines art as a process of revitalizing perception of things that are known to us, of "defamiliarizing" the world, of "making the stone stony" again. Crucial to Shklovsky's understanding of art in this regard, and made explicit elsewhere, is his attention to the role of the past, the literary tradition. Defamiliarization takes old and familiar ways of describing life in art and destroys them in order to renew their perceptibility and significance for the reader or observer. For Tolstoy, the total attentiveness required for monitoring one's present moral behavior pays conscience the price of the past—past art, past habit are, theoretically, subject to destruction in order that we remain aware, even vigilant in our conscious tracking of our behavior. This process is a metaphorical violence.

Though one may take Tolstoy to task for his unreasonable moral expectations, he also sympathetically addresses the effacement of consciousness and conscience through stupefaction as a response to the irresolvable and oppressive contradictions he sees in Russian life. In "Why Do Men Stupefy Themselves?" he blames those who hide from conscience via alcohol and tobacco, but in *The Kingdom of God Is within You*, he recognizes a necessity for hiding from oneself. In this book on the philosophy of nonviolence, Tolstoy's earlier existential angst is given a political justification. Acknowledging the sixty thousand suicides in Europe, Tolstoy remarks that he is surprised there are not more.

> Every man of the present day, if we go deep enough into the contradiction between his conscience and his life, is in a state of despair. Not to speak of all the other contradictions between modern life and the conscience, the permanently armed condition of Europe together with its profession of Christianity is alone enough to drive any man to despair, to doubt of the sanity of mankind, and to terminate an existence in this senseless and brutal world. This contradiction, *which is the quintessence of all the other*

contradictions, is so terrible that to live and to take part in it is only possible
if one does not think of it—if one is able to forget it . . . . tomorrow some
crazy ruler will say some stupidity, and another will answer in the same spirit,
and then I must go and expose myself to being murdered, and murder
men—who have done me no harm—and more than that, whom I love. And
this is not a remote contingency, but the very thing we are all preparing for,
which is not only probable, but an inevitable certainty. To recognize this
is enough to drive a man out of his senses or to make him shoot himself.
And this is just what does happen, and especially often among military
men. A man need only come to himself for an instant to be impelled inevitably to such an end. And this is the only explanation of the dreadful intensity with which men of modern times strive to stupefy themselves, with
spirits, tobacco, opium, cards, reading newspapers, traveling, and all kinds
of spectacles and amusements.[41]

The surface meaning of this passage, to rail against forced conscription, is
apparent. Yet there are two kinds of violence cited, violence perpetrated by the
state and the violence one inflicts on oneself. The latter has a long history in
Tolstoy's writing. Tolstoy pondered the idea of suicide, if not suicide itself, from
the time of *Boyhood.* In *Anna Karenina* and in *A Confession,* suicide is what a
person contemplates when one faces the apparent meaninglessness of life. In
the case of state induced violence, however, the cause of despair is a contradiction of conscience and reality, what one knows to be right and the wrong one is
forced to do. It is no longer a question of the right meaning, which is entirely
accessible to conscience, if not to consciousness, but a question of obedience,
which now remains. By this time the Christianity that briefly served Tolstoy
after *A Confession* is linked too closely with the government to be of use to
an individual man. The repeated refrain in *The Kingdom of God Is within You*
is that one must choose between the Sermon on the Mount and the Nicene
Creed, between the dedication to nonviolence and submission to the rules
of a church.

The tension between struggle and submission clouds Tolstoy's attempts at
artistic clarity in the last phase of his career. His interpretation of stupefaction
as a need to forget, born of the contradiction between modern life and conscience, recalls Nietzsche: "As the man who acts must, according to Goethe, be
without a conscience, he must also be without knowledge; he forgets everything
in order to be able to do something."[42] De Man, who quotes this passage from
Nietzsche, makes this forgetting into a definition of modernism and ultimately
literature itself: "But Nietzsche's ruthless forgetting, the blindness with which
he throws himself into an action lightened of all previous experience, captures

the authentic spirit of modernity."[43] But as practitioners of modernism realize that their forgetting of the past itself will be historicized as a past, the paradox becomes apparent. So, too, with literature: "The distinctive character of literature thus becomes manifest as an inability to escape from a condition that is felt to be unbearable."[44] For Tolstoy, though he would reject entirely de Man's notion of literature, the burden is increasingly a biographical and literary past. What he needs is an aesthetics of complete consciousness, yet such consciousness is morally untenable, as is evident in his discussion of conscription. As a writer who is entirely aware of the shaping role of his readers, moreover, Tolstoy realizes that escape from the past of his authorship, that inevitable hermeneutic background for interpretation, is impossible. *What Is Art?* emerges from this paradox and is caught in it. Tolstoy repeatedly disavows his past literature, but invariably his aesthetic theory relies on knowledge of it in order to be comprehensible. Stupefaction, violence, and aesthetics are thus bound ever more closely in the narrative alibi of *What Is Art?*

WHAT IS ART?

> The chief peculiarity of this feeling [produced by art] is that the receiver of a true artistic impression is so united to the artist that he feels as if the work were his own and not someone else's—as if what it expresses were just what he had long been wishing to express. A real work of art destroys, in the consciousness of the receiver, the separation between himself and the artist—not that alone, but also between himself and all whose minds received this work of art.
>
> —*What Is Art?*

One of the chief arguments of this study has been that Tolstoy cultivates and makes creative use of the space between what an author says and what he leaves unsaid. Tolstoy's relationship to what is not written, we have seen, frequently shapes his authorial identity. Although, in his early years, Tolstoy strived to formulate nontraditional, anti-institutional narrative strategies that would, ideally, convey his thoughts perfectly to readers, "so that others could read me," as he wrote in "A History of Yesterday," Tolstoy never claimed complete intellectual union between author and reader. He maintained what Yurij Lotman would call the necessary asymmetry of semiotic structures in dialogue.[45] How could he craft and maintain an authorial identity to unite and enrich his fiction, if the reader and the author were of one mind? Those gaps of meaning were necessary for the co-creation of Tolstoy's authorial identity.

In Tolstoy's 1896 aesthetic treatise *What Is Art?* such absence-ridden, negative art is denigrated and abandoned in the name of utter communicative transparency and efficiency.[46] Yet there is a crucial paradox in Tolstoy's argument, as Jeff Love perfectly distills it: "The main argument of the treatise involves a thoroughgoing refutation of mediating discourses as such, thereby putting even itself in question as belonging to one such discourse, aesthetics."[47] True understanding of art requires that we not reflect upon it critically, but that is exactly what Tolstoy feels obligated to do at length in *What Is Art?* That perfect comprehension that was once just an ideal of lovers has become a defining requirement of Tolstoy's "genuine" art. Comprehension is authorized by man's relationship to God and brings the community of readers together in their relationship to God. Art is not just an ideal. "Art," Tolstoy writes, "like speech, is a means of communication, and therefore of progress, i.e., of the movement of humanity forward toward perfection."[48] He makes explicit the relation to God in communication: "People talk about incomprehensibility; but if art is the transmission of feelings flowing from man's religious perception, how can a feeling be incomprehensible which is founded on religion, i.e., on man's relation to God? Such art should be, and has actually always been, comprehensible to everybody because every man's relation to God is one in the same."[49] Lost in the exchange for a newer more perfect art, in addition to the lost possibility of romantic love, is all of Tolstoy's own past creative fiction, which Tolstoy disavows.

Nevertheless, knowing the early fiction and understanding how Tolstoy dismantles it is, as I will argue here, absolutely necessary to understand *What Is Art?* The argument for perfect comprehensibility is incomprehensible without that hermeneutic background. Tolstoy dismisses most of his previous fiction, but that does not make *What Is Art?* any less a self-directed document and a crucial statement of authorial identity.[50] Caryl Emerson appraises *What Is Art?* within the context of Tolstoy's interest in psychology: "Tolstoy's views on art have been undervalued in part because they have been misclassified. No one would consider his treatise a descriptive aesthetics of the artistic product. But it should also not be reduced entirely to an ethics. Tolstoy's aesthetics is closer to a psychology. What interests him are the psychological effects of producing and receiving art."[51] This new psychology of artistic communication revises Tolstoy's analytical psychology of characters. It is, in fact, a meta-aesthetic revision of the psychologism of Tolstoy's major fiction, as the aesthetic conditions for understanding narrative analysis of the emotions are now interrogated.

Tolstoy judges both art and his own past. Yet he doubts himself and his judgment, for example, because of his social origins. Gone from this new aesthetics is the aristocratic legitimacy that sustained Levin and removed his doubt: "I belong to the class of people whose taste has, by false training, been perverted. And therefore my old, inured habits may cause me to err, and I may mistake for absolute merit the impression a work produced on me in my youth."[52] Tolstoy blurs the boundary between biographical and literary history—his deformative upbringing shapes his literary influences. And there is a dual meaning in Tolstoy's consciousness of his errors in taste. Though he intends to champion comprehensibility, he has to admit that even *his* taste has likely been perverted by his upbringing, perhaps causing him to look not just at art but at his own past fiction in a mistaken way. As though following the reflexive gesture of Gadamer's historically effected consciousness or the example of some modernist author, he sees that his own history has shaped the way he looks at it. We may trust his aesthetic theory but not always his aesthetic judgment: "My only purpose in mentioning examples of works of this or that class is to make my meaning clearer, and to show how, with my present views, I understand excellence in art in relation to subject matter. I must, moreover, mention that I consign my own artistic productions to the category of bad art, excepting the story 'God sees the Truth,' which seeks a place in the first class [of good art], and 'The Prisoner of the Caucasus,' which belongs to the second."[53] Having committed himself to a complete revision of aesthetic theory, Tolstoy doubts his own taste and judgment and needs to rewrite an entire literary career. The birth of Tolstoy's aesthetic theory is at the expense of the death of Tolstoy's fiction. It is not just an aesthetic theory, however, but an overcoming of an older authorial self without which it would be unthinkable. *What Is Art?* provides the theoretical background to the revisionary authorial project Tolstoy has already embarked upon in his works of fiction and other essays.

Although Tolstoy early and often changed his mind about his authorial career, relishing his literary work and then throwing it overboard altogether, *What Is Art?* constructs an entire aesthetic theory to transcend his individual practices, even as it is predicated on his personal experience. Art, as Tolstoy explains, re-creates the author's experience: "If only the spectators or auditors are infected by the feelings which the author has felt, it is art. *To evoke in oneself a feeling one has experienced, and having evoked it in oneself, then, by means of movements, lines, colors, sounds, or forms expressed in words, so to transmit that feeling that others may experience the same feeling—this is the activity of art. Art is a human activity consisting in this, that one man consciously, by means of certain external signs, hands on to others feelings he has lived through, and that other people are infected by these feelings and also experience them.*"[54] Note first the continued emphasis on consciousness. Real art is grounded in the author's experience, though not the experience of another work of art. Though there is nothing particularly radical or avant-garde in this definition, neither is it a simplistic realism. Having lived through and in his own way participated in the debates on realism in the mid-nineteenth century, Tolstoy comes to regard mimesis skeptically. That is why he focuses on the subjective feeling of an experience rather than the object itself. That feeling must be transmitted (and he assumes that all such feelings may be transmitted) so that others will experience it, too. The conscious experience, we recall from "Why Do Men Stupefy Themselves?" is the bulwark of conscience.

Infection, proselytization even, heighten the communicative demands on art. Communication is as crucial here as it was in Tolstoy's early work, but there are some important changes. In his early work, Tolstoy explored in unusual ways the philosophical repercussions of the entire communicative act. What gets into the work of art and what is left out both affect the constitution of the author's identity and the role of the work of art as an object of pleasure. In this later stage of his aesthetics, distracting details, and the diverting passages that Tolstoy used to ponder whether literature could entertain as well as instruct, are translated into mere noisy interference in the artistic transmission of a particular feeling. He writes: "The ideal of excellence in the future will not be the exclusiveness of feeling, accessible only to some, but, on the contrary, its universality. And not bulkiness, obscurity, and complexity of form, as is now esteemed, but, on the contrary, brevity, clearness, and simplicity of expression. Only when art has attained to that, will art neither divert [забавлять] nor deprave men as it does now."[55] Where the early Tolstoy sought a disintermediated relationship with the reader, now he valorizes an efficient relationship with the reader, which, though related, is not necessarily the same thing. The detailed descriptions of an early work, "Lucerne," for example, are superfluous for the later Tolstoy. Reminding us of his shift away from metonymy, he draws a deliberate comparison between the superfluity of detail and the reader's abundance of wealth: "For people of the wealthy classes, spending their lives in idleness and luxury, demand continual diversion [развлечений] by art."[56] Tolstoy uses metaphors of consumption throughout *What Is Art?* as though to demonstrate that the wealthy classes can afford to grow literarily corpulent on meals of needlessly realistic detail.[57] The impoverishment of upper-class literature leads them to see, in addition, an abundance of literary topics, where in fact those topics are totally exhausted. Here we have Tolstoy's apotheosis of slender literary efficiency, which is evident in his late stories, where the pages number dozens rather than hundreds or thousands.

An alibi, we recall, is necessarily two narratives, if not several, since we readers must keep in mind both the story that is told (the exculpatory evidence) and the negative story that is not told (the perpetration of the crime). The late fiction must be read, by contrast, in relation to Tolstoy's emerging efficient aesthetics. The narrative message is intended to be necessarily singular, since conflicting meanings interfere with the communicative imperative. Nevertheless, one of the paradoxes of Tolstoy's late aesthetic theory, a paradox that has undoubtedly been clear throughout this book, is that, though Tolstoy's late work negates his early work and rewrites it, it is not quiescent or conventional or even univocal in its message. As I have argued regarding "The Kreutzer Sonata" and "The Death of Ivan Ilyich," and as the diverse scholarship itself proves, interpretive meaning is in fact multiple and often disjunctive. Moreover, though Tolstoy bases the entire aesthetics of *What Is Art?* on comprehensibility, the literature he authors after it is not necessarily so easily understood. *Resurrection*, for example, is as unequivocally moral a novel as Tolstoy ever wrote. Yet the wealth of meaning in *Resurrection*, not to mention the novel's popularity, derives from the reader's knowledge of Tolstoy's previous novels, the tradition of the society novel, as well as the model of the wives of the Decembrists, who followed their husbands into exile. (Tolstoy long contemplated writing a novel on the Decembrists—in fact, the end of *War and Peace* points in this direction, as Pierre's politics evolve.) *Resurrection* tantalizes us with sex and violence so that we may share Nekhlyudov's struggle and spiritual rebirth. Even though *Resurrection* fails to meet the literary standard of an *Anna Karenina*, it is certainly not simple or brief. It is understood fully not just in the context of *What Is Art?* but also in the context of what it is not. It is not *The Cossacks*, or *War and Peace*, or *Anna Karenina*. This dual hermeneutic register informs the novel.

Tolstoy did not abandon literary style or give up his war with literary institutions, but he is saddled with his own past authorial identity. That identity itself creates interference in the transmission of Tolstoy's moral message. Such is also the case in *What Is Art?* While railing against the upper classes, Tolstoy quotes and rephrases Voltaire: "Voltaire said that '*Tous les genres sont bons, hors les genres ennuyeux*'; but with even more right one may say of art that *tous les genres sont bons, hors celui qu'on ne comprend pas*, or *qui ne produit pas son effect*, for of what value is an article which fails to do that for which it was intended?"[58] Who, if not upper-class readers, especially those of a certain age, appreciates Tolstoy's quote of Voltaire in the original French? Why does Tolstoy make his own point in French? (There is more French poetry quoted in *What Is Art?* than there is Russian poetry.) And for that matter, just who is Tolstoy's intended audience in *What Is Art?* Not necessarily the wealthy, but also not the peasant and native artists whom he idealizes in his treatise. He may think the peasant women's chorus exemplifies good art, but he is unlikely to hand them a copy of his book. By themselves these are minor points. Yet the aesthetic treatise is doubly encoded. It addresses two audiences, those who know his early work and students of the later moral philosophy, but also aesthetic sinners like himself, who may still be reading Voltaire.[59]

Reaching an audience in the way he wants to, a perennial problem for Tolstoy, continues to shape his work significantly. In a preface to the uncensored English edition, he complains of the original Russian version: "A book has appeared under my name containing thoughts attributed to me which are not mine."[60] The censor had removed and changed the text. One is reminded of Tolstoy's response (in his unsent letter to the editor of *The Contemporary*, Nekrasov) to the changes which were made in his very first publication, *Childhood*. We recall Tolstoy's complaint: who wants to read about *my* childhood? He now chastises himself for not having learned his lesson, for compromising when he should have remained firm: "I have narrated all this [publication history] in such detail because it strikingly illustrates the indubitable truth that all compromise with institutions of which your conscience disapproves—compromises which are usually made for the sake of the general good—instead of producing the good you expected, inevitably lead you, not only to acknowledge the institution you disapprove of, but also to participate in the evil that institution produces. I am glad to be able by this statement at least to do something to correct the error into which I was led by my compromise."[61] Starting out with institutional complaints, Tolstoy returns habitually to matters of authorial identity, to explaining himself. Again, as though in spite of himself, Tolstoy makes more of the communicative event of literature than his formalized late aesthetics allows. Speech to the other (here, the reader) is simultaneously reflexive, as Tolstoy continues to adjust his own relation to the means and mode of literary expression and publication. An implicit, but crucial, answer to the question of what art is remains authorial control over the message and its transmission.

Once we recognize how Tolstoy continues to develop a reflexive authorial identity, even though he has abandoned his past works, we may look to some of the same literary touchstones of Tolstoy's narrative alibi. To start, the use of violence in art is sanctioned, at least in certain circumstances, by Tolstoy's approving example of the Vogul tribe's dramatization of the hunt for reindeer. Confronting violence allows them to live with it.[62] This undercurrent of violence is unsurprising, since, as Michael Denner reminds us: "It is worth noting from the beginning that [Tolstoy's] metaphor of contagiousness is one of sublimated violence."[63] I have already mentioned, moreover, how diverting detail no longer reflects Tolstoy's concern for how literature edifies as it entertains. Third, he also renews and develops his long-standing war against criticism and critics (harkening back, yet again, to the young Tolstoy's distaste for becoming a journalist). As he writes in *What Is Art?* "A friend of mine, speaking of the relation of critics to artists, half jokingly defined it thus: 'critics are the stupid who discussed the wise.' However partial, inexact, and rude this definition may be, it is partly true and is incomparably more just than the definition which considers critics to be men who can explain works of art. 'Critics explain!' What do they explain? The artist, if a real artist, has by his work transmitted to others the feeling he experienced. What is there, then, to explain?"[64] We return here to Tolstoy's early battles against paraphrase, summed up in his defense of *Anna Karenina*:

> If I wanted to say in words all that I had in mind to express by my novel, I should have to write the same novel which I wrote all over again. If nearsighted critics think that I wanted to describe only what I like, how Oblonsky dines and what shoulders Anna has, they are mistaken. In everything, in almost everything I have written, I was guided by the need to bring together ideas linked among themselves, in order to achieve self-expression. But every idea expressed by itself in words loses its meaning, becomes terribly debased when it is taken alone, out of the linking in which it is found. This linking is based not on an idea, I think, but on something else, and to express the essence of that linking in any way directly by words is impossible, but it is possible indirectly, with words describing images, actions, situations.[65]

But this, as I have been arguing, is what is so fascinating about *What Is Art?* Tolstoy claims that his old work is no longer acceptable under his new definition of art. Yet this new aesthetics really becomes fully meaningful only in light of the early narrative techniques of disintermediation. When viewed in terms of Tolstoy's aesthetics over his entire career, critics are not just critics, and criticism is not just mistaken interpretation—these are forms of additional mediation, obstacles of literary communication. He writes in *What Is Art?* that "an artist's work cannot be interpreted. Had it been possible to explain in words what he wished to convey, the artist would've expressed himself in words. He expressed it by his art only because the feeling he experienced could not be otherwise transmitted. The interpretation of works of art by words only indicates that the interpreter is himself incapable of feeling the infection of art."[66] The same words could have been written at almost any time in Tolstoy's career. So at the same time that Tolstoy reinvents himself, he also forges authorial continuity and authority over the literary process and institutions.

Tolstoy's anti-interpretive tirade tells us something about the early aesthetics that we might not have gleaned at first. The inviolability of the early fiction (having to write *Anna Karenina* all over again) relied on a shaky foundation. With his defense of *Anna Karenina*, he turns to the inscrutable notion of "linkages of ideas," the truth of which are in their relation with one another. In *What Is Art?* the irreducible truth of art relies on its religious nature. To repeat an essential quote: "Art, like speech, is a means of communication, and therefore of progress, i.e., of the movement of humanity toward perfection."[67] This march towards perfection, once unimaginable to the author of *War and Peace*, the opponent of notions of historical progress, is the manifestation of man's religious perception: "The movement forward of humanity, that which is voiced by religious perception, has no limits."[68] Tolstoy's ecumenical approach to religion seems a good analogy to his approach to literature. Ideally, religious perception is perfectly comprehensible, just as good art is, but that "every man's relation to God is one and the same" is a poor basis for such a conclusion, especially since many religions preach that every man's relation to God is not at all one and the same. Tolstoy dismisses literary critics, but he fails entirely to address literary competency. Not all readers are capable of such perfect comprehension, despite an author's best intentions. And, similarly, some readers recognize a surplus of meaning, in spite of the author, by virtue of their knowledge of Tolstoy's earlier work.

Love was once Tolstoy's register of perfect comprehension. The analogy still serves Tolstoy, but the degree to which the terms have changed radically dramatizes his aesthetic revisionism. Just as a surplus of detail feeds corpulent upper-class readers, and a surplus of authorial history threatens to undermine Tolstoy's late aesthetic efficiency, so too does a surplus of aesthetic pleasure suggest sexual deviancy. I quote at length Tolstoy's comparison of art to a prostitute:

Awful as the comparison may sound, what has happened to the art of our circle and time is what happens to a woman who sells her womanly attractiveness, intended for maternity, for the pleasures of those who desire such pleasures.

The art of our time and of our circle has become a prostitute. And this comparison holds good even in minute details. Like her it is not limited to certain times, like her it is always adorned, like her it is always salable, and like her it is enticing and ruinous.

A real work of art can only arise in the soul of an artist occasionally as the fruit of the life he has lived, just as a child is conceived by its mother. But counterfeit art is produced by artisans and handicraftsmen continually, if only consumers can be found.

Real art, like the wife of an affectionate husband, needs no ornaments. But counterfeit art, like a prostitute, must always be decked out.

The cause of the production of real art is the artist's inner need to express a feeling that has accumulated, just as for a mother the cause of sexual conception is love. The cause of counterfeit art, as of prostitution, is gain.

The consequence of true art is the introduction of a new feeling into the intercourse of life, as the consequence of the wife's love is the birth of a new man into life.

The consequences of counterfeit art are the perversion of man, pleasure which never satisfies, and the weakening of man's spiritual strength.

And this is what people of our day and of our circle should understand in order to avoid the filthy torrent of depraved and prostituted art with which we are deluged.[69]

It would be easy to criticize Tolstoy over a passage like this. The prostitute appears regularly in religious texts, and is also a metonym in Tolstoy's late work for his own autobiographical succumbing to sexual temptation as a young man. He does not seem to notice, moreover, that inscribing one's aesthetic philosophy onto women's bodies, using the analogies of prostitution, childbirth, and dress, is not likely to communicate it effectively. His provocation gets in the way. One would also have difficulty imagining a more overburdened register of aesthetic theory.

Most striking here, I would like to argue, is Tolstoy's implicit reinterpretation of *Anna Karenina*, which was also an important subtext for "The Kreutzer Sonata." Both *What Is Art?* and "The Kreutzer Sonata" make metonymic detail, and any ornament detracting from the efficiency of infection, into sexual depravity. Anna becomes like art in the novel, but not authentic art. She is seductive, often misleading, and by practicing birth control she severs the connection between her sexual attractiveness and procreation. She writes a children's book at a time when she has little interest in children. The art she embodies is possibly ruinous: Levin narrowly escapes her grasp and returns to Kitty, who is simultaneously child, mother, and perfect interlocutor. But in our first consideration of the novel, Anna seemed merely to embody a kind of modern art that had lost its moorings in reality, drifting perilously into a sea of pure reflection, without object. Anna's suicide, as Tolstoy initially reinterpreted it in *A Confession*, was an act of strength: recognizing the cruel joke of life, she ends her life. And, after all, Anna's art is the most perplexing, dramatic, and mesmerizing of the novel. There is something in Anna that provokes the best art of the entire novel, Mikhaylov's portrait of her. Vronsky's reaction to the portrait is instructive: "'One needed to know and love her as I love her, to find just that sweetest spiritual expression of hers,' thought Vronsky, though he himself had only learnt to know that 'sweetest spiritual expression' through the portrait. But the expression was so true that it seemed both to him and to others that they had always known it."[70] That is to say, Anna's unrepresentable spiritual essence is revealed by the visual representation, and Vronsky therefore *recognizes* that which he has never seen. Vronsky's impossible act of visual recognition, laden with the heavy irony that Vronsky knows neither Anna nor art, conformed to Tolstoy's dissatisfaction with traditional empirical epistemology: empirically, you cannot recognize as true what you have never known. Tolstoy was not a romantic, and Vronsky is not born with the "imprint" of Anna upon his soul. Dropping his irony along the way, Tolstoy reinterprets the aesthetics of this passage in *What Is Art?*. The painting simply reveals something so true that it seems as though he has known it all along. We can rephrase the passage like this: Vronsky recognizes the hidden truth of Anna's expression not the expression itself.

In *What Is Art?*, Tolstoy remakes Vronsky's recognition of Anna's spiritual expression into a statement of the truth of religious art. He writes: "The business of art lies just in this—to make that understood and felt which, in the form of an argument, might be incomprehensible and inaccessible. Usually it seems to the recipient of the truly artistic impression that he knew the thing before but had been unable to express it."[71] Mikhaylov's art of "removing the wrappings" was itself antithetical to Tolstoy's late aesthetics in practice if not in outcome. True art transforms "bad" subjects (as does Tolstoy himself) and in doing so also transforms the recipient of this art. *What Is Art?* adapts and purifies Mikhaylov's aesthetics.

Tolstoy in his later years seems tangled in a web of contradictions. Acutely aware of his own shortcomings, he allows and even encourages others to take him as a moral guide. Although he was resolutely opposed to violence and unwholesome sex, he fills his stories with both. Renouncing both his aristocratic education and the bulk of his literary oeuvre, he writes tracts that cannot be understood without them. And arguing for an efficient communicative relation to one's readers, he diverts and complains about critics. Behind all these strains lies a single dynamic, a paradox of purification, that powers the last work I will discuss. In "Father Sergius," Lev Tolstoy, a man striving for exemplary redemption, describes a character doing the same, and in the description he registers the violence, the lust, the hypocrisy, and the alibis that attend his efforts to be simple and pure.

THE EXAMPLE OF FATHER SERGIUS

While writing "Father Sergius," Tolstoy completed *What Is Art?* The story, fully contextualized by Tolstoy's late aesthetics, thus provides an excellent conclusion for our discussion of violence, narrative alibi, and fiction.[72] The plot is fairly straightforward. Father Sergius is a former aristocrat named Kasatsky who learns that his fiancée was the mistress of the tsar. His pride wounded, he breaks his engagement with her and becomes a monk. Father Sergius is later celebrated for his asceticism, saintly devotion, and for his heroic battle with temptation, when he chopped off his own finger rather than submit to lust (embodied by the divorcee Makovkina). Later in the story, after succumbing to lust for a different woman, he realizes that the true model of sainthood may be found in his cousin Pashenka, a poor wife and mother who toils only for others without recognizing her own sacrifice and without her sacrifice being recognized by others. "Pashenka is what I ought to have been but failed to be," he concludes. "In living for others, she lives for God."[73] Sergius then decides to live out his remaining days not as a celebrated miracle worker but as a poor, religious tramp. He is ultimately arrested and sent to Siberia.

Because it contains such a provocative description of Sergius's self-mutilation, "Father Sergius" makes a compelling example of narrative violence. For one can scarcely imagine this story without the dramatic and violent crescendo of that false ending. "Father Sergius" contains all the markers of Tolstoy's fully evolved aesthetics of a narrative alibi, of presence and significant absences. Like "After the Ball," it demonstrates Tolstoy's purposeful deconstruction of his early narrative aesthetics. Consider, to give a single important example, how the story fractures our expectations of a psychological transparency of self, which was heralded as a goal of Tolstoy's early narrative fiction. The story begins with a tempting narrative riddle: "In Petersburg in the eighteen-forties a surprising event occurred. An officer of the Cuirassier Life Guards, a handsome prince who everyone predicted would become aide-de-camp to the Emperor Nicholas I and have a brilliant career, left the service, broke off his engagement to a beautiful maid of honor, a favourite of the Empress's, gave his small estate to his sister, and retired to a monastery to become a monk. The event appeared extraordinary and inexplicable to those who did not know his inner motives, but for Prince Stepan Kasatsky [the future Father Sergius] himself it all occurred so naturally that he could not imagine how he could have acted otherwise."[74]

This disjunction between the self one knows and the self others know initiates the story, and creates the expectation that it will be resolved by the story's plot. What we know of Kasatsky from the start is that he is focused inward; there are "intense and complex strivings that went on within him."[75] He studies himself and his faults and he ceaselessly works to improve himself and his prospects. If others simply fail to understand him as he understands himself, we would never register that disjunction as revolutionary. (Even idealistic Levin recognizes that he and Kitty will sometimes fail to understand one another.) We may ask more specifically how violence entwines itself in the self-other, authentic-legitimate, mute-communicative oscillation that we have come to know in the preceding chapters on Tolstoy's narrative alibi.

In order to answer that question, we need to examine closely the staggering scene of Sergius's self-mutilation, when he cuts off his own finger, metaphorically castrating himself. The scene is introduced by the theme of monastic temptation and an allusion to the problem of identity as a Cartesian mind-body dilemma. An "inner conflict" surprises Sergius: "The sources of that conflict were two: doubts, and the lust of the flesh. And these two enemies always appeared together. It seemed to him that they were two foes, but in reality they were one and the same. As soon as doubt was gone so was the lustful desire."[76] Belief and sexual desire are articulated in this idiom of personal identity, because the story initially activates Tolstoy's old aesthetics of the legitimate self. Temptation is an effective device in narratives of legitimation, as readers are invited to share or resist the object of desire alongside the subject of the story. Tolstoy continually returns to this trope of sexual desire in narrative so that we may overcome that desire along with the hero and so that Tolstoy may purify his aesthetics, exorcizing the demon of readerly legitimation.

Sergius-Kasatsky seeks knowledge of himself so that others may know him (respect him, revere him). Complete command of the mind will quell desire, and yet the narrative is based on surprises for the self. He says to his fiancée, the tsar's mistress: it is "thanks to you that I have come to know myself."[77] His profession of gratitude is deeply ironic, because in fact he knows neither her (she is the tsar's mistress) nor, it follows, himself. The desire to know and gain command of oneself in order to display it to others provides the story with its narrative events. This command of knowledge of the self and the ability to communicate it are analogues for authorship. When Sergius finally overcomes his doubt and his need for others to legitimate his identity, he successfully completes his spiritual quest (and the story ends). The authentic life is revealed, as is typical for the later Tolstoy, in a recollection of childhood values, embodied by his cousin Pashenka. But the adventures of self-discovery that occupy Sergius forestall his recollection of her.

"Father Sergius" is like Tolstoy's other narratives of romantic desire in that communicativeness as such plays an important role both inside and outside the story. As Makovkina knocks at the door, Sergius looks through the glass window (that metaphor of consciousness, language, and literature), and it first reflects only his image (since he has been searching primarily for himself) before revealing hers. "Their eyes met with instant recognition: not that they had ever known one another, they had never met before, but by the look they exchanged they—and he particularly—felt that they knew and understood one another."[78] He is attracted to Makovkina physically, even socially. She represents the life of ease and pleasure that he has forsaken, and thus she mirrors Sergius's social desire. This misleading past of society life will ultimately be supplanted by his childhood memory of Pashenka. Yet Makovkina also represents an ideal of transparency, appearing as she does through the glass without any doubt as to her intentions. It is as though she manifests the temptation of authorial communication itself: to reach readers yet control the medium of communication. She is unmediated, and soon she is even unclothed. Tolstoy does not deny the communicative link between her and Sergius, but Sergius mutilates himself in order to hear only the voice of the spiritual quest within him, in order to mute all other voices. His inner spirit is subsequently imagined by him in the metaphor of a spring (another key metaphor of literary inspiration, opposed to the mirrored glass), which has dried up in him since he has become famous for his spiritual turn inward. "Sometimes in lucid moments he thought he was like a place where there had once been a spring of living water."[79] The comparison is apt, since the metaphor also projects Sergius's wish for impotency.

Sergius repeatedly defines himself negatively, as a kind of absence. His desire for impotency represents Tolstoy's project of severing narrative from its source in sexual desire. As he writes in *What Is Art?* "From Boccaccio to Marcel Prevost, all the novels and poems invariably transmit the feeling of sexual love in its different forms. Adultery is not only the favorite, but almost the only theme of all the novels."[80] Though we should not get waylaid by the undercurrent of sexual metaphor in the story, that imagery is most important in its narrative relation. Sergius cuts off his finger not just to curtail his lust but to end the conversation. His desire for impotency is also a desire for there to be no story. Violence often represents the limits of narrative potential for Tolstoy, and it creates those limits as well. John Kopper argues that, in the society of utter permissiveness that Tolstoy witnessed, he had to create new kinds of restrictive semiological fields in order for narrative events to demonstrate transgression: "In 'Father Sergius,' 'The Kreutzer Sonata,' and 'The Devil,' Tolstoy takes a narrative situation that presents a rather infertile semiological field. What can be said about a man's sexuality when the man can do what he wants?"[81] Violence dramatizes the celibacy that, were it not threatened, might be devoid of all narrative interest.

Tolstoy places Makovkina and Sergius on opposite sides of doors and other barriers. The narration of a collapse of space between elsewhere and here has been crucial, as we have seen in earlier chapters, to Tolstoy's narrative alibi. The absorbing presence of realism, most striking in the second-person narrative of "Sevastopol in December," accompanies the narrative focus on the discovery of the self. Makovkina's plan to seduce Sergius, to force him to respond to her by crossing that physical barrier, recalls Tolstoy's disintermediating realistic experiments as a young author. Seduction denigrates the ideal of presence in Tolstoy's early realism and recasts it as lust. The lust for sex is the lust for presence. Tolstoy marks the change between that early aesthetics and this late one, however, by dismantling not just presence but totality, in this case the integrity of the desiring body (rather than the integrity of the desired body, as in "After the Ball"—both parties are damaged by illicit sexual desire, would be Tolstoy's point). Sergius does respond to Makovkina's pleas that he come to her. He crosses the boundary that separates them, but not before exacting a vicious disintegration of his own body. Chopping off his finger makes his capitulating presence partial, representing Tolstoy's refusal to make meaning available in this narrative quest for self-understanding and for romance. The story and its resolution are not exhausted by the romantic trope of overcoming obstacles to desire. The old narrative goals of sexual desire are maintained; they propel the story forward, but not without irreparable damage. Tolstoy yields to presence, but only a disintegrated presence, arguing here that romantic desire dehumanizes us, even dismembers us. Sergius's finger is compared to a wooden "stick" easily severed by an ax used to chop wood.

But if the goal of the story is no longer to force meaning to reveal itself in a realistic world, as it was in the early fiction, what is accomplished by the mutilated body of the monk? The missing finger, like a missing puzzle piece, forces interpreters inside the story (e.g., Makovkina) and outside it (us) to reconstitute meaning anew. Makovkina sees the blood of Sergius's hand and she runs into the other room: "There on the floor she saw the bloody finger. She returned with her face paler than his and was about to speak to him, but he silently passed into the back cell and fastened the door. 'Forgive me!' she said. 'How can I atone for my sin?' 'Go away. God will forgive.'"[82] Absence, in other words, no longer fosters narrative curiosity—what may or may not happen next?—but conversion. The absence is a disturbing visual clue of the incompleteness of a person. There is no more story. There is only faith and a need to relinquish the present world. And thus readers are not at all surprised to find that the heretofore mellifluous Makovkina is decisively muted: she does not "utter a word all the way home. A year later she entered a convent as a novice, and lived a strict life under the direction of the hermit Arseny, who wrote letters to her at long intervals."[83] Violence, then, is the negative space that suggests where narrative must end and faith begin. (It is important to note that is related to Tolstoy's repeated muting of feminine sexual desire.)

We recall here that the foundation of the communicative goal of Tolstoy's aesthetics, once idealized by romantic love, was transformed in *What Is Art?* into a shared relationship to God. When Makovkina understands perfectly, she converts. This is what Tolstoy means by authenticity in the later stories—it is the recognition of a true self. Celibacy, represented by her entering the convent, is a return to the presexualized truth of childhood. Her reduction to silence, like Anna Karenina's death, symbolizes being perfectly understood at the end of all the travails of miscommunication. Slivitskaya retells, half jokingly, a misogynistic story of Tolstoy's notion of perfect conversation with a woman. "It is obvious that Tolstoy relates to words with mistrust. 'Yes, laconicism, if not silence,' he writes in his diary. His joking story is not without a serious point: 'At the Chicherins I was brought together with the Baroness von Raden, who was considered a very smart woman. We spent the evening together, and she didn't say a word. I was convinced that she was indeed smart' (M., 2, 58)."[84] Her silence made the case for Tolstoy.

In the end, Sergius, like Tolstoy, lives out the dream of realizing that metaphor of alibi. He goes *elsewhere*, beyond the boundaries of what can be told in the story, though in Tolstoy's case that becomes a sensational newspaper story itself. This conclusion turns the notion of communicating knowledge of oneself, the goal of the story's beginning, entirely on its head. Once Sergius knows himself he stops talking and the story concludes. We never find out his last thoughts. He never does reintegrate his inward knowledge of himself with society's view of him. The implicit promise of the story, that one's sinful identity can be ultimately transcended, abandoned without any metonymic traces to be narrated, is ultimately fulfilled. Sergius goes in his death where Tolstoy never could go, not just into some elsewhere but into another self no longer burdened by the past that follows along, not just into one's own memory but into the memory of others. This, too, is a kind of violence, a suicide, that Tolstoy realizes in his narrative alibi.

ON TOLSTOY'S AUTHORSHIP

For the conclusion of this book, I would like to treat Tolstoy's narrative alibi within the tradition of primarily western theories of authorial intent and identity. Narrative alibi is the term I have been using throughout this study to describe, first, Tolstoy's exculpatory fictions, works like "Father Sergius," where the author looks back at his previous sinful life and creates a narrative arc that leads toward conversion and repentance. I have also used the term *narrative alibi* to characterize the gaps or absences that Tolstoy incribed into his early works. Although all literary texts have gaps, Tolstoy especially worked to make the hidden parts of his early stories and novels crucial to their meaning. Why? Because he wanted to be unique or different, but also because he doubted the value of a literary authorship and refused to identify himself fully with his role as an author. Both aspects of narrative alibi are at work in the latter half of Tolstoy's career, when he takes advantage of the gaps in meaning in his early works and reinterprets them according to his late aesthetics. Crucially, Tolstoy seems to say in this later stage that he *intended* his early works to be read a particular way.

For Tolstoy, authorial intent is always paramount for understanding a work of art. From his earliest writings on literature, such as those unpublished essays in the draft version of *Childhood*, to his late aesthetic treatise, *What Is Art?*, Tolstoy suggested that the work of literature means primarily what the author wants it to mean. *What Is Art?* explicitly defines literature by its transmission of the author's feelings and ideas. Nevertheless, in his own literary authorship, which involved a frequent return to past works and implicit or explicit reinterpretation of them, he treated intention in a more complex manner than is suggested by *What Is Art?* After considering several of Tolstoy's works, his expressions, interpretations, and reinterpretations of given themes and formal devices, I believe that Tolstoy viewed intention as a dynamic and even changeable past to the work of fiction.[1] We are used to saying that great works of art change with the times; I think Tolstoy came to see his own creative intentions about his literary work as similarly flexible and changeable, and oriented toward the future.

Such a view of the past may surprise readers of *War and Peace*, since it differs substantially from Tolstoy's deterministic view of history in that epic novel. Historical events in Tolstoy's *War and Peace*, one recalls, reveal more of their determined nature the further the past recedes from our view. By contrast, I will argue, for Tolstoy a literary intention does not lose its variability or authority and may be renewed creatively as time passes. In *War and Peace* fading memories of battle become ever more fixed in typical, and false, narratives. The fading creative impulse of a past work of fiction, by contrast, may or may not become fixed and frozen in meaning. Tolstoy thus dehistoricizes intention, liberating it in a way that is both radical in his implicit approval of the malleability of the author's meaning for a work and conservative in his explicit reassertion of authorial control over the evolution of a work's meaning. Tolstoy came to conceive intent broadly.

The Western critical tradition has tended to restrict the role of intention. A narrow definition of authorial intention was reinforced by New Criticism, and particularly by Wimsatt and Beardsley's well known essay "The Intentional Fallacy." As they argued against literary interpretation that focused on uncovering the author's intended meaning of a text, they narrowed authorial intention to the genesis of a literary work: "The Intentional Fallacy is a confusion between the poem and its origins, a special case of what is known to philosophers as the Genetic Fallacy [a fallacy in which an argument succeeds or fails because of its source]."[2] In the process they reject numerous, more dynamic notions of authorial intention and creativity that point to a kind of inspirational force that may or may not be fully controlled by the artist. One thinks, for example, of Wordsworth's famous definition of good poetry as the "spontaneous overflow of powerful feelings," and other theories of expressivity.

For Wimsatt and Beardsley the truth of a work of art cannot be verified by comparison with the artifacts of a creator's volitional world. They define authorial intention explicitly in its objective sense: intention "corresponds to *what he intended*. . . . Intention is a design or plan in the author's attitude toward his work . . . the way he felt, what made him write." They reject that intention decisively: "The design or intention of the author is neither available nor desirable as a standard for judging the success of a work of literary art." Thus we should, the argument continues, reject authorial intention for both theoretical and practical-methodological reasons: intention betrays our confusion about the author's role in creation, and it is unclear how we could adequately uncover the author's intended meaning anyway. As to the former: "To insist on the designing intellect as a *cause* of a poem is not to grant design or intention as a *standard*." As for the latter: "If the poet succeeded in doing it, then the poem itself shows what he was trying to do. And if the poet did not succeed, then the poem is not adequate evidence, and the critic must go outside the poem—for evidence of an intention that did not become effective in the poem."[3] The author may be a cause (or agent) in the construction of the text, but are we willing to say he or she is the only source of meaning? Barthes, whom I will discuss below, makes a similar point in his essay "The Death of the Author." The author's intention both realizes and is realized by the text, and therefore makes a bad reference point.

On both theoretical and methodological counts, then, one finds ample reason to agree with the basic argument of Wimsatt and Beardsley. Yet—as was clear in the paradoxes of Tolstoy's *What Is Art?*—our access to authorial intention is further mediated and obscured by the language and expressions we have come to associate with creative impulses, including their unspeakability or irreducibility. The term *authorial intention* as we use it has multiple meanings, each of which may be caught up in our interpretive practices, which may not be reconcilable with one another. To use the term as though it were singular and transparently comprehensible, as Wimsatt and Beardsley do while rejecting it, is to oversimplify. As one might guess, their essay has provoked many replies both for and against authorial intention.[4] Tolstoy believed that authorial intention determined the meaning of a text, but he used the variability of meaning possible in the interpretation of literature as the basis to redefine that intention. This redefinition was possible, as I have argued, because Tolstoy's late creative process embraced in unique and brilliant ways various gaps and unspoken elements in his early narratives. Intent has an orientation toward the future that transcends the mere realization of the text. Two aspects of authorial intention are key to this revisionary aesthetics: a relation to the passage of time, the historical aspect of authorial intention, and a relation to Tolstoy's construction of an authorial identity, a biographical or autobiographical aspect of authorial intention.

Tolstoy is not alone in his revision of the historical specificity of authorial intention. In different ways both Roman Jakobson in his "The Statue in Puškin's Poetic Mythology," with its implied structuralist model, and T. S. Eliot in "Tradition and the Individual Talent," with its emphasis on the timelessness of canonical great works, dehistoricize intention. Jakobson discerns in Pushkin's oeuvre symbolic constants that identify the poet's work as his alone. "In the multiform symbolism of a poetic oeuvre we find certain constant organizing elements which are the vehicle of unity in the multiplicity of the poet's works and which stamp these works with the poet's individuality."[5] To search for "invariants" over the course of many different works, here the motif of the animated statue, is to understand fully the value of individual instances "only in their relation to a whole symbolic system."[6] Biographical, autobiographical, or sociological facts do not bind a work to a static historical point of origin. Authorial intent is replaced by an unbound and dynamic set of symbolic constants that still function to identify the poet. In a brilliant critical insight, Jakobson sees Pushkin exploiting creatively this very tension between static and dynamic in the semiotics of the statue, "the opposition of the *dead, immobile matter* from which a statue is shaped and the *mobile, animate being* which a statue represents."[7] One typically sees the same opposition in literary intention, which animates the literary work but is often construed as a moribund impulse opposed to the dynamic life of the work itself. Jakobson views Pushkin's iteration of the statue symbol in light of a larger system, which identifies the author's work but not his or her creative impulse—to which, I would argue along with Tolstoy, one can return.

For Eliot, like Jakobson, that creative impulse is not bound by its historical origin. Yet Eliot envisions authorship as an act of extreme depersonalization, as the work of art takes its meaning from its relationship to other great works of art in a timeless canon. "What happens is a continual surrender of himself as he is at the moment to something which is more valuable. The progress of an artist is a continual self-sacrifice, a continual extinction of personality."[8] What speaks for the meaning of a work of art are those aspects of tradition that transcend the individual poet. "We dwell with satisfaction upon the poet's difference from his predecessors, especially his immediate predecessors; we endeavour to find something that can be isolated in order to be enjoyed. Whereas if we approach a poet without this prejudice we shall often find that not only the best, but the most individual parts of his work may be those in which the dead poets, his ancestors, assert their immortality most vigorously."[9] Paradoxically, the best expression of authorial identity is found in its extinction.

For Jakobson's Pushkin, meaning is inseparable from identification, from the ways in which the poet's work reveals him as speaker. For Eliot, the extinction of personality is part of the intended act of authorship, and is a willed surrender of what is most identifying to the timelessness of canon. The most individual aspects of a poet are those where impersonal canonical voices speak through the poet. Both Jakobson and Eliot point to one crucial element of the act of authorship: the person who conceived and created the work of art at a particular moment in time is gone in an instant. For Jakobson, Pushkin attaches that moment of historical loss to himself by repeating it symbolically in an animate-inanimate opposition; for Eliot, the poet embraces the extinction of that moment to better prepare for inclusion in the museum of literary tradition. For both, the dehistoricization of intent is bound to a moment of creation as simultaneous, metaphorical death.

Though Jakobson and Eliot differ in their treatment of the expression or extinction of personality in authorship, they share with Tolstoy an interest in how intention loses historical specificity and determination. Repetition is change for Tolstoy—not, as in Eliot, a bid for timelessness. Nor is it an invariant, as it is for Jakobson, which Tolstoy would likely find even less open to creative reinterpretation. Regardless of the model or theorist, gestures of dehistoricization as a lost moment of creation ignore the multiple ways in which the past of a work of literature (genetically, as planning, notes or sketches, key biographical experiences, reading other authors or viewing art, etc.) actually figures prominently in its production. In spite of Wimsatt and Beardsley, one cannot always dismiss the overlap between the genesis of a work of literature and the author's intention toward it. This overlap or intersection between genesis and intention similarly combines the historical and biographical aspects of authorial intention.

It would be difficult to avoid considering Tolstoy's biography when we read his fiction. Russian formalist Boris Tomashevsky takes up the question of traces of biographical information in works of literature in the essay "Literature and Biography" (1923). He begins by citing the irreconcilability of two approaches to the problem. Biographers see the work of literature as just another fact of the author's life; "On the other hand, there are those for whom any kind of biographical analysis is unscientific contraband, a 'back-door' approach" to a kind of illicit interpretation.[10] Describing a model of analysis that by any measure includes a tremendous amount of literary criticism as it has been practiced if not theorized, Tomashevsky provides a middle path between biographical approaches and formalist-scientific approaches that banish all biographical information from literary analysis. Instead he considers the literary functions of biography, for example, of authors such as Voltaire and Rousseau, whose biographies were well known at the time and were part of the background of their literary works. "In fact," Tomashevsky writes, "the knowledge that their biographies were a constant background for their works compelled Voltaire and Rousseau to dramatize certain epic motifs in their own lives and, furthermore, to create for themselves an artificial legendary biography composed of intentionally selected real and imaginary events."[11] When authors use autobiographical information in their literary works, and readers are expected to know that information in order to understand the work fully, then Tomashevsky refers to that information as the biographical "legend." "The biographical legend is

necessary only to the extent that the literary work includes references to 'biographical' facts (real or legendary) of the author's life."[12] Authorial intent is thus
defined in part through interpretation.

With Romantic poets such as Byron, for example, the legend expands to
include much of the poet's life, and the boundaries between the author and
hero of the poem is blurred. The magnitude of the legend also varies from era
to era (and grows maximally, for example, in futurism with poets such as
Vladimir Mayakovsky). Yet the role of the literary historian remains the same.
"Thus, legends about poets were created, and it was extremely important for the
literary historian to occupy himself with the restoration of these legends, i.e.,
with the removal of later layers and the reduction of the legend to its pure
'canonical' form. These biographical legends are the literary conception of the
poet's life, and this conception was necessary as a perceptible background for
the poet's literary works. The legends are a premise which the author himself
took into account during the creative process."[13] This last statement, that the
author himself takes biographical legend into account during the creative process, is patently true in the case of Tolstoy and other authors but should not be
considered in a simplistic way. Our current conception of an author's biographical legend is often constituted by the legend itself. With Tolstoy, for example,
we view the early works with the future gray-bearded philosopher of Yasnaya
Polyana already fully formed in our minds. This mistaken view of Tolstoy may
be impossible to avoid completely, but that is why I have strived to indicate the
evolution of Tolstoy's authorial identity as a dynamic process between younger
and older author, a process that we enter into more as we interpret his work. As
a younger author, when fewer readers knew his biography, Tolstoy could not
have used his authorial identity as part of the background of his literary works
in the way that he later would.

In spite of any shortcomings in Tomashevsky's theory, he shows greater
sensitivity to the issue than Barthes does in his essay on "The Death of the
Author." Both theorists see readerly interpretation as pointing the way out of
the dilemma of intention. Like Eliot, Barthes sees authorship as a profoundly
depersonalizing process. Authorship destroys the very authorial person we think
may be confiding meaning to us: "Writing is the destruction of every voice, of
every point of origin. Writing is that neutral, composite, oblique space where
our subject slips away, the negative where all identity is lost, starting with the
very identity of the body writing." He goes on: "No doubt it has always been that
way. As soon as a fact is *narrated* no longer with a view to acting directly on reality but intransitively, that is to say, finally outside of any function other than that
of the very practice of the symbol itself, this disconnection occurs, the voice

loses its origin, the author enters into his own death, writing begins."[14] Notice the redefinition of literature, which is here reduced to the "practice of the symbol itself." Barthes transforms authorship from a constructive model, in which a biographical person builds meaning in the text, into a performative one, in which meaning is created by the reader enacting it with the text as script. He affirms "the necessity to substitute language itself for the person who until then had been supposed to be its owner. For him, for us too, it is language which speaks, not the author; to write is, through a prerequisite impersonality . . . to reach that point where only language acts, 'performs', and not 'me.'"[15]

Under this revised version of literature, we must change not just our ideas of authorship but also our sense of the reader's role. Both may be better understood with the help of linguistics. Alluding to the notion of the shifter (e.g., "I" or "you"), in which a person occupies temporarily a grammatical space in speech, Barthes writes: "Linguistically, the author is never more than the instance writing, just as *I* is nothing other than the instance saying *I*: language knows a 'subject', not a 'person', and this subject, empty outside of the very enunciation which defines it, suffices to make language 'hold together', suffices, that is to say, to exhaust it."[16] Literature is thus not made by an author at a particular historical time, it is performed by a "scriptor," who is "born simultaneously with the text."[17] The reader's job is to disentangle the web of quotations and references within the text. "The reader is the space on which all the quotations that make up a writing are inscribed without any of them being lost; a text's unity lies not in its origin but in its destination. Yet this destination cannot any longer be personal: the reader is without history, biography, psychology; he is simply that *someone* who holds together in a single field all the traces by which the written text is constituted."[18] In other words, the reader is no more a person than the author is; he or she is a created interlocutor for the speech of the text.

More than anyone surveyed so far, Barthes both dehistoricizes authorship and severs it from biography. In fact, history is largely irrelevant, since in temporal terms Barthes' scriptor is simultaneous with the reading of the text. From Barthes' point of view, it does not matter whether Tolstoy believes he as author has the final word on the meaning of a novel or story. That is not the way literature works. But it is an important part of the way literature works for Tolstoy. Thus for all of Barthes' influence on contemporary theories of authorship, he adds little to our consideration of Tolstoy.

Treating authorial intention as the past of a work of literature does not necessarily entail emptying the author-as-subject of all meaningful agency in creativity. Other theorists describe a more dynamic past of authorial intention in a manner that better contextualizes Tolstoy's own authorial practices. For these theorists, the point is to recombine the genesis of a work of art and its literary evolution with authorial identity. In *The Life of the Poet*, for example, Lipking suggests that, in spite of calls to view poetry after the "death" of the author as almost anonymous, we should not turn away from the notion that the poet's life has a shape, a beginning and an end, that is meaningful and worthy of study in and of itself. "We know far more about the facts of poets' lives, their quirks and torments, their singularities, than we do about the life that all poets share: their vocation as poets. . . . We cannot ignore the evidence that the development of a great many poets follows a consistent internal logic."[19] Like Tomashevsky, who theorized a similar view of literary biography, Lipking aims "to write not the biographies of poets but the biography that gets into poems: the life that has passed through a refining poetic fire."[20] Lipking's work reminds one that while authorial identity often derives from singularity or originality of the author, the way that identity is created and used within literature may be open to generalization. Tomashevsky and Lipking both tell us that authorial biographies figure in crucial, unignorable ways in the works of an author. The career of a real person impinges on the meaning of a text and renders untenable simple notions of authorial intention. Tolstoy's ambivalence toward the profession of authorship tangibly affected how he wrote his early works.

Considering how an author initiates a work of literature, Edward Said differentiates between an origin, which is divine, and a beginning, which is more historical and takes into account intention and influence. According to Said, the latter is an activity implying return and repetition rather than simple linear accomplishment: "Beginning and beginning-again are historical whereas origins are divine. . . . A beginning not only creates but is its own method because it has intention. In short, beginning is *making* or *producing differ-ence*."[21] That is to say, the return and repetition of a beginning do not necessitate sameness but produce an alternate notion of "adjacency." In modernist writers like Joyce, Said sees a necessity "*at the beginning* for them to see their work as making reference, first, to other works, but also to reality and to the reader, by adjacency, not sequentially or dynastically. The true relationship is by adjacency."[22] For example, Joyce's *Ulysses* does not suggest that this is what happens to the Greek idea as it descends to Dublin but rather that Odysseus is like Bloom, Telemachus like Daedalus, and so forth.[23] Thus we have analogues rather than derivations.

The distinction is important for us because Tolstoy forces the reader of his later fiction to resolve whether repeated themes, motifs, or literary devices of his early fiction derive or descend somehow from the early works as amplifications or further clarifications, or whether such returns and repetitions create, in

Said's terms, adjacency. As I have been arguing, I believe that Tolstoy intervenes authoritatively but misleadingly in the reception of his later works by suggesting they are derivations and continuations, further clarifications, of ideas sketched but not fully revealed in the early works. With adjacency, Said maintains intention but makes it flexible. He writes: "An intention, therefore, is a notion that includes everything that later develops out of it, no matter how eccentric the development or inconsistent the result. . . . By *intention* I mean an appetite at the beginning intellectually to do something in a characteristic way. . . . With regard to a given work or body of work, a beginning intention is really nothing more than the created *inclusiveness* within which the work develops."[24] Although this definition of intention is somewhat vague—intention includes everything that develops subsequent to it—Said avoids the deterministic, and insoluble, suggestion that intention is equivalent to a work's meaning. By associating "beginning intention" not just with one work but also with a body of work he also implies an elasticity in intention that is exemplified in our discussion of Tolstoy.

Said follows Foucault, who sees the author's name as characterizing "a particular manner of discourse,"[25] and envisions a wide scope for intention in its authority: "I call these rules of pertinence *authority*—both in the sense of explicit law and guiding force (what we usually mean by the term) and in the sense of that implicit power to generate another word that will *belong to* the writing as a whole (Vico's etymology is *auctor: autos: suis ipsius: propsius: property*)."[26] Tolstoy's authority is demonstrated in his return and reshaping of his intention in his early works. The return suggests authorization—authorization that the early works belong with and should be read alongside later works, even as later works repudiate the early works. He also claims authority in precisely this latter sense, since his restatement of early themes intends to supplant or efface the early meanings. Along the same lines, we can usefully adjust Bloom's *Anxiety of Influence* by considering the context of a *single* author's career, in which the poet's struggle is not with a precursor but with his or her own authorial past. Bloom's term *apophrades* ("the return of the dead"), for example, resonates with Tolstoy's treatment of his early work. Bloom writes of apophrades: "The new poem's achievement makes it seem to us, not as though the precursor were writing it, but as though the later poet himself had written the precursor's characteristic work." In other words, Tolstoy manages to make us think that the early works were written not just by the same person who wrote the later works (it was, after all, unquestionably the same person), but also by the same author—an artist who has devoted himself primarily to didactic and religious nonfiction and, occasionally, fiction. As I have argued, we risk attributing too much continuity to Tolstoy's literary career precisely because his late works deceptively resemble the early works. That false continuity masks Tolstoy's more dynamic approach to the authorial past.

We have thus far examined several theorists who in one way or another have complicated our initial simpler view of authorial intention. I have asserted that Tomashevsky, Lipking, Said, and Bloom are more congenial for our study of Tolstoy because they allow for the flexibility of some change in intention over the course of the author's life and career. It is not entirely clear, however, how changes in intention could be accessed in the text without simultaneously considering the author's direct biographical intervention. Tolstoy returns to his story "Kholstomer" and rewrites it in a way that emphasizes a Christian conclusion, and the initial intent of the story has been reshaped and expanded. Said would have us consider the two iterations of the text as adjacent to one another, but we could not say that the intent of the story shifted in the absence of Tolstoy's actual rewriting of it. Nevertheless, just such a shift in authorial intention without actual rewriting has been the focus of much of the previous chapters. How does one register a change in intent without retreating into the facts of authorial biography? To start, as I have argued, Tolstoy can use techniques or literary devices or scenarios that directly recall or repeat earlier uses, shift his intended meaning, and therefore suggest that we should read the earlier work according to the model of the later work. Are we to read the language of love and romance in *War and Peace* as false and misleading because similar scenes in *Resurrection* suggest Tolstoy ultimately would have us so interpret it? How should we view such shifts in the text of *War and Peace?*

Yuri Tynianov in "On Literary Evolution" (1929) seems to envision just such a problem. Like our other theorists, he makes the crucial distinction between a work's genesis, which too often relies upon the author's psychology, and its literary evolution.[27] Literary evolution is, for Tynianov, the proper way to study literary history. He rejects the simple causality of psychological explanations of the genesis of a work of literature as well as the "history of generals" approach to literary history. Under the influence of Tynianov, we could say neither that Tolstoy writes *War and Peace* to express and reflect the happiness of his early married years nor that he writes it to do one better than Stendhal. For Tynianov, to study a work of literature in its literary evolution is to see its synchronic relation to social, linguistic, and literary orders, as well as to consider its diachronic relation to such orders in the past. With literary evolution Tynianov means to study the "mutation of systems."[28]

Like Jakobson, who influenced him and with whom he collaborated, Tynianov rewrites traditional terms like *influence* and *intention*. He speaks specifically of intention when he describes how the literary order interacts with the nonliterary world. In literary evolution the dominant elements in the literary system differ over time, and this mutability necessarily points to their changing interrelationship with other nonliterary orders. Tynianov refers to those orders as "social conventions," which "are correlated with literature first of all in its verbal aspect."[29] The interrelationship of the verbal function with social conventions is, in Tynianov's terminology, the *ustanovka* (intention or orientation) of the literary work. The term *ustanovka*, which Jakobson introduced as a translation for Husserl's term *Einstellung*, has multiple meanings for Tynianov.[30] Jurij Striedter divides these meanings into three corresponding levels of intentional relation: "For Tynianov, it is only through *ustanovka* that the work as a functional system also becomes a system with an intentional reference, and that the historical or evolutionary aspect becomes a cardinal point in his general theory. He distinguishes three levels of the intentional relation: (1) Every factor of a work of literary art has an intentional relation to the complete work of art as a system. (2) This system has an intentional relation to the system of literature and literary evolution. (3) Literature and literary evolution have, through language, which is both the medium of literary creation and the medium of social communication, an intentional relation to the entire human environment in its historical and social transformations."[31] *Ustanovka* describes the intentional relationship of the individual elements of a work to the whole work, the whole work to the system of literature, and the system of literature to the extraliterary environment.

Tynianov succeeds here, I believe, because he redefines intention as a set of relational functions within the text itself, thus mitigating the danger of reducing authorial intention to biography or to a historically determined event. Because the literary system and cultural conventions change through time, the intention of the text will also change. As Striedter points out, ironically enough, Tynianov was attacked for being both too historical (by Wellek) and not historical enough (by Jauss).[32] In this book, I generally agree with Jauss's appeal to Gadamerian hermeneutics, as I have tried to hold Tolstoy's works to their historical positions in his evolution as an author.[33] I do this not in order to restrict Tolstoy to the meaning he attributed to, say, *Childhood* in the 1850s, but so that we may see his later works in dialogue with the early works (adjacent to them, as Said puts it) rather than deriving from them and superseding them. Tynianov's model of literary evolution is flexible enough to accommodate both my own more historicizing approach to authorial intention as well as Tolstoy's dehistoricizing attitude toward it.

Tolstoy's attitude toward authorial intent, and his creative use of it, remind us of more than the obvious fact that he wanted to assert control over the meaning of his oeuvre. Insofar as we can ascertain through our own interpretation of Tolstoy's fiction, we can see that his genius was not just in authoring great works but also in creating, maintaining, and using his authorial identity in complex and unique ways, even in nonautobiographical works. Although authorial identity is not the same as personal identity, one of the most probing recent philosophical works on subjectivity, personal identity, narrative, and ethics, Ricoeur's *Oneself as Another*, gives us a useful way to describe Tolstoy's authorial identity.

In *Oneself as Another* Ricoeur continues to develop the notion of narrative identity that he introduced in his earlier *Time and Narrative*, but he primarily concentrates on reconciling analytical and continental philosophical treatments of personal identity. Ricoeur separates his work decisively from the Cartesian tradition of understanding the subject as a disembodied, unchanging, rational substance, and claims that "the hermeneutics of the self is placed at an equal distance from the apology of the cogito and from its overthrow."[34] He thus charts a path between the certainty of Descartes' philosophy of the subject and Nietzsche's suspicious rejection of it. There is neither one unchanging thinking substance in personality nor an entirely constructed and variable object. *Oneself as Another* consequently does not fit easily into any one camp in twentieth-century debates on the social construction of the self. But it does provide a vocabulary for describing the conflicted view of Tolstoy's authorial identity as both stable and variable.

Ricoeur proposes two meanings for identity, *idem* and *ipse* ("same" versus "self," depending on which word one uses in Latin for "identity"). The former contains the sense of self-sameness and the latter implies "no assertion concerning some unchanging core of the personality."[35] For Ricoeur selfhood is always ipse-identity, and he uses the terms selfhood and ipse-identity interchangeably. Ipse-identity-selfhood contains the possibility of change for an individual over the course of one's life, and requires a different kind of defining process than idem-identity. Ipse-identity is not the "what" of the self, as Ricoeur frequently says, that is implied in the sameness of idem-identity and the focus of much analytic philosophy, but the "who" of the self that changes over time. Nevertheless, there are models of permanence in time for ipse-identity. Indeed there must be some kind of permanence in time for any notion of personal identity, which has three components: numerical identity, qualitative identity, and uninterrupted continuity between first and last stages of development of an individual.[36]

Ricoeur sees two models of permanence in time for ipse-identity — "character" and "honesty/faithfulness/keeping one's word/self-constancy/self-maintenance" (Ricoeur refers to it variously). Character permits us to reidentify an individual as being the same, as his/her descriptive features compound "numerical identity and qualitative identity, uninterrupted continuity and permanence in time."[37] Character is the way that ipse is most like idem: "Permanence of character expresses almost complete mutual overlapping of the problematic of idem and of ipse, while faithfulness to oneself in keeping one's word marks the extreme gap between the permanence of the self and that of the same and so attests fully to the irreducibility of the two problematics one to the other. I hasten to complete my hypothesis: the polarity I am going to examine suggests an intervention of narrative identity in the conceptual constitution of personal identity in the manner of a specific mediator between the pole of character, where *idem* and *ipse* tend to coincide, and the pole of self-maintenance, where selfhood frees itself from sameness."[38]

As important as character is, however, the notion of keeping one's word is the more crucial model of permanence in time for ipse-identity. "Keeping one's word expresses a *self-constancy* which cannot be inscribed, as character was, within the dimension of something in general but solely within the dimension of 'who'?"[39] Character is how ipse-identity resembles idem-identity, but keeping one's word is a model fully belonging to ipse-identity. Ricoeur embraces it as a form of permanence that requires the mediation of temporality, and that is best expressed in narrative.

Narrative is constantly affirming the permanence of identity and disrupting it. Narrative identity mediates between character and self-maintenance or honesty as a "discordant concordance" in identity at the level of emplotment. That identity "can be described in dynamic terms by the competition between a demand for concordance and the admission of discordances which, up to the close of the story, threaten this identity. By concordance, I mean the principle of order that presides over what Aristotle calls the 'arrangement of the facts.' By discordances, I mean the reversals of fortune that make the plot an ordered transformation from an initial situation to a terminal situation"[40] In other words, retrospectively the identity of the character in the story is the narrative itself, but disruptive possibilities are always present prospectively and emerge with new or unexpected events in the plot. Discordant concordance is the synthesis of heterogeneity in a narrative.

Keeping one's word provides selfhood or ipse-identity freedom from sameness, because it relies on a different kind of intention, one that refers to the future. Ricoeur observes that there are three uses for the term intention: "having done or doing something intentionally, acting with certain intention, intending to. . . . The third use alone contains explicit reference to the future."[41] His main objection to traditional accounts of intention (he discuss the work of Anscombe at some length) are that they seek mainly to discriminate intentional actions from unintentional actions. Looking backward they fail to differentiate between why someone acts, his or her reason for acting, and the cause of an action. When one "intends to" accomplish a certain action in the future, judging the truth becomes problematic. To understand this more crucial form of intention, in which the "why" of the act is more important than its cause, Ricoeur develops the concept of "attestation."

Attestation provides selfhood or ipse-identity a way of verifying identity and the "intention to" in contrast to the verification deployed by science in the consideration of idem-identity. With attestation he intends "to characterize the alethic (or veritative) mode of the style appropriate to the conjunction of analysis and reflection, to the recognition of the difference between selfhood and sameness, and to the unfolding of the dialectic of the self and the other—in short, appropriate to the hermeneutics of the self considered in its three-fold structure."[42] Too complex in its lengthy elaboration to summarize briefly, attestation overlaps with conscience and honesty or keeping one's word. It offers selfhood a model of certainty that one finds in testimonials of belief, and it opposes and substitutes for the certainty of causality in the physical world of science. It is credence. "Attestation is fundamentally attestation of *self*. This trust will, in turn, be a trust in the power to say, in the power to do, in the power to recognize oneself as a character in a narrative, in the power, finally, to respond to accusation in the form of the accusative: 'It's me here' (*me voici!*), to borrow an expression dear to Lévinas."[43] In that sense, attestation is not just a recognition of one's own identity in selfhood, but also a claiming of responsibility, as Ricoeur says, a response to moral accusation.

There are some conclusions we can draw about Tolstoy's view of authorial intent and identity in light of Ricoeur's philosophical arguments. For example, Ricoeur shifts the conversation about intention away from a retrospective, causal point of view, thereby avoiding the problems of genesis we encountered in other theories. The "intention to" that he describes for an action is oriented toward the future and verified by attestation's testimony. Attestation accounts for the ethical stance Tolstoy takes in looking back, not just in order to retell the history of his authorship of a series of literary works but to account for them in a larger narrative of redemption. Tolstoy's reinterpretation of past works is in this way not so much a falsification of what they may have meant in their original context as an assertion of an identity, an attempt to remain true to oneself, to bring the contradictions of identity into productive accord. Ricoeur is fascinated by the paradox that attestation implies: "How can one say at one and the same time 'Who am I?' and 'Here I am!'? Is it not possible to make the gap separating narrative identity and moral identity work to the benefit of their living dialectic? This is how I see the opposition between them transformed into a fruitful tension."[44] In this view, Tolstoy's revisionary late aesthetics do not tell the story of authorship but of the author's redemption.

I have argued that narrative alibi is a process in which the later Tolstoy returns to the lacunae and interpretive gaps of the earlier works, which he originally used to underscore his novelty as an author, in order to reinterpret them creatively and maintain control over his intended meaning. Ricoeur's investigation of intention, narrative, and selfhood suggests a similarly dynamic process more productive than the simple opposition of early career and late career. The incompleteness of "intention to" in ipse-identity, which focuses attention on the changeability of the self, accommodates well a process in which Tolstoy returns to open-ended elements of his authorial identity and provides them with a more stable narrative of a religious philosopher purifying his biography and ideas. But Ricoeur highlights the dialectic of ipse-identity in narrative between its more or less malleable aspects, character and keeping one's word. The process is ongoing.

One may see continuity and further clarification in Tolstoy's development of ideas of romantic love in, for example, *Childhood, The Cossacks, War and Peace, Anna Karenina,* "The Kreutzer Sonata," and *Resurrection,* as though he did not get the ideas quite right and returned again and again to them until he was satisfied. But it is just as clear that Tolstoy was not satisfied. Dismissing the question of genetic explanations entirely, if we were to interpret authorial intention simply as the idea that Tolstoy wished to realize in each work, we would be forced to conclude not just that he failed but that his failure became worse and worse as time passes and his ideas changed. In Ricoeur's terminology, it is as though with each iteration of those narratives of romantic love (*Anna Karenina,* etc.) Tolstoy hoped to convert his desire to "keep his word" into a constitutive part of his "character." That is to say, he returned to and treated the most changeable aspects of his intentions as though they were more permanent components of his authorial identity. But the process itself would suggest otherwise.

Now, alibi and attestation would seem to be incompatible, even contradictory: I was not there! There I was! But both of them, and especially their interaction, were essential to a mind broad enough to recognize the heterogeneity of the self and at the same time to insist on its integrity. The young Tolstoy asks himself "who am I?" and "what can I become?" Ricoeur might call this a "fruitful tension" of self: core and continuous potential, idem and ipse. The old Tolstoy revisits his early works, sees much that is wrong and even sinful, yet wants to redeem in those works some morally sound meaning. Tynianov and

Jakobson might see an evolving structure with dominance shifting from one element to another; Tomashevsky and Lipking could see a fine interweaving of life and text, which enters the past of the writer's life, which makes its way into a new text. Barthes' description of the interaction between depersonalized scriptor, text, and readers sounds oddly reminiscent of Tolstoy on opera: both of them describing something so artificial, clunky, and thoroughly formalized that any notion of "communication" seems ridiculous. When Tolstoy corrected the Gospels, was he grappling with a strong predecessor, as Bloom would have it, or was he, with Said, removing the text from an overmythologized origin and restoring it to its truest beginning, which is adjacent to all humanity?

These theories, in short, are helpful not as a priori conditions for seeing Tolstoy's career, but as lights we can turn toward various aspects of Tolstoy's creation of meaning. What persists in Tolstoy is not a particular semiotic configuration, nor a specific motif, but a self-adjusting process of creating possibilities—including possible meanings—and revising what has already been given. This continuous negotiation of present, future, and past conditioned Tolstoy's authorship of his many texts and of his long life, and did not stop until his death.

Notes

INTRODUCTION

1. See L. N. Tolstoi, *Polnoe sobranie sochinenii* [*PSS*], 90 vols. (Moscow: Gosudarstvennoe izdatel'stvo "Khudozhestvennaia literatura"), 1928–58, 30: 111. Hereafter cited as *PSS* in the notes and in the text. See also, Leo Tolstoy, *What Is Art?* trans. Aylmer Maude (New York: Liberal Arts Press, 1960), 123. Unless indicated otherwise, all Russian quotes by Tolstoy refer to this edition. All English translations are mine unless otherwise noted. I have adjusted quotes from published translations throughout the book for accuracy or to emphasize a particular available meaning.

2. *PSS* 30: 163n1; *What Is Art?* 155n5.

3. Eric de Haard, "Gogol and Tolstoi's Madmen: Dimensions of Intertextuality," *Essays in Poetics: The Journal of the British Neo-Formalist Circle* 28 (Autumn 2003): 51. Needless to say, Tolstoy was not entirely uninterested in literary life. His first visits to St. Petersburg as a newly published author were full of enthusiasm. But he never dedicated himself to literary institutions in St. Petersburg or Moscow in any sustained manner.

4. The concept runs throughout the second half of *Truth and Method*. Hans-Georg Gadamer, *Truth and Method*, trans. Joel Weinsheimer and Donald Marshall, 2nd rev. ed (New York: Continuum, 1989), 335 and passim.

5. Vladimir E. Alexandrov, *Limits to Interpretation : The Meanings of Anna Karenina* (Madison: University of Wisconsin Press, 2004).

6. *What Is Art?* 7–8.

CHAPTER 1. GUILTY STORIES

1. Irtenev is the family name of the hero of the *Childhood* trilogy. Moreover, Tolstoy hid the manuscript from his wife so that she would not recognize in it Tolstoy's (former) lust for Aksynia Bazykina, with whom Tolstoy had an affair and who bore him a son. See *PSS* 27: 718, 722–23.

2. Richard Gustafson, *Leo Tolstoy: Resident and Stranger; A Study in Fiction and Theology* (Princeton, NJ: Princeton University Press, 1986); Gary Saul Morson, *Hidden in Plain View: Narrative and Creative Potentials in "War and Peace"* (Stanford, CA: Stanford University Press, 1987). Isaiah Berlin's famous essay on *War and Peace, The Hedgehog and the Fox*, also belongs here: *The Hedgehog and the Fox: An Essay on Tolstoy's View of History* (New York: Simon and Schuster, 1986).

3. Inessa Medzhibovskaya provides an authoritative examination of Tolstoy's conversion, noting the "striking characteristic normally overlooked in studies of Tolstoy's conversion: this experience was a gigantic philosophical and religious project, the search for a new outlook rather than a crisis-begotten tragic moment" (*Tolstoy and the Religious Culture of His Time: A Biography of a Long Conversion, 1845–1887* [Lanham, MD: Lexington Books, 2008], xv).

4. How a text generates a plurality of interpretations, as well as a limit to them, is the primary concern in Vladimir E. Alexandrov, *Limits to Interpretation : The Meanings of Anna Karenina* (Madison: University of Wisconsin Press, 2004).

5. Boris Eikhenbaum, "The Creative Incentives of Tolstoy," in *Reminiscences on Tolstoy*, ed. Kalpana Sahni (Atlantic Highlands, NJ: Humanities Press, 1980), 115.

6. Gary Saul Morson has written extensively of the way in which Tolstoy embraces contradictions and conflicts between possible events in his narratives, and he elaborates a notion of "sideshadowing" to account for how authors gesture toward alternative narrative possibilities. Morson writes: "sideshadowing conveys the sense that actual events might just as well not have happened. . . . Alternatives always abound, and, more often than not, what exists need not have existed. *Something else* was possible, and sideshadowing is used to create a sense of that 'something else.' . . . Along with an event, we see its alternatives; with each present, another possible present" (Gary Saul Morson, *Narrative and Freedom: The Shadows of Time* [New Haven: Yale University Press, 1994], 118). I am interested more in the way that Tolstoy uses gaps in his narratives to define and redefine his authorial identity.

7. Leo Tolstoy, *Resurrection*, trans. Rosemary Edmonds (New York: Penguin Books, 1966).

8. The distinction shows up in several places, but see, for example, Tolstoy's 1887 essay *On Life* (PSS 26: 313). Conversion is not simply an act of blind faith for Tolstoy, but a process of rational consciousness that leads one in the direction of Christianity: "A person always comes to know everything through reason, and not through faith" (ibid., 439). The mental process of recognizing the true meaning of life is thus frequently emplotted in a story by Tolstoy, as in "The Death of Ivan Ilyich."

9. Tolstoy, *Resurrection*, 117; italics in original (PSS 32: 82–83).

10. (PSS 23: 5).

11. It is standard critical practice to follow Wayne Booth's distinction between the author, the historical person himself or herself, and the "implied author," who "chooses consciously or unconsciously what we read" and who "is the sum of his own choices." These are in turn distinct from the narrator, who is not always the same person as the implied author and who communicates directly with the reader. See Wayne C. Booth, *The Rhetoric of Fiction*, 2nd ed. (Chicago: University of Chicago Press, 1983), 74–75.

The distinction between implied author and author is less useful for Tolstoy, who purposely conflates the two and blurs the boundaries between them.

12. The lacuna in authorial identity that Tolstoy embeds in his fiction and that interests me is not equivalent to that mutable aspect of self that is so important to philosophical definitions of personal identity. In personal identity, there is a combination of changing and unchanging dimensions of the self. As Olga Slivitskaia quotes Tolstoy: "One I is changing, another I is unchangeable" (*PSS* 55: 359). The mutable self emerging in one's experience of the world is full of potential, and provides a key to the barrier between self and world that troubled Tolstoy. Slivitskaia's formulation of the problem is: "It's not a person *in* his relation to another person and the world, but a person *as a relation* to all (that is, to other similar 'relations,' that is, other people) and to the All (that is, to the infinity of the world)." The problem of intercourse-communication (*obshchenie*) with the world is the problem of personal identity for Tolstoy. See Olga Slivitskaia, "*Vojna i Mir*" *L. N. Tolstogo: Problemy chelovecheskogo obshchenia* (Leningrad: Izd-vo Leningradskogo universiteta, 1988), 12–13.

13. *PSS* 60: 308. English translation from Leo Tolstoy, *Tolstoy's Letters*, trans. and ed. Reginald Frank Christian, 2 vols. (New York: Charles Scribner's Sons, 1978), 1: 129.

14. Turgenev swore after hearing Tolstoy abuse Sand that he would break off relations with Tolstoy. This story and others about how Tolstoy would tweak Turgenev and other litterateurs in St. Petersburg are often retold in the biographies. For example, see: A. N. Wilson, *Tolstoy: A Biography* (New York: W. W. Norton, 1988), 137. See also: Justin Weir, "Turgenev as Institution: *Notes of a Hunter* in Tolstoy's Early Aesthetics," in *Turgenev and His Contemporaries*, ed. Joe Andrew and Robert Reid (Amsterdam: Rodopi, 2009).

15. Jeff Love, *Tolstoy: A Guide for the Perplexed* (New York: Continuum, 2008), 1.

16. Compare Love's description of the authority of revelation for Tolstoy: "Nonetheless, Tolstoy seems to stake all on revelation, holding that reason has authority only when subservient to revelation and, even then, this authority is derived, secondary" (ibid., 124).

17. Michael A. Denner, "Accidental Art: Tolstoy's Poetics of Unintentionality," *Philosophy and Literature* (2003) 27: 291. Denner shortly thereafter adds: "In 'On Art' (1889) Tolstoy remarks that in the 'highest degree of craft, all effort is invisible, such that one forgets about the artist. The lowest degree, when a work ceases begin a work of art, is a technique where one ceaselessly sees the effort and it's impossible to forget about the artist" (ibid., 296).

18. See Harold Schefski, "Tolstoy's Urban-Rural Continuum in *War and Peace* and *Anna Karenina*," *South Atlantic Review* 46, no. 1 (1981): 29.

19. Pavel Biriukov, *Biografiia L.N. Tolstogo: V dvukh knigakh*, 2 vols. (Moscow: Algoritm, 2000), 1: 230.

20. N. I. Burnasheva, ". . . *Projti po trudnoj doroge otkrytija* . . .": *Zagadki i nakhodki v rukopisiakh L'va Tolstogo* (Moscow: Flinta, Nauka, 2005), 27.

21. Ibid., 56, and elsewhere.

22. A different and compelling interpretation of the relationship between Tolstoy's writing and personal identity is offered by Irina Paperno, in "'Who, What Is I?': Tolstoy in His Diaries," *Tolstoy Studies Journal* 11 (1999): 32–54.

23. See Boris Tomaševskij, "Literature and Biography," in *Readings in Russian Poetics: Formalist and Structuralist Views*, ed. Pomorska and Matjeka (Ann Arbor: Michigan Slavic Publications, 1978), 47–55.

24. Mikhail Bakhtin, by contrast, uses the model of authorship as a way of understanding personal identity. See his "Author and Hero in Aesthetic Activity," in Mikhail Bakhtin, *Art and Answerability: Early Philosophical Essays*, ed. Michael Holquist and Vadim Liapunov, trans. Vadim Liapunov (Austin: University of Texas, 1990): 4–256. In my concluding chapter, I associate authorial identity with Ricoeur's notion of *ipse*-identity in *Oneself as Another*, trans. Kathleen Blamey (Chicago: University of Chicago Press, 1992).

25. See William K. Wimsatt and Monroe C. Beardsley, "The Intentional Fallacy," *Sewanee Review*, 54 (1946): 468–88; and, for example: Tynjanov, "On Literary Evolution," in *Readings in Russian Poetics: Formalist and Structuralist Views*, ed. Ladislav Matejka and Krystyna Pomorska (Cambridge, MA: MIT Press, 1971; rpt., Ann Arbor: Michigan Slavic Publications, 1978), 66–78.

26. Tynjanov, "On Literary Evolution."

27. N. N. Gusev, *Letopis' zhizni i tvorchestva L. N. Tolstogo* (Moscow: Academia, 1936), 47. In an 1858 letter to Botkin Tolstoy proposes a journal devoted to purely artistic, versus political, works and subjects. The journal was never realized. See: Rimvydas Šilbajoris, *Tolstoy's Aesthetics and His Art* (Columbus, OH: Slavica Publishers, 1990), 21–22.

28. Ibid., 52.

29. Ibid., 129. Biriukov discusses Tolstoy's pedagogical and publishing project more fully (*Biografiia*, 1: 241–68).

30. Eikhenbaum, "Creative Incentives of Tolstoy," 113.

31. November 12, 1851. English translation from Wilson, *Tolstoy*, 88. The letter is mentioned by many others.

32. Lydia Ginzburg, *On Psychological Prose*, trans. Judson Rosengrant, (Princeton, NJ: Princeton University Press, 1991), 244.

33. The idea runs throughout his *Truth and Method*, trans. Joel Weinsheimer and Donald Marshall, 2nd rev. ed. (New York: Continuum, 1989).

34. Barthes' essay is reprinted in Seán Burke, ed., *Authorship: From Plato to the Postmodern; A Reader* (Edinburgh: Edinburgh University Press, 1995), 127.

35. A good example of this is found in "A History of Yesterday," one of Tolstoy's first literary works, which shares in the reflective first-person form style of his diaries. In that work, the narrator finds that he cannot describe yesterday without speaking first of the day before yesterday. As is well known, in his initial plan for *War and Peace* Tolstoy did not envision beginning in 1805, but he found he was unable to describe the war without retreating several years. See Morson, *Hidden in Plain View*, and Kathryn B. Feuer, *Tolstoy and the Genesis of "War and Peace,"* ed. Robin Feuer Miller and Donna Tussing Orwin (Ithaca, NY: Cornell University Press, 1996).

36. Consider Tolstoy's elevation of his failed defense of the soldier Shibunin in 1863 as a key moment in the development of his theory of nonviolence (*PSS* 37: 67). See Walter Kerr, *The Shabunin Affair: An Episode in the Life of Leo Tolstoy* (Ithaca, NY: Cornell

University Press, 1982). Biriukov's biography was a key source for Eikhenbaum's *Young Tolstoi*, since Eikhenbaum did not have access to all of Tolstoy's papers.

37. In Foucault, "What Is an Author?" in *Authorship*, ed. Burke, 234. "The author's name is not a function of a man's civil status, nor is it fictional: it is situated in the breach, among the discontinuities, which gives rise to new groups of discourse and this singular mode of existence" (ibid., 235).

38. Wilson, *Tolstoy*, 88.

39. *PSS* 46: 182, dated October 24, 1853. Often quoted, for example, see Feuer, *Tolstoy and the Genesis*, 17. One can find an echo of this sentiment in the essay "To Readers" from an early variant of *Childhood*. Lev Tolstoi, *Polnoe sobranie sochinenii v sta tomakh* (Moscow: Nauka, 2000), 19: 42. Feuer writes: "*War and Peace* would seem to have been the crisis which broke the fever, for afterward Tolstoy was never again seriously troubled by the question of digressions *and* he never worked again so hard (or to such brilliant effect) at the concealment of the author's view when he was not speaking in his own person" (8).

40. Squaring one's life also has an unexpected twist in Tolstoy's 1886 story "How Much Land Does a Man Need?"

41. Eduard Babaev, *Lev Tolstoi i Russkaia zhurnalistika ego epokhi* (Moscow: MGU, 1978), 13.

42. Walter Moss, *Russia in the Age of Alexander II, Tolstoy and Dostoevsky* (London: Anthem, 2002), 24.

43. De Haard has studied Tolstoy's early fiction extensively. He mentions Turgenev-like passages or allusions to *A Hunter's Sketches* in "The Woodfelling," "Family Happiness," and "Polikushka" (Eric de Haard, *Narrative and Anti-Narrative Structures in Lev Tolstoj's Early Works* [Amsterdam: Rodopi, 1989], 71, 150, 55). See also the excellent section on Turgenev's influence on Tolstoy, in Donna Tussing Orwin, *Consequences of Consciousness: Turgenev, Dostoevsky, Tolstoy* (Stanford, CA: Stanford University Press, 2007), 69–75.

44. From Goldenveizer, July 28, 1902. See Aleksandr Goldenveizer, *Vblizi Tolstogo: Vospominaniia* (Moscow: Zakharov, 2002), 116. Noted in Leo Tolstoy, *Polnoe sobranie sochinenii v sta somakh* (Moscow: Nauka, 2000), 1: 397.

45. Biriukov, *Biografiia* 1: 83. Others included Sterne, *Sentimental Journey*; Rousseau, *Confession, Emile, Nouvelle Heloise*; Pushkin, *Eugene Onegin*; Schiller, *The Robbers*; Gogol, "The Overcoat," "Ivan Iv. and Ivan Nik.," "Nevsky Prospect," "Vy," *Dead Souls*; Druzhinin, *Polinka Saks*; Grigorovich, *Anton-Goremyka*; Dickens, *David Copperfield*; Lermontov, *Hero of Our Time, Taman*; Prescott, *The Conquest of Mexico*. The Sermon on the Mount, Rousseau, and Dickens are listed as *enormously* influential.

46. He had likely been rereading the stories recently republished in a single volume. See Gusev, *Letopis'*, 35.

47. May 30, 1852; ibid., 28.

48. De Haard, *Narrative and Anti-Narrative*, 71. The text is "Zapiski o Kavkaze: Poezdka v Mamakai-Iurt," in *PSS* 1: 330.

49. De Haard, *Narrative and Anti-Narrative*, 71.

50. Boris Sorokin, *Tolstoi in Prerevolutionary Russian Criticism* (Columbus: Ohio State University Press for Miami University, 1979), 159. Sorokin also credits M. O. Gershenzon,

Mechta i mysl' I. S. Turgeneva (Moscow, 1919); repr., Brown University Reprint (Providence, RI: Brown University Press, 1967), 69–73. Orwin, *Consequences of Consciousness*, 73–75.

51. In 1896, as quoted in Gusev, *Letopis'*, 214.

52. Ivan Turgenev, *First Love*, trans. Isaiah Berlin (New York: Penguin Books, 1950), 103.

53. To name a few: Wachtel sees Tolstoy plainly as a myth maker (Andrew Baruch Wachtel, *The Battle for Childhood: Creation of a Russian Myth* [Stanford, CA: Stanford University Press, 1990]); Wilson calls the post–*Anna Karenina* Tolstoy an autobiographical puppet master revealed in all sorts of "completely inconsistent roles: squire, starets, yurodivy, lecher, saint, husband, historian, private landowner, public dissident, etc., etc." (*Tolstoy*, 305); Love mentions that "Tolstoy's autobiographical writings may be interpreted with justice as a sophisticated form of self-fashioning" (*Guide for the Perplexed*, 17).

54. Ernest J. Simmons, *Leo Tolstoy*, special limited ed. (Boston: Little, Brown, 1946), 124. Orwin notes that Turgenev took the epithet "troglodyte" from Schiller's *Ode to Joy* (Orwin, *Consequences of Consciousness*, 198n30).

55. *PSS* 1: 403.

56. Ibid., 1: 402.

57. *PSS* 1: 402, 425.

58. *PSS* 1: 426.

59. Written to the artist-caricaturist L.N. Vaksel.' *PSS* 1: 425.

60. Sorokin, *Prerevolutionary Russian Criticism*, 155–56. Here and elsewhere I benefit much from Sorokin.

61. Ibid. 157.

62. Ibid. According to Sorokin, "Turgenev objected more vigorously to the intruding bias against civilization" (ibid. 159), and, "For Turgenev, Tolstoy was not only an archaic thinker but an anti-intellectual, who tried to lock his readers into a rigid formulaic state of mind by means of repetitive indoctrination" (ibid., 161), and he objected to how Tolstoy made "intelligent, educated women [into] shrews and hypo-crites" (ibid.). After reading *Confession* he writes to D. V. Grigorovich: "This is a piece remarkable through its sincerity, truthfulness, and power of conviction. Yet it is based on faulty premises throughout—and ultimately leads to a gloomy denial of all vitality in human life. . . . This, too, is a nihilism of sorts. By the way, I am surprised that Tolstoy, who, among other things, denies art, nevertheless surrounds himself with artists" (ibid., 166).

63. Simmons, *Leo Tolstoy*, 98–99, 92–93.

64. Gusev, *Letopis'*, 49.

65. Viktor Borisovich Shklovskii, *Lev Tolstoy* (Moscow: Progress Publishers, 1978), 162.

66. See chapter 2 for a discussion of the drafts to *Childhood* and Tolstoy's unsent letter to Nekrasov.

67. Ginzburg, *On Psychological Prose*, 245.

68. Chernyshevsky's praise of Tolstoy's psychological method set the mark for this kind of criticism. See A. K. Knowles, ed., *Tolstoy: The Critical Heritage* (London: Routledge, 1978). Many articles and books address psychology in Tolstoy. There is an argument to

be made that Tolstoy is interpreted this way because of the ascendancy of psychology in the nineteenth and twentieth centuries, which gave readers an easier idiom with which to discuss Tolstoy's profound spiritual searching. Susan Sontag writes: "A large part of the popularity and persuasiveness of psychology comes from its being a sublimated spiritualism: a secular, ostensibly scientific way of affirming the primacy of 'spirit' over matter" (*Illness as Metaphor and AIDS and Its Metaphors* [New York: Anchor Books, 1990], 55–56).

69. Boris Eikhenbaum, *The Young Tolstoi*, trans. Gary Kern (Ann Arbor, MI: Ardis, 1972), 4.

70. These two quotes are from different contexts, though I separated them with only ellipses: Donna Tussing Orwin, ed., *The Cambridge Companion to Tolstoy* (Cambridge: Cambridge University Press, 2002), 49. Orwin goes on to say: "He had another purely personal reason for writing fiction as well. Like many people, he fantasized about life as a means of understanding and controlling it. Very often, therefore, his works are counterpoints to his life at the time he wrote them, and represent imagined solutions to real life problems" (ibid.). Elsewhere Orwin writes similarly that the works are "provisional resolutions of conflicts within Tolstoy, each has a 'personality' more integrated and less contradictory than Tolstoy's own" (Donna Tussing Orwin, *Tolstoy's Art and Thought, 1847–1880* [Princeton, NJ: Princeton University Press, 1993], 10). Rather than suggesting that his works simplify real-life problems, I understand Orwin to suggest that these provisional solutions then participate in the interpretive complexity of art and fiction. Works that require us to unravel the metafictional and self-referential knots created by their ties to the author's biography and his problems create a vast number of interpretive puzzles; that is why authors, such as Tolstoy, who have such complex and even conflicted attitudes toward the authorial image they are presenting, like to write these kinds of works. Fredric Jameson uses the term "containment strategy" to discuss how works provide formal unity, however provisional, to a hidden or repressed contradictory whole. See Fredric Jameson, *The Political Unconscious: Narrative as a Socially Symbolic Act* (Ithaca, NY: Cornell University Press, 1981).

71. Amy Mandelker, *Framing Anna Karenina: Tolstoy, the Woman Question, and the Victorian Novel* (Columbus: Ohio State University Press, 1993).

72. Eikhenbaum, *Young Tolstoi*, 4.

73. Ibid., 4–5.

74. Ibid., 3.

75. Here I follow this article of Carol Joyce Any, "Boris Eikhenbaum's Unfinished Work on Tolstoy: A Dialogue with Soviet History," *PMLA* 105, no. 2 (1990): 234. See also her book on Eikhenbaum, where the relationship to work on Tolstoy is further examined: *Boris Eikhenbaum: Voices of a Russian Formalist* (Stanford, CA: Stanford University Press, 1994).

76. Any, "Boris Eikhenbaum's Unfinished Work," 236. Any resolves the dilemma by considering Eikhenbaum's 1929 *Moi vremennik* (My Periodical), which reveals, as she writes: "the right of writers to maintain independence from political constraints, to define their own personal and literary attitudes toward their social environments" (237).

77. Any discussion of aporia, double-encodings, slippery meanings in language and so forth instantly suggest to many readers the literary critical trend of deconstruction and

its practitioners Jacques Derrida and Paul de Man, among others. Modernist writers discovered and used many of the tricks and contradictions of language and epistemology that deconstructionist critics subsequently caught up to and devoted many books to describing (see Steven Cassedy, *Flight from Eden: The Origins of Modern Literary Criticism and Theory* [Berkeley: University of California Press, 1990]). My experience with Tolstoy suggests that one should not limit that observation to modernist writers.

78. Ginzburg, *On Psychological Prose*, 245.

79. Henry Gifford, *Tolstoy* (Oxford: Oxford University Press, 1983), 9–10.

80. Orwin, *Cambridge Companion to Tolstoy*, 54.

81. Boris Eikhenbaum, *Lev Tolstoi: kniga pervaia: Piatidesiatye gody* (Leningrad: Priboj, 1928), 33–34. Eikhenbaum mentions a "history of today" rather than a history of "yesterday," the more familiar title, because that was how Tolstoy referred to the early fragment in his diary while working on it, for example in the entry for March 25, 1851.

82. The formalists did pay attention to the distinction between the published versus the unpublished in the sense that they noted how the hierarchy of genres may change over time. See Tynianov, "The Ode as an Oratorical Genre," trans. Ann Shukman, *New Literary History* 34, no. 3 (2003): 565–96; also, William Mills Todd, *The Familiar Letter as a Literary Genre in the Age of Pushkin* (Princeton, NJ: Princeton University Press, 1976).

83. Ginzburg, *On Psychological Prose*, 9.

84. Morson views this aspect of Tolstoy, the desire to re-present reality, not just to be realistic in his fiction, as part of the didactic nature of his prose. See "The Reader as Voyeur: Tolstoi and the Poetics of Didactic Fiction," *Canadian-American Slavic Studies* 12 (1978): 465–80. More scholars than one could easily enumerate have had something to say about Tolstoy and mediation, and I refer specifically to several of them in this section. Mediation gets careful consideration in, to name a couple of recent works, Alexandrov's *Limits of Interpretation*, which I discuss below, and Love's *Guide for the Perplexed*.

85. See Krystyna Pomorska, "Tolstoy: Contra Semiosis," *International Journal of Slavic Linguistics and Poetics* 25–26 (1982): 383–90. She extends the linguistic argument: "Tolstoy's attacks against highly developed culture can be viewed as a protest against overextended semiosis" (384).

86. Liza Knapp, "'Tue-la! Tue-la!': Death Sentences, Words, and Inner Monologue in Tolstoy's *Anna Karenina* and 'Three More Deaths,'" *Tolstoy Studies Journal* 11 (1999): 14. Irina Paperno makes a similar point in "'Who, What Is I?'" See also Kathleen Parthe, "Death Masks in Tolstoi," *Slavic Review* 41, no. 2 (1982): 297–305; Kathleen Parthe, "The Metamorphosis of Death in Tolstoy," *Language and Style: An International Journal* 18, no. 2 (1985): 205–14; Kathleen Parthe, "Tolstoy and the Geometry of Fear," *Modern Language Studies* 15, no. 4 (1985): 80–94.

87. See Jahn's discussion of *On Life* and "The Death of Ivan Ilych": Gary R. Jahn, *"The Death of Ivan Ilich": An Interpretation* (New York: Twayne Publishers, 1993), 95.

88. In his absence in 1862, Tolstoy's estate was searched by governmental authorities. His subsequent utter outrage, while valid, reminds us how insulating Tolstoy's estate and fame could be, and how in control of his day-to-day life Tolstoy was and insisted he be.

He wrote angrily to Alexandra Tolstaya that he was going to move to England: "I shall loudly proclaim that I'm selling my estate in order to leave Russia, where it's impossible to know a minute in advance that they won't chain you up or flog you together with your sister and your wife and your mother—I'm going away"; and he later adds: "I frequently tell myself how extraordinarily lucky it was that I wasn't there. If I had been, I should probably be on trial for murder now" (Tolstoy, *Tolstoy's Letters*, 1: 162). Tolstoy wrote to Alexander II a couple of weeks later, citing his ruined reputation and asking whom, in particular, he might blame. Here is a typical example of Tolstoy's insistence that institutional relationships be transformed into personal ones.

89. Paperno, " 'Who, What Is I?' " 32.

90. Compare Bakhtin's analysis of Tolstoy's "Three Deaths," in *Problems of Dostoevsky's Poetics*, vol. 8 of *Theory and History of Literature*, ed. and trans. Caryl Emerson (Minneapolis: University of Minnesota Press, 1984), 69–73.

91. *PSS* 1: 280. English translation from "A History of Yesterday," Leo Tolstoy, *Tolstoy's Short Fiction*, ed. Michael R. Katz (New York: W. W. Norton, 1991), 280.

92. *Tolstoy's Short Fiction*, 279.

93. Gustafson, *Leo Tolstoy*, 203–4.

94. "Just as in any human utterance a sound takes its meaning only from within the total statement, so any Tolstoyan text takes its meaning only from within the complete oeuvre. To understand any part of his life's text, a story or novel, an essay or tract, a diary entry or a letter, we must see the particular set of words in their relationship to all his words" (ibid., 6–7).

95. The critique of empiricism is in chapter 5, ibid. Rimvydas Silbajoris exemplifies the structuralist trend, writing: "The whole of Tolstoy's work, fiction and nonfiction, in all its modes and genres, is not an aggregate of separate categories of texts, but a single text, a complex, dynamic structure of modulations and transitions which constantly interpenetrate each other encoding and re-encoding the same ultimate message" (*Tolstoy's Aesthetics and His Art* [Columbus, OH: Slavica Publishers, 1991], 253).

96. Morson, *Hidden in Plain View*, 131. Morson devotes an entire chapter to "forms of negative narration" in order to describe Tolstoy's strategies for overcoming the inherent falsity of narrative (ibid., 130–89). Love similarly describes Tolstoy's struggle with the inherent deception of narratives, and his attempt to overcome that deception by relinquishing narrative (*Guide for the Perplexed*, 115, 118). I am less interested in how Tolstoy tries to tell truth. I aim to describe how Tolstoy uses the "falsity of all narratives" to invent and reinvent himself, and uses his authorial image in a complex manipulation of the reader's interpretation of his works of fiction.

97. Alexandrov, *Limits to Interpretation*, 53; emphasis in original. Alexandrov's is a thought-provoking meditation on mediation, to say the least. He suggests the connection between his theoretical chapters and his interpretation of *Anna Karenina* is circumstantial: "There is no necessary connection between the method and Tolstoy's novel: I choose it because it is well known, popular, complex, and a personal favorite" (9). I think the connection is, or could be, stronger. *Anna Karenina* is a great book to consider in this theoretical light exactly because Tolstoy himself was fascinated by the dilemmas of mediation.

CHAPTER 2. AN AUTHOR OF ABSENCE

1. Most scholars considering Tolstoy's aesthetics discuss Mikhailov's painting. For a full treatment of vision in Tolstoy, though, see Amy Mandelker, "Illustrate and Condemn: The Phenomenology of Vision in *Anna Karenina*," *Tolstoy Studies Journal* 8 (1995–96): 46–60; Thomas Seifrid, "Gazing on Life's Page: Perspectival Vision in Tolstoy," *PMLA* 113, no. 3 (1998): 436–48; Justin Weir, "Tolstoy Sees the Truth but Waits: The Consequences of Aesthetic Vision in *Anna Karenina*," in *Approaches to Teaching Tolstoy's "Anna Karenina," Approaches to Teaching World Literature*, ed. Liza Knapp and Amy Mandelker (New York: Modern Language Association of America, 2003).

2. *PSS* 19: 42. English translation from Leo Tolstoy, *Anna Karenina*, ed. George Gibian, trans. Aylmer Maude, 2nd ed. (New York: W. W. Norton, 1995), 431.

3. *PSS* 19: 74; Tolstoy, *Anna Karenina*, 458.

4. Richard Gustafson, *Leo Tolstoy: Resident and Stranger; A Study in Fiction and Theology* (Princeton, NJ: Princeton University Press, 1986), 152–53.

5. Gary Saul Morson, "Tolstoy's Absolute Language," *Critical Inquiry* 7, no. 4 (1981).

6. Ibid.

7. Rudolf Arnheim, *Art and Visual Perception: A Psychology of the Creative Eye; The New Version* (Berkeley: University of California Press, 1974), 236.

8. All from *PSS* 18: 3.

9. I am reminded that more than visual imagery supports the introduction of the novel. There is also the acoustic imagery that Nabokov finds in the repetition of the word home, дом, in the novel's opening paragraph: a tolling bell signaling that something is not right in the Oblonsky home. See the lecture on *Anna Karenina* in Vladimir Nabokov, *Lectures on Russian Literature* (New York: Harcourt Brace Jovanovich, 1981).

10. The words "abyss of forgetfulness" contain an allusion to the last poem by Gavriil Derzhavin:

Река времен в своем стремленьи
Уносит все дела людей
И топит в пропасти забвенья
Народы, царства и царей.

А если что и остается
Чрез звуки лиры и трубы,
То вечности жерлом пожрется
И общей не уйдет судьбы.

The current of the river of time
Carries away all the affairs of people
And drowns in an abyss of forgetfulness
Nations, kingdoms, and kings.

And if something remains
Through the sounds of the lyre and horn,

Then it will also be devoured
And will not escape the common fate.

11. *PSS* 32: 310. English translation from Tolstoy, *Resurrection*, trans. Rosemary Edmonds (New York: Penguin Books, 1966), 399; trans. modified.

12. Note that Grigoriev would not yet have read Tolstoy's greatest achievements, *War and Peace* and *Anna Karenina*. A. K. Knowles, ed., *Tolstoy: The Critical Heritage* (London: Routledge, 1978), 69.

13. Ibid. 70.

14. Ibid. 72.

15. For a different view of Tolstoy and nihilism, see Donna Tussing Orwin, *Tolstoy's Art and Thought, 1847–1880* (Princeton, NJ: Princeton University Press, 1993). She writes: "Eikhenbaum calls Tolstoy a 'nihilist' or 'cynic' who dissolved all theories of positive knowledge in the acid of analysis and countered this nihilism only with 'instinct' and 'conviction,' which, moreover, were almost 'biological.' Eikhenbaum at this point misunderstands Tolstoy's position in just the same way Grigor'ev had. Not acknowledging Tolstoy's peculiar form of idealism, neither sees how higher reason, which speaks through feelings in man and orders the chaos of motion in man and nature, both redeems human reason and puts it in its place as 'onesided'" (77).

16. *PSS* 26: 470. Translation from Leo Tolstoy, *Tolstoy's Short Fiction*, ed. Michael R. Katz (New York: W. W. Norton, 1991), 299.

17. This is what intrigues existentialists. See Robert Bernasconi, "Literary Attestation in Philosophy: Heidegger's Footnote on Tolstoy's 'The Death of Ivan Ilyich,'" in *Heidegger in Question: The Art of Existing* (Atlantic Highlands, NJ): Humanities Press, 1993), 76–98.

18. Kathleen Parthe, "Tolstoy and the Geometry of Fear," *Modern Language Studies* 15, no. 4 (1985): 80–94. See also Kathleen Parthe, "Masking the Fantastic and the Taboo in Tolstoj's 'Polikushka,'" *Slavic and East European Journal* 25, no. 1 (1981): 21–33; Parthe, "Death Masks in Tolstoi," *Slavic Review* 41, no. 2 (1982): 297–305; and Ksana Blank, "Lev Tolstoy's Suprematist Icon-Painting," *Elementa* 2, no. 1 (1995): 67–89.

19. I have in mind his diary note from April 27, 1884: "I want to begin and finish something new. Either the death of a judge, or Notes of a madman [Записки несумасшедшего (sic)]" (Gusev, *Letopis' zhizni i tvorchestva L. N. Tolstogo* [Moscow: Academia, 1936], 310).

20. *PSS* 26: 105; *Tolstoy's Short Fiction*, 160.

21. *PSS* 29: 43; *Tolstoy's Short Fiction*, 267.

22. Patrick Fuery provides a useful definition of primary versus secondary absences:

Secondary absences are those which are always derived from a state of presence. They imply presence, acknowledge its relational context, gain their epistemological and ontological structures from it, and indicate sites of presence. They retain, and even reinforce, the binarism of presence and absence. Primary absences, on the other hand, exist outside of any relational context of presence. Primary absences exist in their own right, independent of any sense of presence. . . . Secondary absences suggest presence because the idea of presence is contained within them. An absent person enjoys the status of absence only because the sense of presence is held in readiness, in being. Primary absences operate external to any sense of presence, which is not to deny the possibility of measuring these absences against registers of presences. One of the major differences, however, is that primary absences are defined in terms of the centrality of absence rather than any referential action to a sense of presence and/or re[present] ation.

Patrick Fuery, *The Theory of Absence: Subjectivity, Signification, and Desire* (Westport, CT: Greenwood Press, 1995), 1–2, 2. Eric de Haard has usefully treated many of the ways Tolstoy defeats expectations in his early work as examples of "antinarrative structures." Especially relevant is de Haard's adaptation of Lotman's concept of the "minus device," which, by complicating readers' expectations, makes a work more complex, rather than simple. Eric de Haard, *Narrative and Anti-Narrative Structures in Lev Tolstoj's Early Works* (Amsterdam: Rodopi, 1989).

23. David Sloane, "Rehabilitating Bakhtin's Tolstoy: The Politics of the Utterance," *Tolstoy Studies Journal* 13 (2001): 64.

24. Caryl Emerson, "Bakhtin (Again) on Tolstoy," keynote address presented at a Harvard University symposium, "The Overexamined Life: New Perspectives on Tolstoy," April 2002. Rakhil' Moiseevna Mirkina was, as Emerson puts it, "one of Bakhtin's most diligent and loyal students."

25. Donna Tussing Orwin, ed., *The Cambridge Companion to Tolstoy* (Cambridge: Cambridge University Press, 2002), 49.

26. A. P. Chekhov, *Sobranie sochinenii v dvenadtsati tomakh* (Moscow: Gosudarstvennoe izdatel'stvo khudozhestvennoi literatury, 1962), 8: 297.

27. Here Eikhenbaum refers to "Gooseberries" and Chekhov's work in general, but he could have said the same of Tolstoy. See "Chekhov at Large," in *Chekhov : A Collection of Critical Essays*, Robert Louis Jackson (Englewood Cliffs, NJ: Prentice-Hall, 1967).

28. Boris Eikhenbaum, *The Young Tolstoi*, trans. Gary Kern (Ann Arbor, MI: Ardis, 1972), 23, following Biriukov. Tolstoy is his own literary subject from the very start: "A History of Yesterday," "From the Window," *Childhood*, and even "Sevastopol in May" all convey the "truth" of subjective experience.

29. Foucault writes: "The function of an author is to characterize the existence, circulation, and operation of certain discourses within a society" (in *Authorship: From Plato to the Postmodern; A Reader*, ed. Seán Burke [Edinburgh: Edinburgh University Press, 1995], 235).

30. Leo Tolstoy, *What Is Art?* trans. Aylmer Maude (New York: Liberal Arts Press, 1960), 7–8.

31. See: William Mills Todd, III, *Fiction and Society in the Age of Pushkin: Ideology, Institutions, and Narrative* (Cambridge, MA: Harvard University Press, 1986), 103–4. Todd writes: "Writers such as Pushkin, Lermontov, and Gogol had to contend with the public that Belinsky described in his earlier essay, which he starkly entitled 'Something about Nothing.' They not only had to play the critic's role within their novels, explaining such elementary concepts as 'irony' (Lermontov), 'beauty' (Gogol), and 'the novel'

(Pushkin) to their readers, they had to make model readers for their works *within* those works" (103).

32. From the draft chapter "K tem g[ospod]am kritikam, kotorye zakhotiat priniat' ee na svoj schet," Tolstoy, *Polnoe sobranie sochinenii v sta tomakh*, 19: 137.

33. Boris Eikhenbaum, "The Creative Incentives of Tolstoy," in *Reminiscences on Tolstoy*, ed. Kalpana Sahni (Atlantic Highlands, NJ: Humanities Press, 1980), 114.

34. Although the relationship between intention and autobiography changes over the course of Tolstoy's career (as, for example, in the case of *Childhood*, where the reading public did not yet know the author's identity), Love characterizes well the general dynamic between intention and autobiography: "But, in the case of Tolstoy, there is a formidable desire to impose authorial intention on his readers as well as a tacit recognition of the impossibility of doing so. Tolstoy's attempt to merge fiction with his own life is a clear sign of this desire as is his violent attack on critics of art and literature in *What is Art?* Tolstoy sought to appropriate his own works, to ensure that they not escape him and speak differently to different people" (Jeff Love, *Tolstoy: A Guide for the Perplexed* [New York: Continuum, 2008], 26). Wachtel sees more nuance here in Tolstoy's generalizing assertions that derive from autobiographical specifics: "Specificity was generally autobiographical for Tolstoy: hence the conflict of specific and general often took the form of a simultaneous attempt to reveal and conceal himself." And he, too, notes the problem that the reading public would not have been able to perceive the play of autobiography and fiction in *Childhood* ("History and Autobiography in Tolstoy," in Orwin, *Cambridge Companion to Tolstoy*, 177, 178).

35. The tactic of publishing as a writer, but defending one's rights over a work as a nobleman has a long history. Authorial rights in general developed, as Mark Rose explains, toward the end of the Middle Ages as a matter of honor and reputation, and a commingling of honor and property continued into modern times. "Thus matters of propriety became entangled with matters of property." See *Authors and Owners: The Invention of Copyright* (Cambridge, MA: Harvard University Press, 1995), 82.

36. Tolstoy, *Polnoe sobranie sochinenii v sta tomakh*, 19: 141. He goes on: "In order to achieve that perfection, and all authors hope for perfection, I find only one means: to form for oneself a clear, defined understanding of the mind, qualities and orientation of the proposed reader."

37. G. N. Ishchuk points out that this early desire to be "understood" as an author is the "first phenomenological and terminological step on the path to 'infection'" (22). More generally, he writes: "Tolstoy always thought a lot about the reader, wrote a lot about the reader and, most important, always strove to present the reader as a participant in the creative process. Because of that the problem of readerly perception proved to be connected with his fundamental philosophico-ethical queries and constructions. It was particularly important in the period of the formation of his creative method, at the source of his writerly path" (G. N. Ishchuk, *Problema chitatelia v tvorcheskom soznanii L. N. Tolstogo* [Kalinin: Kalininskii gosudarstvennii universitet, 1975], 17).

38. Ibid., 20.

39. The letter is from June 27–July 9, 1857. Leo Tolstoy, *Tolstoy's Letters*, trans. and ed. Reginald Frank Christian, 2 vols. (New York: Charles Scribner's Sons, 1978), 1: 58.

40. Tolstoy, *Polnoe sobranie sochinenii v sta tomakh*, 19: 137.
41. Tolstoy apparently read a letter from N. M. Longinov to I. I. Panaev that insulted him; so he wrote Longinov a letter challenging him to a duel. The actual content of both letters is unknown. See: Gusev, *Letopis'*, 63. It was prevented by Nekrasov's intercession (Orwin, *Cambridge Companion to Tolstoy*, 5).
42. PSS 2: 172–73. Translation from Leo Tolstoy, *Childhood, Boyhood, Youth*, trans. Rosemary Edmonds (New York: Penguin Books, 1964), 268.
43. Wayne Booth long ago saw the resemblance between attempts to present a perfectly unmediated realism and more intrusive forms of narration (*The Rhetoric of Fiction*, 2nd ed. [Chicago: University of Chicago Press, 1983], 53). He dismisses the notion that conventions of impersonal narration—a nonintrusive narrator—elude signs of omniscience (ibid., 161). Tolstoy seems to make the most of this failed circumscription of omniscience. Tolstoy's impersonal and first-person narrators both insist on telling us about the world authoritatively.
44. Eikhenbaum and Feuer both treat Tolstoy's commentaries in the early works as a matter of authorial digression. Eikhenbaum, as Feuer puts it, "stresses that Tolstoy mixed narrative and expository genres primarily because of artistic dissatisfaction with traditional forms and his constant quest for new ones." Feuer suggests, however: "To Tolstoy digressions meant the intrusion of the author's commenting voice into a fictional narrative, the undisguised use of his own voice. And Tolstoy related the question of how the author's voice was to be used in fiction to the question of how— and when, and whether—the author's voice was to be concealed: 'When one reads a work, especially a purely literary one, the chief interest lies in the character of the author as it expresses itself in the work. But there are some works in which the author pretends to a view, or changes his view several times. Most pleasing are those in which the author somehow tries to hide his personal view and at the same time remains constantly faithful to it wherever it is revealed. The most insipid works are those in which the view changes so frequently it is totally lost'" (Kathryn B. Feuer, *Tolstoy and the Genesis of "War and Peace,"* ed. Robin Feuer Miller and Donna Tussing Orwin [Ithaca, NY: Cornell University Press, 1996], 17). Eikhenbaum sees digressions as a question of literature; Feuer sees them as a question of the author's point of view. I would supplement Feuer by giving additional attention to Tolstoy's conscious and creative manipulation of his authorial persona. Fidelity to his point of view and how it is revealed is crucial, but how readers and critics would come to view the author in light of those revelations is equally important for Tolstoy. Eikhenbaum's influential treatment of Tolstoy goes beyond the early, more restrictive Formalist point that Tolstoy created new forms because he perceived old ones as impoverished. I mean to emphasize that Tolstoy chooses fluid, and unconventional forms in part because they provide him the flexibility of creative revelation of his authorial persona.
45. Leo Tolstoy, *Tolstoy's Short Fiction*, 279.
46. Tolstoy, *Polnoe sobranie sochinenii v sta tomakh*, 1: 11; *Childhood, Boyhood, Youth*, 13.

CHAPTER 3. LEGITIMATE FICTIONS AND NARRATIVE DIVERSIONS

1. *PSS* 3: 216. Quoted by G. N. Ishchuk, *Problema chitatelia v tvorcheskom soznanii L. N. Tolstogo* (Kalinin: Kalininskii gosudarstvennii universitet, 1975), 28.

2. For example, see Lucien Dällenbach, *The Mirror in the Text* (Chicago: University of Chicago Press, 1989); Linda Hutcheon, *Narcissistic Narrative: The Metafictional Paradox* (New York: Methuen, 1980).

3. Wayne C. Booth, *The Rhetoric of Fiction*, 2nd ed. (Chicago: University of Chicago Press, 1983), 137n. Quote originally from Wolfgang Iser, *The Implied Reader: Patterns of Communication in Prose Fiction from Bunyan to Beckett* (Baltimore: Johns Hopkins University Press, 1974), 114–15.

4. Iser, *Implied Reader*, 280, 291.

5. Gary Saul Morson, *Hidden in Plain View: Narrative and Creative Potentials in "War and Peace"* (Stanford, CA: Stanford University Press, 1987), 211.

6. Anne Hruska suggests that the idea of the family, and its consequences for others, is a point of continuity for the early and late Tolstoy: "Even in the early works the storm that will begin to rage at the end of the 1870s is approaching. And the roots of the postcrisis Tolstoyan tearing away of the family is evident even in the idealizations of family happiness that one finds in Tolstoy's early works" (Anne Hruska, "Stradaniia detej i zhestokost' tolstovskoj garmonii," in *L. N. Tolstoi v 1850-e gody: rozhdenie khudozhnika*, ed. Galina Alekseevna [Tula: Iasnaia Poliana, 2002], 49; my trans.).

7. In "Vospominanie," and quoted by Pavel Biriukov, *Biografiia L.N. Tolstogo: v dvukh knigakh* (Moscow: Algoritm, 2000), 41.

8. Lev Tolstoi, *Polnoe sobranie sochinenii v sta tomakh* (Moscow: Nauka, 2000), 1: 483.

9. Ibid., 484.

10. Sandra M. Gilbert and Susan Gubar, *The Madwoman in the Attic: The Woman Writer and the Nineteenth-Century Literary Imagination* (New Haven: Yale University Press, 1979), 4. See also Jakobson's definitive discussion of metaphoric and metonymic poles in his essay on aphasia in Roman Jakobson, *Language in Literature* (Cambridge, MA: Harvard University Press, 1987), 109–14.

11. Did aristocratic children really have the idealized happy childhoods that Tolstoy portrayed in *Childhood*? Wachtel says no, Priscilla Roosevelt says yes. See Andrew Baruch Wachtel, *The Battle for Childhood: Creation of a Russian Myth* (Stanford, CA: Stanford University Press, 1990), 88–96; P. R. Roosevelt, *Life on the Russian Country Estate: A Social and Cultural History* (New Haven: Yale University Press, 1995), 180.

12. *PSS* 4: 16. Translation from Leo Tolstoy, *Tolstoy's Short Fiction*, ed. Michael R. Katz (New York: W. W. Norton, 1991), 13.

13. Orlando Figes, *Natasha's Dance : A Cultural History of Russia*, 1st ed. (New York: Metropolitan Books, 2002), xxix.

14. Translation from Leo Tolstoy, *War and Peace*, trans. Constance Garnett (New York: Modern Library, 1994), 106.

15. *PSS* 9: 123.

16. Jahn discusses Tolstoy's consideration of human being as a split between animal and spiritual selves. See Gary R. Jahn, *"The Death of Ivan Ilich": An Interpretation* (New York: Twayne Publishers, 1993), 94–96.

17. In *The Cossacks* Olenin has a similar experience. When Olenin is in the lair of the deer, "suddenly he was overcome by such a strange feeling of causeless joy and of love for everything he began crossing himself and thanking someone" (Leo Tolstoy, *Great Short Works of Leo Tolstoy*, trans. Louise Maude and Aylmer Maude [New York: Harper and Row, 1967], 164). It seems important that Anna crosses herself from habit and thinks of childhood happiness, whereas, Olenin, by contrast, is happy and then begins to cross himself. In *The Cossacks*, Tolstoy still invites the reader to accompany him and his hero on a search for a legitimate form of life. Anna represents a turning point in several ways. Nothing Anna could do, save be someone she is not, would facilitate her return to happiness in a role society deemed legitimate. Her momentary happiness is the gift of childhood authenticity she recalls before dying.

18. *PSS* 26: 93; *Tolstoy's Short Fiction*, 149–50.

19. A. S. Pushkin. *Polnoe sobranie sochinenii*, 10 vols. (Moscow: Izdatelstvo akademii nauk, 1937–59), 8: 268.

20. Compare Gary Saul Morson, "The Reader as Voyeur: Tolstoi and the Poetics of Didactic Fiction," *Canadian-American Slavic Studies* 12 (1978): 465–80.

21. De Haard details extensively Tolstoy's use of the "minus device" in his early fiction and connects it with his perceived (by contemporaries, as well as Leontiev and Eikhenbaum) nihilism. See Eric de Haard, *Narrative and Anti-Narrative Structures in Lev Tolstoj's Early Works* (Amsterdam: Rodopi, 1989). De Haard quotes Eikhenbaum: "Behind the unmaskings and ironic contrasts stands the negation of literary clichés that shows already in the diaries. Nature is not like they depict it, neither is war, neither is the Caucasus, courage does not show like that, people do not live and think, do not, finally, die like that—such is Tolstoj's nihilism in its early forms. The most fatal, and simultaneously inevitable, "not like that" is approaching: art is not like they write and think about it" (ibid., 23). There can be no question but that Tolstoy's nihilism is related to the missing plots and frustrated expectations he puts in his fiction. However, I draw the opposite conclusion, that Tolstoy's uses these narrative lacunae to invite readers to help constitute, legitimate, an authorial identity conceived of outside institutional literary norms. De Haard for the most part does not address the larger philosophical and thematic questions related to Tolstoy's nihilism, which, to be sure, have long been a mainstay of Tolstoy criticism at least since Grigoriev.

22. Wolfgang Iser, *The Act of Reading: A Theory of Aesthetic Response* (Baltimore: Johns Hopkins University Press, 1978), 225–26.

23. On the *mise en abyme* of the entire code, see: Lucien Dällenbach, *The Mirror in the Text*, trans. Jeremy Whiteley and Emma Hughes (Chicago: University of Chicago Press, 1989), 43.

24. Boris Eikhenbaum, *The Young Tolstoi*, trans. Gary Kern (Ann Arbor, MI: Ardis, 1972), 101. See also Boris Eikhenbaum, "On Tolstoy's Crises," in *Twentieth-Century Russian Literary Criticism*, ed. Victor Erlich (New Haven: Yale University Press, 1975), 97–101.

25. Mandelker's work on *Anna Karenina* addresses this extensively. See Amy Mandelker, *Framing Anna Karenina: Tolstoy, the Woman Question, and the Victorian Novel* (Columbus: Ohio State University Press, 1993).

26. *PSS* 30: 163n1; *What Is Art?* trans. Aylmer Maude (New York: Liberal Arts Press, 1960), 155n5.

27. Tolstoy often took himself to task for working on *Hadji Murad*. See, for example, Simmons's account: "As was usual with him now, he felt that he was wasting time on a mere work of art, and he was by no means pleased with his efforts. When a guest at Yasnaya Polyana was reading part of the novel to a group, Tolstoy kept popping in and out of the room to listen. Once he broke in to declare the work uninteresting, and finally, with some irritation, he asked the reader to quit bothering with such rubbish" (Ernest J. Simmons, *Leo Tolstoy*, special limited ed. [Boston: Little, Brown, 1946], 626–27).

28. Richard Gustafson, *Leo Tolstoy: Resident and Stranger; A Study in Fiction and Theology* (Princeton, NJ: Princeton University Press, 1986), 6–7.

29. He reinterprets the early work specifically, as when he rewrites his early story "The Snowstorm" (1856) in the later "Master and Man" (1895) or in 1885 completes "Kholstomer," which he began in 1863; but also more generally, as he reworks themes of violence, romance, and spiritual searching in such works as "The Kreutzer Sonata," "The Death of Ivan Ilyich," and *Resurrection*.

30. Leo Tolstoy, *Anna Karenina*, ed. George Gibian, Aylmer Maude, 2nd ed. (New York: W. W. Norton, 1995), 750; the Russian may be found in Gusev, *Letopis'*.

31. Leo Tolstoy, *War and Peace: The Maude Translation, Backgrounds and Sources, Criticism*, 2nd ed., Norton critical edition (New York: W. W. Norton, 1996), 1090.

32. *PSS* 48: 67. From Tolstoy's *Diary*, entry for November 6, 1873. Quoted in Donna Tussing Orwin, ed., *The Cambridge Companion to Tolstoy* (Cambridge: Cambridge University Press, 2002), 16.

33. *PSS* 23: 28. Leo Tolstoy, *"A Confession" and Other Religious Writings*, trans. Jane Kentish (New York: Penguin Books, 1987), 46. Note how vitality is paired here with "escape."

34. *PSS* 23: 30; *A Confession*, 47.

35. Donna Tussing Orwin, *Tolstoy's Art and Thought, 1847–1880* (Princeton, NJ: Princeton University Press, 1993), 26. Orwin also illuminates the Hegelian background to Tolstoy's literary reception, and his designation, by turns, as either an analyzer or a synthesizer.

36. Alexandrov focuses explicitly on mediation in literary criticism in Vladimir E. Alexandrov, *Limits to Interpretation : The Meanings of Anna Karenina* (Madison: University of Wisconsin Press, 2004), 10.

37. Gustafson, of all Tolstoy's critics early and late, sees these contradictions best, and he resolves them in a brilliant analysis of the Orthodox icon as an aesthetic model for Tolstoy. See Gustafson, *Leo Tolstoy*, 203–4.

38. Wachtel, *Battle for Childhood*, 8. Wachtel's interpretation of *Childhood* may have been influenced by Tolstoy's later statements on his early fiction, especially his *Reminiscences*, a particularly untrustworthy work, which was written for a favorite

biographer, Pavel Biriukov. In that work, Tolstoy accuses himself of writing *Childhood* too literarily and insincerely (*PSS* 34: 348), suggesting, among other things, that he will now write "the veritable truth [истинная правда]" (*PSS* 34: 345). Eikhenbaum, who notes his lack of access to Tolstoy's archives, also relies on Biriukov, and he says much the same thing: "The idea for a 'novel' in four parts came to Tolstoy and not from a desire to portray the psychological development of a specific personality with its typically individual peculiarities, but from a need to 'generalize,' to formulate an abstract program" (Eikhenbaum, *Young Tolstoi*, 59).

39. Wachtel, *Battle for Childhood*, 13.

40. Leo Tolstoy, *Tolstoy's Letters*, trans. and ed. Reginald Frank Christian, 2 vols. (New York: Charles Scribner's Sons, 1978), 1: 18.

41. Andrew Wachtel, "History and Autobiography in Tolstoy," in *Cambridge Companion to Tolstoy*, ed. Orwin, 185.

42. Ibid., 188.

43. The inherent falsification of narrative—and how Tolstoy thematizes it—is something Morson discuss extensively in *Hidden in Plain View*, 131.

44. Consider Irina Paperno's insightful discussion of Tolstoy's fascination with retrospective dreams—dreams in which, for example, a window slams shut in the real world, but the mind, before waking one up, instantly creates an entire narrative of a dream that ends with a similar banging sound, which then wakes the dreamer up. In other words, a (false) past chain of events is conjured by the mind to explain an event in the present. See Irina Paperno, "'Who, What Is I?': Tolstoy in His Diaries," *Tolstoy Studies Journal* 11 (1999): 32–54.

45. *PSS* 1: 31. Leo Tolstoy, *Childhood, Boyhood, Youth*, trans. Rosemary Edmonds (New York: Penguin Books, 1964), 40.

46. *PSS* 5: 30. Translation from Leo Tolstoy, *Collected Shorter Fiction*, trans. Aylmer Maude, Louise Maude, and Nigel J. Cooper, Everyman's Library (New York: Alfred A. Knopf, 2001), 450, 453.

47. *PSS* 5: 54; *Collected Shorter Fiction*, 474.

48. Sankovitch writes: "In his fiction Tolstoy rarely uses the word *pamiat'* ('memory') to refer to that part of the mind where memories or reminiscences (*vospominaniia*) are, metaphorically speaking, awakened; instead, he uses the word *voobrazhenie* ('imagination')" (*Creating and Recovering Experience: Repetition in Tolstoy* [Stanford, CA: Stanford University Press, 1998], 113). In subsequent pages, Sankovitch addresses music and memory extensively (ibid., 215–24), though not explicitly the notion of false memory. In *The Cossacks*, to give my own example, Tolstoy describes Olenin: "Were they ideas, memories, or dreams that had been flitting through his mind? They were frequently all three" (Tolstoy, *Great Short Works*, 177). Patricia Carden writes that Tolstoy affirmed the notion that "the capacity for remembering is a sign of the expressive capacity of the self" ("The Recuperative Powers of Memory: Tolstoy's War and Peace," in *The Russian Novel from Pushkin to Pasternak*, ed. John Garrard (New Haven: Yale University Press, 1983), 89.

49. *PSS* 55: 116–17; *Diary*, entry for January 20, 1905.

50. *PSS* 27: 61; *Tolstoy's Short Fiction*, 218.

51. PSS 3: 148; *Collected Shorter Fiction*, 267.

52. Medzhibovskaya remarks that *A Confession* was originally intended as the introduction to a longer work accounting for his wrongdoing. Of the first three chapters, she writes: "Already in these early sections one recognizes familiar themes that are often literally repeated from Tolstoy's writings and diaries of his youth and maturity, or taken from his correspondence and literary works" (Inessa Medzhibovskaya, *Tolstoy and the Religious Culture of His Time: A Biography of a Long Conversion, 1845–1887* [Lanham, MD: Lexington Books, 2008], 232, 245).

53. "Recollections of Leo Tolstoy," in *Portable Twentieth-Century Russian Reader*, ed. Clarence Brown (New York: Penguin Books, 2003), 53.

54. Paperno, " 'Who, What Is I?' " 49.

55. *PSS* 34: 116.

56. Gadamer writes: "Collingwood argues thus: We can understand a text only when we have understood the question to which it is an answer. But since this question can be derived solely from the text and accordingly the appropriateness of the reply is the methodological presupposition for the reconstruction of the question, any criticism of this reply from some other quarter is pure shadow boxing. It is like understanding works of art. A work of art can be understood only if we assume its adequacy as an expression of the artistic idea. Here too we have to discover the question which it answers, if we are to understand it as an answer. This is, in fact, an axiom of all hermeneutics: we described it above as the 'fore-conception of completeness' " (Hans-Georg Gadamer, *Truth and Method*, trans. Joel Weinsheimer and Donald Marshall, 2nd rev. ed. [New York: Continuum, 1989], 370).

57. I consider "The Kreutzer Sonata" and "After the Ball" at length in the next chapter.

58. *PSS* 2: 25; *Childhood, Boyhood, Youth*, 128; emphasis added.

59. Both Nabokov (in *The Gift*) and Tolstoy shared an interest in debunking Chernyshevsky's simplistic but influential theories of realism. Both thought they made for bad art and bad social activism. Nabokov's lecture on *Anna Karenina* may be found in Vladimir Nabokov, *Lectures on Russian Literature* (New York: Harcourt Brace Jovanovich, 1981).

60. Especially later in *What Is Art?* but see also Gary Saul Morson, "The Reader as Voyeur: Tolstoi and the Poetics of Didactic Fiction," *Canadian-American Slavic Studies* 12 (1978): 465–80.

CHAPTER 4. SOLDIERS' STORIES

1. Gary Saul Morson, "The Reader as Voyeur: Tolstoi and the Poetics of Didactic Fiction," *Canadian-American Slavic Studies* 12 (1978): 465–80; reprinted in Tolstoy, *Tolstoy's Short Fiction*, ed. Michael R. Katz (New York: W. W. Norton, 1991), 379–94; for this citation, 380–81.

2. The theory Morson works with (Goffman, Foucault) proposes that literary texts are always already "aesthetically framed," that as readers we approach them with "a set of conventions," and that, in some sense, we cannot avoid doing so.

3. *PSS* 4: 5; *Tolstoy's Short Fiction*, 4–5; *PSS* 4: 6; *Tolstoy's Short Fiction*, 5; *PSS* 4: 13; *Tolstoy's Short Fiction*, 10.

4. *PSS* 4: 7; *Tolstoy's Short Fiction*, 6; *PSS* 4: 15; *Tolstoy's Short Fiction*, 13; *PSS* 4: 16; *Tolstoy's Short Fiction*, 13.

5. It is common to note an important shift between the two stories. See Kathryn B. Feuer, *Tolstoy and the Genesis of "War and Peace,"* ed. Robin Feuer Miller and Donna Tussing Orwin (Ithaca, NY: Cornell University Press, 1996), 16. De Haard writes: "It has often been remarked that "Sevastopol' v mae" is quite different from "Sevastopol' v dekabre" in many respects. "Sevastopol' v mae" is new in Tolstoj's development in that he uses an omniscient, strongly authorial narrator for the first time." Eric de Haard, *Narrative and Anti-Narrative Structures in Lev Tolstoj's Early Works* (Amsterdam: Rodopi, 1989), 79.

6. *PSS* 4: 24; *Tolstoy's Short Fiction*, 17.

7. *PSS* 4: 59; *Tolstoy's Short Fiction*, 43; emphasis added.

8. E. N. Kupreianova, *Estetika L. N. Tolstogo* (Moscow: Nauka, 1966), 48.

9. *PSS* 4: 25; *Tolstoy's Short Fiction*, 18.

10. *PSS* 4: 26; *Tolstoy's Short Fiction*, 19.

11. "Э сеси у аште" *PSS* 4: 56; *Tolstoy's Short Fiction*, 41.

12. *PSS* 3: 145; *Collected Shorter Fiction*, 263.

13. "Nostalgia (from *nostos*—return home, and *algia*—longing) is a longing for a home that no longer exists or has never existed. Nostalgia is a sentiment of loss and displacement, but it is also a romance with one's own fantasy." Svetlana Boym, *The Future of Nostalgia* (New York: Basic Books, 2001), xiii.

14. *PSS* 3: 174; *Collected Shorter Fiction*, 298.

15. *PSS* 3: 174; *Collected Shorter Fiction*, 298.

16. *PSS* 3: 177–78; *Collected Shorter Fiction*, 302.

17. *PSS* 9: 273–74. Leo Tolstoy, *War and Peace*, trans. Constance Garnett (New York: Modern Library, 1994), 249.

18. *PSS* 6: 7; *Great Short Works of Leo Tolstoy*, trans. Louise Maude and Aylmer Maude (New York: Harper and Row, 1967), 89–90. "Young man" is actually well rendered as "un jeune homme" in this translation.

19. For the broader view, see Susan Layton, *Russian Literature and Empire : Conquest of the Caucasus from Pushkin to Tolstoy* (Cambridge; New York: Cambridge University Press, 1994).

20. *PSS* 6: 7–8; *Great Short Works of Leo Tolstoy*, 90.

21. *PSS* 6: 77; *Great Short Works of Leo Tolstoy*, 165.

22. *PSS*, 6: 153–268. Feuer mentions this (*Tolstoy and the Genesis*, 13).

23. *PSS* 6: 141; *Great Short Works of Leo Tolstoy*, 234.

24. *PSS* 6: 72; *Great Short Works of Leo Tolstoy*, 159.

25. *PSS* 6: 24; *Great Short Works of Leo Tolstoy*, 107.

26. *PSS* 6: 63. *Great Short Works of Leo Tolstoy*, 149.

27. *PSS* 6: 88; *Great Short Works of Leo Tolstoy*, 176.

28. *PSS* 6: 40; *Great Short Works of Leo Tolstoy*, 124.

29. *PSS* 6: 91; *Great Short Works of Leo Tolstoy*, 179.

30. *PSS* 6: 90; *Great Short Works of Leo Tolstoy*, 179.

31. *PSS* 6: 75; *Great Short Works of Leo Tolstoy,* 162–63.
32. *PSS* 6: 76–77; *Great Short Works of Leo Tolstoy,* 164.
33. *PSS* 6: 146; *Great Short Works of Leo Tolstoy,* 238.
34. *PSS* 6: 8; *Great Short Works of Leo Tolstoy,* 90.
35. Richard Gustafson, *Leo Tolstoy: Resident and Stranger; A Study in Fiction and Theology* (Princeton, NJ: Princeton University Press, 1986), 60. The original passage refers to *PSS* 6: 123.
36. "The one point about Tolstoj on which contemporary critics agree is nature's role as a moral standard." Donna Tussing Orwin, "Nature and the Narrator in Chadzi-Murat," *Russian Literature* 28, no. 1 (1990): 125.
37. *PSS* 12: 205; *War and Peace,* 1257.
38. Jeff Love, *The Overcoming of History in "War and Peace"* (Amsterdam: Rodopi, 2004), 5–6. I turn to Gary Saul Morson, *Hidden in Plain View: Narrative and Creative Potentials in "War and Peace"* (Stanford, CA: Stanford University Press, 1987), and Love's *Overcoming of History* for comprehensive accounts of the relation between Tolstoy's historical philosophy and the narrative structure of his novel. Especially pertinent regarding calculus is Love's detailed treatment of the topic (58–95).
39. *PSS* 12: 66; 11: 357; *War and Peace,* 1123, 1027.
40. *PSS* 9: 84; *War and Peace,* 73.
41. *PSS* 11: 250; *War and Peace,* 924.
42. See Gary Saul Morson, "Prosaics and *Anna Karenina*," *Tolstoy Studies Journal* 1 (1988).
43. *PSS* 12: 69; *War and Peace,* 1126.
44. *PSS* 12: 338; *War and Peace,* 1383.
45. For this I draw on unpublished work by Timothy Langen, as well as Love's, *Overcoming of History.*
46. *PSS* 9: 349; *War and Peace,* 321.
47. *PSS* 12: 147; *War and Peace,* 1201.
48. *PSS* 9: 350; *War and Peace,* 321.
49. *PSS* 9: 355; *War and Peace,* 326.
50. *PSS* 9: 355; *War and Peace,* 326.
51. *PSS* 9: 356; *War and Peace,* 327.
52. *PSS* 10: 117–18; *War and Peace,* 437.

CHAPTER 5. FAMILY HISTORIES

1. Kathryn B. Feuer, *Tolstoy and the Genesis of "War and Peace,"* ed. Robin Feuer Miller and Donna Tussing Orwin (Ithaca, NY: Cornell University Press, 1996), 24.
2. *PSS* 9: 42; Leo Tolstoy, *War and Peace,* trans. Constance Garnett (New York: Modern Library, 1994), 33.
3. *PSS* 9: 42; *War and Peace,* 34.
4. *PSS* 9: 47; *War and Peace,* 39.
5. Victor Shklovsky, "Art as Technique," in *Russian Formalist Criticism: Four Essays,* trans. and intro. Lee T. Lemon and Marion J. Reis (Lincoln: University of Nebraska Press, 1965), 16–17.

6. *PSS* 10:327. *War and Peace*, 642.

7. *PSS* 9: 250. *War and Peace*, 180.

8. *PSS* 10: 329–30; *War and Peace*, 645.

9. *PSS* 10: 330; *War and Peace*, 645.

10. *PSS* 10: 23, *War and Peace*, 272.

11. *PSS* 10: 340; *War and Peace*, 655.

12. *PSS* 10: 112; *War and Peace*, 336.

13. *PSS* 10: 321; *War and Peace*, 636.

14. *PSS* 10: 324–25; *War and Peace*, 639–40.

15. "There were moments when I became so deranged by this idée fixe that I would glance sharply round in some opposite direction, hoping to catch unawares the void (the *néant*) where I was not" (*PSS* 2: 57; Leo Tolstoy, *Childhood, Boyhood, Youth*, trans. Rosemary Edmonds [New York: Penguin Books, 1964], 159).

16. *PSS* 18: 175. Leo Tolstoy, *Anna Karenina*, ed. George Gibian, trans. Aylmer Maude, 2nd ed. (New York: W. W. Norton, 1995), 151.

17. This process seems to work best when the character is autobiographical. Feuer writes: "With the achievement of Andrei and Pierre as autobiographical heroes, Tolstoy made a return to his earlier works in more than the continuation of one of their fundamental techniques. For although this change did not entirely eliminate the novel's political conception, it did subordinate the political to the moral and spiritual as it converted the novel from an account of *other* men's 'errors and misfortunes' into another of Tolstoy's 'epochs of growth' and self understanding." Kathryn B. Feuer, *Tolstoy and the Genesis of "War and Peace,"* ed. Robin Feuer Miller and Donna Tussing Orwin (Ithaca, NY: Cornell University Press, 1996), 23–24.

18. *PSS* 18: 175–76; *Anna Karenina*, 152.

19. Earlier in the novel, in Tolstoy's take on the *Symposium*, Stiva and Levin similarly discuss two forms of love. See Irina Gutkin, "The Dichotomy between Flesh and Spirit: Plato's *Symposium* in *Anna Karenina*," in *In the Shade of the Giant: Essays on Tolstoy*, ed. Hugh McLean (Berkeley: University of California Press, 1989), 84–99. Richard Gustafson mentions Tolstoy's apophatic conception of God, formulated most explicitly late in his life: "It is most important first of all to accept the apophatic correction Tolstoy always subjected himself to. He fills his diaries not only with statements of the type 'God is . . .' but also the negatives of those statements: 'God is not love' (58, 143; 1910); 'the concept of life is not attributable to God' (54, 135; 1902); 'the conception of the eternal, infinite being of God as a conscious being is just as incorrect as the conception of Him as a physical being' (54, 159; 1903). This apophaticism helps Tolstoy eliminate the anthropomorphic tendencies in his phenomenological method." Richard Gustafson, *Leo Tolstoy: Resident and Stranger; A Study in Fiction and Theology* (Princeton, NJ: Princeton University Press, 1986), 93.

20. *PSS* 18: 176; *Anna Karenina*, 152.

21. *PSS* 18: 176; *Anna Karenina*, 152.

22. *PSS* 18: 177; *Anna Karenina*, 153.

23. *PSS* 18: 177; *Anna Karenina*, 153.

24. *PSS* 18: 180; *Anna Karenina*, 156.

25. *PSS* 18: 180; *Anna Karenina*, 156.

26. Feuer, *Tolstoy and the Genesis*, 29, 30.

27. *PSS* 18: 181–82; *Anna Karenina*, 157.

28. *PSS* 18: 182; *Anna Karenina*, 157.

29. *PSS* 18: 179; *Anna Karenina*, 155.

30. Introduction to Ralph Matlaw, ed., *Tolstoy: A Collection of Critical Essays* (Englewood Cliffs, NJ: Prentice-Hall, 1967), 11–12. Donna Orwin states the same more recently: "His genius is narrow but deep: no man has lived a more sincere life than he did, or one more dedicated to serving the needs of the individual. This consistency produced a great artist, and also a flawed thinker and activist who contributed to the tragic political history of his country." Donna Tussing Orwin, ed., *The Cambridge Companion to Tolstoy* (Cambridge: Cambridge University Press, 2002), 60.

CHAPTER 6. THE RECOVERY OF CHILDHOOD

1. Gary L. Jahn, "The Role of the Ending in Lev Tolstoi's 'The Death of Ivan Ilych,'" *Canadian Slavonic Papers-Revue Canadienne des Slavistes* 24, no. 3 (1982): 237.

2. See E. D. Hirsch, *Validity in Interpretation* (New Haven: Yale University Press, 1967). The idea of using Hirsch's categories in reference to "The Death of Ivan Ilyich" emerged in a Tolstoy seminar offered by Gary Jahn at the University of Minnesota in 1991.

3. The point is Jahn's. See Gary R. Jahn, "'The Death of Ivan Il'ic': Chapter One," in *Studies in Honor of Xenia Gasiorowska*, ed. Lauren G. Leighton (Columbus, OH: Slavica Publishers, 1983), 42–43.

4. *PSS* 26: 62. Leo Tolstoy, *Tolstoy's Short Fiction*, ed. Michael R. Katz (New York: W. W. Norton, 1991), 124.

5. *PSS* 26: 62; *Tolstoy's Short Fiction*, 124.

6. *PSS* 26: 93; *Tolstoy's Short Fiction*, 149.

7. *PSS* 26: 68; *Tolstoy's Short Fiction*, 129.

8. Inessa Medzhibovskaya, *Tolstoy and the Religious Culture of his Time: A Biography of a Long Conversion, 1845–1887* (Lanham, MD: Lexington Books, 2008), 304.

9. *PSS* 26: 79; *Tolstoy's Short Fiction*, 138.

10. *PSS* 26: 68; *Tolstoy's Short Fiction*, 129. Translations usually add "*therefore* most terrible." The "therefore" does not actually exist in the Russian, but here and elsewhere Tolstoy alludes to logical constructions.

11. See, for example: H. K. Schefski, "Tolstoj's Case against Doctors," *Slavic and East European Journal* 22 (1978): 569–73.

12. *PSS* 26: 113; *Tolstoy's Short Fiction*, 166–67.

13. Medzhibovskaya notes that the character Ivan Ilych appears in the Tolstoy's unfinished dramatic satires begun in 1856, "The Noble Family," and "Man of Affairs," as well in the autobiographical tragicomic dialogue *Interlocutors* from 1877 (*Tolstoy and the Religious Culture*, 296).

14. Jahn, "Role of the Ending," 235.

15. Medzhibovskaya, *Tolstoy and the Religious Culture*, 310.
16. For a discussion of the decreasing chapter sizes, and "parallel decrease in the spatial dimensions of the story," see Jahn, "Role of the Ending," 231, passim.
17. *PSS* 26: 112; *Tolstoy's Short Fiction*, 166.
18. *PSS* 26: 107; *Tolstoy's Short Fiction*, 161.
19. Note also the repetition of the word жить (to live): "Чего ж ты хочешь теперь? Жить? Как жить? Жить, как ты живешь в суде, когда судебный пристав провозглашает: "Суд идет!" Суд идет, идет суд, — повторил он себе. — Вот он, суд! Да я же не виноват! — вскрикнул он с злобой. — За что?" (*PSS* 26: 107); *Tolstoy's Short Fiction*, 161–62.
20. *PSS* 26: 64; *Tolstoy's Short Fiction*, 125.
21. See Donna Tussing Orwin, "Nature and the Narrator in Chadzi-Murat," *Russian Literature* 28, no. 1 (1990): 125–44. I agree with her judgment of Hadji Murad in this respect, but wonder whether she overvalues the rational model of the framing narrator.
22. *PSS* 35: 583.
23. The frame narrative of the novella enters the manuscript drafts early and stays there, regardless of Tolstoy's other compositional decisions. Orwin says of the framing narrator: "The writer-narrator of *Chadzi-Murat* differs from all the other characters in the work in that, while they remain essentially self-centered, he, through the action of reason, truly puts himself in their places" ("Nature and Narrator," 139). His rationality supports his moral authority.
24. *PSS* 35: 594. The quote is taken from Tolstoy's diary entry for March 21, 1898 (*PSS* 53: 188).
25. *PSS* 53: 187. Noted in the commentary (ibid.), specifically while he was working on *Resurrection*. Most critics writing on *Hadji Murad* mention the "peep show" and "fluidity" as characterological concerns for Tolstoy.
26. *PSS* 35: 599.
27. *PSS* 35: 596–97.
28. Orwin writes: "This is the ineradicable, subrational, completely particular stuff of individuality, which Tolstoj celebrates from his very first works" ("Nature and Narrator," 135). Orwin does not mention that the story of Hadji Murad's mother rejecting her role as wet nurse is fictive.
29. David Herman has an excellent essay on silence in the story. See David Herman, "Khadzhi-Murat's Silence," *Slavic Review* 64, no. 1 (2005). The article is brilliant and moving, though I disagree with the conclusion. Herman's basic idea is, in part, that *Hadji Murad* represents Tolstoy's resignation that "you cannot teach others in life" (14). There is: "Finally silence: Khadzhi-Murat dies and that is all. The event is, as it were, simple, but remarkable for what it lacks—*God is not there*" (19). "Khadzhi-Murat casts into disarray the philosophy and aesthetics Tolstoi otherwise embraced— no wonder, in a final muting, Tolstoy arranged for its publication only after his death" (23). Ultimately, Herman asks us to believe that the missing moralizing in *Hadji Murad* means, not that the novella was a guilty pleasure for an aging author, but that in this one unpublished work Tolstoy acknowledges that God is missing from the world. It is a thought-provoking and compelling interpretation.

30. *PSS* 35: 611–12.
31. Lev Tolstoi, *Sobranie sochinenii* (Moscow, 1983), 14: 496.
32. *PSS* 35: 68. Leo Tolstoy, *Great Short Works of Leo Tolstoy*, trans. Louise Maude and Aylmer Maude (New York: Harper and Row, 1967), 616.

CHAPTER 7. THE WORLD AS LOVE AND REPRESENTATION

1. I first explored this topic in "Anna Incommunicada: Language and Consciousness in *Anna Karenina*," *Tolstoy Studies Journal* 8 (1997): 99–111, but there are a number of noteworthy books and articles coming both before and after. Especially important is Patricia Carden, "The Expressive Self in *War and Peace*" *Canadian-American Slavic Studies*, 12, no. 4 (Winter 1978): 519–34. See also, Malcolm V. Jones, "Problems of Communication in *Anna Karenina*," in *New Essays on Tolstoy*, ed. Malcolm V. Jones and R. F. Christian (Cambridge: Cambridge University Press, 1978), 85–108. Gary Saul Morson draws extensive connections between Tolstoy's view of language and use of narrative in *Hidden in Plain View: Narrative and Creative Potentials in "War and Peace"* (Stanford, CA: Stanford University Press, 1987). Olga Slivitskaia (*"Vojna i Mir" L. N. Tolstogo: Problemy chelovecheskogo obshchenia* [Leningrad: Izd-vo Leningradskogo universiteta, 1988]) discusses the problem on the large umbrella of human relatedness. Eric de Haard considers Tolstoy's antinarrative tendency more broadly; see his *Narrative and Anti-Narrative Structures in Lev Tolstoj's Early Works* (Amsterdam: Rodopi, 1989). More recently, Liza Knapp and David Herman have explored the subject, both touching on the semiotic implications of Tolstoy's art and language. See Knapp, "Language and Death in Tolstoy's *Childhood* and *Boyhood*: Rousseau and the Holy Fool," *Tolstoy Studies Journal* 10 (1998): 50–62; and "'Tue-La! Tue-Le!': Death Sentences, Words, and Inner Monologue in Tolstoy's *Anna Karenina* and 'Three More Deaths,'" *Tolstoy Studies Journal* 11 (1999): 1–19. See Herman, "Stricken by Infection: Art and Adultery in *Anna Karenina* and 'Kreutzer Sonata,'" *Slavic Review* 56, no. 1 (1997): 15–36.
2. A hermeneutics of "suspicion" is elaborated by Paul Ricoeur in his: *Freud and Philosophy: An Essay on Interpretation*, trans. Denis Savage (New Haven: Yale University Press, 1970). I discuss the concept further in chapter 9.
3. *PSS* 1: 279. Leo Tolstoy, *Tolstoy's Short Fiction*, trans. and ed. Michael R. Katz (New York: W. W. Norton, 1991), 279.
4. *PSS* 1: 281; *Tolstoy's Short Fiction*, 281.
5. Ibid.
6. Ibid.; emphasis mine.
7. Ibid.
8. *PSS* 1: 282; *Tolstoy's Short Fiction*, 282.
9. Leo Tolstoy, *Childhood, Boyhood, Youth*, trans. Rosemary Edmonds (New York: Penguin Books, 1964), 159.
10. See Rischin's discussion of Beethoven: Ruth Rischin, "Allegro Tumultuosissimamente: Beethoven in Tolstoy's Fiction," in *In the Shade of the Giant: Essays on Tolstoy*, ed. Hugh McLean (Berkeley: University of California Press, 1989), 12–60. Also Z. G. Palijukh and A. N. Prokhorov, eds., *Lev Tolstoj i muzyka* (Moscow: Sov. Kompozitor, 1977).

11. Liza Knapp makes a study of Tolstoy's conceptions of language and their debt to Rousseau that I find very convincing. Knapp traces Tolstoy's view of language from its origin in Rousseau's idealized history of a shared community of language, through its stratification into differing languages of the family and household in the *Childhood* trilogy; there in the figure of the holy fool Grisha, according to Knapp, Tolstoy develops a precursor of inner speech and ultimately an image of the "other" of systematic Saussurean language. In subsequent articles Knapp argues that Anna acquires this antisemiotic language of the holy fool. See Knapp, "Language and Death," and " 'Tue-La! Tue-Le!' "

12. Barbara Hardy writes: "Vronsky, Oblonsky, and Levin are all strongly sexed men whose sexual vitality is communicated in their energy, whether this is displayed in eating, working, or riding a horse." Barbara Hardy, "Form and Freedom: Tolstoy's *Anna Karenina*," in *Anna Karenina*, ed. George Gibian, trans. Aylmer Maude (New York: W. W. Norton, 1970).

13. *PSS* 19: 48. Leo Tolstoy, *Anna Karenina*, ed. George Gibian, trans. Aylmer Maude, 2nd ed. (New York: W. W. Norton, 1995), 436.

14. Galina Galagan, for example, writes: "The opposition of the condition of liveliness and unity in the world of nature to the static artificial integrity in the world of people is structurally-meaningful in the half-story, half-treatise 'Lucerne' (1857)." See G. Ia. Galagan, *L. N. Tolstoi: Khudozhestvenno-eticheskie iskaniia* (Leningrad: Nauka, 1981), 62.

15. Eric de Haard, *Narrative and Anti-Narrative Structures in Lev Tolstoj's Early Works* (Amsterdam: Rodopi, 1989), 117.

16. Boris Eikhenbaum, *Lev Tolstoi*, reprint of Leningrad 1928 31st ed. (Munich: Wilhelm Fink Verlag, 1968), 313. Simmons also calls it Tolstoy's "first moralistic tract," and remarks that it is "a slight thing in the totality of Tolstoy's vast literary creations, but it is a highly important signpost pointing the direction of much of his future thought." Ernest J. Simmons, *Leo Tolstoy*, special limited ed. (Boston: Little, Brown, 1946), 157.

17. Olga Slivitskaia, "Fraktal'nyi kharakter tvorchestwa molodogo Tolstogo 'Lucerne,'" in *L. N. Tolstoi v 1850-e gody: Rozhdenie khudozhnika*, ed. Galina Alekseeva (Tula: Iasnaia Poliana, 2002), 16.

18. Quoted by Eikhenbaum, *Lev Tolstoi*, 308.

19. Donna Orwin writes: "Nekhliudov is long-winded, because he enunciates ideas that his creator is just in the process of digesting," ideas originating with Goethe, as Orwin convincingly argues. Donna Tussing Orwin, *Tolstoy's Art and Thought, 1847–1880* (Princeton, NJ: Princeton University Press, 1993), 78.

20. *PSS* 5: 4. Translation from Leo Tolstoy, *Collected Shorter Fiction*, trans. Aylmer Maude, Louise Maude, and Nigel J. Cooper, Everyman's Library (New York: Alfred A. Knopf, 2001), 420.

21. Patricia Carden, "The Expressive Self in *War and Peace*," *Canadian-American Slavic Studies* 12, no. 4 (Winter 1978): 520.

22. The story honors negation in one additional way, though. De Haard writes: "This occurrence [the mockery of the Tyrolese], which forms the central motif of "Ljucern" is the total negation, an exact inversion of one short episode of [Karamzin's] *Pis'ma*

russkogo putesestvennika which takes place in Berne [cf. Lotman & Uspenskij 1984: 532]" (de Haard, *Narrative and Anti-Narrative Structures*, 119).

23. *PSS* 5: 3; *Collected Shorter Fiction*, 419

24. *PSS* 5: 26; *Collected Shorter Fiction*, 444.

25. *PSS* 5: 20; *Collected Shorter Fiction*, 437.

26. My emphasis. Galagan, *L. N. Tolstoi*, 62.

27. *PSS* 19: 340; *Anna Karenina*, 687 (citations here from the 1995 edition unless otherwise stated).

28. "несообщительность, основанные не на гордости, но на отсутствии потребности сближения." *PSS* 5: 5; *Collected Shorter Fiction*, 421.

29. *PSS* 5: 6; *Collected Shorter Fiction*, 422.

30. The plot is similar to *The Cossacks*, and one sees in both how well Richard Gustafson's paradigmatic story of the "stranger" trying to become a "resident" fits much of Tolstoy's fiction. See, for example Gustafson, *Leo Tolstoy: Resident and Stranger; A Study in Fiction and Theology* (Princeton, NJ: Princeton University Press, 1986), 51.

31. Morson makes this point about the metaliterary tendency of Tolstoy's moralistic fiction. See Gary Saul Morson, "The Reader as Voyeur: Tolstoi and the Poetics of Didactic Fiction," *Canadian-American Slavic Studies* 12 (1978): 465–80.

32. *PSS* 5: 8; *Collected Shorter Fiction*, 424.

33. *PSS* 5: 9; *Collected Shorter Fiction*, 425; trans. modified.

34. The English translator, as often happens, characteristically eliminates Tolstoy's idiosyncratic repetition of words, but then also mistakes the last все for "everyone" instead of "everything." Thus: "They all seemed to experience the same sensation that I did, and stood in silence round the singer, listening attentively. All were quiet."

35. *PSS* 5: 10–11; *Collected Shorter Fiction*, 427.

36. *PSS* 5: 11; *Collected Shorter Fiction*, 428.

37. *PSS* 5: 17; *Collected Shorter Fiction*, 434; *PSS* 5: 19; *Collected Shorter Fiction*, 436; *PSS* 5: 19; *Collected Shorter Fiction*, 436.

38. *PSS* 5: 21; *Collected Shorter Fiction*, 438.

39. *PSS* 5: 26; *Collected Shorter Fiction*, 444.

40. *PSS* 5: 26; *Collected Shorter Fiction*, 444.

41. *PSS* 5: 26; *Collected Shorter Fiction*, 444.

42. Contemporary readers of Tolstoy no doubt enjoyed the additional self-referential allusion appearing earlier in the story: "I think that if the waiters and porter had not been so yielding I should have enjoyed a fight with them, or could have whacked the defenceless young English lady on the head with a stick. Had I been in Sevastopol at that moment I would gladly have rushed into an English trench to hack and slash at them" (*PSS* 5: 20; *Collected Shorter Fiction*, 437). One hardly fails to note the intertextual allusions also to Pushkin's "Egyptian Nights," its improvisatore and overtones of "art for art's sake." The concluding rejoinder of the singer's voice in "Lucerne" reminds one also, as Orwin mentions (*Tolstoy's Art and Thought*, 72), of the conclusion of Turgenev's "The Singers."

43. From our contemporary perspective, it is difficult to imagine that, though she was eight years his junior (twenty at the time), Valeriya Arsenyeva might genuinely have

been moved by such "love" letters, which are equal parts egotistical musing, condescending instruction, and jealous accusation. Tolstoy himself would occasionally even assume the role of different personalities in his letters, as in this one.

44. Leo Tolstoy, *Tolstoy's Letters*, trans. and ed. Reginald Frank Christian, 2 vols. (New York: Charles Scribner's Sons, 1978), 1: 65.

45. *PSS* 19: 124; *Anna Karenina*, 500.

46. *PSS* 19: 127; *Anna Karenina*, 504.

47. *PSS* 19: 132; *Anna Karenina*, 507.

48. *PSS* 19: 134; *Anna Karenina*, 510.

49. *PSS* 19: 136; *Anna Karenina*, 511.

50. *PSS* 19: 135; *Anna Karenina*, 510.

51. Mandelker's interpretation of this scene is just the opposite: "Tolstoy counters Victorian victimizing conventions, both literary and social, with a native Russian version of the courtship plot, an 'anti-proposal' scene: the mushroom-picking episode where Varenka does not receive Koznyshev's marriage proposal." Amy Mandelker, *Framing Anna Karenina: Tolstoy, the Woman Question, and the Victorian Novel*, (Columbus: Ohio State University Press, 1993), 169.

52. *PSS* 19: 138; *Anna Karenina*, 512.

CHAPTER 8. ANNA INCOMMUNICADA

1. For an earlier version of this argument, see: Justin Weir, "Anna Incommunicada: Language and Consciousness in *Anna Karenina*," *Tolstoy Studies Journal* 8 (1997): 99–111.

2. N. G. Chenyshevsky, *Polnoe sobranie sochinenii*, 16 vols. (Moscow: Khudozhestvennaia literatura, 1947), 3: 427.

3. See Gary Saul Morson, "Tolstoy's Absolute Language," *Critical Inquiry* 7, no. 4 (1981): 667–87. See also Caryl Emerson, "The Tolstoy Connection in Bakhtin," *PMLA* 100, no. 1 (1985): 68–80.

4. *PSS* 18: 4; *Anna Karenina*, ed. George Gibian, trans. Aylmer Maude, 2nd ed. (New York: W. W. Norton, 1995), 2.

5. *PSS* 18: 449; *Anna Karenina*, 389.

6. Ibid.

7. Ibid.

8. Here I will rely more or less on Gustafson's analysis. He sees prayer in Tolstoy's oeuvre as a form of "recollective consciousness." Prayer "assesses." "It glances backward and forward. . . . Whether [this] prayer of assessment takes the form of reaffirmation or supplication, however, it has the function of recollection of identity and clarification of vocation." As an assessment of human reality in the context of the Divine, prayer supersedes ordinary, communicative language in the constitution of self; it is an ideal language for Tolstoy. Richard Gustafson, *Leo Tolstoy: Resident and Stranger; A Study in Fiction and Theology* (Princeton, NJ: Princeton University Press, 1986), 331.

9. *PSS* 18: 157; *Anna Karenina*, 135.

10. For a Wittgensteinian reading of Tolstoy, see Martin Price, *Forms of Life: Character and Moral Imagination in the Novel* (New Haven: Yale University Press, 1983).

11. *PSS* 19: 348; *Anna Karenina*, 695.

12. Gustafson, *Leo Tolstoy*, 331.

13. *PSS* 8:52; *Anna Karenina*, 38–39.

14. *PSS* 18: 46; *Anna Karenina*, 39.

15. *PSS* 18: 46; *Anna Karenina*, 39.

16. *PSS* 18: 5; *Anna Karenina*, 2.

17. *PSS* 18: 9; *Anna Karenina*, 6.

18. *PSS* 18: 7; *Anna Karenina*, 4.

19. *PSS* 18: 451; *Anna Karenina*, 390.

20. Malcolm V. Jones, "Problems of Communication in *Anna Karenina*," in *New Essays on Tolstoy*, ed. Malcolm V. Jones and R. F. Christian (Cambridge: Cambridge University Press, 1978), 89.

21. Grossman accounts for this loss of communication in the context of the society tale background to *Anna Karenina*: "One striking feature of the relationship between Anna and Vronsky is the degree to which both are forced out of accustomed modes of thinking and feeling. As each begins to function at new and deeper emotional levels, habitual patterns of communication become less possible and communication itself becomes more problematic." Joan Delaney Grossman, " 'Words, Idle Words': Discourse and Communication in Anna Karenina," in *In the Shade of the Giant: Essays on Tolstoy*, ed. Hugh McLean (Berkeley: University of California Press, 1989), 117.

22. *PSS* 18: 158; *Anna Karenina*, 136.

23. *PSS* 18: 308; *Anna Karenina*, 266.

24. *PSS* 19: 281; *Anna Karenina*, 636.

25. In another context, Slivitskaia says the look (*vzgliad*) in Tolstoy's world is "incomparably significant": "It expresses the content of mental life that has no counterpart in language" (Olga Slivitskaia, "Vojna i Mir" L. N. Tolstogo: Problemy chelovecheskogo obshchenia, [Leningrad: Izd-vo Leningradskogo universiteta, 1988], 141). Looks may express things words cannot, but the inexpressible can also be dangerously hermetic and multivalent, which is, I think, Tolstoy's point here with Anna.

26. *PSS* 19: 27; *Anna Karenina*, 418.

27. *PSS* 19: 28; *Anna Karenina*, 419.

28. *PSS* 19: 33; *Anna Karenina*, 423.

29. *PSS* 19: 109; *Anna Karenina*, 488–89.

30. *PSS* 18: 306; *Anna Karenina*, 264.

31. *PSS* 19: 188; *Anna Karenina*, 556.

32. *PSS* 19: 219; *Anna Karenina*, 582.

33. *PSS* 19: 327; *Anna Karenina*, 676; my ellipses.

34. *PSS* 19: 329; *Anna Karenina*, 678.

35. Amy Mandelker, *Framing Anna Karenina: Tolstoy, the Woman Question, and the Victorian Novel* (Columbus: Ohio State University Press, 1993), 84.

36. Knapp writes that Levin, like Anna, mistrusts language, especially when he is confronted with death. Liza Knapp, " 'Tue-la! Tue-la!': Death Sentences, Words, and

Inner Monologue in Tolstoy's *Anna Karenina* and 'Three More Deaths,'" *Tolstoy Studies Journal* 11 (1999): 11.

37. It is worth noting that in 1880, three years after the completion of *Anna Karenina*, Tolstoy was writing *A Confession, A Criticism of Dogmatic Theology*, and *A Translation and Harmonization of the Four Gospels*.

38. *PSS* 19: 379; *Anna Karenina*, 721–22.

39. My reading of Levin is influenced by the analysis of personal identity in Richard Wollheim, *The Thread of Life: William James Lectures, 1982* (Cambridge, MA: Harvard University Press, 1984). "I have now returned twice to the question, What is it to lead the life of a person: once from the question, What is a person? once from the question, What is a person's life? . . . Whether we start with the thing or the product, inquiry returns us to something intermediate between the two, or to the process, which takes place in the thing and results in the product" (21; my ellipses).

CHAPTER 9. THE POETICS OF ROMANTIC BETRAYAL

1. For more on jealousy in Tolstoy, see Jean Bessiere, *La jalousie: Tolstoi, Svevo, Proust* (Paris: Champion, 1996); Pierre Brunel, "Ecrire la jalousie," in *L'écriture romanesque de la jalousie: Tolstoï ("La Sonate à Kreutzer"), Svevo ("Senilità"), Proust ("Un amour de Swann")*, ed. Pierre Brunel (Paris: Didier Erudition—CNED, 1996), 23–27. Philippe Chardin, "La jalousie ou les deplaisirs de l'exagération," *Litteratures* 35 (1996): 149–65; Harold K. Schefski, "Tolstoy and Jealousy," *Irish Slavonic Studies* 10 (1989): 17–30.

2. Brunel, "Ecrire la jalousie," 46. This formulation recalls Todorov's definition of the fantastic as a hermeneutic hesitation between the marvelous and the uncanny: Tzvetan Todorov, *The Fantastic: A Structural Approach to a Literary Genre*, trans. Richard Howard (Ithaca, NY: Cornell University Press, 1975).

3. John R. Searle, *Intentionality: An Essay in the Philosophy of Mind* (Cambridge: Cambridge University Press, 1983). For a discussion of intention in relation to literary theory, see John Searle, "Literary Theory and Its Discontents," *New Literary History* 25, no. 3 (1994): 637–67.

4. Paul Ricoeur, *Freud and Philosophy: An Essay on Interpretation*, trans. Denis Savage (New Haven: Yale University Press, 1970), 34; emphasis in original.

5. *PSS* 5: 116. Translation from Leo Tolstoy, *Tolstoy's Short Fiction*, ed. Michael R. Katz (New York: W. W. Norton, 1991), 95.

6. Malcolm V. Jones, "Problems of Communication in Anna Karenina," in *New Essays on Tolstoy*, ed. Malcolm V. Jones and R. F. Christian (Cambridge: Cambridge University Press, 1978), 94.

7. Tim Langen, "The Poetics of Listening in *Anna Karenina*," presented at a Harvard University symposium, "The Overexamined Life: New Perspectives on Tolstoy," April 2002.

8. *PSS* 32: 317. Translation from Leo Tolstoy, *Resurrection*, trans. Rosemary Edmonds (New York: Penguin Books, 1966), 407.

9. PSS 5: 79; *Tolstoy's Short Fiction*, 64.

10. Gary Saul Morson, *Hidden in Plain View: Narrative and Creative Potentials in "War and Peace"* (Stanford, CA: Stanford University Press, 1987), 256. The addition of "conventional" is my reading of Morson.

11. PSS 10: 31. Translation from Leo Tolstoy, *War and Peace*, trans. Constance Garnett (New York: Modern Library, 1994), 355, 357.

12. PSS 10: 65; *War and Peace*, 388.

13. PSS 32: 253–54; *Resurrection*, 331.

14. PSS 32: 256; *Resurrection*, 333.

15. PSS 32: 286; *Resurrection*, 369; PSS 32: 286; *Resurrection*, 370; PSS 32: 287; *Resurrection*, 371.

16. PSS 32: 288; *Resurrection*, 372.

17. PSS 32: 288; *Resurrection*, 372.

18. PSS 32: 288; *Resurrection*, 373.

19. This "hypothetical observer" point of view was part of the narrative solution for Tolstoy in *War and Peace*. See Kathryn B. Feuer, *Tolstoy and the Genesis of "War and Peace,"* ed. Robin Feuer Miller and Donna Tussing Orwin (Ithaca, NY: Cornell University Press, 1996), 23.

20. PSS 32: 289; *Resurrection*, 373.

21. PSS 32: 303; *Resurrection*, 391.

22. PSS 27: 481. Leo Tolstoy, *Great Short Works of Leo Tolstoy*, trans. Louise Maude and Aylmer Maude (New York: Harper and Row, 1967), 305.

23. PSS 27: 483; *Great Short Works of Leo Tolstoy*, 307.

24. PSS 27: 513–14; *Great Short Works of Leo Tolstoy*, 347; first ellipses mine.

25. PSS 27: 514; *Great Short Works of Leo Tolstoy*, 348.

26. PSS 27: 515; *Great Short Works of Leo Tolstoy*, 348.

27. PSS 27: 517; *Great Short Works of Leo Tolstoy*, 350.

28. PSS 19: 346. Leo Tolstoy, *Anna Karenina*, ed. George Gibian, trans. Aylmer Maude, 2nd ed. (New York: W. W. Norton, 1995), 693.

29. PSS 27: 513; *Great Short Works of Leo Tolstoy*, 347.

30. PSS 27: 494; *Great Short Works of Leo Tolstoy*, 321–22; my ellipses.

31. PSS 27: 498; *Great Short Works of Leo Tolstoy*, 327.

32. PSS 27: 499; *Great Short Works of Leo Tolstoy*, 329.

33. PSS 27: 502; *Great Short Works of Leo Tolstoy*, 333.

34. PSS 27: 510; *Great Short Works of Leo Tolstoy*, 343.

35. PSS 27: 507; *Great Short Works of Leo Tolstoy*, 339.

36. Lev Vygotsky, *Thought and Language*, rev. ed., trans. Alex Kozulin (Cambridge, MA: MIT Press, 1986), 33.

37. Ricoeur, *Freud and Philosophy*, 34.

38. PSS 19: 367. *Anna Karenina*, 818–19; my emphasis and ellipses.

39. Style is not always the determining factor. Creating an "event," constructing the plot out of nothing, is part of Tolstoy's challenge in the later stories about sex, as John Kopper argues. "In 'Father Sergius,' 'The Kreutzer Sonata,' and 'The Devil' Tolstoy takes a narrative situation that presents a rather infertile semiological field. What can

be said about a man's sexuality when the man can do what he wants? The author makes each story into an experiment answer to his narrative dilemma." "Tolstoy and Narrative of Sex: A Reading of 'Father Sergius,' 'The Devil,' and 'Kreutzer Sonata,'" in *In the Shade of the Giant: Essays on Tolstoy,* ed. Hugh McLean (Berkeley: University of California Press, 1989), 178.

40. *PSS* 19: 376; *Anna Karenina,* 828.

41. Pozdnyshev is not the narrator, but he tells most of the story. By keeping him at one narrative remove from the story itself, Tolstoy is able to depict both its production and its reception. Lucien Dallenbach would call this a *mise en abyme* of the whole code. See Dallenbach, *The Mirror in the Text* (Chicago: University of Chicago Press, 1989), 43.

42. David Herman, "Stricken by Infection: Art and Adultery in *Anna Karenina* and 'Kreutzer Sonata,'" *Slavic Review* 56, no. 1 (1997): 34.

43. *PSS* 27: 7; *Tolstoy's Short Fiction,* 173.

44. *PSS* 27: 77, 74; *Tolstoy's Short Fiction,* 231, 228.

45. *PSS* 27: 19; *Tolstoy's Short Fiction,* 183; *PSS* 27: 18; *Tolstoy's Short Fiction,* 182; *PSS* 27: 21; *Tolstoy's Short Fiction,* 184; *PSS* 27: 24; *Tolstoy's Short Fiction,* 186; *PSS* 27: 24; *Tolstoy's Short Fiction,* 186; *PSS* 27: 30; *Tolstoy's Short Fiction,* 191.

46. *PSS* 27: 40; *Tolstoy's Short Fiction,* 203.

47. *PSS* 5: 126; *Tolstoy's Short Fiction,* 103.

48. *PSS* 27: 44; *Tolstoy's Short Fiction,* 203.

49. *PSS* 27: 44; *Tolstoy's Short Fiction,* 203.

50. Charles Isenberg, *Telling Silence: Russian Frame Narratives of Renunciation* (Evanston, IL: Northwestern University Press, 1993), 83.

51. Golstein writes: "Similar to that quintessential paranoid text, *Mein Kampf,* the Pozdnysev story quickly departs from autobiography and gets lost in hysterical attacks on others." Vladimir Golstein, "Narrating the Murder: The Rhetoric of Evasion in 'The Kreutzer Sonata,'" *Russian Literature* 40, no. 4 (1996): 454.

52. Harold Bloom, *The Anxiety of Influence: A Theory of Poetry* (London: Oxford University Press, 1973), 5, and passim.

53. Consider J. M. Coetzee's interpretation. Because Pozdnyshev does not "doubt himself when there are obvious grounds for doing so," he lacks authority as one who makes a confession. Coetzee believes Tolstoy grew weary of the traditional mechanics of narrative and placed the "truth" in Pozdnyshev's mouth. J. M. Coetzee, "Confession and Double Thoughts: Tolstoy, Rousseau, Dostoevsky," *Comparative Literature* 37, no. 3 (1985): 205, 232.

54. Isenberg, *Telling Silence,* 97. Isenberg provides an excellent example, but his subtle account by no means represents a schematic application of Freudian theory.

55. It is worth noting that in a kind of wordless mutual comprehension, almost a negative image of love, men in Tolstoy's fiction often recognize in each other their shared animal baseness. Even if they cannot communicate with one another, they have a psychological explanation available for one another's base deeds.

56. *PSS* 32: 286; *Great Short Works of Leo Tolstoy,* 348–49.

57. Though I arrived at my interpretation of "The Kreutzer Sonata" separately, through a consideration of romance narratives, I recognize that it extends Jackson's comparison of Pozdnyshev and the underground man, as well as of Golstein's remarkable essay on "The Kreutzer Sonata." Golstein writes: "Indeed, it is my contention that the novella focuses less on articulating Tolstoy's views on sexuality, or aesthetics, than on the portrayal of a paranoid and unrepentant murderer, a man who hysterically accuses everything that mirrors his own ugliness" (Golstein, "Narrating the Murder," 451). The main difference between my interpretation and Golstein's, a significant one, I think, is that I believe Pozdnyshev is actually making everything up. See Robert Louis Jackson, "Tolstoj's 'Kreutzer Sonata' and Dostoevsky's *Notes from the Underground*," in *American Contributions to the Eighth International Congress of Slavists, Zagreb, and Ljubljana, September 3–9, 1978*, ed. Victor Terras (Columbus, OH: Slavica Publishers, 1978).
58. See the chapter on "Notes from Underground" in Michael Holquist, *Dostoevsky and the Novel* (Princeton, NJ: Princeton University Press, 1977).
59. *PSS* 27: 564.
60. *PSS* 27: 15; *Tolstoy's Short Fiction*, 179.
61. *PSS* 27: 61; *Tolstoy's Short Fiction*, 218.
62. Ruth Rischin, "Allegro Tumultuosissimamente: Beethoven in Tolstoy's Fiction," in *In the Shade of the Giant: Essays on Tolstoy*, ed. Hugh McLean (Berkeley: University of California Press, 1989), 43. She amplifies this insight: "In exposing the erotic component in social relations, in driving a polemic against equivocation in music, Tolstoy paradoxically restricts the power of language as an instrument of truth. In this respect Pozdnyshev's story can be read as a metaphor for an aggression against linguistic ambiguity—it can even be understood as a crime of passion against the duplicity of language" (ibid., 48).
63. Herman writes in "Stricken by Infection": "Tolstoi's almost paranoid discovery of adultery on all sides in not entirely perverse. Tolstoi is in fact waging war against adulterousness in the name of a powerful ideal which he only dimly descries and which he cannot bring himself to embrace fully except while writing *Kreutzer Sonata*, but which he nonetheless finds powerfully attractive throughout his life. *It is an ideal of human purity, and hovering in the background a still more inclusive ideal of what might be called semiotic purity . . .*" (20–21; my ellipses and emphasis).
64. The reference for the diary entry is *PSS* 50: 47. Golstein, "Narrating the Murder," 453.
65. Isenberg, *Telling Silence*, 84.
66. *PSS* 27: 78. One thinks also here of the conclusions to "The Death of Ivan Ilyich" and "Master and Man."
67. Tolstoy actually began writing that essay even before he was assailed by countless letters asking him to clarify his own beliefs.
68. *PSS*, 29: 70.
69. N. N. Gusev, *Letopis' zhizni i tvorchestva L'va Nikolaevicha Tolstogo, 1891–1910* (Moscow: Gosudarstvennoe izdatel'stvo khudozhestvennoj literatury, 1960), 728; emphasis mine.

CHAPTER 10. AFTER LOVE AND LANGUAGE

1. Quoted in: N. N. Gusev, *Letopis' zhizni i tvorchestva L. N. Tolstogo* (Moscow: Academia, 1936), 214.

2. Ivan Turgenev, *First Love*, trans. Isaiah Berlin (New York: Penguin Books, 1950), 103.

3. Gusev, *Letopis*,' 449. This often-quoted remark was from 1903, just a couple of months before he began writing "After the Ball."

4. For an earlier version of this argument see Justin Weir, "Tema liubvi v pozdnoj proze Tolstogo," in *Lev Tolstoy i mirovaia literatura: Materialy mezhdunarodnoi nauchnoi konferentsii*, ed. Galina Alekseeva and Nikolai Sviridov (Tula: Izdatel'skii Dom "Yasnaya Polyana," 2007), 63–70.

5. *PSS* 34: 117. All translations from the Russian are mine.

6. "After the Ball" seems to have been written about less frequently than several of Tolstoy's other later moralistic tales, but there are a couple of important exceptions. See Alexander Zholkovsky's "Before and after 'After the Ball': Variations on the Theme of Courtship, Corpses, and Culture," in *Text Counter Text: Rereadings in Russia Literary History* (Stanford, CA: Stanford University Press, 1994), by Alexander Zholkovsky, 59–87. See also Stephanie Sandler, "Pleasure, Danger, and the Dance: Nineteenth-Century Russian Variations," in *Russia, Women, Culture*, ed. Helena Goscilo and Beth Holmgren (Bloomington: Indiana University Press, 1996), 247–72. The "visit to the bordello" sequence appears again in *Anna Karenina*. See Ronald LeBlanc, "Levin Visits Anna: The Iconology of Harlotry," *Tolstoy Studies Journal* 3 (1990): 1–20.

7. See Neil Cornwell, ed., *The Society Tale in Russian Literature: From Odoevskii to Tolstoi* (Atlanta: Rodopi, 1998).

8. The model for this kind of analysis is Jakobson's "The Statue in Pushkin's Poetic Mythology," reprinted in Roman Jakobson, *Language in Literature* (Cambridge, MA: Harvard University Press, 1987), 318–67.

9. Burnasheva has demonstrated that Colonel B. is a direct literary descendant of Nikolai Rostov. See: N. I. Burnasheva, ". . . *Proiti po trudnoi doroge otkrytiia*. . . ." *Zagadki i nakhodki v rukopisiax L'va Tolstogo* (Moscow: Nauka, 2005), 348. The connection furthers my main contention that Tolstoy uses "After the Ball" to comment on his earlier work.

10. *PSS* 34: 116, 125.

11. *PSS* 34: 551–53.

12. *PSS* 34: 116.

13. See Chekhov's 1892 "Ward No. 6" for lengthy discussion of environment (*sreda*) versus the life of the mind.

14. From "Environment," written in 1873. See: Fyodor Dostoevsky, *A Writer's Diary, Volume One: 1873–1876*, trans. Kenneth Lantz (Evanston, IL: Northwestern University Press, 1993), 135–36.

15. Daniil Kharms named many of his absurdist miniature stories *sluchai*, thus rendering better the redundancy of the possible English translation "chance event."

16. *PSS* 34: 118, 120.

17. *PSS* 34: 117.
18. *PSS* 34: 116.
19. Ekphrasis is the literary description of a visual object, usually a work of art. See Amy Mandelker, *Framing Anna Karenina: Tolstoy, the Woman Question, and the Victorian Novel* (Columbus: Ohio State University Press, 1993).
20. *PSS* 34: 118.
21. *PSS* 34: 124.
22. *PSS* 34: 125.
23. *PSS* 34: 125.
24. *PSS* 34: 117.
25. Boris Eikhenbaum, *The Young Tolstoi*, trans. Gary Kern (Ann Arbor, MI: Ardis, 1972), 30.
26. Roman Jakobson writes: "Following the path of contiguous relationships, the Realist author metonymically digresses from the plot to the atmosphere and from the characters to the setting in time and space." "Two Aspects of Language and Two Types of Aphasic Disturbances," in *Language in Literature*, ed. Krystyna Pomorska and Stephen Rudy (Cambridge, MA: Harvard University Press, 1987), 111.
27. *PSS* 34: 120.
28. My ellipses. Zholkovsky, *Text Counter Text*, 66. Zholkovsky sees folkloric formulas here. Either the tortured Tatar is a bride, subdued for her wedding night by the beating, or he represents Ivan himself, undergoing a rite of initiation (83–84). Ultimately, Zholkovsky interprets "After the Ball" as Tolstoy's activation and problematization of a latent cultural plot, "enacting a symbolic transition from the paganism of official culture to his own version of Christianity" (86), whereas I view the story more as a different kind of assault on traditional narrative itself and therefore a radically less productive cultural text. For example, Zholkovsky sees Ivan as having undergone a "spiritual conversion" (62–63, 85); yet, on the contrary, it seems to me that Tolstoy goes out of his way to demonstrate that Ivan has learned little from his experience. He still believes many years later, for example, that perhaps the colonel knew something about the Tatar that he did not.
29. Peter Brooks, *Body Work: Objects of Desire in Modern Narrative* (Cambridge, MA: Harvard University Press, 1993), 19.
30. Ibid. 20.
31. *PSS* 34: 118.
32. *PSS* 34: 118.
33. *PSS* 34: 121.
34. Stephanie Sandler writes of "After the Ball": "In this story women play no role important enough to merit punishment. Varen'ka initially seems an important memory, but only in a trivialized, debased form of the cycle of error and reproof" (Sandler, "Pleasure, Danger, and the Dance," 262).
35. *PSS* 34: 122.
36. *PSS* 34: 123.
37. Liza Knapp, "Tolstoy on Musical Mimesis: Platonic Aesthetics and Erotics in 'The Kreutzer Sonata,'" *Tolstoy Studies Journal* 4 (1991): 25–42; and Ruth Rischin, "Allegro

Tumultuosissimamente: Beethoven in Tolstoy's Fiction," in *In the Shade of the Giant: Essays on Tolstoy*, ed. Hugh McLean (Berkeley: University of California Press, 1989), 12–60, both point out that the following quote by Pozdnyshev rephrases a passage from *Childhood*. Nikolai remarks: "I well remember the feelings [those pieces] aroused in me. They resembled memories—but memories of what? It almost seemed as if I were remembering something that had never been." *PSS* 1: 31. Translation in Leo Tolstoy, *Childhood, Boyhood, Youth*, trans. Rosemary Edmonds (New York: Penguin Books, 1964), 40.

38. *PSS* 27: 61; *Tolstoy's Short Fiction*, ed. Michael R. Katz (New York: W. W. Norton, 1991), 217.

39. From her essay, "Tolstoy's Aesthetics," in *The Cambridge Companion to Tolstoy*, ed. Donna Tussing Orwin (Cambridge: Cambridge University Press, 2002), 249.

40. *PSS* 34: 124.

41. *PSS* 34: 116.

42. *PSS* 34: 123.

43. *PSS* 34: 123.

44. Sandler, "Pleasure, Danger, and the Dance," 263. Tolstoy's wife, Sonya, accused Tolstoy of a homosexual relationship with Chertkov as late as 1910 (Ernest J. Simmons, *Leo Tolstoy*, special limited ed. [Boston: Little, Brown, 1946], 741).

45. De Haard sees antinarrative structures in the early fiction, but he has more in mind Tolstoy's unconventional plots (and missing plots). See Eric de Haard, *Narrative and Anti-Narrative Structures in Lev Tolstoj's Early Works* (Amsterdam: Rodopi, 1989). I am thinking primarily of how Tolstoy undermines literary communication altogether.

46. Donald Fanger, "Nazarov's Mother: On the Poetics of Tolstoi's Late Epic," *Canadian-American Slavic Studies* 12 (1978): 574.

47. Ibid., 576.

48. Tolstoy's diary entry relating to "After the Ball" notes merely: "Story about a ball and through the line" (*Rasskaz o bale i skvoz' stroj*). Gusev, *Letopis'*, 455. In *Hadji Murad* Nikolai punishes a student by having him run a gauntlet of a thousand men twelve times ("Thank God, we have no capitle [*sic*] punishment," he writes). The narrator comments: "Nicholas knew that twelve thousand strokes with the regulation rods were not only certain death with torture, but were superfluous cruelty, for five thousand strokes were sufficient to kill the strongest man. But it pleased him to be ruthlessly cruel and it also pleased him to think that we have abolished capital punishment in Russia." Nikolai additionally requests that all the students be there to witness the punishment. *Great Short Works of Leo Tolstoy*, trans. Louise Maude and Aylmer Maude (New York: Harper and Row, 1967), 621.

CHAPTER 11. THE ROLE OF VIOLENCE IN ART

1. I am indebted here to a notion from David Herman's interpretation of "The Kreutzer Sonata," in which he matches the late Tolstoy's ideal of human purity with an ideal of "semiotic purity." "Stricken by Infection: Art and Adultery in *Anna Karenina* and

'Kreutzer Sonata,'" *Slavic Review* 56, no. 1 (1997): 21. I do not discuss Tolstoy's *The First Step* (1897), in which he makes an argument for vegetarianism by way of an extremely explicit and detailed description of his visit to an abattoir. Violence and self-purification are obviously and openly linked, though not in the meta-aesthetic manner that has drawn most of my attention in this study. See Ronald D. LeBlanc, "Unpalatable Pleasures: Tolstoy, Food, and Sex," *Tolstoy Studies Journal* 6 (1993): 1–32. See also Ronald D. LeBlanc, *Vegetarianism in Russia: The Tolstoy(an) Legacy*, Carl Beck Papers in Russian and East European Studies, no. 1507 (Pittsburgh: University of Pittsburgh Press, 2001).

2. Mary Carruthers discusses the use of lurid images by monks in order to remember the details of complex prayers or meditative practices, in *The Book of Memory: A Study of Memory in Medieval Culture* (Cambridge: Cambridge University Press, 1990).

3. Contrast this situation of no past or future, just a present, with the situation of the diaries Irina Paperno describes, where there is a past and a future but no present. "'Who, What is I?'": Tolstoy in His Diaries," *Tolstoy Studies Journal* 11 (1999): 32–54.

4. *PSS* 2: 40–41. Translation in Leo Tolstoy, *Childhood, Boyhood, Youth*, trans. Rosemary Edmonds (New York: Penguin Books, 1964), 143.

5. Maxim Gorky, *My Childhood* (New York: Penguin Books, 1966), 181.

6. *PSS* 26: 242. Leo Tolstoy, *Plays: Volume Two, 1886–1889*, trans. Marvin Kantor with Tanya Tulchinsky, intro. Andrew Baruch Wachtel (Evanston, IL: Northwestern University Press, 1996), 90. *Vlast' t'my* is often translated *The Power of Darkness*. Kantor and Tulchinsky choose "realm" for "vlast.'" Wachtel notes: "The word 'power,' however, tends to connote some kind of outside force, whereas what Tolstoy seems to have had in mind was that evil can be inherent in human nature. Thus, his focus is on the entire closed world in which the crimes described in this play were committed rather than on any external power. That is why we have opted for 'realm' here" (ibid., xi).

7. See Donskov's bibliography in his *Essays on L. N. Tolstoj's Dramatic Art* (Wiesbaden, Germany: Harrassowitz Verlag, 1988).

8. Donskov (ibid., 69) argues that Tolstoy used dialect not just for comic but also for serious effect.

9. As Andrew Wachtel writes: "With its constant use of peasant dialect and its shocking violence, *The Realm of Darkness* stands practically alone in the Russian dramatic tradition" (Wachtel, introduction to *Plays*, xiii).

10. *PSS* 26: 706. See: N. Gudzii "'Vlast' t'my': Istoriia pisaniia, pechataniia i postanovki na stsene 'Vlasti t'my,'" *PSS* 26: 705–36. Among literary influences, Wachtel discusses Pisemsky's drama *A Bitter Fate* (1859) and Dostoevsky's *Crime and Punishment* (Wachtel, introduction to *Plays*, viii, x). George Steiner sees a reflection of Raskolnikov's confession in the scene where Nikita admits his sins before the wedding crowd (*Tolstoy or Dostoevsky: An Essay in the Old Criticism* [New York: Alfred A. Knopf, 1959], 128). Tolstoy clearly has Raskolnikov's crime in mind during these years. He discusses the question of why Raskolnikov kills the old pawnbroker and her sister in an essay from a few years later, "Why Do Men Stupefy Themselves?" (1890), which I discuss below.

11. Gudzii, "'Vlast' t'my,'" 706.

12. Ibid., 713.

13. Ibid., 706–7.

14. Neil Carruthers, "The Paris Première of Tolstoy's *Vlast' t'my* (*The Power of Darkness*)," *New Zealand Slavonic Journal* (1987): 83.

15. See W. Gareth Jones, "Tolstoy Staged in Paris, Berlin, and London," in *The Cambridge Companion to Tolstoy*, ed. Donna Tussing Orwin (Cambridge: Cambridge University Press, 2002), 142–60.

16. Ibid., 143.

17. Quoted by Donskov (*Essays*, 19). Originally from an interview in *Teatr i iskusstvo* 34 (1908): 580–81.

18. Donskov, following Christian, is right to reject oversimplification: "Reference has been made to Tolstoj's statement that one must not 'make him [the character] think [on the stage] and call up memories. . . . A ready-formed state of mind, ready-formed resolutions, must be presented to the public.' This assertion that characters must be already formed, and that there is no room for them to think anew or to develop into something different is, according to R. Christian, an absurdly constricting one. But in practice, it was not so simple since Tolstoj's heroes do digress into the past and they certainly do develop" (*Essays*, 22). Donskov references R. F. Christian, *Tolstoy: A Critical Introduction* (Cambridge: Cambridge University Press, 1969), 257–58.

19. An often-repeated anecdote, but see, for example: A. N. Wilson, *Tolstoy: A Biography* (New York: W. W. Norton, 1988), 61.

20. Tolstoy did write several more plays, notably *The Fruits of Enlightenment* (1889) and *The Living Corpse* (1900).

21. PSS 18: 156; translation from *Anna Karenina*, ed. George Gibian, trans. Aylmer Maude, 2nd ed. (New York: W. W. Norton, 1995), 135–36.

22. Donskov, *Essays*, 25.

23. PSS 26: 130; *Plays: Volume Two, 1886–1889*, 8.

24. PSS 26: 123; *Plays: Volume Two, 1886–1889*, 1.

25. PSS 26: 123; *Plays: Volume Two, 1886–1889*, 1.

26. PSS 18: 46; *Anna Karenina*, 39.

27. PSS 26: 143; *Plays: Volume Two, 1886–1889*, 18.

28. Gustafson's work provides the key insight here with his analysis of prayer in Tolstoy as a form of "recollective consciousness," an assessment of human vocation in the context of the divine. See *Leo Tolstoy: Resident and Stranger; A Study in Fiction and Theology* (Princeton, NJ: Princeton University Press, 1986), 331.

29. Simmons remarks that as Tolstoy's attention turned from trying to stage *The Power of Darkness*, he became consumed with completing *On Life*. See: Ernest J. Simmons, *Leo Tolstoy*, 2 vols. (New York: Vintage Books, 1960), 2: 420.

30. PSS 26: 183; *Plays: Volume Two, 1886–1889*, 46.

31. PSS 26: 196; *Plays: Volume Two, 1886–1889*, 55; PSS 26: 197; *Plays: Volume Two, 1886–1889*, 56.

32. PSS 27: 269. Leo Tolstoy, *Selections: "Why Do Men Stupefy Themselves?" and Other Writings*, trans. Aylmer Maude, ed. Meredith Murray et al. (Blauvelt, NY: Strength Books, 1975), 40.

33. *PSS* 27: 270; "Why Do Men Stupefy Themselves?" 55.

34. *PSS* 27: 273; "Why Do Men Stupefy Themselves?" 45.

35. *PSS* 27: 275–76; "Why Do Men Stupefy Themselves?" 52.

36. *PSS* 27: 280; "Why Do Men Stupefy Themselves?" 58, 60.

37. Morson reads the passage on Bryullov and the "tiny bit" as crucial for Tolstoy's "prosa-ics," as well as his view of life and love: "For Tolstoy, true love and true life are experi-enced in moments that are barely noticeable at all. . . . Tolstoy is the artist of tiny alterations." Gary Saul Morson, *Anna Karenina in Our Time: Seeing More Wisely* (New Haven: Yale University Press, 2007), 77–78. I agree that much of the creative aesthetics of Tolstoy's major novels are affected by his interest in the small details of everyday life. Nevertheless, the tiny bit of this essay ultimately serves to undermine the major fiction.

38. *PSS* 27: 280; "Why do Men Stupefy Themselves?" 60; my emphasis.

39. *PSS* 27: 282; "Why do Men Stupefy Themselves?" 64.

40. Victor Shklovsky, *Russian Formalist Criticism: Four Essays*, trans. Lee T. Lemon and Marion J. Reis (Lincoln: University of Nebraska Press, 1965), 12.

41. *PSS* 28: 104. Leo Tolstoy, *The Kingdom of God Is within You: Christianity Not as a Mystic Religion but as a New Theory of Life*, trans. Constance Garnett (Lincoln: University of Nebraska Press, 1984), 131–32; my emphases.

42. Quoted in Paul de Man, *Blindness and Insight: Essays in the Rhetoric of Contemporary Criticism*, 2nd ed. (London: Methuen, 1983) 147.

43. Ibid.

44. Ibid., 162.

45. See: Yuri M. Lotman, *Universe of the Mind: A Semiotic Theory of Culture*, trans. Ann Shukman (New York: I. B. Tauris, 2001), 143.

46. An uncensored version was published in translation in 1898. See Leo Tolstoy, *What Is Art?* trans. Aylmer Maude (New York: Liberal Arts Press, 1960).

47. Jeff Love, *Tolstoy: A Guide for the Perplexed* (New York: Continuum, 2008), 143. Michael Denner writes: "Thus the practical aesthetics, the model for the production of art in *What Is Art?* hinges on a paradox: The key to creating an authentic work of art is the absence of any intention to produce art." Michael A. Denner, "Accidental Art: Tolstoy's Poetics of Unintentionality," *Philosophy and Literature* 27 (2003): 292.

48. *PSS* 30: 151; *What Is Art?* 142.

49. *PSS* 30: 109–10; *What Is Art?* 97.

50. One need look no further than the subtext of Rousseau for proof of this self-directedness, as Thomas Barran argues in his: "Rousseau's Political Vision and Tolstoy's *What Is Art?*" *Tolstoy Studies Journal* 5 (1992): 1–12. Tolstoy continues to revise his relationship to the great philosopher of his youthful aesthetics. Barran reminds us of a political dimen-sion, which, as we have seen, is present also in the revision *The Kingdom of God Is within You* provides for "Why Do Men Stupefy Themselves?"

51. Caryl Emerson, "Tolstoy's Aesthetics," in *Cambridge Companion to Tolstoy*, ed. Orwin, 248–49.

52. *PSS* 30: 163 fn 1; *What Is Art?* 155 fn 5.

53. Ibid.

54. *PSS* 30: 65; *What Is Art?* 51; emphasis in original.

55. *PSS* 30: 185; *What Is Art?* 179–80.

56. *PSS* 30: 112; *What Is Art?* 100.

57. There are many instances of the comparison, especially in Tolstoy's discussion of taste. For example: "To value a work of art by the degree of its realism, by the accuracy of details reproduced, is as strange as to judge of the nutritive quality of food by its external appearance" (*PSS* 30: 116–17; *What Is Art?* 104).

58. *PSS* 30: 111; *What Is Art?* 99.

59. Tolstoy's criticism of the consumption of art by members of his own class is iconoclastic. Compare Gamboni's description: "Nevertheless, compared to the Byzantine iconoclasm, the ethical, social, political and aesthetic elements of the Reformation were far more explicit, and certainly, weightier. There was the critique of art as luxury and of artistic investment as economic waste detrimental to the interests of the poor, an argument that has remained central to the reception of public patronage down to the present." Dario Gamboni, *The Destruction of Art: Iconoclasm and Vandalism since the French Revolution* (London: Reaktion Books, 1997), 29.

60. Tolstoy, *What Is Art?* 7.

61. Tolstoy, *What Is Art?* 7–8.

62. Emerson writes: "It would be easier for them, of course, if they could justify this violent activity by automatizing it, or by persuading themselves that deer were somehow so different from human beings that killing them was not murder. But for this very reason, in order to forestall such comfortable psychological accommodation and to allow the heart to feel anguish is the drama necessary in their culture." Emerson, "Tolstoy's Aesthetics," 242.

63. Denner, "Accidental Art," 284. Denner goes on: "I think he means to emphasize the latent, etymological meaning of the *zarazit,*' to infect, the root of which is *razit,*' to strike, a military term that likely resonated with Tolstoy, a war veteran" (ibid.).

64. *PSS* 30: 122–23; *What Is Art?* 111.

65. *PSS* 62: 268–69; *Anna Karenina*, 750.

66. *PSS* 30: 111; *What Is Art?* 123.

67. *PSS* 30: 151; *What Is Art?* 142.

68. *PSS* 30: 86; *What Is Art?* 72.

69. *PSS* 30: 178–79; *What Is Art?* 172–73.

70. *PSS* 19: 45; *Anna Karenina*, 434.

71. *PSS* 30: 109; *What Is Art?* 97.

72. Tolstoy never published "Father Sergius," nor did he publish other important works, such as *Hadji Murad*. Although I have argued that authorship involves the manipulation of a public identity shared with readers, these works are not the contradiction they seem to be. Tolstoy is caught in a paradox of gesturing toward authorial silence through the voice of texts that ring all the more loudly having been written by the famous Tolstoy. I find David Herman's resolution of this paradox convincing (see his "Khadzhi-Murat's Silence," *Slavic Review* 64, no. 1 [2005]: 1–23). Not publishing these texts allows Tolstoy to arrive at the aesthetic conclusion within his literature, yet activate that conclusion in his refusal to publish. As with other self-imposed rules, he tended

to break this one. He publishes *Resurrection* for profit, for example, in order to help relocate the Dukhobors to Canada. And the overall point I hope to convey in this chapter is that Tolstoy's attempts to transcend his authorship are invariably noisy, multivalent, and intextual—not at all as silent as he would have us believe.

73. PSS 31: 44. Translation in *Great Short Works of Leo Tolstoy*, trans. Louise Maude and Aylmer Maude (New York: Harper and Row, 1967), 544–45.
74. PSS 31: 5; *Great Short Works*, 503
75. PSS 31: 7; *Great Short Works*, 505.
76. PSS 31: 19; *Great Short Works*, 517–18.
77. PSS 31: 9; *Great Short Works*, 507.
78. PSS 31: 21; *Great Short Works*, 519–20.
79. PSS 31: 30; *Great Short Works*, 529.
80. PSS 30: 88; *What Is Art?* 75.
81. *In the Shade of the Giant: Essays on Tolstoy*, ed. Hugh McLean (Berkeley: University of California Press, 1989), 178.
82. PSS 31: 26; Tolstoy, *Great Short Works*, 525.
83. Ibid.
84. Olga Slivitskaia, "*Vojna i Mir*" *L. N. Tolstogo: Problemy chelovecheskogo obshchenia* (Leningrad: Izd-vo Leningradskogo universiteta, 1988), 144–45.

CHAPTER 12. ON TOLSTOY'S AUTHORSHIP

1. Morson draws attention to what he calls "processual intentionality" in Dostoevsky (*Narrative and Freedom: The Shadows of Time* [New Haven: Yale University Press, 1994], 142–45), and in Tolstoy (*Hidden in Plain View: Narrative and Creative Potentials in "War and Peace"* [Stanford, CA: Stanford University Press, 1987], 218–23). For Morson (and for Dostoevsky and Tolstoy) the complexity of human psychology and behavior defies narrow definitions of intention. I believe that Tolstoy comes to reconceptualize authorial intention because it offers him a means to retain control of the meaning of his literary texts and to redefine his authorial identity. These views of psychology and of authorship are compatible, though they do not imply one another.
2. From William K. Wimsatt and Monroe C. Beardsley, "The Affective Fallacy," in *The Norton Anthology of Theory and Criticism*, ed. Vincent B. Leitch (New York: W. W. Norton, 2001), 1388.
3. The Wimsatt and Beardsley quotes refer to *The Norton Anthology of Theory and Criticism*, 1374–75.
4. There is a string of articles responding to Steven Knapp and Walter Benn Michaels's "Against Theory," *Critical Inquiry* 8, no. 4 (1982): 723–42, which embraced intentionalism for literary interpretation. The essays were gathered by W. J. T. Mitchell in *Against Theory: Literary Studies and the New Pragmatism* (Chicago: University of Chicago Press, 1985). An exceptionally clear minded and useful rejoinder to Knapp and Michaels may be found in John Searle, "Literary Theory and Its Discontents," *New Literary History* 25, no. 3 (1994): 637–67.

5. "The Statue in Pushkin's Poetic Mythology," in Roman Jakobson, *Language in Literature*, ed. Krystyna Pomorska and Stephen Rudy (Cambridge, MA: Belknap Press of Harvard University Press, 1987), 318.

6. Ibid., 319.

7. Ibid., 353.

8. Eliot, "Tradition and the Individual Talent," in *Authorship: From Plato to the Postmodern: A Reader*, ed. Seán Burke (Edinburgh: Edinburgh University Press, 1995), 76.

9. Ibid., 74.

10. Boris Tomaševskij, "Literature and Biography," in *Readings in Russian Poetics: Formalist and Structuralist Views*, ed. Ladislav Matejka and Krystya Pomorska (Cambridge, MA: MIT Press, 1971; rpt., Ann Arbor: Michigan Slavic Publications, 1978), 47.

11. Ibid., 49.

12. Ibid., 52.

13. Ibid., 51–52.

14. Ibid., 125; Barthes, "The Death of the Author," in *Authorship: From Plato to the Postmodern*, 125.

15. Ibid., 126.

16. Ibid., 127.

17. Ibid.

18. Ibid., 129.

19. See Lawrence Lipking, *The Life of the Poet: Beginning and Ending Poetic Careers* (Chicago: University of Chicago Press, 1981), viii.

20. Ibid., x.

21. Emphasis in original. See Edward W. Said, *Beginnings: Intention and Method* (New York: Columbia University Press, 1985), xvii.

22. Ibid., 10.

23. Ibid.

24. Ibid., 12.

25. Michel Foucault, "What Is an Author?" in *Authorship*, ed. Burke, 235.

26. Ibid., 16.

27. See Jurij Tynjanov, "On Literary Evolution," in *Readings in Russian Poetics*, ed. Matejka and Pomorska, 67.

28. Ibid.

29. Ibid., 73.

30. Jurij Striedter, *Literary Structure, Evolution, and Value: Russian Formalism and Czech Structuralism Reconsidered* (Cambridge, MA: Harvard University Press, 1989) 59.

31. Ibid., 60.

32. Ibid., 70.

33. Jauss is interested in a form of reader response criticism. See Hans Robert Jauss, "Literary History as a Challenge to Literary Theory," in *Toward an Aesthetic of Reception*, trans. Timothy Bahti (Minneapolis: University of Minnesota Press, 1982), 3–45.

34. Paul Ricoeur, *Oneself as Another*, trans. Kathleen Blamey (Chicago: University of Chicago Press, 1992), 4.

35. Ibid., 2.
36. Ibid., 116–17.
37. Ibid., 119.
38. Ibid., 118–19.
39. Ibid., 123.
40. Ibid., 141.
41. Ibid., 68; ellipses in original. The Anscombe work referred to is: G. E. M. Anscombe, *Intention* (London: Basil Blackwell, 1979).
42. Ibid., 21.
43. Ibid., 22.
44. Ibid., 167.

INDEX

Absolute language, 35

Abyss versus abundance, 36–38, 41

Adjacency, 223

Adultery. *See* Poetics of suspicion; Romantic betrayal; Sexuality

Aesthetic distance, 69

Aesthetic pleasure, 4, 58, 67, 111, 203, 207–8, 249n60

Aesthetics: of absence and Tolstoy's outsider status, 5–6, 17; anticommunicative aesthetics, 146; of antinarrative, 177; and art for art's sake, 44, 128, 257n42; and artistic "sincerity," 16; and authenticity, 95; and authorial intent, 179; and boundary between reality and fiction, 69; communicative goal of, 128–29, 152, 201, 203–5, 209, 214; of complete consciousness, 200; of early fiction, 63, 69, 73, 210; efficient aesthetics of Tolstoy's later fiction, 124, 201, 203–4, 207, 209; Ginzburg on, 30; of "infection," 45, 63, 99, 202–3, 205, 206; intimacy of aesthetic reception, 6–7, 45; of later fiction generally, 7, 63, 110, 203–4; and mediation, 30, 33; and memory as spiritual, 193; moral aesthetics, 179, 191; and narrative alibi, 4–8; and psychology, 120, 175, 201; of realism, 99, 144–45, 173–74; and

resistance to institutions, 7, 43, 205; and romantic narrative, 91, 147, 149; and selectivity, 48; theory of, in *What Is Art?*, 200–209; and Tolstoy's past literature, 60, 200–202; and violence, 178, 181–82. See also *What Is Art?* (Tolstoy)

Aesthetic structure, 30

Aesthetic vision, 35

"After the Ball" (Tolstoy): beginning of, 65–66, 167–68; body in, 171, 173–74, 176–77; challenges to Ivan's story in, 170–71; chance events in, 171–72; compared with Tolstoy's other fiction, 169–71, 173, 176–78; critics on, 177, 264n6, 265n28, 265n34; dancing in, 169–73; digressions and descriptive detail in, 172–77; ekphrasis in, 170–71; ending of, 176; female characters in, 265n34; framing and genre markers in, 167, 170, 176; identity based on false memory in, 66; influences on, 166; Ivan's relationship with Varen'ka in, 169, 171, 172–77; juxtaposing past and present in, 79; love story in, 169, 171, 173–77; metahistory of authorial identity in, 79; mirroring circularity in, 170, 171; music in, 175, 189; narrative alibi in, 169; narrators of, 170, 171, 176; political context of, 166; and "return of the

Diaries of Tolstoy: on abuses of language,
164; on "After the Ball," 266n48; on
"The Death of Ivan Ilyich," 241n19; on
"The Devil," 157; Eikhenbaum on, 29;
Ginzburg on, 30; on God, 252n19; on
habitualization, 198; and *Hadji Murad*,
118; on his own lack of talent, 23; on
literature and authorship as career, 25;
on music, 65, 126; on penchant for
destruction, 34; readers' lack of access
to, 20; and search for true self, 31;
self-analysis and introspection of, 19,
20–21, 25, 26, 28, 29, 31; on silence, 214;
on suicidal temptations, 65; on
Turgenev, 23; as writer's workshop, 29;
writing of fiction versus, 17–18, 20, 22,
25, 26, 30
"Diary of a Madman" (Gogol), 33, 39, 173
The Diary of a Writer (Dostoevsky), 168
Dickens, Charles, 235n45
Digressions: in "After the Ball," 173, 176; in
Anna Karenina, 103–7; descriptive detail
in, 172–77, 203, 208; Eikhenbaum on,
244n44; narrative diversions versus,
71–72, 86; in "Sevastopol in May," 72;
on violence in *Boyhood*, 184–86, 187,
193, 194; in *War and Peace*, 235n39
Dionysius the Areopagite, 104
Diversions. *See* Narrative diversions
Doctors, 113
Donskov, Andrew, 190, 267n8, 268n18
Dostoevsky, Fyodor: Bakhtin on, 41;
compared with Tolstoy, 11, 163; dialogue
in, 41; Eikhenbaum on, 27; on
environmental determinism, 168–69; as
influence on Tolstoy, 166; narrative
techniques of, 69; Tolstoy on, 166,
195–96, 267n10; and Underground
Man, 158, 163, 176; and utopian
ideas, 151
—works: *Brothers Karamazov*, 169; *Crime
and Punishment*, 169, 195–97, 267n10;
House of the Dead, 23; *Notes from the
Underground*, 151

Drama: challenge of showing characters'
thoughts in, 189; *The Realm of
Darkness/The Power of Darkness* as,
186–93; Tolstoy on limitations of,
188–89; Tolstoy's plays, 186–93, 268n20
Dreams. *See* Retrospective dreams
Drug use, 193–200
Druzhinin, A. V., 15–16, 128, 235n45
Dueling, 45–46, 77, 153, 190, 244n41

"Egyptian Nights" (Pushkin), 58, 257n42
Eikhenbaum, Boris: Any on, 237nn75–76;
on Chekhov, 242n27; on *Childhood*,
248n38; on crisis in Russian literature,
60; on diaries of Tolstoy, 29; on
digressions in Tolstoy's fiction, 244n44;
on "Family Happiness," 44; on
Formalism, 27; on "A History of
Yesterday," 238n81; on "Lucerne," 127;
on nihilism of Tolstoy, 241n15, 246n21;
and overcoming psychological approach
to Tolstoy, 26–30; on social engagement
of Tolstoy, 44; on Tolstoy's interest in
problem of description, 172; on "Two
Hussars," 44; *The Young Tolstoi* by, 27,
28, 29, 235n36, 242n28
Ekphrasis, 170–71, 265n19
Eliot, T. S., 19, 217, 218
Emerson, Caryl, 40, 175, 201, 242n24,
270n62
Empiricism, 32
Ergol'skaia, Tatiana, 19–20, 55, 189
Estrangement as literary device, 98
Evgeny Onegin (Pushkin), 71

Family: in *Anna Karenina*, 102–8; and
aristocratic tradition, 56–57, 245n11; in
"The Death of Ivan Ilyich," 115; in
Tolstoy's early and late fiction generally,
245n6; in *War and Peace*, 85, 97–102.
See also "Family Happiness" (Tolstoy)
"Family Happiness" (Tolstoy): abyss
imagery in, 37; Eikhenbaum on, 44; first
person narrator of, 151; love in, 151,

transparency of, 71, 124, 134, 136, 144, 145, 150, 151; Vygotsky on, 158

Legitimation: and aristocratic tradition in Tolstoy's works, 56–57; and *Childhood*, 49; compared with narratives of authenticity, 55; and metaphoric connections based on similarity, 56–57; readerly participation and, 6, 45, 49, 51, 53–58, 69; and realism, 76; and selfhood, 55; theme of legitimacy and illegitimacy in Tolstoy's works, 55–56

Leontiev, Konstantin, 246n21

Lermontov, Mikhail: and critics, 43, 44; death of, 45–46; *A Hero of Our Time* by, 43, 235n45; on military life, 79; narrative techniques of, 69; and readership, 242–43n31; romanticism of, 27; and tales of the Caucasus, 54

The Life of the Poet (Lipking), 222

Lipking, Lawrence, 222, 224, 230

Literary critics. *See* Critics

The Living Corpse (Tolstoy), 268n20

Longinov, N. M., 244n41

Looks and visual cues. *See* Nonverbal communication

Lotman, Yurij, 200, 242n22

Love, Jeff: on authority of revelation, 233n16; on deception of narratives, 239n96; on mediation, 238n84; on relationship between intention and autobiography, 243n34; on Tolstoy's autobiographical writings, 236n53; on Tolstoy's search for authority, 16; on *War and Peace*, 86, 251n38; on *What Is Art?*, 201

Love and love stories: in "After the Ball," 169, 171, 173–77; in *Anna Karenina*, 121, 126, 133–46, 151, 229; and community, 151; in *The Cossacks*, 84–85, 229; and epistemology, 125; and "Family Happiness," 151, 152–53; and happiness, 136; and "A History of Yesterday," 124–25; and language, 100, 123–25, 133–34, 136, 145, 149–53; and music,

126–34; and presentness generally, 121; Tolstoy and Christian love, 54, 55; Tolstoy's "love" letter to Arsenyeva, 132–33, 152, 257–58n43; Tolstoy's rejection of, in later works, 147, 149; in *War and Peace*, 37, 38, 98–102, 229. *See also* Romantic betrayal; *Tolstoy's specific works*

"Lucerne" (Tolstoy): compared with *The Cossacks*, 257n30; critics on, 126–27, 129, 256n16, 256–57n22; descriptive detail in, 203; ending of, 129, 132, 257n42; first-person narrator of, 127, 129; full title of, 126; love story in, 7, 126–32; music in, 64, 126–32, 164, 257n42; and nature philosophy, 127–28, 256n14; Nekhlyudov's isolation in, 130; origin of, 45, 127; pantheistic despair in, 38; plot of, 127, 130–32, 257n30; readerly participation in, 128–29; second-person narration in, 131; self-referential allusion in, 257n42; Turgenev on, 127

The Madwoman in the Attic (Gilbert and Gubar), 56

Mandelker, Amy, 26–27, 142, 144, 247n25, 258n51

"Man of Affairs" (Tolstoy), 253n13

Marx, Karl, 150

"Master and Man" (Tolstoy): childhood in, 57; death in, 35, 40; ending of, 263n66; and negative creation, 35; oppositions and double encodings in, 11; plot of, 40; rewriting of "The Snowstorm" in, 54, 167, 247n29; snowstorm in, 40

Matlaw, Ralph, 107

Mediation, 30–33, 60, 238n84, 239n97, 247n37

Meditations (Descartes), 132

Medzhibovskaya, Inessa, 112, 115, 232n3, 249n52, 253n13

Memory: in *Anna Karenina*, 137–38; Carden on, as sign of expressive

—plot details and characters (*continued*)
Nekhlyudov's relationship with his
sister, 152; Nekhlyudov's spiritual
rebirth, 13, 204; plot of, 13
Retrospective dreams, 248*n*44
Ricoeur, Paul, 150, 158, 226–29,
234*n*24, 255*n*2
Rischin, Ruth, 164, 263*n*62, 265–66*n*37
Romance narratives. *See* Love and love
stories; Poetics of suspicion; Romantic
betrayal
Romantic betrayal: in "After the Ball," 7,
166–78; in "The Devil," 7, 11, 21, 155–59;
in "Family Happiness," 7, 151, 161; in
"The Kreutzer Sonata," 7, 21, 151, 159,
160–65, 175, 263*n*63; language and
"poetics of suspicion," 124, 125–26, 144–46,
153–65; and language as fragmented and
untrustworthy, 144–46; in *Resurrection*, 7,
21, 154–56; in Tolstoy's fiction generally, 3,
7, 147; Tolstoy's rejection of adultery,
263*n*63; in Turgenev's "First Love," 166;
in *War and Peace*, 153
Romanticism: and emotional connections,
133; and military life, 79; and natural
life of natives, 116; and nature, 127–28,
134; and poetry, 220; and Romantic
existentialism, 78; and self as tragically
isolated, 150; and self-created soul, 84;
Tolstoy versus Romantic tradition, 60,
79, 116; and *War and Peace*, 91
Roosevelt, Priscilla, 245*n*11
Rose, Mark, 243*n*35
Rousseau, Jean-Jacques: on education, 29;
as influence on Tolstoy, 29, 51, 85,
235*n*45, 256*n*11, 269*n*50; on language,
256*n*11; literary functions of biography
of, 219; on music, 126; on natural life of
natives, 116; readers' familiarity with, 129
Russian Formalists, 18, 238*n*82

Said, Edward, 222–23, 224, 225, 230
Sand, George, 16, 22, 233*n*14
Sandler, Stephanie, 177, 265*n*34

Sankovitch, Natasha, 65, 248*n*48
Saussure, Ferdinand de, 256*n*11
Schiller, Friedrich, 235*n*45, 236*n*54
Schopenhauer, Arthur, 63, 123
Searle, John R., 153, 260*n*3, 271*n*4
Secondary versus primary absences, 40,
241–42*n*22
Second-person narrators. *See* Narrators
Semiotic purity, 164, 263*n*63
"Sevastopol in December" (Tolstoy):
compared with "Sevastopol in May,"
250*n*5; dissolution and repentance in,
68–69; diversionary tactics in, 2; ending
of, 70–71; framing techniques in, 49;
music in, 70–71; narrative
experimentation in, 71; and need for
revisiting one's interpretation, 70;
present tense in, 69–70, 75, 100;
publication of, 71; readerly participation
in, 6, 54, 59, 68–69; second-person
narration in, 2, 47, 54, 59, 68, 69–71,
212–13; similarity between fiction and
reality in, 56; translation of, into
French, 19; war in, 68–71
"Sevastopol in May" (Tolstoy): compared
with "Sevastopol in December," 250*n*5;
complex narrative of, 72–73; digression
on vanity in, 72; ending of, 59, 64,
73–74; failure to look at death in, 75;
final meandering chapter in, 74–75;
first-person narrator in, 73; framing
techniques in, 49, 59; Mikhaylov's
forebodings in, 74; misleading passages
in, 74; and narrative alibi, 75; narrative
diversion in, 74–75; narrative
experimentation in, 71–72; omniscient
narrator of, 72, 73, 250*n*5; opposition
between said and unsaid in, 30, 31–32;
as precursor of *War and Peace*, 72;
present tense in, 75; publication of, 71;
readerly participation in, 6, 54; themes
of, 72–73; third-person voice in, 73;
Truth as hero of, 6, 59, 64, 71, 72, 73, 75;
war in, 74–75

RUSSIAN LITERATURE AND THOUGHT

Strolls with Pushkin
Abram Tertz (Andrei Sinyavsky)

Untimely Thoughts: Essays on Revolution, Culture, and the Bolsheviks, 1917–1918
Maxim Gorky

Abram Tertz and the Poetics of Crime
Catharine Theimer Nepomnyashchy

Dostoevsky and Soloviev: The Art of Integral Vision
Marina Kostalevsky

Toward Another Shore: Russian Thinkers Between Necessity and Chance
Aileen M. Kelly

Liberty, Equality, and the Market: Essays by B. N. Chicherin
Edited and translated by G. M. Hamburg

Pushkin's Historical Imagination
Svetlana Evdokimova

Rereading Russian Poetry
Edited by Stephanie Sandler

View from the Other Shore: Essays on Herzen, Chekhov, and Bakhtin
Aileen M. Kelly

See No Evil: Literary Cover-Ups and Discoveries of the Soviet Camp Experience
Dariusz Tolczyk

Philosophy of Economy
Sergei Bulgakov
Translated, edited, and introduced by Catherine Evtuhov

The Little Tragedies
Alexander Pushkin
Translated, with Critical Essays, by Nancy K. Anderson

A Voice from the Chorus
Abram Tertz (Andrei Sinyavsky)

1920 Diary
Isaac Babel

Earthly Signs
Marina Tsvetaeva

Problems of Idealism: Essays in Russian Social Philosophy
Translated, edited, and introduced by Randall A. Poole

Five Operas and a Symphony: Word and Music in Russian Culture
  Boris Gasparov

"Anna Karenina" in Our Time: Seeing More Wisely
  Gary Saul Morson

Leo Tolstoy and the Alibi of Narrative
  Justin Weir